Market Denial and International Fisheries Regulation

Publications on Ocean Development
Volume 70

A Series of Studies on
the International, Legal, Institutional and Policy Aspects
of Ocean Development

General Editors: Vaughan Lowe and Robin Churchill

The titles published in this series are listed at www.brill.nl/pood

Market Denial and International Fisheries Regulation

The Targeted and Effective Use of Trade Measures Against the Flag of Convenience Fishing Industry

By
Darren S. Calley

MARTINUS
NIJHOFF
PUBLISHERS

LEIDEN • BOSTON
2012

This book is printed on acid-free paper.

Library of Congress Cataloging-in-Publication Data

Market denial and international fisheries regulation : the targeted and elective use of trade measures against the flag of convenience fishing industry / edited by Darren S. Calley.
p. cm. — (Publications on ocean development, 0924–1922 ; v. 70)
Includes bibliographical references and index.
ISBN 978-90-04-20278-8 (hardback : alk. paper) 1. Fishery law and legislation. 2. Foreign trade regulation. 3. Flags of convenience I. Calley, Darren S.
K3895.M37 2011
343'.07692—dc23

2011030847

ISSN: 0924-1922
ISBN: 978-90-04-20278-8

Contents

Acknowledgements

As a 'product' of the School of Law, the University Essex, it is only correct that all due thanks go to the institution that has nurtured my academic development and has overseen my progress from undergraduate student, to postgraduate student, and eventually to lecturer. In the few years that I have been at Essex all of my lecturers – many of whom are now colleagues, some of whom, sadly, no longer are – have been a constant source of information, inspiration and, most important of all, friendship. Not only have my colleagues provided the ethereal support one might expect from an institution of Essex's academic standing, many thanks, too, go to those colleagues whose practical assistance has been so invaluable. Despite some reluctance to single out any individual colleagues for special mention, it is only appropriate to pass on particular thanks Dr Karen Hulme and Mr David Ong for all the support, assistance and advice they have given me over the years. For many, many hours spent analysing vessel histories and commercial data, so invaluable to Chapter Two, I would like to thank Christopher Luff.

Funding for the PhD thesis that, in the fullness of time and after quite an extensive re-write, eventually became this present work, was provided by the Arts and Humanities Research Council, who between 2004 and 2006 provided the author with a full research award. I would very much like to acknowledge and thank the AHRC for this financial aid. Without this source of funding it is entirely possible that the Thesis and, by extension, this book may not have seen the light of day. Further in this regard many thanks are due to my PhD examiners, Professor Duncan French (the University of Sheffield) and Mr Peter Davies (the University of Nottingham).

And for pretty much everything, thanks go to Penny Brearey-Horne.

Acronyms and Abbreviations

AIDCP	Agreement on the International Dolphin Conservation Programme
CCAMLR	Convention for the Conservation of Antarctic Marine Living Resources
CCBSP	Commission for the Conservation and Management of Pollock Resources in the Central Bering Sea
CCSBT	Commission for the Conservation of Southern Bluefin Tuna
CDS	Catch Documentation Scheme
CITES	Convention on the International Trade in Endangered Species
Code of Conduct	United Nations Code of Conduct for Responsible Fisheries
COFI	United Nations Committee on Fisheries
COLTO	Coalition of Legitimate Toothfish Operators
Compliance Agreement	Agreement to Promote Compliance with International Conservation and Management Measures by Fishing Vessels on the High Seas
COP	Conference of the Parties
DCD	*Dissostichus* Catch Document
DML	Dolphin Mortality Level
DWFN	Distant Water Fishing Nation
E-CDS	Electronic Catch Documentation Scheme
ECJ	European Court of Justice
EEZ	Exclusive Economic Zone
EJF	Environmental Justice Foundation
EPO	Eastern Pacific Ocean
FFA	Forum Fisheries Agency
FOC	Flag of Convenience
FONC	Flag of Non-Compliance
GATT	General Agreement on Tariffs and Trade
GDP	Gross Domestic Product
GFCM	General Fisheries Commission for the Mediterranean
HSBT	High Seas Bottom Trawling
HSFA	High Seas Fishing Act (Belize, 2003)
HSTF	High Seas Task Force
IATCC	Inter-American Tropical Tuna Commission

ICCAT	International Commission for the Conservation of Atlantic Tunas
ICES	International Council for the Exploration of the Sea
ICJ	International Court of Justice
IEL	Centre for International Environmental Law
IIL	Institute of International Law
ILO	International Labour Organisation
IMCO	Inter-Governmental Maritime Consultative Organisation
IMMARBE	International Merchant Marine Registry of Belize
IMO	International Maritime Organisation
IOTC	Indian Ocean Tuna Commission
IPOA	International Plan of Action
ITF	International Transport Workers' Federation
ITLOS	International Tribunal for the Law of the Sea
IUCN	World Conservation Union
IUU	Illegal, Unreported and Unregulated (Fishing)
IWC	International Whaling Commission
JISS	Joint Inspection and Surveillance Scheme
JWG	Joint Working Group
MCS	Monitoring, Control and Surveillance
MMPA	Marine Mammal Protection Act (USA)
MRAG	Marine Resources Assessment Group
MTA	Multilateral Trade Agreement
NAFO	Northwest Atlantic Fisheries Organisation
NASCO	North Atlantic Salmon Conservation Organisation
NEAFC	North-East Atlantic Fisheries Commission
NMFS	National Marine Fishery Service (USA)
NPA	National Plan of Action
OECD	Organisation for Economic Co-operation and Development
OSPAR	The Convention for the Protection of the Marine Environment of the North-East Atlantic
RFMO	Regional Fisheries Management Organisation
SEAFC	South-Eastern Atlantic Fisheries Commission
SPRFMO	South Pacific Regional Fisheries Management Organisation
TAC	Total Allowable Catch
TBT	The Agreement on Technical Barriers to Trade
TREM	Trade-Restrictive Environmental Measure
UNCBD	United Nations Convention on Bio-Diversity
UNCCRS	United Nations Convention on the Conditions for the Registration of Ships
UNCLOS	United Nations Convention on the Law of the Sea
UNEP	United Nations Environmental Programme
UNFAO	United Nations Food and Agriculture Organisation

UNFSA	Agreement for the Implementation of the Provisions of the United Nations Convention on the Law of the Sea of 10 December 1982 Relating to the Conservation and Management of Straddling Fish Stocks and Highly Migratory Fish Stocks
UNGA	United Nations General Assembly
VCLT	Vienna Convention on the Law of Treaties
VMS	Vessel Monitoring System
WCPFC	Western-Central Pacific Fisheries Commission
WIOTO	Western Indian Ocean Tuna Organisation
WTO	World Trade Organisation

Chapter One

Introduction

1.1 *The Present Study: the Problem, the Solution and the Methodology*

The central thesis of this study can be succinctly stated. It will consider the ability of States, acting together under the auspices of Regional Fisheries Management Organisations (RFMOs), to adopt trade restrictive measures against the unregulated fishing fleet of the high seas. Flouting the freedom of the oceans, these vessels engage in activities that 'responsible' States decry as being contrary to the international law of the high seas, harmful to the natural environment, and murderous to countless marine dependent species. All the while these vessels operate with seeming impunity whilst they continue to take refuge under the convenient flags of States that are ignorant of, ambivalent to, or just unable to implement and enforce the international laws and codes of conduct designed to prevent these destructive practices. Although straightforward in its aims, the theory posited herein does rest upon numerous key points that require further and detailed explanation. For instance, what are the inadequacies in the contemporary international law of the marine environment that allow so-called flag of convenience (FOC) vessels to operate in contravention of the standards applicable to 'respectable' vessels with seeming impunity? What are the harms caused by these vessels? How has international law traditionally responded to these types of problem, and with what degree of success? More pertinently, what is the international community doing right now and what more could be done?

Over the course of the next three hundred or so pages, these central questions will be addressed and in so doing a framework under which the FOC industry is contextualised, analysed and criticised will be laid out. To do this in a way that adequately demonstrates the machinations of the industry beyond the 'merely theoretical', the study will adopt a methodology that utilises case studies of specific fishing vessels, State practice and environmental harms throughout. The purpose of these case studies is to bring the reality of the flag of convenience industry and its consequent harms into stark relief. Statistics and theory, while fundamental to underpinning the academic integrity of the present work, cannot always convey the practicalities of any problem when devoid of case-in-point examples: consequently it is hoped that the reader's interest in and understanding of the subject-matter will be heightened by the use of these occasional vignettes.

This book is, of course, an academic study first and foremost, however, and no amount of extraneous narratives can act in substitution of scholarly rigour and sound methodology. Thus, the first part of this study will attempt to explain the flag of convenience industry as a historical precept and globally important industry. It will also isolate the FOC fishing fleet from the generality of amorphous convenient shipping fleet in order to establish precisely how and why this sub-industry can flourish. In terms of 'how' it is too often the case, in the author's opinion, that the international community treats the issue of flags of convenience solely as a 'State-based' problem, in that once a State has been discouraged from engaging with the FOC industry (usually by political pressure) then the problem is solved. This is not the case: vessels engaged in FOC fishing do not simply cease to operate once their temporary regulatory haven ceases to be convenient. The owners of these boats will easily find another State of registry. And whilst the existing literature alludes to this, there has been, to the author's knowledge, no vessel-specific audit of this problem before now. Thus the present work will utilise empirical and illustrative examples of specific vessel registries and the fishing boats themselves whenever applicable so as to evidence this practice.

In terms of the 'why' vessels engage in FOC fisheries the answer is, perhaps, obvious: they do so to gain a competitive advantage over their rival commercial entities. Nevertheless some further, albeit brief, explanation may be warranted at this juncture because only once the motivating factors behind a perceived problem are understood is it possible to begin to posit a potential solution. As the following chapters will go on to show, the motivating factors behind the FOC fishing fleet are fiscal – both direct and indirect financial advantages are to be had by vessel owners by registering their vessels with flag of convenience States.

It is the indirect advantages that most inform the central thesis of the book and it is to these that the reader's attention is alerted. Whilst the direct fiscal advantages in terms of reduced shipping costs are often not insignificant, it is the indirect fiscal advantages offered by a regulatory-free climate that really appears to motivate the FOC fishing fleet. These indirect fiscal advantages allow the unregulated FOC fleet access to markets and it is this point that is most strongly emphasised: once market access is denied there becomes no incentive to continue the activity. Therefore this study will posit a theory that can sit alongside 'traditional' regulatory and enforcement measures that will effectively deny access to the most financially lucrative markets for fish and fisheries products.

The theoretical framework envisaged herein is, therefore, somewhat of an exercise in 'working backwards' and opposite to the method of 'traditional' fisheries regulation. As will be shown, the regulation of fisheries has generally tended to begin at source – that is, the regulation of the boats themselves. The theory posited here suggests that regulation should target the market-place and then work back along the history of the fishing cycle. If no market exists for the FOC fisheries produce then there will be no incentive to engage in the practice of FOC fishing. This, of course, echoes the ethos of the regulation in the trade of endangered flora and fauna under the 1973 Washington Convention on the International Trade in Endangered Species (CITES) and so consideration must necessarily be given to this Convention's role in respect of fisheries – both as a theoretical framework and as a complementary system of management.

Although the primary focus of the present study is to posit and evaluate a workable framework under which a pressing issue of global importance might be addressed, it is also hoped that the reader is provided with an overview of many of the contemporary issues relevant to the international law of the marine environment. In terms of the latter it is hoped that the reader will be informed of the fact that the challenges posed by flag of convenience vessels extend beyond the obvious threat to the over-exploitation of an increasingly scarce resource, and that these vessels can, and do, harmfully impact upon all that stand in their way.

In terms of the primary goal of the study it should be noted what the author's intent in this regard is not. The present work does not suggest that the solution proffered should be any more than a framework by which concerned States, acting together, can take action. Nothing contained herein should be taken to read that the use of market-based measures is mandatory and must be applied by all States at all times. Instead, one complementary method of regulation is suggested, to be used in conjunction with many other measures such as traditional flag State controls (discussed in Chapter Four) and Monitoring, Control and Surveillance (discussed briefly below). Trade measures can only be used as part of a concerted and harmonised strategy whereby States give effect to their obligations under international law to protect and preserve the marine environment.[1]

1.2 *The Structure of the Study*

So as to fully appreciate the engrained and industrialised nature of flags of convenience, Chapter Two will chart the rise of the FOC industry over its long and inglorious history. This chapter will demonstrate that as well as being

[1] Article 192 of the United Nations Convention on the Law of the Sea, 21 I.L.M. 1261; (1982).

entrenched in political and economic imperatives, the FOC industry is almost as much of a maritime tradition as the principle of the freedom of the seas itself. Following this glance back to history, the chapter will then contextualise the industry in contemporary terms by considering the incentives to both vessels owners and States. These incentives, as has been mentioned above, are two-fold. First, vessel owners and States of registry can gain enormous and important financial advantages by engaging with the convenient shipping industry, and second, and perhaps even more important, vessel owners benefit enormously from the less regulated FOC registry. Thus, following this analysis of the "industry" generally, the chapter will turn its attention to the specific issue convenient fisheries, and consider the relationship between FOCs and the issue of Illegal, Unreported and Unregulated (IUU) Fisheries. Prior to its conclusion Chapter Two will posit examples from Belizean, Bolivian, Cambodian and Georgian maritime registries at the turn of the millennium and beyond. These examples are included as they evidence in clear terms the hypothesis that single State initiatives cannot adequately curtail the activities of the FOC fleet. When erstwhile FOC States accede to international norms (either voluntarily or as a result of external pressures) little effect is felt by the vessels actually engaged in IUU/FOC activity – they can and will find another all-too-willing short-term State of registry.

Chapter Three will then expand upon the machinations of the industry and analyse it in terms of the harms caused by unregulated fishing. Clearly the immediate and most obvious harm is that of stock depletion, but the consequences of the IUU/FOC industry do not stop there. Having previously considered the justification for FOCs in terms of fiscal advantages to States, individuals and the global economy in Chapter Two, Chapter Three will demonstrate that the unregulated FOC industry poses a disproportionate threat to the marine environment. As well as the aforementioned stock depletion, these threats include the threat posed to marine dependent wildlife, such as sea-birds and marine mammals, the sea bed itself and humankind. Therefore Chapter Three will engage with these threats and consider some particular contemporary issues within the fisheries sector and demonstrate how FOC vessels exacerbate the problems. Specifically, Chapter Three, following a purely numerical evaluation of the IUU/FOC fleet, will then consider some of the more deleterious fishing activities. When these activities are viewed through a legal lens, and when they are considered in conjunction with the aforementioned justifications, underpinnings and realities of the FOC industry, a rather bleak conclusion is arrived at. As the international community wakes up to some of these pressing problems and embarks upon a program of regulation in the high seas, the FOC industry will remain one step ahead. Thus, responsible States may subject themselves to laws curtailing certain deleterious practices. While there remain a few convenient registries ready, willing and able to provide refuge for the countless long-liners, purse seiners and bottom trawlers seeking to evade regulation, it is suggested that the efficacy of these regulations will be seriously undermined.

With these issues in mind Chapter Four turns its attention to the principle of the freedom of the seas under which these vessels flourish and considers the 'traditional' method by which international law has attempted to deal with the problem of flags of convenience. Chapter Four will begin, therefore, by considering the principle of exclusive flag State jurisdiction. In short, this principle states that, subject to one or two noted exceptions, the only means by which laws may be imposed upon vessels on the high seas is through the State of registry. Thus, as Chapter Three has already demonstrated, States that do not accede to international treaties on marine conservation become very attractive havens for unscrupulous fishing entities irrespective of any genuine historical or commercial link between vessel and State. The chapter will therefore chart a century of jurisprudence and catalogue the numerous failed attempts to regulate the unregulated, by which the international community has attempted to define and apply the concept of the 'genuine link' between vessel and State of registry. Chapter Four will then suggest that even if in the unlikely event of an acceptable definition of the genuine link being arrived at and applied, then this would have only a limited impact upon the flag of convenience industry and would not completely rid the oceans of these harmful vessels.

Chapter Five will therefore move away from general international law to the more specific provisions of the many international agreements promulgated to reduce the incidences of IUU fishing within the international fishing fleet. Of chief focus in this chapter will be the issue of regional co-operation. Chapter Five will thus initially focus upon the basis for co-operation and consider the generality of the law of the sea which mandates that States act together to achieve the goal of a healthy marine environment. The study will then move to consider regional implementation of the principles enshrined in those 'hard law' agreements which mandate co-operation and the interaction between these hard laws and the soft laws which dictate many of the specific goals to be achieved by this co-operation. This study will demonstrate that not only is there an obligation for States to act together but that there is also a minimum standard of governance expected by these States when acting under the auspices of Regional Fisheries Management Organisations. Whilst there are many different means of control available to these regional bodies, many of which are utilised, most germane to this study will be the manner in which States may operate a principle of market denial in respect of vessels which do not comply with internationally agreed best practice. The chapter will consider the manner in which one regional organisation – the Commission for the Conservation of Antarctic Marine Living Resources (CCAMLR) – has implemented trade and market restrictive measures through its Catch Documentation Scheme (CDS). The study of the CCAMLR CDS will examine how it operates, to which States it currently applies, and the circumstances under which permits to trade are granted and consider some of the practical issues relevant to the use of such 'permit to trade schemes'. The study will, perhaps most importantly, assess the way in which the CDS is able to deal with environmental harms such as those noted in Chapter Three within the CCAMLR area of competence. Chapter Five will conclude by noting the influence of the CCAMLR CDS and assess the manner in which various other RFMOs have adopted similar schemes.

To build upon the analysis begun in the latter part of the previous chapter, Chapter Six describes the way in which the regional schemes such as CCAMLR's may be expanded in State coverage, as one problem associated with such schemes is that they only bind State parties to each regional scheme and only operate within fixed geographical bounds, and often with regard to specified species only. Consequently this Chapter will consider the role that the Washington Convention on the International Trade in Endangered Species (CITES) may have in expanding the coverage of schemes such as the CDS. In order to highlight the attraction of CITES in this regard, the Chapter will pay close attention to how CITES works as an institution, as well as a Convention, in regulating other types of international wildlife trade. The Chapter will then move to a discussion of some of the recent initiatives to involve CITES in the management of fisheries trade and consider recent attempts to place commercially important fish stocks within the competence of CITES. This analysis will involve consideration of both the very real practical/political aspects of such an endeavour as well as the legal hurdles which must first be overcome. The correlative to the attraction of CITES as a fisheries management tool, of course, is the inherent limits to CITES. Can this Convention adequately deal with all the consequences of unregulated fishing – especially those indirect harms highlighted in Chapter Three? The penultimate aspect of the analysis of CITES will centre around its ability to deal with the Convention's inherent and practical limits. The Chapter will conclude by suggesting that the best way forward appears to be straight ahead: the recent initiatives which appear to be pushing CITES towards a role of expanding the coverage of regional regulation schemes such as CCAMLR's CDS offer the chance of the most comprehensive coverage – both in terms of State participation and regulatory scope.

1.3 *Necessary Omissions*

Finally in this introduction it is worth mentioning a few topics that will not be covered by this work. For reasons of space it has not been possible to consider in depth a number of issues that the reader might consider worthy of mention. First there is the issue of monitoring, control and surveillance (MCS): that is, the physical detection by States of illegal or unregulated fishing vessels. This very important analysis has not been discussed for two pertinent reasons. First, MCS is extremely well covered in existing literature and the reader's attention is drawn to the large volume of literature on this subject. Specifically in this regard Rosemary Rayfuse's *Non-Flag State Enforcement in High Seas Fisheries*[2] is a most comprehensive analysis of many of the existing enforcement mechanisms available in the fight against IUU fishing activities. The second reason for this omission is that the principle of market denial must be seen as complementing the existing controls over vessel activity and the thesis preferred here should not, therefore, be read in such a way as to suggest any trade or market-based solutions should replace the valuable deterrent of MCS.

Likewise, we shall not consider, beyond this Introduction, US Lacey Act-type legislation.[3] This piece of legislation criminalises the importation of fisheries products to the territory of the USA that has been acquired illegally within the jurisdiction of another State. The value of this particular Act, in terms of preventing the trade in unlawfully harvested fisheries produce, cannot be underestimated and has been cited as another of the key weapons to be used against IUU operations. Such is the potential for Lacey Act-type of legislation that the High Seas Task Force, a Ministerially-led initiative by numerous States, has recommended the use of such provisions by all concerned States[4]. There are, however, two important reasons why the Lacey Act shall not be further considered herein. This study concerns the international law of the marine environment and it is probably beyond its competence to consider purely domestic legislation such as the Lacey Act. Whilst the Act itself is a reaction to a pressing issue of international law, its provisions end at the borders of the USA and thus should be considered an internal issue, which whilst wholeheartedly applauded, cannot impact into the realm of public international law.

The second reason that no further consideration will be paid to Lacey Act-type legislation may, at first blush appear more semantic than principled. Law is law, however, and nuances are ignored at the lawyer's peril. The US Act makes it unlawful to import fish products harvested illegally within the territory of another State. This poses a problem in international law because the Act's provisions can only be used in the context of international fisheries when any

2 Martinus Nijhoff Publishers, Lieden, 2004. The reader's attention is also drawn to the many UNFAO Technical Papers issued on this subject since 1981, which include, most recently, P. Flewwelling, *An Introduction to Monitoring, Control and Surveilance Systems for Capture Fisheries*, UNFAO Technical Paper 338, UNFAO, Rome, 2004; Flewwelling, Cullinan, Balton, Sautter and Reynolds, *Recent Trends in Monitoring, Control and Surveillance Systems for Capture Fisheries*, UNFAO Fisheries Technical Paper 415, UNFAO, Rome, 2002.

3 The Lacey Act Amendments of 1981. 16 United States Code § 3371.

4 *Closing the Net: Stopping Illegal Fishing on the High Seas*, Final Report of the Ministerially-led Task Force on IUU Fishing in the High Seas, High Seas Task Force, March 2006, at p. 33 and p. 81.

internationally agreed conservation standards have been directly transposed into domestic legislation. When dealing with flag of convenience fisheries the Lacey Act is rendered impotent by the fact, as Chapter Two notes in some detail, the flag of convenience vessels that form the basis of the present work are not actually engaged in illegal fishing in another State's territory but unregulated fishing beyond the scope of national jurisdiction.

Chapter Two

The Flag of Convenience Industry: Its Historical and Economic Pedigree, Contemporary Context and Relationship to High Seas Fishing

2.1 *Introduction*

Without an understanding of the long established tradition of the use of flags of convenience and their undoubted importance to the wider maritime world, any analysis of convenient fishing registries and any attempt to curb their more harmful activities will fall short. Likewise, if we fail to recognise all the circumstances that have led to the creation of the enormous fleet of fishing vessels plundering the oceans in a seemingly unregulated manner then no viable solution can be found. To avoid the pitfalls presented by the challenge of ridding the oceans of these harmful vessels we must recognise that they form one part of a much larger picture: flags of convenience are entrenched in both maritime history and economic necessity – benefiting vessel owners, States of registry, and say some, the global economy.

Bearing in mind these imperatives we must be able to see the whole picture whilst at the same time concentrating our efforts on the micro. To rid the world of flag of convenience fishing vessels the international community could, if so inclined, rid the world of flags of convenience generally. This, it is contended, is not likely to happen. Too many dollars are invested in these fleets – not just by vessel owners or shipping registrars but by businesses, corporations and governments. To demonstrate this, the first part of this Chapter, *A Brief History of Flags of Convenience*, will chart the rise of the flag of convenience phenomenon and will demonstrate the historical pedigree of the convenient registry. This will show that for at least two hundred years they have been utilised by governments and industries alike when the perception of necessity or the economic imperative demands.

Flag of convenience registers offer vessel owners an advantage – clearly, if they did not they would cease to be convenient. In a market as competitive as the merchant marine industry advantages count: if a vessel can operate more efficiently than its rival and therefore offer potential customers a more economical service then clearly that vessel operates at an advantage. Many flags of convenience offer vessel owners the chance to operate at such an advantage. From cheap registration and tax advantages, to a "hands off" management strategy and the avoidance of the regulatory shackles placed on their rivals, flags of convenience assist businesses in their primary goal of money-making. The next section of the Chapter, *The Economic Drivers of Flags of Convenience*, will focus upon the fiscal advantages to be had by both 'sides' of the flag of convenience industry. Whilst most of the emphasis is placed upon the advantages to be had by the vessels owners, we must not forget that this arrangement is a multi-partite one: not only do the owners gain but so do the States of registry. Thus the advantages to be had by States are considered in *The Economic Incentives for States to Operate as Flags of Convenience.*

The Chapter will then proceed to consider, in *Flags of Convenience and their Relationship with IUU Fishing*, the link between flags of convenience and the fishing industry. This will allow the industry be to contextualised within the wider sphere of Illegal, Unreported and Unregulated (IUU) fishing. In what way, for example, does unregulated fishing differ from illegal fishing? Is there a significant interaction between the trio of harmful activities labelled IUU fishing? And where precisely do we posit flags of convenience in this equation?

In order to demonstrate the fluidity of the flag of convenience industry, the concluding aspects of this Chapter draw upon the examples of the maritime registries of Belize, Bolivia, Cambodia and Georgia. Beginning with *A Rogue State Come Good? How Belize is Cleaning up its Act, but How the Vessel Owners Are Not* the Chapter will demonstrate that throughout the last decade many States have succumbed to the need for valuable foreign investment by opening up their marine registries to those vessel owners who might wish to take advantage of lax regulatory standards. In terms of highlighting the machinations of the industry these States are prime examples as they all fit the template of a 'typical' flag of convenience State. All have a pressing need for foreign investment, either because of an inherent inability to generate sufficient income by alternative means, or because these States have recently emerged from a turbulent history of factionalism or international isolation. What also links these States, and perhaps more germane to this study, is the fact that they have all acted as links in the FOC chain – any study of the movements of vessels between States, as has been conducted as part of this Chapter, will reveal that the vessels registered with a flag of convenience demonstrate an unerring ability to hunt out the next potential FOC State and seek haven there when troublesome regulations appear on the horizon. For these States the FOC industry can be perceived to be a lifeline and assist in rebuilding troubled economies, and in that context flags of convenience are extremely beneficial. Thus the Chapter will proceed to show, in *The On-going Links in the FOC Chain: Bolivia, Cambodia and Georgia*, how vessel owners and States in most need of foreign investment – for instance those

States emerging from international isolation or internal strife – work together to ensure that the FOC phenomenon is perpetuated.

As the following Chapter will demonstrate, convenient fisheries are a relatively small, albeit important, aspect of the flag of convenience industry. The economic imperatives driving fishing boat operators may be the same as for any other vessel owner in that they may wish to minimise costs so as to maximise profits, but, in the unique world of marine capture, many other factors may come into play in the decision to flag out to a convenient registry. In the world of fish stocks management countless regulations are there to be evaded and those vessels not adhering to the rules will always be at a short-term advantage. Whilst these vessels may pose a significant threat to many of the world's fish stocks and the marine environment, they must compete for the legislator's attention with the many other threats to our oceans. The enormity of the task of curtailing each and every harm inflicted upon fish stocks and the wider marine environment should not be underestimated: a significant proportion of the world's fishing fleet is currently engaged in so-called Illegal, Unreported and Unregulated fishing. So we must focus upon the precise nature of the problem to formulate a workable solution. Whilst there may be a consensus within the more responsible international community that rogue fishing vessels must be brought to account or compelled to comply with agreed rules and regulations, there are enormous hurdles to be overcome in turning this consensus into an effective regulatory regime.

2.2 *A Brief History of Flags of Convenience*

Although the phenomenon of flag of convenience fishing is relatively new, the general use of such flags has a long and inglorious history. It is widely stated that flags of convenience date back to the days of the Roman Empire,[1] and although the actual evidence and first hand accounts of this practice are fairly scarce, it is certainly not inconceivable that the Roman flag would have become the flag of protection utilised by many mariners throughout the Empire. During the more recent history of man's use of the ocean space – since the 1800s, at least – the rise of the flag of convenience has been quite well documented. As the legal order of the oceans became codified in the post-*Grotian* era and the principle of flag state jurisdiction recognised (discussed below), ship owners

[1] See, for instance: Z. Oya Özçayir, *Flags of Convenience and the Need for International Co-operation*, International Maritime Law, Vol. 7, Issue 4, May 2000, at p. 111.

sought to avoid national flag State laws by re-registering their vessels to another State unbound by these rules and regulations. Flag of convenience States, or open registries,[2] simply expedite this process by allowing vessels with no previous connection to the State, owned by companies not incorporated into that State, to join their shipping registers. More often than not this process is simple and straightforward with proprietary bodies, often private franchises, facilitating the necessary paperwork. Vessel owners need not even travel to exotic locations to register their vessels there – many flags of convenience have their offices in major commercial centres.[3]

Although not the first example of this practice, the means by which the trans-Atlantic slavers of the 19th century avoided fledgling international prohibition provides a stark and insidious illustration. Early in the 1800's several nations, notably Great Britain and the USA,[4] sought to abolish the slave trade and to this end "negotiated" a number of bilateral agreements with interested States, and by the 1817 Congress of Vienna the leading slave trading nations – Spain, Portugal, France and the Netherlands – had all agreed, in principle and rhetoric, to cease the practice of trans-Atlantic slave trade. These bilateral and multilateral arrangements did, however, fall crucially short of designating the slave trade as equal to piracy under international law – ergo a crime against all nations and subject to universal jurisdiction. Unfortunately therefore only vessels flying the flags of State parties to the specific treaties and agreements permitting such actions could be legitimately searched or detained.[5] The United States, however, refused to allow for search and detention powers to be exercised against its vessels by other States, with the "damaging consequence" that "any slaver flying the American flag could continue to trade with impunity unless arrested by a US vessel."[6]

In the subsequent decades, therefore, the slave trade embarked upon a familiar pattern – ships continued their diabolical trade between West Africa and ports such as Havana, going to extraordinary lengths to conceal the true identities of the vessels and foil the patrols – often the ships would carry not just spare convenient flags and documents, but also spare crews of convenient nationali-

[2] The technical distinction between the terms 'flags of convenience' and 'open registries' is recognised later in this Chapter.

[3] For example the Bahamian register is operated from London, Honduras from New York, Liberia from Virginia, Cambodia from Singapore.

[4] Whilst the *trade* in slaves became prohibited, and the US Government agreed to several measures to prevent such trade, slavery itself remained lawful in the USA for a number of years. Similarly Great Britain only totally abolished slavery when the Abolition of Slavery Act 1833 came into practical force in 1838.

[5] *Le Louis Case* (1817) 2 Dods, 210.

[6] Stephen Sedley, *Ashes and Sparks: Essays on Law and Justice*, Cambridge University Press, Cambridge, 2011, at p. 12.

ties, and depending on the nationality of the perceived threat would alternate between several different national identities:

> American-built ships from Portland, Maine, to Savannah, Georgia, operated in the trade and flew the American flag, knowing that for the most part such display would prevent British warships from stopping them. The determination of a vessel's identity often involved highly elaborate efforts at disguise. If a U.S. Navy vessel chased what seemed to be a slaver its ostensible 'captain' would hoist the Spanish flag, substitute Spanish registration papers, and might even carry a Spanish crew hidden below decks. This stratagem would be exactly reversed if apprehended by a British man of war.[7]

Only in the latter decades of the 20th century did a complete and effective international prohibition on slavery close the loopholes so ruthlessly exploited by the slavers, by allowing for the visit and search of any vessel suspected of slave transportation by any warship on the high seas.[8] Pessimism aside, the fact that international law took well over a century to effectively implement laws prohibiting the slave trade following the first initial moves to do so may not instil confidence in the ability of the international community to react swiftly and decisively in matters of grave concern. This, however, is often the very nature of international law – as subsequent sections of this book will show, the international law-making process does not necessarily lend itself to immediacy and efficacy. The consensual nature of the law of treaties will, perhaps, always allow for States to opt out of international norms, and it is only when practices attract sufficient State opposition that the often slow processes of customary law and *jus cogens* will begin to emerge as norm-creating rules, irrespective of the wishes of certain States.

By the turn of the 20th century, during the USA's prohibition era in the 1920s, a further use for flags of convenience was stumbled upon when the owners of American cruise liners registered their vessels on Panamanian lists and thus circumvented US domestic legislation regarding the consumption of alcohol.[9] By virtue of the 18th Amendment to the US Constitution it became illegal to manufacture, sell, or transport "intoxicating liquors within… the United States

[7] Calvin Lane, *The African Squadron: The US Navy and the Slave Trade 1820–1862.* Reproduced at http://amistad.mysticseaport.org/discovery/themes/lane.navy.html.

[8] UNCLOS Art. 110(1): "…a warship which encounters on the high seas a foreign ship…is not justified in boarding it unless there is reasonable ground for suspecting that…(b) the ship is engaged in the slave trade." This article is "generally regarded as codifying customary international law" and will, as such, apply to all States – Churchill and Lowe, *The Law of the Sea*, 3rd Ed. at p. 212 (herein after "Churchill and Lowe"). This particular Article replicates, almost verbatim, Article 22(1) (b) of the High Seas Convention 1958.

[9] Jane Marc Wells, *Vessel Registration in Selected Open Registries*, (1981) 6 Mar. Law 221, at p. 225 (herein after "Wells").

and all territory subject to the jurisdiction thereof for beverage purposes…"[10] Panama, along with Honduras and Liberia, seeing the obvious advantages to their national economies, in terms of licensing fees and taxes, soon began to operate open registries and found a ready-made market of vessels wishing to avoid regulation and control. For the cost-conscious vessel owner, there was also the bonus of the cheaper operating costs offered by the so-called Panlibhon States. Indeed, in the years preceding World War II the flag of convenience market was largely, although not exclusively, driven by fiscal considerations. US labour laws required that US registered vessels should employ American officers and crew, and as a result of trade union pressure these crews soon became expensive and added to the high operating costs of US registered vessels. Flag States such as Panama had neither the legislative requirements that indigenous crews should be employed nor strong trade union movements with the related expense of adequate training, conditions or wages.[11]

A further fillip for the growing flag of convenience industry came with the threat of imminent war in Europe in the late 1930s. In keeping with the tradition of flying the flags of neutral states in times of conflict[12] US based companies, notably Esso, re-registered their vessels previously registered to the potentially belligerent states under the Panamanian flag.[13] With the outbreak of hostilities in 1939 flag of convenience States received a further boost to their registers with the enactment of the US Neutrality Act. Under the provisions of this Act no US vessels were permitted to enter certain specified combat areas and or to carry "passengers or any articles or materials to any state named…"[14] Consequently, the Panamanian register of vessels continued to expand apace, with European vessels joining their US counterparts in order to escape requisition towards the war effort.[15]

---

[10] 18th Amendment to the US Constitution, Section 1.

[11] Boleslaw Adam Boczek, *Flags of Convenience: An International Legal Study*, Harvard University Press, Cambridge, Massachusetts, 1962, at p. 10 (herein after "Boczek").

[12] This practice can be evidenced in both modern and historical times. For example during the Napoleonic Wars British vessels flew the flag of obscure German Principalities (Elizabeth R. DeSombre, *Convenient Fishing: Participation in International Fishery Management*, Paper for presentation at the International Studies Association Annual Meeting, March 2002, New Orleans, at p. 2 (herein after "DeSombre")). More recently, during the 1990s Kuwaiti and Croatian vessels re-flagged to foreign registries to avoid aggression: Vukas and Vidas, *Flags of Convenience and High Seas Fishing* in *Governing Highs Fisheries: The Interplay of Global and Regional Regimes*, ed. Olav Scram Stokke, at p. 55 (herein after "Vukas and Vidas").

[13] Boczek, at pp. 10–11.

[14] US Neutrality Act, November 4th 1939, 76th Congress, 2nd Session, Public Resolution No. 54, ss 2–3.

[15] Boczek, at p. 11.

By the turn of the 21st century the Panamanian registry was the world's largest, weighing in at over 100million gross tons or 13,500 vessels.[16] Post-war the imperative was no longer conflict fed necessity, but saw a return to flags of convenience in terms of pure fiscal expediency and the avoidance of international norms. For every regulation enacted to curb or control or prohibit activities on the oceans, vessel owners could find a willing partner State prepared to allow them onto their unregulated shipping registries, and by the latter half of the century two parallel, and seemingly mutually exclusive, worlds appeared to have evolved.

On the one hand was the "official line" agreed by States in determining the contents of the definitive set of rules writ large in the Law of the Sea Convention and its progeny: the freedom of the high seas remains the norm but the regulation of certain determined activities will be required, and States must not undermine each other's efforts to ensure this goal. In this world industrialised nations call for a genuine link between vessel and State of registry and also call for greater flag State controls and regulation.

But as the birth of the modern age of flags of convenience shows, these calls are distinctly muted. The flight from the US registry to that of Panama in the middle of the last century was not frowned upon but approved or even encouraged by the US government of the time[17] who recognised then, and whose successors recognise now, that there is also the *laissez-faire* reality of market economies. In this world many multinational corporations effectively constitute larger economies than many States,[18] and Westernised consumers have the buying power to ensure that the commodities they demand are shipped around the globe as quickly and as cheaply as possible. For this, flags of convenience States, peddling their minimally regulated registries are not simply necessary for the ship owners and transport companies but are also necessary to ensure the continuous, efficient and inexpensive movement of goods worldwide. Let us not forget that half the world's merchant fleet sails under flags of convenience[19]

[16] Jessica K. Ferrell, *Controlling Flags of Convenience: One Measure to Stop Over-fishing of Collapsing Fish Stocks*, (2005) 35 Envtl. L. 323.

[17] Boczek, pp. 11–12.

[18] According to a report issued in 2000 by the Institute for Policy Studies, 51 of the top 100 economies were corporations. For example, General Motors had a larger GDP than Denmark. Sarah Anderson and John Cavanagh, *Top 200. The Rise of Corporate Global Power*, December 2000. Available at http://www.ips-dc.org/downloads/Top_200.pdf.

[19] Tony Lane, *Flags of Convenience: Is it Time to Redress the Balance?* Seafarer's International Research Centre, Cardiff University, at http://www.sirc.cf.ac.uk/Other%20pubs/Flagcon.pdf in which Professor Lane states that "Flags of convenience have become the ultimate embodiment of deregulatory principles in international shipping since they came into vogue in the last 30 years" and asks in this article whether "with more than half the world's fleet operating under FOCs... has *laissez-faire* gone too far?".

and, as such, this is simply another aspect of the common business practice of "jurisdiction shopping" in which corporations are compelled to seek out the laxest regulatory requirements in order to minimise costs, and a failure to so do represents a lost opportunity to maximise profits.[20]

Without flags of convenience, critics of regulation claim, all of us, developed and developing worlds alike, will pay a price: the global economy will slow, goods will rise in price and fewer and fewer trickle-down dollars will reach the producers of goods in the remote lands of the Far East and Africa.[21] This is also bad news for industry, governments and, ultimately, consumers. As a result of the maritime industry increasing its overheads to compensate for the greater the regulatory requirements of a less open market place, consumers pay more for their coffee, oil and tea. Monopolistic State registries, without facing competition in the market place and without the incentive to provide a value-for-money service, will hinder or even reverse the recent economic trends, again with consumers paying the ultimate price.[22]

With this economic imperative in mind, it is worth considering the factors which drive the FOC industry and which any attempt to rid the seas of unregulated vessels of all sorts, be they tramps or trawlers, longliners or passenger liners, must recognise and address. But before these factors are considered one important caveat must be inserted: the terms "flag of convenience" and "open registry", although often used together or in substitution of each other, are slightly distinct concepts. As Rayfuse points out "although [the term flag of convenience is] often used coextensively with the term 'open registries' the terms are not necessarily synonymous. The latter are ships registries that are set up for financial gain to 'attract considerable tonnage without adequate administrative or governmental facilities for regulating and enforcing the necessary

[20] Robert Hinckley, *How Corporate Law Inhibits Social Responsibility*, Business Ethics: Corporate Social Responsibility Report, January/February 2002.

[21] It is certainly true that transportation costs for such commodities have declined in the modern age of FOC registries. For instance, based on a constant dollar analysis the cost of transporting a tonne of tea from Sri Lanka to Europe has fallen from US$217 to US$80 in the last forty years. Likewise a tonne of coffee from Brazil to Europe in 1996 cost $50 to transport compared to the 1970 price of $129, see David Hummels, *Have International Transportation Costs Declined?* Journal of International Economics, Volume 54 (1), Table 1. This decline in transportation cost may not be solely due to the reduced costs of unregulated vessels: it is more likely to be a reflection of economies of scale and the increase in vessel capacity compared to crew cost ratio, as well as increased and more efficient port capacity. See Michael Mussa, *Factors Driving Global Economic Integration*, Presentation Paper for Symposium, *Global Economic Integration: Opportunities and Challenges*, August 2000, at http://www.kansascityfed.org.

[22] Daniel J. Mitchell, *The Threat to Global Shipping From Unions and High Tax Politicians: Restrictions on Open Registries Would Increase Consumer Prices and Boost the Cost of Government*, Prosperitas, The Centre for Freedom and Prosperity, August 2004, Vol. 9, Issue 2, at http://www.freedomandprosperity.org/Papers/shipping/shipping.shtml.

standards at sea'. The former can refer to any flag which is adopted for the purposes of political and/or practical expediency."[23] This political or practical expediency can be the failure of any State, and not necessarily one operating an open registry, to bind itself to international norms, in which case the term 'flag of non-compliance' is often used.[24] Nevertheless, for many States and vessels there can be a significant overlap between the economic advantages offered by "open registries" strictly defined and the political or practical expediency of "flags of non-compliance". Therefore for the immediate purposes of this Chapter both will be referred to as "flags of convenience" in its generic sense.[25]

2.3 *The Economic Drivers of flags of Convenience*

The very first economic advantage for ship owners of registering a vessel to a flag of convenience or an open registry is the low cost of registration. This is typically a one-off registration fee and a relatively low annual fee based upon the tonnage of the vessel. Local taxation on the income generated by the activities of the vessel – if levied at all, which it often is not – will be very low and often supported by guarantees of future exemptions or reductions.[26] In terms of the overall annual budgetary requirements to be borne in mind by vessel operators and owners when embarking upon the decision to flag out to open registries, the low cost of registration is only one very small factor, however.[27] Of greater significance in the economic equation are the lower start-up and running costs of the vessels themselves under the national legislations of the flag of convenience registries.

[23] Rosemary Rayfuse, *Non-Flag State Enforcement in High Seas Fisheries*, Martinus Nijhof, Utrecht, 2004, at p. 25 (herein after "Rayfuse (2004)").

[24] Rayfuse (2004), at p. 35. See also Agnew and Barnes, at p. 169.

[25] According to the International Transport Workers' Federation those States perceived as convenient for the purposes of fisheries, ergo 'flags of non-compliance' are also 'open registry' States in the more general sense, see ITF See *More Troubled Waters: Fishing, Pollution and Flags of Convenience*, Major Group Submission to the 2002 World Summit on Sustainable Development in Johannesburg, August 2002, ITF, London, 2002, at p. 16 (herein after "More Troubled Waters") and ITF, *FOC Countries*, at http://www.itfglobal.org/flags-convenience/flags-convenien-183.cfm. Nevertheless, Rayfuse's point that fisheries specific flags of convenience are not *necessarily* open registries is accepted.

[26] Wells, at p. 222.

[27] In fact one analysis of the economic incentives in this decision claims that this factor is "insignificant" – see Tony Alderton and Nik Winchester: *Regulation, Representation and the Flag Market*, Journal of Marine Research, September 2002, at p. 6 (herein after "Alderton and Winchester").

To begin with, many vessels operating under flags of convenience are generally older than the average age of the rest of the world's fleet.[28] As a consequence, the purchase price of these vessels and any loan payments on mortgages will be lessened. This is not to say that *all* flag of convenience vessels are older than the norm[29] but it provides a strong indication that vessel owners intending to register with flags of convenience will often opt for the oldest, ergo cheapest, available vessels. Generally flag of convenience States are sympathetic to these concerns and allow commercial vessels of extreme age on to their registers. For instance, Panama requires "that vessels of over 20 years old will have to pass a special inspection by an authorized Panamanian inspector in order to obtain the Permanent Registration"[30] but has no formal maximum age limit. Similarly, Malta requires that the vessel passes an inspection by an authorised flag State inspector prior to registration, but also has no upper age limit for vessels.[31] Mauritius caps the upper age limit at 15 years, however for vessels older than this "a special application is needed to the Director [of the registry] for exemption which can be given on such conditions as he thinks fit."[32] Cambodia requires that owners of vessels over 25 years of age produce a certificate of seaworthiness but no age of vessel is excluded from the registry.[33]

---

[28] See International Transport Workers' Federation, *What do FOCs Mean to Seafarers?* at http://www.itfglobal.org/flags-convenience/flags-convenien-184.cfm.

[29] In a 2004 document published by the ITF, however, the statistical breakdown of the *average* age of vessels on FOC registries does compare favourably to the *average* age of vessels on non-FOC registries: For instance the average age of vessels registered in both Panama and Vanuatu is 17 years, 16 years in Bermuda, 15 years in the Bahamas, and in Liberia, the Marshall Islands and Antigua & Barbuda it is 12 years. Belize, Honduras and St. Vincent & the Grenadines average slightly older with ages of 23 years, 30 years and 24 years respectively. By way of comparison with Western non-FOC States the figures are: United Kingdom – 20 years, United States – 24 years, Italy and Germany – 22 years, Sweden – 30 years, Norway – 27 years and France – 21 years, see ITF Annual Report 2004, *ITF Campaign Against Flag of Convenience and Sub-Standard Shipping*, 2004, ITF, London. This statistical breakdown may not reflect the true age of many vessels on FOC registries, however, due to the increasing tendency of many of the owners of newly built fishing vessels to register these vessels to a flag of convenience registry immediately upon launch, see Gianni and Simpson, *The Changing Nature of High Seas Fishing: How Flags of Convenience Provide Cover for Illegal, Unreported and Unregulated Fishing*, Australian Department of Agriculture, Fisheries and Forestry, International Transport Workers' Federation, and WWF International, 2005, at p. 20 (herein after "Gianni and Simpson (2005)") in which the authors note that between 2001 and 2003 the number of newly built large-scale (over 24m long) vessels immediately registered to a flag of convenience State was 12% of the total of all large-scale fishing vessels built.

[30] *The Advantages of the Panamanian Registry*, at http://www.embassy-avenue.jp/panama/adva.htm.

[31] Merchant Shipping Directorate, Malta Maritime Authority, at http://malta.co.uk/malta/shipreg1.htm.

[32] Republic of Mauritius' Ministry of Public Infrastructure, Land Transport & Shipping, at http://www.gov.mu/portal/site/mpisite/menuitem.c665e7efbc57b2368b1dd210a0208a0c/.

[33] http://www.flagsofconvenience.com/page.php?pID=51.

Perhaps of more significance in terms of economic output are the day to day running costs of the vessel and will include the crew's wages, insurance and compliance with national minimum safety standards. In these regards flags of convenience registries can prove to be highly attractive for vessel owners. Certainly, as already demonstrated by Panama during the inter-war years, cheap non-indigenous, non-union labour can drastically reduce operating costs and those open registries currently reaping the benefit of increased registrations have no requirement that nationals of the flag state crew the vessel.[34] Consequently vessel operators will be able to crew their vessels with the cheapest available labour. Only twenty percent of all vessels registered to flags of convenience have shown any willingness to adhere to the International Transport Workers' Federation minimum wage determination and in the absence of any statutory minimum wage guarantee in the flag State, crew costs can be very low for operators.[35] Consequently crew members from developing States on board a typical flag of convenience fishing vessel can expect to earn in the region of US$100 per month[36] compared to the starting salary of a UK deckhand on a fishing boat of US$1,400 per month.[37]

Alongside the poor wages paid to crews of flag of convenience vessels are the poor conditions that they may be subjected to during their tenure onboard. Often these crews may not reap the benefits of decent and safe working conditions. Quarters may be sparse, food basic and working hours long – indeed in one case before the International Tribunal of the Law of the Sea, *The Camouco*, the conditions under which the crew were forced to subsist were described as akin to slavery.[38] Again, like wages, substandard conditions on board vessels are ultimately the responsibility of the flag State[39] and in the case of flag of convenience States the evidence does appear to show that these obligations are often not fulfilled.[40] For instance, numerous international conventions exist governing the on-board and employment conditions of maritime workers, covering both

[34] Wells, at n. 20.

[35] H. Edwin Anderson, *The Nationality of Ships and Flags of Convenience: Economics, Politics and Alternatives*, 21 Mar. Law. 139, at p. 157 (herein after "Anderson").

[36] Agnew and Barnes, at pp. 181–182.

[37] See www.connexions.gov.uk/jobs4u this figure correlates to the "bench mark" figure set by the International transport Workers' Federation in 2001.

[38] Panama v France, Case Number 5, ITLOS Press Release 34, 3 February 2000.

[39] UNCLOS Art. 94(2)(b) "[Every State shall] . . . assume jurisdiction under its internal law over each ship flying its flag and its master, officers and crew in respect of administrative, technical and social matters concerning the ship."

[40] International Transport Workers' Federation, *Steering the Right Course: Towards an era of Responsible Flag State and Effective International Governance of Oceans and Seas*, ITF, June 2003, at p. 22 (herein after "Steering the Right Course").

general minimum shipboard conditions[41] as well as more specific issues. Thus several conventions came into being in the latter half of the twentieth century, all issued under the auspices of the International Labour Organisation (ILO), that dealt with specific and detailed issues of shipboard standards. For example, the ILO conventions set the minimum standards to be expected in terms of the standard of food supply onboard vessels,[42] the payment of wages,[43] an entitlement to paid holidays,[44] the minimum standards of accommodation,[45] the prevention of accidents[46] and the permissible hours of work and minimum manning requirements of ships.[47] Only extremely rarely have any of these conventions been embraced by flag of convenience States.[48]

It is precisely this "hands-off" attitude that makes the registry particularly attractive to rogue and exploitative vessel owners in the first place – "[t]here is a strong correlation between inefficient regulation and inferior working conditions for seafarers. Where the aim of the owners flagging to weak regulatory regimes is, invariably, to cut costs, then this has measurable, and significant, effects upon the working conditions and safety of those who toil at the sharp end of the maritime industry."[49]

Once any vessel owner has worked out the economic advantages to his enterprise offered by a State registry that will not subject him to troublesome legislative or regulatory requirements, he will realise that there are indeed economic advantages to be had by flagging out. In practice these economic advantages correlate to an average reduction in operating costs for FOC vessels of between

[41] *Merchant Shipping (Minimum Standards) Convention*, 1976, International Labour Organisation, C/147.

[42] *Food and Catering (Ship's Crews) Convention*, 1946, International Labour Organisation, C/68.

[43] *Wages, Hours of Work and Manning (Sea) Convention*, 1958, International Labour Organisation, C/109.

[44] *Paid Vacation (Seafarers) Convention*, 1949, International Labour Organisation, C/91.

[45] *Accommodation of Crews (Fishermen) Convention*, 1966, International Labour Organisation, C/126.

[46] *Prevention of Accidents (Seafarers) Convention*, 1970, International Labour Organisation, C/134.

[47] *Seafarers' Hours of Work and the Manning of Ships Convention*, 1997, International Labour Organisation, C/180.

[48] For instance, 25 States have ratified the *Food and Catering (Ship's Crews) Convention* – only one of which (Panama) is a recognised FOC State. Likewise, the *Paid Vacation (Seafarers) Convention* has been ratified by 24 States, none of which are FOCs. The *Accommodation of Crews (Fishermen) Convention* has more FOC representation in terms of ratifications, with Belize, Panama and Liberia to be found amongst the 46 State parties. Similarly 2 FOCs (Belize and Liberia) number amongst the 52 ratifications of the *Merchant Shipping (Minimum Standards) Convention*, whilst Malta is the only FOC State out of 20 States to have ratified the *Seafarers' Hours of Work and the Manning of Ships Convention.*

[49] Steering the Right Course, at p. 21 (quoting Winchester and Alderton, *Globalisation and De-Regulation in the Maritime Industry*, 2002).

12 and 27 per cent as compared to non-FOC registered vessels.[50] With these cost-savings in mind, it is no wonder that the FOC option becomes an attractive one.

2.4 *The Economic Incentives for States to Act as Flags of Convenience*

Although 32 States are currently labelled as flags of convenience, the main convenient fisheries registries are – according to the International Transport Workers' Federation[51] – Panama, Malta, Mauritius,[52] Belize,[53] Cambodia, Bolivia, and Equatorial Guinea.[54] To this list the United Nations Food and Agriculture Organisation adds a further 20 or so States "operating open registries that include…fishing vessels."[55] The benefits to these States in terms of fiscal gains to their national economies are, for the most part, the reason that they open their registries to "foreign" vessels. Of these 32 States operating convenient registries a significant proportion are classed as developing States,[56] and the benefits to their national economies are, therefore, "not insignificant."[57]

For instance, the income generated for Panama by its shipping registry amounts to almost US$20m, of which over US$730,000 is from fishing vessels alone; Malta's registry is worth nearly US$5m, with fisheries accounting for US$23,000; Belize reaps over US$2.8m to its national economy, of which

[50] S. Tolofari, *Open Registry Shipping: A Comparative Study in Costs and Freight Rates*, Gordon and Breach Science Publishers, London, 1989.

[51] International Transport Workers' Federation, *FOC Countries*, at http://www.itfglobal.org/flags-convenience/flags-convenien-183.cfm. Although the ITF classes these States as "States" for the purposes of their FOC list, several are not "States" at all but dependent territories, crown dependent territories or administrative departments of other States (UK-Bermuda, Cayman Islands, Gibraltar, Isle of Man; New Zealand – Cook Islands; The Netherlands – Netherlands Antilles; France – Kerguelen).

[52] Although it should be noted that these registries are said to be in the decline. See More Troubled Waters, at p. 16.

[53] Due, in no small part to an increased regulation of fisheries activities by the authorities in Belize, the number of fishing vessels on its register has shown a rapid decrease over the last few years. See United Nations Food and Agriculture Organisation Fisheries Department, *The State of World Fisheries and Aquaculture 2004*, UNFAO, Rome, 2004, at p. 27 (herein after "The State of World Fisheries 2004"). A more detailed analysis of the actions taken by the authorities in Belize can be seen later in this Chapter.

[54] More Troubled Waters, at pp. 16–17.

[55] Judith Swan (2002), *Fishing Vessels Operating Under Open Registries and the Exercise of Flag State Responsibilities – Information and Options*, Fisheries Circular No. 90, FIPP/C980, UNFAO, Rome, 2002, at Appendix 1 (herein after "Swan (2002)").

[56] At least 15 of these States are classed as Small Island Developing States by the UNFAO, see http://www.un.org/esa/sustdev/sids/sidslist.

[57] Swan (2002), Part III, *The Rationale for the Operation of Open Registries.*

US$500,000 comes from fishing vessel registration; Equatorial Guinea's fisheries register accounts for US$121,000 of the total income generated of US$163,000; while Honduras is by far the biggest beneficiary of fisheries registration levies, gaining over US$1m from a total of US$3.4m.[58] And although these sums are relatively small in terms of GDP,[59] in terms of much sought after foreign investment the revenues generated by all vessels are extremely important, especially when it is considered that these figures are almost certainly underestimates and the income generated by registration fees can, in some cases, be doubled by additional documentation charges.[60] If, on the other hand, we consider the revenues generated by fishing vessels in isolation perhaps the same cannot be said for the revenue accrued by this industry: in terms of their contribution to the national economies of the States, the revenues generated by these vessels are certainly not large, and with the exception of Honduras no State amasses more than US$1m.

2.5 *Flags of Convenience and their Relationship with IUU Fishing*

In the context of the fisheries industry, flags of convenience have become synonymous with the broader harms caused by the deleterious practices known as Illegal, Unreported and Unregulated (IUU) fishing. In turn IUU has, at the turn of the 21st century, seemingly become the vogue in describing all manner of unsavoury fishing practices, of which flags of convenience are simply one component. The term 'IUU' was first coined by the Commission for the Conservation of Antarctic Marine Living Resources (CCAMLR) in 1997[61] but for the purposes of this present study, and seemingly most contemporary work on the subject, the accepted definition will be that provided by the United Nations Food and Agriculture Organisation (UNFAO) in its 2001 International Plan of Action, which states:

> Illegal fishing refers to fishing activities:
>
> (1) conducted by national or foreign vessels in waters under the jurisdiction of a State, without the permission of that State, or in contravention of its laws and regulations;
> (2) conducted by vessels flying the flag of States that are parties to a relevant regional fisheries management organization but operate in contravention of

[58] Swan (2002), Appendix 9, Table 3.

[59] Panama's GBP is US$13b, Malta's US$7b, Belize's US$1b, Equatorial Guinea's US$2.2b and Honduras' US$7.2. UK Foreign and Commonwealth Office, *Country Profiles*, at www.fco.gov.uk.

[60] Swan (2002), Part III, *The Rationale for the Operation of Open Registries.*

[61] CCAMLR 16th Meeting of the Parties, 1997. Cited in Agnew and Barnes, at pp. 171–172 and Rayfuse (2004), at p. 37.

the conservation and management measures adopted by that organization and by which the States are bound, or relevant provisions of the applicable international law; or
(3) in violation of national laws or international obligations, including those undertaken by co-operating States to a relevant regional fisheries management organization.

Unreported fishing refers to fishing activities:

(1) which have not been reported, or have been misreported, to the relevant national authority, in contravention of national laws and regulations; or
(2) undertaken in the area of competence of a relevant regional fisheries management organization which have not been reported or have been misreported, in contravention of the reporting procedures of that organization.

Unregulated fishing refers to fishing activities:

(1) in the area of application of a relevant regional fisheries management organization that are conducted by vessels without nationality, or by those flying the flag of a State not party to that organization, or by a fishing entity, in a manner that is not consistent with or contravenes the conservation and management measures of that organization; or
(2) in areas or for fish stocks in relation to which there are no applicable conservation or management measures and where such fishing activities are conducted in a manner inconsistent with State responsibilities for the conservation of living marine resources under international law.[62]

Clearly a number of distinct situations and types of fisheries are covered by the above definition. Illegal fishing can be broken down into three types. The first type of illegal fishing concerns unauthorised fishing in waters under coastal State jurisdiction – such as, for instance, Exclusive Economic Zones, or authorised fishing conducted in an unauthorised manner or in violation of any rules enacted by Coastal States governing such activities. The second and third types of illegal fishing relate to activities taking place in areas beyond national jurisdictions, such as the high seas. In the first of these situations the flag State of the vessel concerned will have acceded to regional treaties and conventions governing fisheries activities in any particular area, and the vessel in question will be operating in a manner inconsistent with the rules laid down by these regional agreements. In the final example, the vessel will be operating in violation of the national laws enacted by its flag State.

Unregulated fishing, however, is not illegal fishing because there are no precise laws governing the activities of the particular vessel in question. This can

[62] Paragraph 3 of the FAO *International Plan of Action to Prevent, Deter and Eliminate Illegal, Unreported and Unregulated Fishing*, UNFAO, Rome, 2001 (herein after "IPOA-IUU").

occur for two main reasons. First, there is so-called "third-party free riding"[63] where regional or international laws have, in fact, been developed but the flag State of the vessel engaged in activities contrary to these laws has not acceded to a relevant convention or treaty. The second situation concerns geographical areas beyond any form of explicit regulation when fishing vessels engage in activities contrary to international norms.

Both illegal and unregulated fishing activities may go unreported, and in addition to these, unreported fishing also includes legitimate and lawful harvests, that, for a variety of reasons, go unreported or, indeed, misreported. A typical example of unregulated/unreported fishing can be found in relation to the toothfish fishery, considered in Chapter Five whereby in order to circumvent regional regulations and conservation measures vessel owners will harvest toothfish within a regulated area but report the catch as being harvested from the high seas beyond the control of the Regional Fisheries Management Organisations.

Illegal/unreported fishing operates on the same basis – that is to say, the fraudulent laundering of harvests, but may also take place because of numerous additional reasons. For instance, a vessel owner might not wish to report the discard of by-catch, and in so doing they will circumvent restrictions on non-target by-catch throwing the evidence of his infraction back into the oceans.[64] Or the vessel owner may not wish to report incidents of discarded target species. The latter instance of discard might take place, for instance, due to a vessel dumping its first catch if it can replenish its holds with more valuable larger fish of the same species.[65] Finally, and perhaps the most straightforward of circumstances, the vessel owner may not wish to declare the fact that they have fished in excess of their allocated quota.

Whilst it is not suggested that there are any easy solutions to these problems, the purpose of this book is to concentrate on unregulated fishing rather than illegal and unreported fishing. Certainly at a theoretical level, if not a practical one, the problem of illegal and unreported fishing is less complex: where rules exist and these rules are breached there is at least a framework under which miscreants may be brought to justice. Obviously there are the major practical considerations of engaging in effective policing in vast ocean spaces,

---

[63] Kevin Bray, *A Global Review of Illegal, Unreported and Unregulated Fishing*, at http://www.affa.gov.au/corporate_docs/publications/pdf/fisheries/eciouuf/IUU6.pdf.

[64] Many Regional Fisheries Management Organisations will impose limits on the level of non-target fisheries, which typically will be discarded due to their low commercial value.

[65] UNGA Resolution 57/142 of 26th February recognised this problem and urged States to take action against such problems. For further see Marine Resources Assessment Group, *Review of the Impacts of Illegal. Unreported and Unregulated Fishing on Developing Countries*, July 2005, MRAG, London, (herein after "MRAG July 2005").

but, provided that luck or judgment works in favour of enforcement agencies, then prosecutions and sanctions may be brought to bear. Much does depend, however, firstly upon the will of the State obliged to bring the miscreants to justice and secondly upon the area of sea space in which the illegal activity has taken place.

As we will see in subsequent Chapters, the oceans are divided into a number of jurisdictional zones, and depending upon the nature of the offence and the area in which that offence occurred enforcement jurisdiction may lie with either the flag State of the vessel, the coastal State in whose waters the offence occurred, or a State having power vested in it by virtue of an agreement with the flag State of the offending vessel. Nevertheless, the risk of capture exists for illegal fishing vessels and this risk of capture must be factored in to the decision to engage in such activities. In the last few years statisticians have developed increasingly sophisticated methodologies for calculating and factoring in this risk of detection into the economics of IUU fishing.[66] Put simply, the risk must be worth taking when considering the following:

(1) benefits that can be realised by engaging in the illegal activity;
(2) the probability that the illegal activity is detected or the detection likelihood driver. This depends mainly on the level of enforcement or the set of regulations in place;
(3) the penalty the fisher faces if caught;
(4) the cost to the fisher in engaging in avoidance activities...;
(5) the degree of the fishers' moral and social standing in society and how it is likely to be affected by engaging in IUU fishing.[67]

Unregulated fisheries provide a different and slightly more vexed set of problems. How, for instance, does the international community respond when vessels are engaged in activities, which, although harmful and contrary to the laws that responsible States subject their vessels to, are not in violation of any obligation to act in a lawful manner due to the non-acceptance of international or regional rules by the flag State of the vessels? Likewise, do the factors of risk-avoidance form as relevant an aspect of the decision to engage in unregulated fishing as they do in the decision to engage in illegal fishing? As this Chapter has already shown, flags of convenience offer vessel owners a competitive advantage by driving down the costs of their operations, and it is contended that whilst for the

---

[66] See for instance, Sumaila, Alder and Keith, *Global Scope and Economics of Illegal Fishing*, Marine Policy 30 (2006) 696–703, (herein after "Sumaila *et al.*"); Agnew and Barnes, *Economic Aspects and Drivers of IUU Fishing: Building a Framework*, in *Fish Piracy: Combating Illegal, Unreported and Unregulated Fishing*, OECD, Paris, 2004; OECD Secretariat, *Economics of IUU Fishing Activities*, in *Why Fish Piracy Persists: The Economics of Illegal, Unreported and Unregulated Fishing*, OECD, Paris, 2005.

[67] Sumaila *et al.*, at p. 697.

illegal fisher the above listed factors will have a significant impact upon their decision-making process, the same logic does not apply to the unregulated or flag of convenience fisher.[68] For the unregulated fisher the primary goal is the avoidance of regulation: after all if you are not subject to the laws in the first place then your activities cannot be deemed illegal.

The next section of this Chapter will therefore demonstrate how the avoidance of regulation works in practice and show that when one State of registry ceases to be convenient another will be there to fill the void.

Whilst generally considered a phenomenon unique to the post-UNCLOS decades, incidences of fish piracy and the use of flags of convenience in fisheries and marine capture can be traced back hundreds, if not thousands of years. For instance Upton and Vangelis state that "pirate fishing in Athenian waters by fleets based in the Asia Minor Greek cities in 260 BC…helped trigger a series of mini-conflicts…"[69] In slightly more modern times, in the late 1800s, the proceedings before the Panel in the *Behring Fur Seal Arbitration*[70] inadvertently gave rise to a particularly overt example of flag-hopping by seal hunters anxious to escape the regulation of their activities.[71] Faced with a declining population of seals found off the coast of Alaska, the USA asserted a right of protection over the herds of fur seals and enacted laws aimed at conserving the species. Over a number of years Canadian seal hunters had been operating on the high seas, in contravention of these US laws, and were arrested, detained and fined. In order to establish the legality of these (and other detentions) the USA and Great Britain submitted the matter to arbitration. During this arbitration, Great Britain (for Canada) argued that the USA had no right of protection and that the fur seals, being found on the ice flows of the high seas, were either *res communis* or *res nullius* (owned by all or owned by no-one). In response to this the USA argued that the freedom of the high seas extended to only inoffensive use: that is to say, use that was not "injurious to the just interests of any nation that borders it" and that it had, in any event, an obligation of protection and a right of property over the seals, due to their annual

[68] As will be shown in Chapters Five and Six the proposed method by which the economic scales can be weighted against the unregulated or FOC fisher is to deny a market for their wares: thus if they cannot sell their product there is no incentive to engage in the activity.

[69] Upton and Vangelis, *Stopping the High Seas Robbers: Coming to grips with Illegal, Unreported and Unregulated Fisheries on the High Seas*, Round Table on Sustainable Development, OECD, 6th June 2003, cited in Bertrand Le Gallic, *Using Trade Measures in the Fight Against IUU Fishing*, Paper Presented to International Institute of Fisheries Economics and Trade Conference, Japan, 2004, at p. 1 (herein after "Le Gallic"), available at: http://www.oecd.org/dataoecd/31/44/34227035.pdf.

[70] *Moore's International Arbitration Awards*, I (1898), 811. Reproduced in 1 *Int. Env. Law Reps.* (2000), 43.

[71] Birnie, Boyle and Redgwell, *International Law and the Environment*, 3rd Edition, Oxford University Press, Oxford, 2009 at pp. 707–708 (herein after "Birnie, Boyle and Redgwell").

migration to US territory. The Arbitral Panel, however, was not impressed by the United States' arguments and found for Great Britain.

Following the judgment of the Panel both parties to the dispute requested that regulations for the future conservation of the fur seals be promulgated by the Panel, a request with which the Panel duly obliged, thus regulating the activities of seal hunting vessels of both UK/Canadian and US ownership in the area. Unfortunately this agreement did not bind the two other States with an interest in seal hunting in that area, Japan and Russia, thus "the US and Canadian vessel owners re-registered their vessels under Japanese and other flags to evade the US and Canadian regulations."[72]

More recently still, during the 1950s, flags of convenience became inexorably linked with marine capture by the infamous *Olympic Challenger* – a whaling vessel owned by Aristotle Onassis' Olympic Whaling Company that sought to avoid International Whaling Commission (IWC) regulations by flying the flag of Panama. Due to Panama's non-membership of the IWC the *Olympic Challenger* was able to violate nearly every IWC rule with absolute impunity.[73] In conjunction with its sister ships, many of which flew Honduran flags, the *Olympic Challenger* accounted for over 4500 unregulated catches of South Atlantic humpback whales in the period between 1951 and 1956.[74] Over the next half century the fishing and flag of convenience industries continued their courtship so that by the dawn of the millennium a significant proportion of the world's fishing fleet was engaged in unregulated activities.[75]

For these vessels, however, the economic advantages to be had by the cheaper running and registration costs of the wider merchant fleet could be described as an added bonus. The traditional image of the ancient and rusting boat, operating so close to the edge of bankruptcy so that the imposition of minimum standards of safety and conditions would be its economic *coup de grace* may still hold true for many fishing vessels, but clearly there is also another aspect to the FOC fishing problem. For the owners of less down-at-heel vessels, the decision to flag out may have been made as a result of weightier considerations.[76]

---

72 *Ibid.*

73 DeSombre, at p. 5.

74 Ken Findlay, *Historic Whaling in the Southern Hemisphere*, Indo-South Atlantic Consortium on Humpback Whales http://www.ISACH.org/.

75 The precise extent of the FOC fishing industry, in terms of the number of vessels and landings will be discussed in the following Chapter.

76 One report notes that "[a]n increasing number of young and recently constructed vessels are moving to open registries. Consequently, the 'flag of convenience' fleet is not an old and aging fleet as had been previously thought." *Report of the Expert Consultation on Fishing Vessels Operating Under Open Registries and Their Impact on Illegal, Unreported and Unregulated Fishing*, UNFAO Fisheries Report No. 722, Rome, 2004, at p. 25 (herein after "UNFAO Fisheries Report No. 722").

Over-capacity within the legitimate fisheries sector is often cited as one such example. Capacity, put simply, is the ability of a vessel, or more usually a fleet of vessels, to catch fish and therefore over-capacity is when there are too many vessels or too much fishing effort in a fleet to be satisfied by the available fish stocks.[77] Consequently when over-capacity exists, unless vessel owners are offered incentives to do otherwise, they will move their vessels from traditional fishing grounds rather than accept less of a stake in the available stocks.[78] Likewise, when regulations encroach into once "free" seas displaced fishers may seek out new grounds in the high seas where regulations may be avoided by the use of a convenient flag.[79] Or, as the example of the *Olympic Challenger* shows, vessel owners may simply wish to avoid regulatory norms from the outset and for many of the newly built vessels registering straight onto flags of convenience this would seem to be the logical rationale.

Open registries exacerbate the problem of flags of convenience due to the ease with which vessels may enter and, significantly, leave them and are particularly valuable to those vessel operators whose decision to flag out may have been driven equally by economic incentives discussed above and the avoidance of international standards. Generally, for those companies owning the vessels, incorporation into the State of registry, and thus providing a "genuine link" to that State simply means having a representative – usually an agent or lawyer with power of attorney – in that State. Consequently moving from flag State to flag State involves little more than paying any deregistration and registration fees due, submitting the necessary documentation (usually application forms, certificates of seaworthiness, notarised bill of sale, etc.) and appointing a representative in the new State of registration. To facilitate this many registries will recommend suitable representatives, and the entire process may be carried out by one visit to proprietary websites such as www.flagofconvenience.com

[77] *Report of the Technical Consultation on the Measurement of Fishing Capacity*, UNFAO Fisheries Report No. 615, Rome, 2000, at paragraph 38.

[78] United Nations General Assembly Report, *Sustainable Fisheries*, A/60/189, 2nd August 2005, at paragraph 76; The Economics of IUU Fishing, at p. 38.

[79] It is often claimed that the growth in FOC fisheries and related harms can often be traced to the creation of the EEZ by UNCLOS, the rationale being that coastal States, under the principle of sovereign rights of exploitation of resources as laid down in Article 56 UNCLOS, would reserve all available stocks for its own vessels under Article 62 UNCLOS. See, for instance, UNFAO Fisheries Report No. 722. In relation to a less "traditional" flag of convenience situation, David Balton notes that this precise occurrence lead to the Bering Sea crisis when following stakes of sovereignty by the USSR and the USA over large areas of the former high seas zones in the Bering Sea under UNCLOS's EEZ regime many distant water fishing nation vessels simply decamped to the high sea "donut hole" and proceeded to decimate the Pollock stocks found therein, see David A Balton, *The Bering Sea Doughnut Hole Convention*, in Olav Schram Stokke, *Governing High Seas Fisheries*, Oxford University Press, Oxford, 2001.

or www.maritimechain.com. In many cases this process can take as little as 24 hours.[80]

Ex hypothesi, vessels may, for instance, fly the flag of State 'A' for the convenient purposes of avoiding one set of regulations or conservation measures. When the sought after stock has been fully exploited the vessel will move on to more fertile grounds and fall within the reach of another regulatory body. At this point, the flag currently being flown may cease to be convenient – for instance, the flag State could be party to the regulatory agreement governing that geographical area or catch. Or, perhaps, the flag State of registration ceases to be convenient due to subsequent adherence to international standards by that State. The ease by which vessels can transfer registration means that such events are, at most, a slight inconvenience, and provided that the vessel can stay one step ahead of the game by seeking out a new flag whenever regulations rear their head, they can continue this process almost indefinitely all the while engaged in potentially or actually harmful fishing practices.

The fishing vessel *El Marquez*[81] provides a perfect example of the relative ease of movement between flag of convenience registries. Built in 1973 by Coast Shipbuilding Corporation of Biloxi, Mississippi, the 659 ton *John Mavar Sr*, as the vessel was originally known, was a mainstay of the USA's shrimp fishing fleet for a quarter of a century, operated by the family-run Mavar Shrimp and Oyster Company and its subsidiary the Mavar Boat Company of Biloxi. In the late 1980s, after over 60 years of independent trading, Mavar Shrimp and Oyster was, however, no more. Bought out by StarKist,[82] (a subsidiary of Heinz Foods) in 1988, the company's 6 fishing vessels continued to operate in the Gulf of Mexico, under the management of the Mavar family, as stipulated in the take-over agreement, supplying the raw ingredients for the pet food industry.[83] In the late 1990s, however, the ageing *John Mavar Sr* was sold on and left the US shrimping fleet. Renamed the *Don Italo* and registered to Belize, the vessel was now owned and operated by Megainvest, an Ecuadorean registered tuna fishing company.[84]

For the next five years the *Don Italo* was engaged in purse seine tuna fisheries in the Eastern Pacific[85] under the management of Megainvest, and whilst during this period its management remained more or less constant, its registration

---

[80] The aforementioned websites provide a full list of registration requirements for a number of FOC States.

[81] Vessel history unless otherwise stated is taken from Lloyd's Register of Shipping.

[82] This would be the first of the *El Marquez's* links to the tuna fishing industry, Star-Kist were later to one of the companies to label their tuna products as "Dolphin Safe".

[83] *Star-Kist Foods Enters Agreement to Acquire Mavar Companies*, PR Newswire, November 30, 1987.

[84] Lloyd's Registry of Shipping.

[85] Inter-American Tropical Tuna Commission Quarterly Report July–September 2001.

did not. After its initial entrance into the flag of convenience market place with its registration in Belize in 1998, its owners seemingly found it difficult to settle upon a suitable State of registration. Consequently from 1998 until 2003 the *Don Italo* flag hopped between most of the notorious flag of convenience States. Belize, Honduras, Bolivia, Ecuador, Belize (again) and finally Panama all played host to the *Don Italo* in this unsettled period in the old vessel's history. Although it was now thirty-two years old it still seemingly represented a good investment for the Mantayara Fisheries Corporation who purchased it and gave the *El Marquez* its present name and function and apparently hoped to squeeze a few more years of service from its ancient hull.[86] In 2003 observers from the Inter-American Tropical Tuna Commission spotted the *Don Italo/El Marquez* fishing in "clear violation" of regionally agreed rules.[87] Since then, however, it seems that the vessel's owners decided to legitimise its activities and the *El Marquez* has, as of 2011, no record of further infractions of fisheries laws.

2.6 *A Rogue State Come Good? How Belize is Cleaning Up its Act, but Vessel Owners Are Not*

So far in this Chapter Belize has been portrayed as one of the key IUU/FOC States. This is not an entirely inaccurate portrayal as clearly Belize does have an open, international register and benefits to the tune of almost US$3m per annum from registry fees alone, and equally historical evidence clearly points to Belizean registered vessels engaging in deleterious activities in many of the world's ocean spaces in the past.[88] But one should not be blind to the fact that as a traditional flag of convenience Belize appears to be on the decline. From its heyday in the late 1990s, when the Belizean fishing registry was synonymous with illegal fishing, a decade later in 2011, no Belizean vessels appeared on the IUU lists of all of the major regional fisheries management organisations.[89] To chart this increase in the legitimacy of the Belizean vessel registry the following section will consider the decline of its involvement in the FOC industry from both a numerical and analytical perspective – how many vessels have left the Belizean register and why did they leave. Of additional crucial significance will

[86] Lloyd's Register of Shipping.

[87] International Dolphin Conservation Program/Inter-American Tropical Tuna Commission, Joint Working Group on Fishing By Non-Parties, 3rd Meeting, Lima, June 2004, Document No. JWG 03/05. The regional rules that the *Don Italo* violated were those relating to the protection of dolphins under the mandate of the Agreement on the International Dolphin Conservation Program. This Agreement is discussed in the next Chapter.

[88] See *infra* n. 93.

[89] For further on RFMO IUU lists see Chapter 5.

be the question of what happens to the vessels leaving the Belize register – are they simply being scrapped, or have they gone the way of the aforementioned *El Marquez* and found a less exacting registry to allow them to continue their activities unmolested by regulation?

With 386km of Caribbean coast line and flanked by Mexico to the northwest and Guatemala to the south, Belize is typical of many Central American States. Its major agricultural products of sugar and bananas, coupled with its fledgling second industry of tourism struggle to generate sufficient foreign investment to prevent its national economy running into deficit. For the 280,000 Belizeans life can be harsh – average unemployment is close to 13% and with 33% of the population living below the poverty line, it is perhaps understandable that it has been tempted to sell its flag to foreign shipping companies.[90]

Facilitating this sale, the Belizean Shipping Register is run from Belize City by the International Merchant Marine Registry of Belize (IMMARBE). IMMARBE is the quasi-governmental body operating under the powers conferred by the 1989 Registration of Merchant Ships Act (Amended 1996)[91] to which all foreign vessel owners must apply in order to have their ships registered. In the 1990s IMMARBE was a very busy enterprise indeed, as in that period the Belizean Register grew steadily: in 1989 only three ships were registered with IMMARBE, but during the following decade a staggering increase had taken place so that by 1999 there were 1631 ships registered to Belize,[92] of which 409 were fishing vessels. Two years later the Belize register had swollen to its high water mark of 455 fishing vessels.[93]

Many of these Belizean fishing vessels were not thought to be playing by the rules, however, with many of them deemed to be undermining the conservation measures agreed by the International Commission for the Conservation of Atlantic Tuna (ICCAT). Despite being warned to ensure its vessels' compliance with these conservation measures by ICCAT, Belize did not act.[94] Consequently, by the late 1990s the Belizean registry had begun to attract such vociferous and scathing criticism that sanctions were imposed on Belize by ICCAT. Belizean ships, said ICCAT, along with vessels from Honduras, were seriously undermining the effectiveness of conservation measures for Bluefin tuna and as such all ICCAT member States were urged to prohibit the import

[90] Social and economic data accurate as of 2011, see: https://www.cia.gov/library/publications/the-world-factbook/geos/bh.html.

[91] The Laws of Belize, Revised Edition 2000, Chapter 236.

[92] Alderton and Winchester, p. 3.

[93] Agnew and Barnes, p. 81.

[94] *Recommendation by ICCAT Regarding Belize and Honduras Pursuant to the 1994 Bluefin Tuna Action Plan Resolution*, Recommendation 96/11, Preamble, 3rd Recital.

of Bluefin tuna and its products from these States.[95] Given the powerful membership of ICCAT – which includes the USA, Japan, Canada, the EU, Russia and China – and the near unanimous opinion that Belize was "one of the worst flags in the world...by almost any statistical indicator"[96] the Belizean authorities faced a stark choice: to continue with their policies in almost total international isolation or reform and clean up their act. IMMARBE chose the latter.

From August 2001, IMMARBE, in conjunction with the Belizean Ministry of Agriculture and Fisheries, undertook a number of initiatives to rid Belize of its tarnished image. Chief of these initiatives was the High Seas Fishing Act of 2003 (HSFA) which signalled Belize's commitment to adhere to many of the international fisheries standards enunciated in international agreements, such as the 1982 United Nations Convention of the Laws of the Sea (UNCLOS),[97] the FAO Compliance Agreement,[98] and the Fish Stocks Agreement.[99] Interestingly, perhaps, the reforming measures introduced by Belize side-stepped almost a century of juridical debate and the 'best method' for curtailing harmful FOC practices, and made no reference whatsoever to the concept of a genuine link between State and vessel in terms of beneficial ownership, seats of corporations or the constitution of the officers and crew of the vessel.[100]

Although Belize did have fisheries laws prior to the HSFA, notably the Revised Fishing Act of 2000,[101] the HSFA introduced for the first time a number of licensing requirements for IMMARBE registered vessels wishing to fish on the high seas areas beyond national jurisdiction. Thus, the HSFA imposes conditions as to where, when and how Belizean high seas fishing operations are to be undertaken. Specifically, the Act introduces the licensing requirement that the issuing officer must be satisfied that Belize will be able to "effectively exercise its responsibilities under the [FAO Compliance] Agreement."[102] Quite how the issuing officer is to ascertain if sufficient flag State control might, in fact, be exercised over the vessel is not detailed by the Act. Nor is the Compliance

---

95 *Ibid.*

96 Lloyd's List, February 2005, Issue 58845, p. 10.

97 The requirements of UNCLOS, in respect of high seas fishing, are discussed in Chapter 5.

98 *Agreement to Promote Compliance with International Conservation and Management Measures by Fishing Vessels on the High Seas*, the Food and Agriculture Organisation of the United Nations, Rome, 1993. For further on this agreement, see Chapter 5.

99 *The United Nations Agreement for the Implementation of the Provisions of the United Nations Convention on the Law of the Sea of 10 December 1982 relating to the Conservation and Management of Straddling Fish Stocks and Highly Migratory Fish Stocks*, for further discussion of the relevant principles contained within this agreement see Chapter 5.

100 See Chapter Four for a comprehensive analysis of the so-called "genuine link" requirement between vessel and State of registry.

101 The Laws of Belize, Volume V, Title XVIII, Chapter 210.

102 Belize High Seas Fishing Act (BHSFA) 2003, s.7(3).

Agreement itself a great deal more helpful in this regard – the only guidance issued is that States such as Belize should take into consideration the links between the vessel and States during the determinative process. The existence of enforcement powers under Part V of the Act, however, is indicative of the ability of the State to ensure compliance – although the efficacy of these enforcement powers is, of course, subject to the obvious need for sufficient resources and adequately trained personnel to be made available. Thus, the first few years of the millennium witnessed a whole-scale expansion of Belize's enforcement capacity; so that by 2005 the number of fisheries inspectors had almost tripled to a figure of 181 compared with the figure of 62 in 2001.[103] The powers vested in these inspectors are fairly broad and permit at-sea stop-and-search inspections and seizures[104] so that the legitimacy of any fishing activity can be ascertained.[105] Following an examination of the facts of the alleged misconduct of the fisher, the Director General or Senior Deputy Registrar may issue a warning, or a fine or may revoke the licenses of miscreants.[106] Only upon payment of a security may any seized vessel be returned to its owner or master prior to any hearing. The amount of this security is to be determined by the Director General or Senior Deputy Registrar.[107] Supplemental to these means of "hands-on" enforcement, all Belizean fishing vessels are required to use functioning electronic satellite tracked Vessel Monitoring Systems (VMS) so that the precise whereabouts of each vessel may be known by IMMARBE at any given time.[108]

To a large extent the HSFA operates on a rather self-referencing basis: it requires that all high seas fishing activities are licensed, that licenses are issued only when appropriate, and that a failure to adhere to the terms of that license or any Regulations issued under the Act constitutes a violation of the Act.[109] Thus, the Act is somewhat lacking in substantive proscriptions. Other than the offences of "the obstruction of authorised officers"[110] and the aforementioned self referencing "contravention of the provisions of the Act" sections, the Act's only other substantive prohibition is the enormously broad requirement that "no Belizean fishing vessel shall engage in any activity on the high seas which

---

[103] Pers. Comm. from Angelo Mouzouropoulos, Director of IMMARBE, to author, August 2005.

[104] BHSFA, s.12(1)(i)(j).

[105] *Ibid.*, s.12(1).

[106] *Ibid.*, s.14.

[107] *Ibid.*, s.13.

[108] IMMARBE Fishing Vessel Circular, FVC-08/06, *Vessel Monitoring Systems*, November 2008.

[109] BHSFA, s.18. This section also deals with, *inter alia*, attempted and repeated offences and aiding and abetting.

[110] *Ibid.*, s.17.

undermines the effectiveness of international conservation and management measures."[111]

Presumably to avoid the need for the Masters of Belizean registered fishing boats to demonstrate, as part of the licensing process, an understanding and knowledge of each and every international conservation and management measure in operation at any given time, in any given locale, the Act confers powers upon the Minister of State to proscribe any activities that may undermine these international measures.[112] Taking the form of Fishing Vessel Circulars, often issued on an annual basis and under the aegis of Regional Fisheries Management Organisation (RFMO) regulations or recommendations, these fisheries circulars flesh out the rather bare bones of the HSFA. For example, it is an internationally agreed priority that the incidental mortality of, *inter alia*, seabirds and turtles is reduced. To this end the UNFAO has issued various international plans of action[113] and guidelines[114] which have been transposed into law and given a degree of regulatory force by numerous RFMOs. Thus it is a requirement for all members of the Indian Ocean Tuna Commission (IOTC), for example, to adhere to the requirements contained within the relevant IOTC resolutions on these matters.[115] Being a member of IOTC since 2007, Belize has fulfilled its obligation under the IOTC resolutions and, in turn, implemented the UNFAO guidance and plan of action in respect of seabirds and turtles by issuing Fishing Vessel Circular 08/01.[116] There are currently six of these fisheries circulars operating to underpin the provisions of the HSFA. Thus fisheries circulars augment the HSFA to fulfil Belize's international and regional obligations in the sphere of fishing vessel identification,[117] the identification and marking of fishing gear,[118] vessel voyage reports,[119] transhipment activities

[111] *Ibid.*, s.7(5)(c).

[112] *Ibid.*, s.16(1)(2).

[113] International Plan of Action for Reducing Incidental Catch of Seabirds in Longline Fisheries, UNFAO, 1999, Rome.

[114] *Guidelines to Reduce Sea Turtle Mortality in Fishing Operations*, UNFAO, 2005 (Re-issued 2009, 2010), Rome.

[115] IOTC Resolution 10/06 on Reducing the Incidental Bycatch of Seabirds in Longline Fisheries; IOTC Resolution 09/06 on Marine Turtles.

[116] IMMARBE FVC-08/01, *Measures to Mitigate the Impact of Fishing for all Fish Stocks on Seabirds and Sea Turtles.*

[117] IMMARBE Fishing Vessel Circular, FVC-08/02 which implements FAO Standard Specifications for the Marking and Identification of Fishing Vessels.

[118] IMMARBE Fishing Vessel Circular, FVC-08/03 which implements the FAO Proposed System for the Marking of Fishing Gear, the FAO Proposed Standard System of Lights and Shapes for the Identification and Location of Fishing Gear.

[119] IMMARBE Fisheries Circular, FVC-08/04.

between vessels on the high seas,[120] the use of VMS technology,[121] and the aforementioned seabirds and turtles circular.

As already mentioned, the new Belizean fisheries management regime does not require a genuine link between vessel and registry by demanding mandatory connections with the State in terms of crews and corporate headquarters. And given the terms of reference under which IMMARBE operates – it is, after all, the *international* merchant marine registry – it would be surprising (and self-defeating) if this were the case. The HSFA has, however, created a link between State and vessel with regards the requirement that the State effectively exercises jurisdiction and control over the vessel. Whilst failing to adhere to the traditional requirement of a genuine link, as demonstrated herein in Chapter Four, the High Seas Fishing Act of 2003 does ensure, if properly implemented, that Belize exercises its flag State responsibilities under the relevant provisions of UNCLOS – that is to say, "effectively exercise its jurisdiction and control in administrative, technical and social matters over ships flying its flag."[122]

The efficacy of the measures taken by the Belizean authorities can be clearly seen by the size of the Registry: within three years the total Belizean merchant fleet had reduced in size by two thirds in 2004, with its fishing fleet diminishing in size by 50% due to the deregistration of 330 vessels deemed as being non-compliant with the HSFA.[123] In view of these facts the international community was sufficiently impressed by Belize's actions that in January 2004 the ICCAT trade sanctions were removed[124] and by 2010 Belize had become a contracting party to ICCAT, a contracting party to IOTC, a co-operating non-contracting party to the Inter-American Tropical Tuna Commission (IATTC) and a co-operating non-contracting party to the North East Atlantic Fisheries Commission (NEAFC).

Clearly then Belize has taken significant steps to come in from the cold, and quite rightly should be congratulated on its initiatives and efforts. Unfortunately, however, the story does not have an entirely happy ending, as there is clear

120 IMMARBE Fisheries Circular, FVC-09/01 which applies, variously and distinctly, to transhipments in the areas covered by several RFMOs and specifically implements the requirements of the North East Atlantic Fisheries Commission (NEAFC), the International Commission for the Conservation of Atlantic Tuna (ICCAT), and the Indian Ocean Tuna Commission (IOTC). The circular also applies a default position for all other (non-specified) RFMOs that all transhipments must be undertaken with the permission that particular RFMO.

121 *Supra*, at n. 108.

122 UNCLOS Article 94(1). For further on this requirement and the link between exercising jurisdiction and the genuine link between vessel and State see Chapter Four.

123 In May 2006 the author contacted IMMARBE requesting information as to how many of the vessels deregistered in Belize were expelled and how many voluntarily deregistered. IMMARBE responded by stating that it was unable to provide this information.

124 *Recommendation by ICCAT Concerning the Importation of Atlantic Bluefin Tuna, Atlantic Swordfish and Atlantic Bigeye Tuna and Their Products From Belize*, Recommendation 02/16.

evidence to suggest that the owners and masters of the vessels leaving the Belizean register do not intend to go meekly into the night. And fortunately for them they do not have to expend too much time and effort in finding a registry that will take them. After all, if an example of a State filling a void was needed we need look no further than Belize itself. From the mid 1980s until 1993 vessels from Panama and Honduras were the chief exponents of IUU/FOC fisheries in the Northwest Atlantic Fisheries Organisation (NAFO) regulatory area, but following diplomatic pressure from the NAFO States both Panama and Honduras de-registered many of the IUU vessels. These vessels immediately registered to Belize and continued their unregulated activities in NAFO waters.[125] In this respect Belize was simply one link of an inexorable and never ending chain that, albeit for a few years,[126] guarantees vessel owners a regulatory free environment.

To evidence this point the author conducted two appraisals of ex-Belizean fishing vessels – one in 2005, and one in 2010 – utilising data taken from Lloyd's Registry of Shipping, to ascertain precisely the registration status of the vessels either expelled by IMMARBE or those which have voluntarily left the Belizean registry. The results of this audit, whilst admittedly far from conclusive,[127] do show an emerging pattern of "new entry" States as well as traditional flags of convenience making not insignificant gains in terms of ex-Belizean registrations.[128] For example, Bolivia,[129] Cambodia,[130] Comoros,[131] Equatorial Guinea,[132]

[125] Vukas and Vidas, p. 56.

[126] On a crude analysis of the Panama/Honduras and Belize experience it is possible to estimate a cycle of seven to ten years from the time a registry becomes an important refuge for IUU fishing boats to the time that diplomatic pressure causes a reappraisal of the conditions of registry. Panama/Honduras held out for eight years between 1985 and 1993. Belize lasted a similar length of time, from 1993 to 2000/2001.

[127] Of the 290 vessels located by the author, 138 were classified, as of December 2010, as "State of Registry Unknown" by Lloyd's.

[128] For a full list of the vessels identified as being ex-Belizean, for the purposes of this audit, see Appendix One this book.

[129] 5 vessels, 1 of which, *Lien Tai*, was previously suspected of IUU longlining activities – *The Importance of Taking Co-operative Action Against Specific Fishing Vessels That Are Diminishing Effectiveness of Tuna Conservation and Management Measures*, Masayuki Komatsu, Expert Consultation Paper on IUU Fishing, prepared for the Government of Australia and the UNFAO, May 2000, Document AUS:IUU/2000/5. 2000, Appendix 3 – *List of Longline Vessels Believed to be Engaged in Unregulated and Unreported Activities*, (herein after "Komatsu, Appendix 3").

[130] 23 vessels.

[131] 4 vessels, 2 of which (*TS Elegance* and *TS Excellence*) have been determined as vessels engaged in IUU activities by the Indian Ocean Tuna Commission, IOTC List of Vessels Determined as IUU, at http://www.iccat.es/IUU.htm, (herein after "IOTC IUU List").

[132] 8 vessels, 2 of which (*Chin Cheng Pong* and *Shin Kuo 2*) have been determined to be engaged in IUU longlining activities, Komatsu, Appendix 3.

Georgia,[133] Sierra Leone,[134] Togo,[135] and Vanuatu[136] have all welcomed ex-Belizean vessels onto their registers in the period between 2001 and 2005. Similarly many vessels found refuge in more established and traditional registries such as Panama,[137] as well as those not traditionally known as a flag of convenience, such as Uruguay.[138] And whilst the numbers of recorded and evidenced transfers of registration are admittedly small, when the 138 vessels currently of "unknown registration" are factored in to the equation then it is possible that within months of the Belizean purge over half the vessels expelled had found a new flag of convenience to fly, unmolested by regulation.[139]

---

[133] 9 vessels.

[134] 7 vessels.

[135] 5 vessels, 2 of which (*Condor* and *Tiphoon*) are designated as IUU toothfish vessels by the Coalition of Legal Toothfish Operators' Wanted Campaign, see http://www.colto.org/vessels.htm (herein after "COLTO, Wanted Campaign"). The *Condor* is also to be found on CCAMLR's list of IUU vessels, see http://www.ccamlr.org/pu/E/sc/fish-monit/iuu-vess-list.htm (herein after "CCAMLR IUU List"). 1 further vessel known to have conducted IUU operations by Greenpeace, see: http://blacklist.greenpeace.org/vessel/show/180 (herein after "Greenpeace IUU List").

[136] 13 vessels, 5 of which (*Shinn Mann No. 11, Shinn Mann No. 21, Shinn Mann No. 666, Chun I No. 316* and *Chun Ying No. 777*) were previously suspected of IUU longlining activities, Komatsu, Appendix 3.

[137] 13 vessels, 1 of which (*Yes Sir*) is Blacklisted by the North-East Atlantic Fisheries Commission as a vessel which has "taken part in fishing operations that contravene regulatory measures as laid down by RFMOs." See Norwegian Fisheries Directorate, *Blacklisted Vessels*, at http://www.fiskeridir.no/fiskeridir/ressursforvaltning/blacklisted_vessels, (Herein after "Norwegian Fisheries Directorate Blacklist").

[138] 5 vessels, of which 3 (*Lua, Vega* and *Viarsa 1*) are Blacklisted by the Commission for the Conservation of Antarctic Marine Living Resources as vessels which have "taken part in fishing operations that contravene regulatory measures as laid down by RFMOs," Norwegian Fisheries Directorate Blacklist. *Vega* and *Viarsa 1* are also to be found on COLTO's Wanted Campaign.

[139] The author's strong suspicion is that many of these vessels are likely to be flying flags of convenience and potentially engaged in IUU fishing activities. This suspicion is based upon the fact that Lloyd's Registry's known history of many of these vessels shows a pattern of moving between flag of convenience States prior to their arrival in and expulsion by Belize – 40 vessels had previously sailed under two or more flags of convenience prior to their status becoming unknown, (Author's research of Lloyd's Registry, September 2005). Additionally, of the remaining 98 "unknown" vessels 48 were registered to Belize immediately after launch and in the period when Belize's reputation as a haven for IUU FOC fishing was at its height, (Author's research of Lloyd's Registry, September 2005). For a comprehensive list and history of these vessels see Appendix One of this book. Furthermore, and perhaps more importantly, 25 of these vessels have a track record of suspected IUU longlining activities whilst on the Belize register when cross-referenced with lists of suspected IUU vessels. See Appendix One for details of the vessels. Likewise, see, in relation to ICCAT Region, *Trade and Market Related Instruments to Reinforce Fisheries Management Measures to Promote Sustainable Fishing Practices*, Cathy A. Roheim and Jon G. Sutinen, Report for the International Centre for

2.7 *The On-going Links in the FOC Chain: Bolivia, Cambodia and Georgia*

One such new entry flag of convenience State is Bolivia. Landlocked Bolivia perhaps might not be one's first choice of a major sea going nation, but in recent years its fleet has dramatically increased in size since the launch of its open registry in 1997.[140] By the time of the registry's third anniversary at the turn of the millennium 155 vessels were flying the Bolivian flag,[141] and by 2006 Bolivia's reputation as a notorious flag of convenience could be evidenced by its abject failure to adhere to a significant number of essential performance indicators adopted by the shipping industry.[142] Similarly Bolivia's representation in the fisheries industry has expanded correspondingly. From its single vessel registered in 1999, through to 11 vessels in 2001, to 24 in 2003,[143] and although by 2005 the number of fishing vessels had fallen to 16[144] the registry had picked up by 2006 to include 43 fishing vessels[145] of which a handful were those escaping/expelled from the Belizean registry. Nevertheless, although the vessels actually identified as being on the Bolivian register are comparatively small these vessels potentially represent the tip of a very large and destructive ice-berg.[146]

First it must be remembered that due to the secretive nature of FOC vessels many of the vessels currently listed as "Flag Unknown" *may* be registered to Bolivia.[147] Whilst this is admittedly capable of being considered conjecture and hypothesis there is a degree of evidence to support any assertion that Bolivia has played theoretical home to many of the world's most destructive fishing vessels.

Trade and Sustainable Development and OECD-High Seas Force, March 2006, (herein after "Roheim and Sutinen"), at p. 16.

140 The Economist, *Bolivia Waves the Flag*, May 27, 2000.

141 Alderton and Winchester, p. 3.

142 *Shipping Industry Flag State Performance Table*, Maritime International Secretariat Services Ltd (in conjunction with BIMCO, Intercargo, International Chamber of Shipping, International Shipping Federation, Intertanko), London, 2006, (herein after "Flag State Performance Table"). Available at: http://www.marisec.org/flag-performance/FlagStatePerformanceTable06.pdf.

143 Agnew and Barnes, p. 81.

144 Gianni and Simpson (2005), p. 13.

145 Statement by the Bolivian Representative to the 74th Meeting of the Inter-American Tropical Tuna Commission, Minutes of the 74th Meeting, Appendix 6(f), p. 51.

146 Gianni and Simpson (2005) claim that Bolivia ranks among the top 14 IUU/FOC fishing States, p. 13.

147 Lloyd's Register of Shipping relies for a large part of its data upon sightings of vessels. Although Art. 94(2)(a) of UNCLOS obliges States to maintain a register of ships, there is no obligation upon States for make their shipping registries open to public scrutiny.

The so-called "Alphabet Boats"[148] provide a good example of such vessels. In the early years of the new millennium this fleet of pirate longliners operated in the Southern Oceans and were, it was alleged, engaged in IUU toothfish fishing.[149] Whilst detailed and accurate information about these vessels is hard to come by it is certain that all of the ten vessels in the fleet were, in 2002–2003 – during their heydays as IUU vessels – registered in Bolivia.[150]

The attraction of Bolivia as a flag of convenience generally, and specifically in relation to fisheries, can be clearly demonstrated by reference to any established criteria for defining a flag of convenience. Bolivia ticks all the right boxes in terms of the avoidance or non-implementation of on-board standards, ease of registration and the lack of any regulatory framework to govern the activities of vessels on its registry. In the race to the bottom in which new entry flags of convenience States compete with one another to offer the most attractive registry,[151] Bolivia is very well placed. The economic attraction of Bolivia is not dissimilar to that of any other flag of convenience State, in that in terms of registration fees and local taxation, capital outlay to enter the register is not a significant sum. Whilst the maximum age of vessel requirement may not be high on the list of priorities for any potential IUU/FOC vessel owner, and indeed, the Bolivian legislative requirements in terms of age are hard to ascertain,[152] owners of older vessels may have no difficulty in registering their vessels in Bolivia. For example, following its expulsion from Belize in 2003, the 30 year old *Mirentzu* provides evidence that even vessels of an extreme age may be welcomed onto the Bolivian registry.[153] Similarly, and again with the important caveat inserted regarding the scarcity of first hand national legislation, it is worth noting that Bolivia is not a party to any of the aforementioned ILO Conventions on wages,

148 So called because the vessel names correspond to letters of the alphabet: *Austin, Boston, Champion, Darwin, Eva, Florence, Georgia, Hunter, Isabella, Jackson, etc.* see Austral Fisheries, *The Alphabet Boats: A Case Study of the Toothfish Poaching in the Southern Ocean*, Austral Fisheries Pty Ltd., 2002, Mount Hawthorn, Australia, p. 1. (Herein after "Austral Fisheries (2002)").

149 Australian Government Fisheries Department, *Australian National Plan of Action to Deter Illegal, Unreported and Unregulated Fishing*, p. 63. (Herein after "Australia IUU/NPA").

150 Austral Fisheries (2002), p. 1. Further research of vessel registration movements at this time confirmed that 2 vessels, *Georgia* and *Hunter* remained on the Bolivian registry in September 2005, Lloyd's Registry of Shipping.

151 Indeed it is this niche market of the worst offenders, unable to gain or sustain their registration on the more established flag of convenience registries due to the greater implementation of minimum international standards by these States, that allow new-entry FOCs to flourish. See Nik Winchester, *How the Squeeze on Standards Enables Small Flags to Flourish*, "The Sea", Issue 151, May/June 2001, Seafarers International Research Centre.

152 Despite a fairly exhaustive search for this data none was found.

153 Lloyd's Registry of Shipping.

conditions or safety on board vessels. Thus the immediate economic attraction to vessel owners is obvious.[154]

In terms of fishing vessels in particular, the attraction of Bolivia for potential IUU/FOC vessel owners is equally apparent. Bolivia has neither the obligation, nor indeed, the practical ability to implement or enforce any specific international or regional regulations concerning any fish stocks or methods of harvest. Despite its ratification of UNCLOS in 1995[155] and its overarching obligations, *inter alia*, to co-operate with other States for the conservation and management of the living resources of the high seas,[156] Bolivia has not implemented these obligations in any serious or meaningful way in terms of entering into regional fisheries management organisations or strategies. Thus, Bolivian registration allows IUU/FOC vessel owners to operate in a manner contrary to almost all regional norms with relative impunity on the high seas.[157] Likewise, other than the aforementioned ratification of UNCLOS, Bolivia has not shown any willingness to enter into global agreements for the conservation of fish stocks or the wider marine environment.[158]

Like Bolivia, Cambodia is another recent entry into the flag of convenience sector. From its humble beginnings in 1995 through to 1999 only 6 fishing vessels were found on the Cambodian registry. By 2005 over 3.5% of the world's flag of convenience fishing vessels were registered in Cambodia.[159] Like Bolivia, Cambodia's remarkable expansion in to the flag of convenience sector appears to have been driven by the twin attractions of low cost and low regulation. In its 2003 "Flag State Audit" the Seafarer's International Research Centre[160] ranked Cambodia as the joint poorest flag State (along with St Vincent &

---

154 The Flag State Performance Table lists as essential for responsible flag State the requirements of, for instance, the ratification of international conventions on health and safety on board ships, marine pollution, etc. Likewise a "negative indicator" on the Flag State Performance Table will result from a State allowing vessels of extreme age on to its shipping register. In both regards Bolivia receives a "negative indicator".

155 http://www.un.org/Depts/los/reference_files/chronological_lists_of_ratifications.htm#The%20United%20Nations%20Convention%20on%20the%20Law%20of%20the%20Sea.

156 Section II of Part VII, Articles 116–120 UNCLOS.

157 Bolivia is not a member of any Regional Fisheries Management Organisations.

158 The failure of Bolivia to embrace international norms includes both hard law such as the United Nations Agreement for the Implementation of the Provisions of the United Nations Convention on the Law of the Sea of 10 December 1982 relating to the Conservation and Management of Straddling Fish Stocks and Highly Migratory Fish Stocks ("The Straddling Stocks Agreement"); the Code of Conduct for Responsible Fisheries, Rome, 1999; the Agreement to Promote Compliance with International Conservation and Management Measures by Fishing Vessels on the High Seas, Rome, 1995 ("The Compliance Agreement").

159 Gianni and Simpson (2005), p. 13.

160 Flag State Audit, *Nik Winchester and Tony Alderton*, Seafarer's International Research Centre, 2003.

the Grenadines) in terms of regulatory capacity, leading the Audit's author to comment that "[i]n these newest flag states we can see the almost total lack of regulation. These super unregulated registers, such as Cambodia...mop up those vessels deemed too risky to the more established open registers, such as Panama and Liberia, thereby extending the working life of such vessels in an almost regulatory-free manner."[161] The Flag State Audit used as its parameters administrative factors such as the cost to vessel owners of Cambodian registry (low), the responsibilities of the administration in ensuring vessel safety and crew welfare (limited), crewing requirements and inspections (lacking) and the eligibility of foreign entities to register in Cambodia (unrestricted).[162] The Audit also considered detentions and inspections conducted under the Tokyo and Paris Memoranda of Understanding on Port State Control (which allow for the inspection and detention of vessels by port States so as to "eliminate sub-standard shipping") in which Cambodian vessels ranked far higher than regional averages.

Similarly the Shipping Industry Flag State Performance Table, complied in 2005, portrayed Cambodia's registry in a less than flattering light and ranked it as one of "the flag States with the highest number of negative performance indicators" in the report, along with other FOCs such as Bolivia, Costa Rica, Honduras and Sao Tome & Principe.[163] The Flag State Performance Table used as its parameters factors such as vessel detentions and inspections under the Paris and Tokyo Memoranda of Understanding, compliance with International Labour Organisation reporting requirements and International Maritime Organisation meeting attendance.[164]

Within the strict confines of the avoidance of fisheries norms, Cambodia fares little better. It is not party to any International or regional fisheries management organisation and nor has it signed, ratified or acceded to the UN Fish Stocks Convention or the Compliance Agreement, and so for the owners of ex-Belizean vessels wishing to escape that State's increased regulation in the early years of the millennium, Cambodia might have represented a suitable flag of convenience. In terms of alleged IUU activity by Cambodian registered vessels, however, no consistent pattern emerges, because whilst Cambodia profited from the registration of ex-Belizean vessels initially following IMMARBE's clean-up,[165] little evidence remains that Cambodian registered vessels pose a

161 Dr Nik Winchester, Seafarer's International Research Centre, Cardiff University, at http://www.sirc.cf.ac.uk/fsa.htm.

162 Flag State Audit, p. 83.

163 Review of the Flag State Performance Table conducted by the High Seas Task Force, *How Well Are Flag States Performing?*, Meeting of the HSTF, Paris, March 2005.

164 Flag State Performance Table.

165 23 ex-Belizean vessels re-registered to Cambodia during the period 2003–2006.

significant threat in terms of IUU fishing, with only 4 vessels "blacklisted" by RFMOs as having engaged in IUU fishing in the immediate years following their entry onto the Cambodian register.[166] None of these vessels are known to have links with the Belizean register.

This, of course, begs the question as to why Cambodia has fared so relatively well in ensuring that fishing entities do not currently use its register as a haven for IUU activities. The answer, it is suggested is two-fold: first, when the Cambodian registry began to swell with IUU vessels after the launch of the registry in 1995, regional and international bodies acted swiftly against imports of fish and fish products from Cambodia. By 1998, it had become obvious that certain IUU fishing vessels were evading measures imposed upon erstwhile irresponsible flag States such as Belize, Honduras and Panama by embarking upon a textbook course of flag hopping and transferring their flags to other States and entities so as to "avoid the trade restrictive measures" operating under ICCAT Recommendation 96/11.[167] ICCAT further requested those States and entities acting as havens for the IUU vessels to take "all necessary measures so as not to diminish the effectiveness of the ICCAT conservation and management measures..."[168]

It had become apparent by 2001, however, that numerous States of registry, including Cambodia, were not acting as requested by ICCAT's earlier Recommendation, with the effect that the conservation measures enacted in the ICCAT region for bigeye tuna were being seriously undermined. Thus ICCAT recommended that all its Contracting Parties prohibit the imports of bigeye tuna and its products from Cambodia, as well as Belize, Honduras and St Vincent & the Grenadines.[169] Similarly, the European Community (EC) embarked upon a series of prohibitions to implement ICCAT's Recommendation and Resolution with the effect that all imports of bigeye tuna originating in Cambodia *et al.* should be prohibited.[170]

---

166 NAFO and NEAFC listed the Cambodian registered "Ice Bay" (IMO No. 8028424) until 2009, and IATTC listed "Dragon III" (IMO No. unknown) and "Tarzan XVIII" (IMO No. unknown) in its IUU list in 2006. CCAMLR has listed the Cambodian, ex-Panamanian "Turuman" (IMO No. 7235733) in its 2005 blacklist.

167 Recommendation by ICCAT Regarding Belize and Honduras Pursuant to the 1994 Bluefin Tuna Action Plan Resolution.

168 Resolution 18/98 by ICCAT Concerning the Unreported and Unregulated Catches of Tunas by Large-Scale Longline Vessels in the Convention Area.

169 Recommendation 00/15 by ICCAT Regarding Belize, Cambodia, Honduras, and St Vincent & the Grenadines Pursuant to the 1998 Resolution Concerning the Unreported and Unregulated Catches of Tuna by Large-Scale Longline Vessels in the Convention Area.

170 Council Regulation (EC) No. 1036/2001, repealed by Council Regulation (EC) No. 827/2004. The latter Regulation did not, however, repeal the substance of the earlier prohibition in relation to Cambodian originating bigeye tuna.

By 2005, however, both ICCAT and the EC had begun to recognise "the efforts made by Cambodia to address the concerns of the Commission" and citing, *inter alia*, the efforts of Cambodia in "deregistering those vessels previously identified as conducting illegal, unregulated and unreported fishing activities..." ICCAT and the EC consequently lifted their prohibitions against imports of Cambodian bigeye tuna.[171]

The second reason for the shift in Cambodian policy, however, may not solely have been due to ICCAT's sanctions and may equally have been brought about by a dramatic change in regime. Like Belize a few years earlier, Cambodia appears to have had a change of heart as to the direction that its vessel registration policy was taking and in 2002 embarked upon a dramatic U-turn, not just in its vessels registration policy but in its entire foreign and international policy. For years, explained Cambodia's first ever delegate to attend an ICCAT Meeting,[172] Cambodia had struggled against civil war and unrest. When it emerged from two decades of turmoil in the late 1990s it was a priority of that country to begin the process of rebuilding and catching up with the rest of the world. As part of this rebuilding process, claimed the delegate, Cambodia would enter the international fold and would attempt to co-operate with all international organisations and "take any measure necessary to control its flagged vessels..."[173]

Irrespective of this second justification for its change of heart, the Cambodian example demonstrates both the manner in which vessel owners can and will take advantage of any opportunity to flag hop so as to avoid international regulation and the manner in which international or regional action can, albeit slowly, effect change in those States which rely heavily on international support.

By 2006 the international community was beginning to turn its attention to the former Soviet Republic of Georgia, a State whose vessel registry has grown steadily in recent years by taking advantage of those vessels fleeing first the Belizean clean up and then Cambodia's purge. Ranking the world's 5th largest flag of convenience fishing registry in 2005 the Georgian registry thus far seems to have avoided the fluctuations noticed by many other FOCs in the last decade. Whilst the registries of Belize, St Vincent & the Grenadines, Equatorial Guinea and Bolivia generally reached their high water mark in or around 2002–2003, the Georgian fishing vessel registry has grown consistently since 1999, and more importantly has become a significant entity in the IUU/FOC market.

---

171 Recommendation 04/15 by ICCAT Concerning the Lifting of Bigeye Tuna Trade Restrictive Measures Against Cambodia; Council Regulation (EC) 919/2005.

172 New Orleans, Louisiana, November 2004.

173 Reproduced in ICCAT Report of the Biennial Period, 2004–05, Part I (2004), Vol. 1.

Georgian vessels are consistently to be found on RFMO blacklists, and whilst the numbers are not high, in terms of representing both a proportion of the Georgian registry and the global fleet as a whole, it can be seen that Georgian flagged vessels pose an enormously disproportionate threat to fisheries conservation and management. For instance, almost 25% of the vessels listed as engaging in IUU activity by the Inter-American Tropical Tuna Commission in 2006 were Georgian registered.[174] Similarly both NAFO and NEAFC listed a whole fleet of Georgian registered vessels on their blacklists, all of which (bar one vessel) are known to have fled the purge of the Belizean registry.[175] Georgian flagged vessels have also been found on CCAMLR's blacklist[176] and whilst no individual vessels are listed by ICCAT, the evidence of Georgian involvement in IUU activities prompted ICCAT to recommend its Contracting Parties to adopt sanctions against all bigeye tuna imports from Georgia.[177]

The Georgian success story may, however, be an inadvertent one. According to the UNFAO "Georgia has no fisheries laws"[178] and, like Cambodia, the attraction of Georgia could conceivably by dictated by extrinsic factors such as the State's natural wish to regenerate following internal strife.[179] Nevertheless this example shows, as do those of Bolivia and Cambodia, that whatever the rationale or basis to a convenient flag, vessel operators waste no time in exploiting all available loopholes in order to stay one step ahead of regulations, and, as is borne out by an analysis of recent vessel movement trends, individual vessels are already beginning to move away from the Georgian registry. Perhaps sensing that Georgia will soon no longer provide a refuge, due to its flirtations with the European Union in recent years, some vessels are already moving off to pastures new. Some of these vessels registries may pose a much greater challenge to the international community than the previous generations of flags of

---

[174] IATTC IUU Vessel List, June 2006. Available at: http://www.iattc.org/VesselRegister/IUU.aspx?Lang=ENG. Although it should be noted that by 2011 only one Georgia vessel was to be found on this list.

[175] NAFO IUU Vessel List, available at http://www.nafo.int/fisheries/frames/fishery-iuu.html; NEAFC IUU 'A' Vessel List, available at http://www.neafc.org/measures/iuu-a-list.htm, NEAFC IUU 'B' Vessel List, available at http://www.neafc.org/measures/iuu-b.htm. It should be noted that Georgian involvement in these lists had diminished somewhat by 2011, with only one vessel (Dolfin, IMO No. 8422852, an ex-Georgian, now Russian stern trawler) being noted by NAFO.

[176] CCAMLR IUU Vessel List, available at http://www.ccamlr.org/pu/E/sc/fish-monit/iuu-list-06.pdf.

[177] ICCAT Recommendation 03/18 for Bigeye Tuna Trade Restrictive Measures Against Georgia. These measures remain implemented in the EC by Council Regulation (EC) 919/2005.

[178] United Nations Food and Agriculture Organisation, Country Profiles, available at http://www.fao.org/fi/fcp/en/GEO/profile.htm.

[179] Georgia, of course, endured a far from stable period in its history prior to it becoming a haven for IUU fishing vessels.

convenience, because unlike the insecure economies of Belize and Cambodia *et al.*, the new registry States are relatively independent and more resilient in the face of international opposition and condemnation.

Two such States are the Peoples' Republic of China and the Russian Federation. There are indications that China has now become yet another link in the chain of convenient vessel movements and is now the host to numerous ex-Belizean, Cambodian, Bolivian and Georgian vessels. Vessels such as the *West Ocean*, and its sister ships the *North Ocean* and *East Ocean* are known to have spent time on the registries of Bolivia and Georgia but now reside on the Chinese registry. Although the beneficial ownership of these vessels is also Chinese,[180] this factor may be negated by the fact that all of these vessels are currently listed as engaging in IUU activity.[181] Similarly the Russian Federation is becoming an increasingly popular choice of registry for the IUU vessels operator.[182] Although by 2011 the Russian presence on RFMO blacklists was almost non-existent, it is an inescapable fact that much of the current Russian fishing fleet are vessels that have moved between flags of convenience throughout the last decade.[183]

And if it was not worrying enough that IUU vessels were hunting out super-powers with which to register their vessels, the indications are that the whole flag of convenience cycle might be beginning all over again: according to one study the original modern flag of convenience – Panama, having ridden the storm generated in the 1990s[184] – is now seen as an extremely attractive haven for IUU vessels.[185] This worrying conclusion is also borne out by even the most cursory of glances at the blacklists produced by many RFMOs: it is impossible not to notice that Panamanian registered vessels are known to have engaged in IUU fishing activities in areas as diverse as the North Atlantic to the South Pacific.[186]

---

[180] Thus "genuinely linking" the vessel to that State and indicating that these vessels are no longer pure flag of convenience ships, see Chapter Four.

[181] Greenpeace IUU List, March 2007.

[182] Greenpeace IUU List, March 2007 shows that 4 Russian registered vessels (some of which are obvious refugees from the Belizean purge – see, for example, the *Eridan*) are currently engaged in IUU activity.

[183] Nearly ten per cent of the vessels that left the Belizean register between 2001 and 2006 are now resident on the Russian registry. While many of these vessels went directly from Belize to Russia, many took a more circuitous route, and spent time on the registries of the 'usual suspects' of Cambodia and Panama prior to arriving in Russia.

[184] During this time Panama was viewed as one of the worst offenders, in terms of allowing unregulated fishing vessels onto its registry.

[185] Environmental Justice Foundation, *ICCAT's Fight Against the Tuna Pirates*, at http://www.ejfoundation.org/page268.html.

[186] See, for instance, NEAFC IUU 'B' List, on which 4 of the 10 vessels found are Panamanian; the same is true of NAFO IUU Vessel List.

2.8 *Conclusion*

This Chapter has shown that the flag of convenience phenomenon should not be taken lightly. It has shown that the problem is based upon a deeply ingrained tradition embracing all types of maritime activities and, more importantly, is still being utilised for the avoidance of all manner of regulations. In the context of fisheries the increasing regulation of international marine capture has ensured a new role for the flag of convenience registry, and, as such, vessel owners must stay one step ahead of these regulations by constantly searching out new flags to take the place of those States which fall in line with international norms. This Chapter has shown that this can be done and that there is always a hiding place for errant vessels, if only for a relatively short period of time. Unless the international community can act once and for all to close the loopholes and ensure that vessels cannot simply flag-hop at a moment's notice this phenomenon will continue, and consequently the deleterious and harmful practices and by-products of the global IUU/FOC fleet will remain unchecked. With this in mind the following Chapters will consider first these deleterious and harmful practices and the "traditional" international response to the problem of flags of convenience generally, and the response to the specific and discrete problem of IUU/FOC fishing.

Chapter Three

The Consequences of Flags of Convenience on the Marine Environment and Fisheries Sector

3.1 *Introduction*

Now that its pedigree has been established and its context defined the analysis will turn to some of the more specific and contemporary issues surrounding flags of convenience and the fishing industry. The scope of the problem will be identified in terms of the number of vessels currently operating under convenient flags in *How Great is the Problem of Flag of Convenience Fishing*, and, more importantly (considered in *What Type of Environmental Damage is Caused by Flag of Convenience Vessels*) what type of damage is done by unregulated fishing practices to the legitimate fishing industry and the marine environment. Certainly no assertion is made that this section of the Chapter provides an exhaustive list of the deleterious aspects of unregulated fishing, but by the use of a few choice and wide ranging examples, some of the main concerns will be identified. The use of one such example – the negative environmental impacts associated with high seas bottom trawling – is included as an example of a flag of convenience problem in the making. Further examples are provided in the section entitled *The Impact upon Individuals Employed in the Flag of Convenience Sector* to show that flags of convenience do not just harm legitimate fisheries and the marine environment but can also have a negative impact upon the crews of those vessels themselves.

Throughout the Chapter a recurring theme will be present: the "traditional" methods of ocean governance simply do not work to combat deleterious flag of convenience fisheries. The greater regulation of fisheries activities in areas beyond national jurisdictions can only be achieved by flag States, and States not wishing to comply with international standards cannot be compelled to do so. As noted in relation to Belize in Chapter Two, for some States diplomatic pressure may, occasionally, be sufficient for them to succumb and regulate their marine industries, but the vessels engaged in deleterious activities do not disappear. They simply join the new wave of more resilient flag States, eager for foreign currency and the short term advantages offered by selling their flags, each fighting it out in a more and more competitive arena by promises of less and less State regulation.

3.2 *How Great is the Problem of Flags of Convenience Fishing?*

In terms of their consequences flags of convenience have been described as a "serious menace" to the entire maritime world[1] and "a clearly recognised threat to the sustainable development of marine transport, the protection of the marine environment and the sustainable utilisation of marine living resources."[2] In the period following the entry into force of UNCLOS in 1994 there has been an explosion of fishing boats flagging out as vessel owners head for the relatively free spaces of the high seas both as a consequence of the obvious depletion of coastal stocks and in order to escape the newly recognised and regulated Exclusive Economic Zones of coastal States.[3]

In terms of accurately gauging the numbers of vessels engaged in flag of convenience fisheries – and more importantly, the amount of stocks harvested – inherent difficulties arise due to the very fact that flag of convenience fishing goes largely unreported and the vessels operate in secret. There are, however, a number of methodologies that can be utilised in order to arrive at approximate conclusions as to how great the general problem of IUU and flags of convenience fishing is.

Most obvious is self reporting. In 2002 the UNFAO undertook surveys of many of the known or perceived open registries and collated the responses in its Fisheries Circular 980.[4] Unfortunately, the secretive nature of FOC States ensured that of the 25 States polled, less than half responded. To complete the picture the author of the Circular made use of public documents available at Lloyds Register of Shipping which yielded the UNFAO with information indicating that 1500 fishing vessels were registered with "certain open registries."[5] This survey, whilst providing the analyst with data regarding the number of vessels engaged in fisheries activities, and therefore allowing certain assumptions and calculations to be made as to their likely impacts on the marine environment, does not complete the story. In order to assess these impacts more guile is required.

---

1 EU Fisheries Commissioner Franz Fischler, *Illegal Fishing – A Threat to Our Common Heritage.* http://europa.eu.int/comm/archives/commission_1999_2004/fischler/illfish_en.htm.

2 International Transport Workers' Federation, *More Troubled Waters: Fishing, Pollution and FOCs*, ITF, 2002, London.

3 Vukas and Vidas, p. 55. In which the authors claim that in the immediate years following UNCLOS, from 1994 to 1997, 10% of the world's total merchant fleet re-flagged, and in the same period over 70% of all fish stocks were either fully exploited, over exploited or in a recovery stage.

4 Judith Swan (2002), *Fishing Vessels Operating Under Open Registries and the Exercise of Flag State Responsibilities – Information and Options*, Fisheries Circular No. 980, FIPP/C980, UNFAO, Rome, 2002, (herein after "Swan (2002)"), Appendices 5 and 9.

5 Swan (2002), Appendix 9.

Trade-based statistical analysis is one way of estimating the global or regional market for IUU fisheries generally, and the importance of this endeavour should not be overlooked. Without an accurate assessment of the extent of the problem those seeking solutions would, without doubt, find their efforts hampered by any lack of information both at the outset when plans are being formulated, and during assessment periods when the efficacy of those plans in action are being estimated.[6] One method of trade analysis is to compare the estimated global harvest of any particular species against known trade data – how much of that species is in the international market place at any given time. There are, as a cautionary note, a number of pitfalls to be avoided in this methodology. For instance "double counting" when fish products have been imported, exported and re-imported is an obvious trap that the unwary statistician might fall into. Likewise, when incorrect conversion factors are used when comparing live weight as against filleted, headless, or gutted (or, in fact, any combination of the three) fish products an inaccurate conclusion might be arrived at. Or the data can be rendered entirely useless by something as simple as the use of a regional name which does not correspond with the normal trade name of the species.[7]

Provided that the above mentioned pitfalls have been avoided, and adequate and detailed statistics are available, the trade analyst will be able to determine, up to a point, the level of IUU fisheries for the particular species in question. Put simply, where there is a greater number of any particular fish stock in the international market place than can be legitimately accounted for then the level of IUU fishing of that stock will, conservatively, be of a comparable level.[8]

Similarly, a comparison of known import and export data may provide evidence of IUU fisheries. For example, if the export figures generated by the main harvesting nations of a certain fish stock are less than import figures generated by the main consumer States of that stock, then again, it may be fair to say that the surplus figure will have circumvented official trade channels and been illegally harvested.[9]

Additionally, monitoring and surveillance evidence may be helpful in estimating the number of flag of convenience vessels operating in any particular region.

---

6 Anna Willock, *Using Trade and Market Information to Assess IUU Fishing Activities*, in *Fish Piracy: Combating Illegal, Unreported and Unregulated Fishing*, OECD, Paris, 2004 (herein after "Willock (2004)"). It should be noted that Willock's methodology does not specifically deal with flags of convenience fisheries but IUU fisheries in general. Further analysis of the trade and market statistics, a project beyond the scope of the present work, would be required to break down the figures to paint an accurate picture of flags of convenience fisheries specifically.

7 Willock (2004), p. 69.

8 Willock (2004), p. 69.

9 Willock (2004), p. 70.

As well as vessel sightings by official surveillance vessels and vessels engaged in legitimate fisheries, evidence of IUU fishing activities may also be found in the discarded gear of these vessels.[10] In addition to this anecdotal evidence changes in patterns of vessel registration, of the type evidenced in Chapter Two, are also indicative of the growth in flag of convenience vessels: according to one study undertaken towards the end of the last millennium, flag of convenience vessels accounted for 10% of the entire global fisheries effort.[11] By 2002 the problem had shown no signs of abating, and according to Greenpeace the number of vessels engaged in flag of convenience fishing had reached 15%, and that figure was still on the increase.[12]

Whilst the figure of 15% may be the global average,[13] in areas where large stocks of commercially valuable fish are found the level of IUU and flag of convenience fishing is by far in excess of this percentage – in fact, in certain regions, the level of illegitimate harvesting is equal to or even greater than lawful catches. For instance, in the southern oceans, within the Commission for the Conservation of Antarctic Marine Living Resources (CCAMLR) region, unlawful and unregulated catches of Patagonian toothfish (*Dissostichus eleginoides*) were, at one time, estimated to account for over half of the total harvest.[14] In terms of depriving legitimate fishermen of potential income IUU fishing in the CCAMLR region has been conservatively estimated to have been worth over US$500 million cumulatively over the period 1997 until 2003.[15]

---

[10] Denzil GM Miller, *Patagonian Toothfish: The Storm Gathers*, in *Fish Piracy: Combating Illegal, Unreported and Unregulated Fishing*, OECD, Paris, 2004, at p. 131 (herein after "Miller").

[11] Vukas and Vidas, at p. 55 (Citing *Review of Measures Taken by Regional Marine Fisheries Bodies to Address Contemporary Fishery Issues*, FAO Fisheries Circular, 940 (1998), 74.

[12] Press Conference on Flags of Convenience, World Summit on Sustainable Development, Johannesburg, 30th August 2002. See http://www.un.org/events/wssd/pressconf/020830conf9.htm.

[13] Since 2002 there have been very few further studies as to the size of the global IUU fleet, Traffic International have, however, suggested that since 2003 IUU global landings have fallen by 25%: see Mary Lack, *Continuing CCAMLR's Fight Against IUU Fishing for Toothfish*, WWF Australia and Traffic International, Cambridge, 2008, at p. 19 (herein after "Lack (2008)").

[14] Traffic International press release, *Illegal Fishing Continues to Threaten Patagonian Toothfish*, 14th August 2001. See http://www.traffic.org/toothfish/. There are those who suggest that illegal and unregulated catches of Patagonian toothfish account for as much as 80% of the global market, see Adrienne J. Oppenheim, *The Plight of the Patagonian Toothfish: Lessons From the Volga Case*, 30 Brooklyn J Int'l L. 293, at p. 295. Data available as of autumn 2006 shows that the level of IUU toothfish capture may be significantly dropping since the introduction of the CCAMLR Catch Documentation Scheme (discussed in Chapter Five) and may account for around 25% of the total harvest, see *Why Fish Piracy Persists: The Economics of Illegal, Unreported and Unregulated Fishing*, OECD, Paris, 2005, at p. 132 (herein after "The Economics of Illegal, Unreported and Unregulated Fishing").

[15] Miller, at p. 111. It should be noted that Miller questions the precise accuracy of these figures and acknowledges the inherent difficulties arriving at trade and market based analysis of harvests.

Although to a lesser extent than in the CCAMLR area, the North-East Atlantic Fisheries Commission (NEAFC) has reported IUU fishing activities by non-contracting State vessels to be well above the global average. In 2002 27% of all Oceanic redfish *(Sebastes montella)* catches within the NEAFC regulatory area were taken by IUU vessels, including "a handful of vessels of flags of convenience."[16] Similarly IUU catches have a "significant impact" in the region covered by the International Commission for the Conservation of Atlantic Tuna (ICCAT), who estimate that around 10% of all catches are either illegal, unreported or unregulated.[17] Unregulated fishing, that is to say IUU/FOC fishing, is an especially large problem for the Commission for the Conservation of Southern Bluefin Tuna (CCSBT) whose most recent figures point to a level of one third of the total allowable catch falling prey to pirate fishers.[18] IUU plaice, cod and redfish captured in the Northwest Atlantic Fisheries Organisation's (NAFO) area of competence has also been a major problem and accounted for an estimated 10 000 tonnes in 2001.[19]

Clearly these statistics, whilst varying from region to region, and methodology to methodology, show that a significant percentage of the world's fish stocks are being harvested in an unregulated and unlawful manner of industrial proportions. And an industry it is. It would be a mistake to believe that the flag of convenience fisheries sector comprises a number of individual "rogue" vessels acting independently. Vessels rarely operate in isolation and usually hunt in packs, with a sophisticated support infrastructure of supply ships, relief crews, reefers (refrigerated cargo vessels), and, in some cases, processing vessels, all of which ensure that the fishing vessels themselves rarely, if ever, need to land at port and be subject to invasive inspections and scrutiny.[20]

3.3 *What Type of Environmental Damage is Caused by Flags of Convenience Vessels?*

No reasonable person can escape the fact that these vessels are bad for the fishing industry and almost universally condemned by governments, NGOs and

[16] Kjartan Hordal, *IUU Fishing in the NEAFC Area: How Big is the Problem and What Have We Done?*, in *Fish Piracy: Combating Illegal, Unreported and Unregulated Fishing*, OECD, Paris, 2004, at p. 161.

[17] *The Economics of Illegal, Unreported and Unregulated Fishing*, at p. 128.

[18] *The Economics of Illegal, Unreported and Unregulated Fishing*, at p. 130. These figures, however, represent the year until 1999 and unfortunately represent the most up-to-date available at the time of writing.

[19] *The Economics of Illegal, Unreported and Unregulated Fishing*, at p. 136.

[20] David J. Agnew and Colin T. Barnes, *Economic Aspects and Drivers of IUU Fishing: Building a Framework*, in *Fish Piracy: Combating Illegal, Unreported and Unregulated Fishing*, OECD, Paris, 2004, at pp. 89–96 (herein after "Agnew and Barnes").

all concerned, but what is the basis for this condemnation? Is it simply because the very existence of flags of convenience offends notions of equity and fairness? Without doubt they do – after all, nation States which go to the trouble and expense of negotiating and enforcing treaties and agreements regulating the harvest of marine wildlife might rightly feel aggrieved at other States perceived as taking more than their fair share and not playing by the rules. It is, however, contended that the problem of flags of convenience goes well beyond notions of fairness. This next section will highlight some of the current problems associated with flags of convenience and their impact on the marine environment and demonstrate that vessels operating under the protection of these flags pose a real and serious threat not just to the sustainable use of valuable and scarce fish stocks but to the wider province of ocean management and dependent communities.

The state of the world's fisheries, even without the additional problem of FOC vessels, is not particularly healthy. Vast numbers of fish stocks are seriously threatened by over-capacity in the fishing industry and by some of the deleterious practices employed. To compound these direct human interventions, there is data to suggest that indirect human activities such as marine pollution and climate change, coupled with environmental factors and natural phenomena such as the *El Niño* weather cycle can have a grave impact upon the sustainability of fish stocks.[21] While headlines such as those along the lines of "Fish stocks face extinction" propagated by many environmental organisations may be dismissed as a little alarmist, it is impossible to escape the reality that many stocks are indeed in danger of serious over-exploitation and are being, or have been, harvested at an unsustainable rate.

According to the UNFAO's 2010 Report, 53% of all fish stocks are currently fully exploited and have reached their maximum sustainable limits of harvest and a further 32% of all stocks are either overexploited, depleted or recovering.[22] This global average is, however, not replicated evenly throughout the oceans and per species: for instance in the Eastern Central Pacific only 33% of stocks are over or fully exploited, whilst 100% of stocks in the Western Central and Northeast Atlantic sectors and the Western Indian Ocean have reached or exceeded their maximum sustainable harvest limits.[23] Similarly the International Council for the Exploration of the Sea estimate that in its area, which covers most of the North Atlantic, the Barents Sea and the North Sea, 84% of stocks fall beyond safe biological limits. Within the OSPAR region, again covering

[21] The State of World Fisheries and Aquaculture 2004, UNFAO, Rome, 2004, p. 33 (herein after "World Fisheries (2004)").

[22] The State of World Fisheries and Aquaculture 2010, UNFAO, Rome, 2010, p. 35 (herein after "World Fisheries (2010)").

[23] World Fisheries (2004), p. 34; World Fisheries (2010), p. 38.

areas of the Northeast Atlantic, only 29% of fisheries are within these limits.[24] According to Greenpeace these areas are particularly susceptible to the unregulated activities of FOC fishing vessels and a 2005 press release claims that in the area known as the Barents Sea "high sea loophole", illegal and unregulated cod catches alone account for 150,000 tonnes per annum – equivalent to one third of the total legal catch.[25]

For those areas falling within areas of national jurisdiction and the Exclusive Economic Zones of coastal States stock recovery plans can be fairly readily designed, and given sufficient will and resources, be equally readily implemented by coastal States.[26] On the high seas, however, where regulation is less of an exact science and more of an aspiration, over-exploitation can be even more of a threat to the sustainability of fragile fish stocks.

Firstly, and most obviously, any fishing vessel flagged to a State not obliged or unwilling to implement any regional or international agreement regulating amounts or methods of catch is likely to have chosen that register for that very reason. Whilst concerned States may recognise the demise of the stocks and enact multilateral conservation measures to prevent collapse, convenient States may not. Equally, whilst responsible States may recognise particular methods of harvest as being particularly harmful in terms of by-catch or environmental degradation and enact measures to limit those harmful consequences, again convenient States may show no such concerns. Ergo, it might be fanciful to suggest that such vessels will voluntarily adhere to those agreements, as this would entirely undermine one of the very reasons for joining that registry in the first place.

Clearly then, unshackled by regional, multilateral or even widely accepted international agreements, those unregulated vessels may pose a disproportionate threat to stocks and the wider environment. One study has shown that in terms of environmental degradation and by-catch, flags of convenience vessels cause twenty times more harm than regulated vessels.[27] Due to the inevitable linkage between flag of convenience and unreported fishing there are obvious difficulties in estimating the proportion of the threat posed to stock levels. As previously mentioned there are ways in which the levels of unreported catches may be assessed using trade data and there are ways of gauging the numbers

---

[24] The Royal Commission on Environmental Pollution, *Turning the Tide: Addressing the Impact of Fisheries on the Marine Environment*, December 2004, Cm 6392, p. 90.

[25] *Greenpeace Exposes Pirate Fishing on the Arctic High Seas*, Greenpeace Press Release, 19th September 2005, available at press-releases-bounces@mailman.greenpeace.org.

[26] Under Article 61 UNCLOS it is, in fact, a correlative duty of the rights of exclusivity over natural resources that coastal States undertake measures to ensure the conservation of the living resources found within their EEZs.

[27] CCAMLR, *Incidental Mortality of Seabirds in Fisheries, Particularly Longline Fisheries*, at http://www.ccamlr.org/pu/E/e_pubs/am/p6.htm (herein after "CCAMLR Seabirds").

of vessels engaged in FOC fishing, but, unfortunately, these methodologies do not allow us to readily ascertain the precise amount of harvesting done by each FOC vessel compared to a lawful one. Much of the reason for this is the fact that this industry, taking advantage of the openness of open registries, is a very fluid one in which "vessels [change their] names and flags easily and frequently, moving from fishery to fishery."[28] Nevertheless, even without precise data it is obvious that FOC vessels are taking more and more of the stocks available to legitimate fishermen and it is almost universally accepted that the amount of stock taken unlawfully undermines conservation and management measures.[29]

As well as the more obvious deleterious consequences to target species and their conservation, flag of convenience fisheries can also have dire implications for marine dependent wildlife and non-target species. IUU fishermen do not simply ignore or evade regulations concerning stock levels. The international regulation of fisheries goes beyond the setting of catch limits and quotas – there are numerous treaties and guidelines promulgated by the international community aimed at protecting the marine environment from the harmful effects of irresponsible fishing. Whilst responsible States will adhere to these treaties and guidelines, flag of convenience States and the vessels they harbour may be entirely ambivalent towards them. Not only will the following sections catalogue some of the more prevalent environmental harms caused by irresponsible fisheries, but it will also consider the attempts by the international community to reduce the damage caused by these practices. This latter endeavour shows, however, that certain of the attempts of the international community might simply exacerbate the flag of convenience problem. Although it has been stated before, it is worth repeating: additional regulation that relies purely on flag State control *can* and *does* promote the attraction of the flag of convenience States that refuse to implement those regulations.

3.3.1 *Longlines and Seabird Mortality*

An obvious example of irresponsible fisheries can clearly be evidenced by the use of longlines and the damage caused by this method of fishing to marine dependent seabirds, including albatross, fulmars and gulls.[30] The Royal Society

---

[28] Swan (2002), Part I, *Introduction.* See also, UNFAO Fisheries Report No.772, *Report of the Expert Consultation on Fishing Vessels Operating Under Open Registries and Their Impact on Illegal, Unreported and Unregulated Fishing*, UNFAO, Rome, 2004, at p. 74 (herein after "UNFAO Fisheries Report No. 772").

[29] Swan (2002), Part IV, *Effective Flag State Control*, which states that seven of the main RMFOs polled voiced concerns over the levels and methods of harvest by IUU/FOC vessels.

[30] Kim Rivera, *Incidental Catch of Seabirds in Longline Fisheries*, US National Marine Fisheries Service, Alaska, April 2002, http://www.waterbirdconservation.org/plan/rpt-NPOA.pdf (herein after "Rivera").

for the Protection of Birds estimates that over 100,000 seabirds die every year on flag of convenience longlines.[31] Appalling as this figure is when viewed in isolation, the tragedy of seabird by-catch is compounded when one considers the already precarious nature of many of the species doomed to die on unregulated longlines. At least 23 of the 74 different species of seabirds known to have died on longlines are already a threatened species according to established criteria.[32] Compounding this, too, is the fact that for every adult bird hooked on a longline there may well be several dependent chicks doomed to starvation as their parent drowns on the line.[33]

Longlines are nonetheless the preferred method by which a variety of fish are caught. Utilised in the harvest of Patagonian toothfish, tuna, swordfish, several varieties of cod, haddock and halibut to name but a few species,[34] they are, in crude terms, baited and barbed steel cables straddling the oceans. Longlines are indeed long – sometimes up to 100km in length with a number of subsidiary lines running from the central section. Each line may have thousands of hooks attached. Efficient as they may be in harvesting the target species, these baited longlines have proven to be extremely attractive to surface feeding and scavenging seabirds, with the result that these seabirds are hooked on the barbs of the line, where they will face an inevitable and drawn-out death. Prompted by the intolerably high level of seabird mortality due to longline fisheries, the UN's Food and Agriculture Organisation, as part of its Code of Conduct for Responsible Fisheries, drafted its 1999 International Plan of Action for Reducing Incidental Catch of Seabirds in Longline Fisheries (IPOA-Seabirds).[35] Although voluntary in application and falling short of an outright prohibition of longlining, IPOA-Seabirds urges States and "fishing entities"[36] engaged in longline fisheries to assess the deleterious consequences of their activities and to adopt national plans of action (NPOA) to reduce incidental catches of seabirds. Unfortunately by 2011, a full decade after the required implementation date,[37]

---

[31] See http://www.rspb.org.uk/international/albatross_appeal/illegal_fishing/index.asp. This figure correlates to the estimation of 333,000 seabirds which perished on longlines laid by "pirate" toothfish vessels in the Southern Ocean during the three year period between 1997 and 2000: see *infra* n. 32, at p. 7.

[32] American Bird Conservancy, *Sudden Death on the High Seas – Longline Fishing: A Global Catastrophe for Seabirds*, at p. 6. Available at www.abcbirds.org/policy/seabird_report (herein after "American Birds Conservancy").

[33] American Birds Conservancy, at p. 3.

[34] Rivera, at p. 1.

[35] Food and Agriculture Organisation of the United Nations, Rome, 1999.

[36] The use of the term "fishing entities" in the IPOA is a deliberate one. The FAO envisaged the recommendations contained within the IPOA to apply to all States – members and non-members of the FAO, *and* private fisheries undertakings.

[37] IPOA-Seabirds, Article 13.

no flag of convenience State had implemented any form of NPOA despite clear evidence that vessels registered in these States were engaged in harmful longline fisheries.[38]

For example, in the Atlantic catches of bigeye tuna by flag of convenience long-liners has "increased sharply in the last decade" to reach almost a quarter of the total catch.[39] Likewise, in the last decade "FOC-IUU fleets became major producers of long-line yellowfin [tuna] catches" and account for almost 20,000 tonnes out of a total catch of 140,000 tonnes.[40] Similarly in the Indian Ocean longline vessels from Honduras, Belize, Equatorial Guinea, Panama, and "other FOC-IUU" vessels harvest approximately a quarter of all albacore caught by this method. This figure is repeated as regards the bigeye tuna catch. Perhaps more alarming, however, is the fact that a staggering 10,000 tonnes of non-target, by-catch swordfish find their way onto the longlines of vessels from Belize, Honduras and Equatorial Guinea.[41]

The failure of any FOC States to embrace the IPOA could well be explained by its very content. The IPOA lists a number of cognitive, technical and operational measures that could be adopted in order to reduce the negative impacts of irresponsible longline fisheries. These measures include urging States to engage in the research and development of efficient and cost-effective measures, deterrents and mitigating procedures. States should also educate fishermen engaged in longlining as to the need to reduce incidental catches of seabirds and, significantly, States should provide technical and financial assistance in the furtherance of the aims of the NPOA. The technical and operational means by which incidental seabird mortality may be avoided or reduced are found in the final section of the IPOA. In order to reduce the length of time that the baited lines spend on the water's surface it is suggested that lines could be weighted, or that the bait could be thawed, or that the swim bladders of the fish bait could be punctured to reduce buoyancy. Alternatively fishermen could equip themselves with proprietary underwater line setting or bait casting machines. Scavenging seabirds can be deterred from feeding on the bait in a number ways – acoustic deterrents are one possibility, as are water cannons, bird scaring curtains and "tori poles". Operationally, fishermen could be encouraged to set their lines at

[38] Documents lodged with the UNFAO include those from the USA, Australia, New Zealand, Brazil, South Africa, Uruguay, Canada, Japan and Argentina, see: http://www.fao.org/fishery/ipoa-seabirds/npoa/en.

[39] Makoto Peter Miyake, Naozumi Miyabi and Hideki Nakano, *Historical Trends of Tuna Catches in the World*, UNFAO Fisheries Technical Paper 467, UNFAO, Rome, 2004, Chapter 2 "Development of the Atlantic Tuna Fisheries." (herein after "UNFAO Fisheries Technical Paper 467").

[40] UNFAO Fisheries Technical Paper 467, Chapter 2 "Development of the Atlantic Tuna Fisheries".

[41] UNFAO Fisheries Technical Paper 467, Chapter 3 "Development of the Indian Ocean Tuna Fisheries".

night when the bait is less visible to sea birds,[42] or reduce the attractiveness of the vessel to scavengers by discarding waste at times or in ways where it is least likely to attract seabirds.

The measures suggested by the IPOA, whilst diverse and ranging in likely efficiency, have at least two common features – effort and expense. The avoidance of these common features, it is suggested, are two of the very reasons why vessels have historically attached themselves to flag of convenience registries. Indeed, as history has shown any State adopting these measures will rapidly cease to be an attractive State of registration for irresponsible fishermen, as chief among the reason for registering vessels with any given State is that State's disregard for international obligations or guidelines.[43] Consequently it is envisaged that no flag of convenience State will wish to lose the revenue generated by its foreign registry by implementing, either practically or theoretically, such voluntary codes of conduct unless compelled to – or to put it another way "[t]he *raison d'être* behind the existence of… [flag of convenience]… registers is the offering of a regulatory free environment for the ship owner. The very success of the flag depends on the continued and anticipated maintenance of this environment."[44] Likewise, the financial imperative of education, training and economic assistance to fishermen is also likely to dissuade flag of convenience States from implementing the IPOA – as again, the economic benefits of the flag of convenience model operate for the benefit not just of the vessel owners but the State of registry too. Why would any State operating a convenient registry willingly incur additional and unnecessary expense?[45]

---

42 Although it should be noted that one study found that this practice did, in fact, increase the incidence of *Procellaria aequinoctialis* (white chinned petrels) being caught. See CCAMLR Seabirds.

43 As was noted in the example of Belize in Chapter Two – unfortunately, despite repeated requests for this information the Belize vessel registry was unable to provide the author with precise information concerning voluntary de-registrations as opposed to expulsions from the registry.

44 Alderton and Winchester, at p. 10.

45 Indeed, evidence suggests that the increased regulation of longline fisheries by organisations such as CCAMLR in the 1990s was a contributing factor in the expansion of the IUU longline fleet operating in the Southern Oceans. See Joint Nature Conservation Committee, *Seabird Bycatch* at http://www.jncc.gov.uk/page-1565. Similarly in the ICCAT region increased regulation has been observed to correlate with increases in the size of the flag of convenience fleet, see *Problems in the Fisheries Management of International Tuna Fisheries and its Relation With Fishery Subsidies*, Yuji Ouzumi and Shingo Ota, paper presented to UNEP Fisheries Workshop, Geneva, February 2001, at p. 4.

3.3.2 *Purse Seine Fisheries and Dolphin Mortality*

Akin to longline fisheries is the practice of purse seine capture. These large purse-shaped nets are used in the harvest of a variety of fish stocks from small sardines to yellowfin tuna, but have, in the past, proven to be indiscriminate in regards to non-target species. These non-target species can range from juvenile fish and those too small to be of economic value to the notorious incidence of dolphin mortality in the tuna industry.

For many years fishermen in search of yellowfin tuna in the Eastern Pacific Ocean have noticed and exploited the phenomenon, unique to this part of the ocean, by which large harvests of tuna are found swimming beneath schools of dolphin. By encircling the dolphins with their mile long nets, the fishermen know that they will have also encircled the tuna, and once this process is complete the bottom of the net is pulled together like a purse. At this point neither the tuna, nor many of the dolphins can escape the nets.

So successful was this method of tuna capture that by the 1970s the majority of vessels in the Eastern Pacific, most of which were US-flagged, had changed gears from bait boating to purse seining,[46] with the resultant tragedy that the number of dolphins doomed to drowning or mutilation in the nets reached over six million in the heyday of purse seining from the late 1950's onwards.[47] Concerned at this rate of dolphin mortality, and under pressure from environmental groups, the US government brought in legislation to curb purse seining by US flagged vessels. Instead of an outright ban, however, the 1972 Marine Mammal Protection Act (MMPA) attempted to limit dolphin by-catch by requiring that all vessels engaged in the seining tuna industry were licensed.[48] The conditions of any licence specified, *inter alia*, that vessels must adhere to any regulations issued in pursuance of the MMPA's aspiration that the incidental dolphin mortality or the incidental infliction of serious harm to marine mammals during purse seining should be reduced to "insignificant levels approaching a zero mortality and serious injury rate."[49] In practice, however, permits were issued to the largest tuna fisheries organisation as a matter of routine with no limit set as to levels of permitted by-catch.[50] This unfettered

---

[46] UNFAO Fisheries Technical Paper 467, p. 67.

[47] Deirdre McGrath, *Writing Different Lyrics to the Same Old Tune: The New (and Improved) 1997 Amendments to the Marine Mammal Protection Act*, 7 Minnesota Journal of Global Trade 431, Summer 1998, (herein after "McGrath") Purse seining technology was first introduced in this area in 1957, see James Joseph, *The Tuna-Dolphin Controversy in the Eastern Pacific Ocean: Biological, Economic and Political Impacts*, 25 Ocean Devel. and Int'l L. 1, 21 (1994).

[48] Marine Mammal Protection Act 1972 (Amended 2007), s.104(a).

[49] *Ibid.*, s.101(a)(2).

[50] S. 101(a)(2) cited in Rachel C. Hampton, *Of Dolphins and Tuna: The Evolution of an International Agreement*, 10 Fordham Envtl. Law J. 99, p. 111, (herein after "Hampton").

granting of permits and the seemingly unlimited levels of tolerable by-catch alarmed environmental campaigners and, in 1976, the legality of this process was successfully challenged in the Washington courts.[51] The National Marine Fishery Service (NMFS), the governmental agency in charge of implementing the MMPA, responded by introducing a quota system for dolphin by-catch, provisionally to allow for the by-catch of almost 80,000 dolphins per annum. By 1981 this figure had declined to 20,500 dolphin deaths per year when the MMPA was formally amended to include the provision for the setting of an annual quota at this level by the NMFS.[52]

On the face of things the MMPA appeared to be an enormous success. From the early levels of almost exclusive US dominated dolphin mortality in seining in the 1960's, by the 1980's US involvement in yellowfin tuna harvest in the Eastern Pacific – and consequently US vessels involved in incidental dolphin deaths or serious injury – had fallen to a mere 35%. US involvement in the industry continued to diminish in the following decade and by 1991 only 11% of all vessels engaged in purse seining in the Eastern Pacific were US registered.[53] Unfortunately, the reduction in US registered vessels did not entirely correlate to a similar reduction in vessels actually engaged in dolphin mortality in the purse seine industry. Although some US flagged vessels decamped to the Western Pacific in search of bigeye, skipjack and yellowfin tuna, many purse seine operators, following the best traditions of any vessel owner facing a troublesome regulatory curtailment of their activities, did what vessel owners in this situation seemingly always do and found themselves another flag to fly under.

Fortunately for the seining industry the governments of Ecuador, Venezuela, Vanuatu and Mexico were not, at least initially, as sentimental about the well-being of marine mammals and a little more resolute in the face of environmental pressure than their US counterparts. Consequently, following the introduction of strict quotas in the US fleet in 1981 these States offered a convenient refuge for US vessels, until regulations again encroached upon their activities in the early 1990s. Since 1981, when the Mexican fleet began significant harvest of yellowfin tuna in the Eastern Pacific, vessels flying that flag have consistently accounted for over 100,000 tonnes of stocks per annum up until the turn of the millennium. In the same time period Venezuela closely mirrored Mexico's consistency on a smaller scale, averaging approximately 50,000 tonnes per annum, whilst Vanuatu and Ecuador each harvest around 20,000 tonnes

[51] *Committee for Humane Legislation Inc v Elliot L Richardson et al.*, 540 F.2d 1141 (D.C. Cir. 1976).

[52] Hampton, p. 111.

[53] Hampton, p. 105.

per annum.[54] When these combined catches are compared to US vessel capture in the heyday of their fleet in the 1970s it is clear that no significant decrease in harvest has taken place – in fact the opposite is apparent. Purse seiners from the four aforementioned States annually account for 30,000 tonnes more yellowfin tuna captured in the Eastern Pacific than the US fleet ever did.[55]

Similarly the rates of dolphin mortality in the first decade following the 20,500 limit imposed upon US flagged vessels in 1981 had only marginally improved throughout the entire yellowfin fishery, due to the lack of efforts of Mexico *et al.* Throughout the 1980s dolphin mortality was consistently around the 100,000 per annum region, that is to say, for every "set" on a shoal of yellowfin tuna, by which the shoal is encircled, an average of eight dolphins were to die.[56]

These levels of mortality went neither unnoticed by, nor were acceptable to, environmental organisations and, crucially, the consumers of tuna. Faced with consumer boycotts of their products three of the largest canning operations, the US based "Bumblebee", "Starkist" and "Chicken of the Sea" announced in April 1990 that they would no longer purchase "tuna caught in association with dolphins." Major canneries in Europe followed suit and soon the phrases "Dolphin Friendly" and "Dolphin Safe" became the watch words for the ethical consumer.[57] US domestic laws followed close behind, with the Dolphin Protection Consumer Information Act 1990, revisions to the Marine Mammal Protection Act 1992 and the International Dolphin Conservation Act 1992. These domestic US laws specify, respectively, the conditions under which the tuna should be caught in order to qualify as "Dolphin Safe,"[58] prohibit the sale of "non-Dolphin Safe" tuna and tuna products and impose an embargo upon the import of tuna not captured in a "Dolphin Safe" way.

In the wake of such pressure the major purse seining States embarked upon a two-pronged strategy: Mexico instigated proceedings before the dispute resolution Panel set up under the General Agreement on Tariffs and Trade (GATT)

[54] UNFAO Fisheries Technical Paper 467, Part IV, *The Development of the Pacific Tuna Fisheries.*

[55] UNFAO Fisheries Technical Paper 467, Part IV, *The Development of the Pacific Tuna Fisheries.*

[56] Inter American Tropical Tuna Commission/Agreement on the International Dolphin Conservation Programme, at http://www.iattc.org/DolphinSafeENG.htm.

[57] The Whale and Dolphin Conservation Society, *An Introduction to the Tuna-Dolphin Issue*, available at: http://www.wdcs.org.

[58] Jennifer Ramach, *Dolphin Safe Tuna Labelling: Are the Dolphins Finally Safe?* (1996) 15 Va. Envtl LJ 743. *(d) Further Legislation: The Advent of Dolphin Safe Labelling.* (herein after "Ramach").

claiming that the 1992 Acts violated international trade rules,[59] and under the banner of the Inter American Tropical Tuna Commission (IATTC), the major States began to develop methods by which tuna harvests could be maintained and satisfy the public demand for dolphin safe tuna. These measures would eventually result in the La Jolla Agreement.[60]

The La Jolla Agreement had a remarkably similar goal to that of the US MMPA a full twenty years earlier, in that its stated aim was to "(1)…progressively reduce dolphin mortality in the Eastern Pacific Ocean (EPO) fishery to levels approaching zero through the setting of annual limits and (2), with a goal of eliminating dolphin mortality in this fishery, seeking ecologically sound means of capturing large yellowfin tunas not in association with dolphins while maintaining the populations of yellowfin tuna in the EPO at a level which will permit maximum sustained catches year after year, and to limit and, if possible, eliminate the mortality of dolphins in the fishery of the EPO…"[61] The catch limits imposed by the La Jolla Agreement were on a diminishing scale, starting at 19,500 for the first year of operation to under 5,000 by 1999. These stated aims were all achieved with remarkable and "better than expected" success with dolphin mortality for the period in question consistently half that envisaged and permitted.[62] This success was accomplished by requiring that all participating States allow observers on board all "qualifying vessels"[63] engaged in purse seining[64] and assigning vessel-by-vessel Dolphin Mortality Levels.[65] Once the vessel's DML had been achieved the observer was empowered to inform the

[59] *United States – Restrictions on the Imports of Tuna (Report of the Panel)*, 30 ILM 1594 (1991), *Tuna-Dolphins 1.* Mexico was successful in part in its proceedings: the mandatory requirements under the International Dolphin Protection Act were said to violate GATT rules, whilst the voluntary code established by the revised Marine Mammal Protection Act did not. Despite this victory the Mexican government did not pursue the matter further, preferring instead to negotiate with US officials to enact a mutually acceptable agreement, see McGrath, *(b) Defining Dolphin Safe* and *(c) The GATT Incident.*

[60] Ramach, *(e) The International Reaction and Status of Proposed Amendments.*

[61] La Jolla Agreement for the Reduction of Dolphin Mortality in the Eastern Pacific Ocean, April 1992.

[62] The Whale and Dolphin Conservation Society, *The La Jolla Agreement: International Steps to Control Dolphin Fishing*, at http://www.wdcs.org/dan/publishing.nsf/allweb/2C5AE8A85CD67CE980256E1B003F367D.

[63] Vessels with a "carrying capacity greater than 400 tonnes" that the government under which jurisdiction in vested "has reasonable cause to believe will set on tunas associated with dolphins…" La Jolla Agreement, s.1.

[64] La Jolla Agreement, s.12.

[65] La Jolla Agreement, s.2. The manner in which each DML was arrived at was simply to divide the annual mortality limit by the number of vessels engaged in tuna fisheries posing a risk to dolphins.

captain of the vessel to cease activities imperilling dolphins[66] and States were obliged to ensure the co-operation of vessels under their jurisdiction.[67] Of the ten signatories in April 1992, all of the major States engaged in yellowfin tuna purse seining in the Eastern Pacific were represented, including those States that had stepped in so quickly to fill the gap left by the US in 1981.

Unfortunately, whilst it appeared for some time that La Jolla and its heir, the Agreement on the International Dolphin Conservation Program (AIDCP),[68] had rid the Eastern Pacific of destructive tuna harvests by ensuring the compliance of the relevant States,[69] by the early years of the new millennium vessels from the latest generation of FOC States slowly began to appear on the horizon. For instance, IATTC reported that whilst the observance of its general measures for the conservation and management of stocks in the Eastern Pacific, as well as under the specific provision for dolphin mortality under the AIDCP, had been good, vessels flying the flag of Bolivia ignored its December 2002 closure of pure seine fisheries for tuna in the Eastern Pacific Ocean.[70] Similarly the International Dolphin Conservation Program noted at its La Jolla meeting of October 2004 that "there is a possibility that vessel owners engaged in... [IUU]... fishing activities may have re-flagged their vessels to avoid compliance with AIDCP management and conservation measures." To counter the serious threat posed by such vessels, AIDCP and IATTC proposed in 2004, and subsequently adopted by IACTT's 73rd Meeting in June 2005, a blacklist of all ships presumed to have engaged in activities undermining conservation and management measures. So as to give bite to these provisions the flag States of these IUU vessels were required to take measures, including de-registration, to prevent further occurrences of IUU fishing in the AIDCP region.[71]

---

66 La Jolla Agreement, s.14.

67 La Jolla Agreement, s.15.

68 Introduced by the Panama Declaration of 1995, AIDCP's avowed aims are broadly similar to that of La Jolla in that it aims to reduce dolphin by-catch in the Eastern Pacific. However, the two agreements differ in some key features. AIDCP is binding upon its State Parties, as opposed to the voluntary application of La Jolla, but, unlike La Jolla and, indeed, the Panama Declaration itself, AIDCP sets no goal as to the total elimination of incidental dolphin mortality, but instead initially aspired to the "progressive reduction" of dolphin mortality to "levels approaching zero." Article III(2) of the Agreement (amended in October 2004) states that the Agreement's objective is "the elimination of dolphin mortality in this fishery."

69 I.e., those States previously assigned as convenient for the purposes of evading US legislation.

70 Report for the International Dolphin Conservation Program and the Inter American Tropical Tuna Commission Joint Working Group on Fishing by Non-Parties, 2nd Annual General Meeting, Antigua (Guatemala), June 2003, JWG 02/06 FAO/IUU/IPOA.

71 AIDCP, 12th Meeting of the Parties, La Jolla, California, October 2004, *Draft Resolution to Establish a List of Vessels Presumed to Have Carried Out Illegal, Unreported and Unregulated Fishing Activities in the Agreement Area*, Document MOP-12–08, also IACTT *Resolution*

Certainly at the time of writing it is too soon to judge the precise level of the threat or the efficacy of these latest measures to combat this new chapter of IUU/FOC fisheries. As the 2005 Resolution recognises, the vessels may disappear for a while only to return under new names and registries. Whilst the cloak of secrecy shrouding vessel movements on and off registries continues to render the IATTC IUU list impotent it is impossible to accurately gauge the current level of threat. This list – despite being proclaimed as the "primary tool to deter IUU fishing" by IATTC[72] – is little more than a collection of vessel names, lacking detail or IMO numbers,[73] and is, in large, part, badly out of date. Perhaps even worse is the lack of any meaningful sanction for vessels found on the list: other than the "discouragement" (not the prohibition) of trade with IUU vessels, inclusion on the IATTC list carries with it few additional consequences. Although the levels of dolphin mortality may be at an all time low, insofar as legitimate vessels are concerned,[74] we can only speculate as to the level of IUU/FOC activity taking place in the Eastern Central Pacific. And given the fact that to play within the (IATTC/AIDCP) rules involves effort and expense, and there is little disincentive to engage in IUU activity in the IATTC region, is it going too far to suggest that many IATTC member State flagged purse-seiners might be wishing to re-flag to a State not covered by this regional agreement?

3.3.3 *High Seas Bottom Trawling*

Labelled "the world's most destructive type of fishing" in a recent study,[75] High Seas Bottom Trawling (HSBT) can have terrible repercussions for deep sea coral reefs and its associated marine life. As marine technology improves scientists utilising the very latest in submersible vehicles are beginning to discover huge forests of coral deep in the world's oceans, in water so deep that sun light cannot permeate and where temperatures can be as little as 30°F.[76] Nevertheless these coral forests have flourished for many hundreds and occasionally

---

C-05–07 to Establish a List of Vessels Presumed to Have Carried Out Illegal, Unreported and Unregulated Fishing Activities in the Agreement Area.

72 *Progress made in respect of the Course of Actions for RFMOs from the Joint Meeting of Tuna RFMOS in Kobe*, IATTC Secretariat, January 2007, paragraph 6.

73 A vessel's IMO number is its unique identifier – while the vessel name, flag and owner may easily change, its IMO number will stay constant. Thus it is particularly important that IUU vessels are identified by their IMO number.

74 *Annual Report of the Inter-American Tropical Tuna Commission 2008*, IATTC, La Jolle, 2008, p. 25.

75 Deep Sea Conservation Coalition, *Why the World Needs A Time-Out On High Seas Bottom Trawling*, DSCC. June 2005, at http://www.savethehighseas.org/publicdocs/TimeOut_english.pdf (herein after "*Time-Out on Bottom Trawling*").

76 Oceana, *Deep Sea Corals; Out of Sight, But No Longer Out of Mind* at http://www.savecorals.com/news/oceana_coral_report.pdf at p. 2 (herein after "*Deep Sea Corals*").

thousands of years, feeding upon microscopic animals in the surrounding waters, imperceptibly growing to enormous reefs, which, in turn, provide shelter and habitat for a number of commercially important fish stocks.[77]

Unfortunately for these coral reefs it is precisely because of the fish stocks that they harbour, coupled with the scientific advances in deep sea technology that has allowed man to view them, which may be placing their very future in jeopardy.[78] As the fisheries industry wakes up to the enormous potential benefits offered by the reefs in terms of fish stocks, and as shallower, regulated coastal zones show signs of stock depletion, more and more efficient and destructive techniques in harvesting these stocks are being developed.[79]

Untainted by jargon, bottom trawling is exactly what it sounds like – vast nets are dragged along the ocean floor reaping all life in their huge gaping mouths. These nets are weighted by heavy steel doors which keep the nets open; often these heavy doors, themselves weighing several tonnes,[80] are linked with chains, steal bearings and large diameter rollers. Little or no life remains unmolested by their gargantuan jaws: non-target fish species, mammals, turtles and coral reefs all meet the same fate – annihilation. As the bottom trawling vessels target newer, deeper dwelling species, the destruction becomes magnified. Capable of operating in depths of over 6,000 feet[81] the need for more robust and heavier nets increases, and as a consequence, so does the environmental degradation found in their wake. These nets are, it is estimated, able to move 18 ton rocks[82] – no little wonder that delicate coral reefs are simply pulverized to the point where if they do ever recover this process will take many hundreds of years.[83]

From an ecological standpoint the destruction of the deep sea coral reefs may be bad enough in itself – after all some corals are said to be many thousands of years old[84] and undoubtedly important and beautiful life forms in their own right – but to fully appreciate the impacts of the destruction of the coral forests it is also necessary to understand the role they play in the wider marine envi-

---

[77] Oceana, *European Trawlers are Destroying the Oceans*, Oceana, Madrid, 2004, at p. 31 (herein after "*European Trawlers are Destroying the Oceans*").

[78] *Deep Sea Corals*, at pp. 10–11.

[79] Bunny McDiarmid, Martini Gotje and Karen Sack, *The Northwest Atlantic Fisheries Organisation: A Case Study in How RFMOs Regularly Fail to Manage Our Oceans*, Greenpeace, June 2005, at p. 2 (herein after "Greenpeace NAFO Case Study").

[80] The Deep Sea Conservation Coalition estimates the weight of the doors to be 7 tonnes each, whereas Oceana put this figure to be more like 5 tonnes. Either way they are very heavy objects.

[81] *Deep Sea Corals*, at p. 11.

[82] *Deep Sea Corals*, at p. 11.

[83] Oceana, *What Threat Does Trawling Pose?* At http://www.savecorals.com/trawling.html.

[84] *Deep Sea Corals*, at p. 2.

ronment. Cold water corals are essential to the survival of a myriad of species, providing "habitat, feeding grounds, recruitment and nursery functions" for not just the targeted commercially important species, but an unknown number of other species dependent upon the corals.[85]

Certainly there is a bitterly ironic circularity in the fact that the ruinous methods of harvesting the targeted fisheries are ensuring that the sustainability of these target species is far from guaranteed. In a classic example of killing the goose that laid the golden egg, the HSBT industry is not simply destroying the world's ocean floor it is also ensuring its own extinction. From halibut, Pacific cod and shrimp hiding amongst the *Primnoa* and *Paragorgia arborea* (Red Trees and Bubblegum corals) of the North Atlantic and North Pacific to the molluscs and crustaceans residing in the shelter of the *Lophelia Pertusa* found in several areas of the Atlantic,[86] without the protection of the reefs themselves, these demersal fish stocks and sedentary species – or those remaining once the trawlers have cut their ruthless swathe – face an uncertain future. Once the shelter of the coral has gone the ability of theses species to replenish their stock levels will be seriously compromised.[87]

Likewise, grave fears have been expressed that the destructive practices of bottom trawling vessels operating in the extremes of the depths of the oceans may result in hundreds or even thousands of habitats and species, as yet unknown to science, vanishing before they, and their potential benefits for mankind and the environment, can be studied.[88] What is known, however, is that many thousands of species, unimportant to the fisheries sector as catch, but vital in the food chain, will be lost if their natural environments fall prey to destructive bottom trawling.[89] And unfortunately many of these natural environments have already fallen prey. Whilst most reefs on which studies have been undertaken

---

[85] United Nations Environmental Program, *Cold Water Coral Reefs: Out of Sight, No Longer Out of Mind*, at http://www.unep.org/cold_water_reefs/comparison.htm (herein after "UNEP Cold Water Coral Reefs").

[86] *Deep Sea Corals*, at p. 4.

[87] International Council for the Exploration of the Seas, *Report of the Working Group on the Ecosystem Effects of Fishing Activities*, ICES CM 2002, ACE; 03.

[88] UN Convention on Biological Diversity, 7th COP, Kuala Lumpur, February 2004, Working Paper prepared by the Subsidiary Body on Scientific, Technical and Technological Advice, *Management of Risks to the Biodiversity of Seamounts and Cold-Water Coral Communities Beyond National Jurisdiction*, UNEP/CBD/COP/7/INF/25, at p. 2 (herein after "Kuala Lumpur Working Paper").

[89] Kuala Lumpur Working Paper, at p. 3.

show signs of physical damage,[90] some have already been completely destroyed by the heavy jaws of the world's bottom trawling fleet.[91]

The same sad cycle is equally true in relation to seamounts. Seamounts are underwater mountains, sometimes standing alone, sometimes forming great chains – usually volcanic in origin – rising from the seabed to a height of up to 1000 metres and are particularly important marine features due to their micro-environment. These "hotspots" of biological diversity are, in many ways, sub-ecosystems within the oceans. Due to their size they have their own tidal cycle and due to the strong swells generated in the locality of seamounts these areas demonstrate an abundance of plankton biomass and prey organisms. These organisms, in turn, can attract large numbers of predatory species, ranging from all manner of fish to marine mammals, sharks, cephalopods and seabirds. Like deep water coral reefs seamounts are particularly susceptible to the "boom and bust" practices of the fishing industry, and the industry has not been slow in realising the potential of these underwater oases. And, like deep water coral, it is not simply the depletion of the target species that is the sole problem. Many of the same hazards applying to coral reefs are prevalent with regards to seamounts – the heavy trawling gear simply destroys the structure of the mount and the coral substrate found on the surrounding seabed.[92] The true extent of the loss of this habitat in terms of biodiversity may never be quantified. The limited sampling that has taken place on seamounts has shown, however, that due to the unique aquatic climate in these areas they are hotspots not just of known biodiversity, but also of the unknown. Seamounts provide refuge for ancient species and newly evolving ones alike, and are said to be "stepping stones" for species to propagate the oceans.[93]

With these potentially terrible consequences in mind, one may be tempted to analyse the bottom trawling industry in terms of cost and benefit. There could well be a strong case to be put forward in favour of bottom trawling if the industry was spurred on by necessity and the harm done to the environment was in some way commensurate with the benefits accrued. This, however, is unlikely to be the case. The benefits of bottom trawling, in terms of harvested stocks, are minimal. Bottom trawling accounts for less than one per cent of the global catch of fish stocks,[94] and with most fish harvested by bottom trawling

[90] Whilst the main threat to Cold Water Corals is undoubtedly due to high seas bottom trawling, human interventions in the form of oil exploration, the laying of pipelines and cables and pollution, dumping and research activities are also factors in their degradation, see UNEP Cold Water Coral Reefs.

[91] UNEP Cold Water Coral Reefs.

[92] ICES, *Seamounts – Hotspots of Marine Life*, at http://www.ices.dk/marineworld/seamounts.asp.

[93] Kuala Lumpur Working Paper, at p. 3.

[94] *Time-Out on Bottom Trawling*, at p. 4.

destined for the tables of American, European and Japanese consumers, the catch has very little impact on global food security.[95]

Although high seas bottom trawling is not a phenomenon caused exclusively by flags of convenience it does, nevertheless, provide a fertile breeding ground for these vessels. The main States involved in bottom trawling at present are not those "usual suspects" of States associated with flag of convenience fisheries but historically important and "responsible" distant water fishing nations. In the short term this could prove to be positive as those States currently operating large fleets of bottom trawlers (Spain, Russia, Portugal, Norway, Estonia, Denmark, Japan, Lithuania, Iceland, New Zealand and Latvia)[96] could well prove themselves responsible by complying with any international regulation of bottom trawling. Whilst past performance is no guarantee of future conduct, the more optimistic of analysts may take comfort from the past actions of many of the States with large numbers of bottom trawlers in relation to similar threats to biodiversity. Certainly few States have unblemished records in the murky waters of international fisheries, and when the words "fishing" and "Spain" or "Russia" or "Poland" or "Japan" are mentioned in the same sentence perhaps one would be forgiven if one's first thoughts tend not to be positive, but, in the past these States have demonstrated an ability to engage with the international fishing community to find solutions to serious threats to marine biodiversity.[97]

At present, international society is, perhaps slowly, waking up to the problems caused by bottom trawling the high seas. Noting the potentially disastrous consequences of bottom trawling activities, the scientific community and environmental pressure groups have led calls, as is often the case, for an immediate moratorium on bottom trawling.[98] Similarly the Kuala Lumpur Conference of Parties to the Convention on Biological Diversity, noting the threat to biodiversity posed by destructive bottom trawling, heard calls for States to properly

[95] *Time-Out on Bottom Trawling*, at p. 4.

[96] *Time-Out on Bottom Trawling*, at p. 4: Matthew Gianni, *High Seas Bottom Fisheries and Their Impacts on the Biodiversity of Vulnerable Deep Sea Ecosystems*, IUCN, Gland, Switzerland, 2004, at p. viii (herein after "Gianni").

[97] Examples could include the Bering Sea Doughnut Hole "crisis" when several DWFNs listed as HSBT States (notably Poland and Japan) engaged with the former Soviet Union and the United States to reach a compromise in the form of the Convention on the Conservation and Management of Pollock Resources in the Central Bering Sea. For a thorough overview of the negotiations leading to the Convention see David A. Balton, *The Bering Sea Doughnut Hole Convention*, in Olav Schram Stokke, *Governing High Seas Fisheries*. Likewise the Grand Banks controversy between Canada and the EC (notably Spain and to a lesser extent, Portugal) found resolution through NAFO. Again, for more information see Christopher C. Joyner, *Canadian activism in the Grand Banks*, also in Stokke.

[98] *Time-Out on Bottom Trawling:* "1,136 scientists from 69 nations…call for an immediate worldwide moratorium on…deep sea bottom trawling…".

and collectively address the issue. The final published Declaration, COPVII/5, recognised the environmental harms caused by destructive fishing practices to cold water corals and sea mounts and called upon the international community to "urgently take the necessary short term, medium term and long term measures to eliminate/avoid destructive practices...in marine areas beyond the limits of national jurisdiction, in particular areas with seamounts...and cold water corals."[99] These measures should, where appropriate and based upon scientific knowledge and precaution, include an interim prohibition of these destructive practices.[100] Likewise the UN General Assembly has made calls on an annual basis since 2005 for States and regulatory bodies to take urgent action to protect seamounts, cold water corals, etc from the destructive practices associated with bottom trawling activities.[101] In part a response to these UNGA Resolutions the UNFAO issued, in September 2008, its *International Guidelines for the Management of Deep-Sea Fisheries in the High Seas*, which, *inter alia*, call upon States to assess and guard against the most deleterious impacts of bottom fishing in Vulnerable Marine Ecosystems such as seamounts and cold water corals.

Whether or not this will prove to be too little too late for many threatened habitats and species remains to be seen and the results of the international community's actions are to be awaited. Clearly though plans are afoot to regulate the bottom trawling of the high seas. Other than the CBD initiatives there are a number of management plans currently operated by Regional Fisheries Management Organisations. As these plans come to effective fruition there may be no finer contemporary example of the subtle shift between unregulated fisheries as found in sub-paragraph (2) of the FAO definition and unregulated fishing as defined in sub-paragraph (1) of the same. It will be recalled that the former type of unregulated fishing was defined by the FAO as "fishing activities...in areas or for fish stocks in relation to which there are no applicable conservation or management measures and where such fishing activities are conducted in a manner inconsistent with State responsibilities for the conservation of living marine resources under international law."[102] In contrast, the latter type,

[99] Kuala Lumpur Working Paper, at paragraphs 28 to 32. These include "hard law" such as UNCLOS, the Convention on Biodiversity itself, and the Fish Stocks Agreement, as well as non-binding "soft law" such as the Code of Conduct for Responsible Fisheries, the Plan of Implementation of the World Summit on Sustainable Development, Chapter 17 of Agenda 21, and a variety of UNGA Resolutions.

[100] UNCBD, COPVII/5, *Marine and Coastal Biodiversity*, paragraphs 59–61.

[101] See, for instance, UNGA Resolution 59/25 of January 2005, at paragraph 66, reaffirmed by UNGA Resolution 60/31 of March 2006, at paragraphs 68–73; UNGA Resolution 61/105 of March 2007, at paragraphs 80–90; UNGA Resolution 62/177 of February 2008, at paragraphs 97–101, and; UNGA Resolution 63/112 of February 2009, at paragraphs 102–107.

[102] FAO International Plan of Action to Prevent, Deter and Eliminate Illegal, Unreported and Unregulated Fishing, FAO, Rome, 2001, paragraph 3.3.1.

according to the FAO, is "fishing activities in the area of application of a relevant regional fisheries management organization that are conducted by vessels without nationality, or by those flying the flag of a State not party to that organization, or by a fishing entity, in a manner that is not consistent with or contravenes the conservation and management measures of that organization."[103] Thus, whereas bottom trawling activities may have once been 'technically' classified as unregulated fisheries due to the absence of regulation, post-RFMO action on this issue certain vessels might be engaged in 'unregulated fishing-proper' due to those vessels flying the flag of non-party States. This is, of course, a fairly nuanced distinction, but one that is sufficiently important in the context of flag of convenience fishing to warrant further close analysis.

The North-East Atlantic Fisheries Commission, for example, at its 23rd Annual Meeting in November 2004 announced that it would temporarily suspend bottom trawling in a number of sectors of the huge Reykjanes Ridge area of the Atlantic for a period of three years beginning on 1st January 2005.[104] Further to this, NEAFC closed off additional areas to HSBT activities in 2007 to include the fisheries zones of Hatton Bank and Rockall,[105] and again in 2009 to include five further mid to north Atlantic fisheries zones. Between 2009 and 2011 NEAFC extended the 2005 temporary closures of the Reykjanes Ridge zones until 2016[106] and the Hatton Bank and Rockall Zones closures were extended, again, until 2012.[107] For all NEAFC zones that remain 'open' for HSBT activities a two-fold strategy of management applies, with separate arrangements being made for 'existing fisheries' (where, presumably the damage has already been done) and new or exploratory fisheries. Rather than curtailing existing fisheries (other than in the aforementioned closed areas) NEAFC Recommendation XVI of 2008 imposes an obligation upon States to map and chart areas that have already been used for bottom fishing.[108] In all areas not identified as existing fisheries, or – in existing fisheries areas – following significant changes in the "conduct or technology" of the fisheries, or in the event of any new scientific information indicating that an existing fishing ground should be classified as vulnerable, the fisheries will be classified as 'exploratory' and thus fall within the regulatory procedures enunciated in Articles 4–7 of NEAFC Recommendation XVI of 2008.[109] These regulatory procedures require

[103] *Ibid.*, paragraph 3.3.2.

[104] NEAFC Recommendation for the Protection of Vulnerable Deep Water Habitats, 23rd Annual Meeting.

[105] NEAFC Recommendations IX of 2007 and XI of 2008.

[106] NEAFC Recommendation on the Protection of Vulnerable Marine Ecosystems from Significant Adverse Impacts in the NEAFC Regulatory Area, 2009 (PV).

[107] NEAFC Recommendation XIV of 2011.

[108] NEAFC Recommendation XVI of 2008.

[109] As amended by NEAFC Recommendation XV of 2011.

that following a risk assessment undertaken by NEAFC's Permanent Committee on Management and Science (PECMAS), the fisheries will be either subject to strict regulation or closed, depending upon the severity of the threat posed and the vulnerability of the ecosystem. The strict regulation envisaged in these exploratory areas is found in Annex One and requires that any bottom fisheries activities can only be undertaken upon receipt of detailed plans pertaining to the harvesting of the stock, the mitigation measures in place, catch monitoring and data collection. Thus, for vessels flagged to NEAFC contracting States (the Faeroe Islands and Greenland, Estonia, Poland, Iceland, Norway and the European Community) the regional regime has closed off or regulated huge swathes of vulnerable ocean floor.

Like NEAFC, the Commission for the Conservation of Antarctic Marine Living Resources has adopted measures to militate against many of the worst excesses of the bottom trawling industry. And again like NEAFC, CCAMLR implements a multi-pronged strategy that falls short of an outright prohibition of all bottom trawling activities in all fishing zones. Instead, in the generality of cases CCAMLR limits and regulates bottom trawling. Thus, under CCAMLR Conservation Measure 22–06 of 2010, flag States can only allow their vessels to engage in bottom trawling activities when so authorised by the CCAMLR Commission.[110] Informing the Commission's decision to authorise any bottom trawling activities is the risk assessment carried out by CCAMLR's Scientific Committee which, in turn, considers the likely impact of the bottom trawling on the marine environment.[111] During the course of any assessment or following 'encounters' with vulnerable marine ecosystems during the course of any bottom trawling activity, the CCAMLR Commission may determine that that particular fisheries ground should be subject to further conservation measures.[112] In certain geographical areas, however, bottom trawling is entirely prohibited, so that, for instance, bottom trawls cannot be utilised in any fisheries for *Champsocephalus gunnari* (mackerel or icefish) in CCAMLR statistical sub-area 48.3 (a rectangle of the southern Atlantic surrounding South Georgia).[113] Likewise, in all high seas areas within CCAMLR's remit, bottom trawls are prohibited unless CCAMLR has enacted specific control regulations

[110] CCAMLR Conservation Measure 22–06 (2010), *Bottom Fishing in the Convention Area*, Article 6.

[111] *Ibid.*, Article 7.

[112] *Ibid.*, Article 10.

[113] CCAMLR Conservation Measure 42–01 (2010) *Limits on the fishery for* Champsocephalus gunnari *in Statistical Subarea 48.3 in the 2010/11 season.* Although subject to annual review, this measure has been in place, in various guises, since at 2001.

for that area.[114] These measures apply to all CCAMLR member States' vessels and Non-Member State Parties.[115]

Although the aforementioned HSBT States currently operating bottom trawlers may well adhere to any agreed regulation of the industry, it is probably not too contentious to speculate as to the future practices of the vessels themselves. As regulation increases and encroaches, what might the less-than scrupulous vessel owner do? Should they remain flagged to States that require strict adherence to these regional requirements? Or should the vessel owner attempt to circumvent these regulations by flagging their vessel to a non-contracting State. This is precisely the manner in which any new flag of convenience fishing industry begins – the vessels owners will leave the Spanish, Russian, Portuguese, etc registers and flag out to convenient States not party to any of the aforementioned agreements. One-time Spanish, Portuguese, Russian and Japanese registered vessels may soon be swelling the registries of non-CCAMLR or NEAFC party States such as Bolivia, Cambodia or Saint Vincent and the Grenadines. If so, the measures adopted by the RFMOs will not apply to those vessels engaged in bottom trawling on the high seas, and to that extent it would take only a handful of States, or indeed one State, to seriously undermine those conservation and management measures.

3.4 *The Impact on Individuals Employed in the Flag of Convenience Sector*

As well as considering the above mentioned environmental consequences of IUU and flag of convenience fisheries, one must also remember that people are directly harmed by deleterious methods of fisheries. This harm can take the form of the more obvious and direct threats to livelihoods and jobs in the legitimate fisheries sector, the loss of revenue for fisheries dependent communities and physical harm to legitimate fishermen. Additionally, the plight of those individuals crewing flag of convenience vessels should not be overlooked, for evidence shows that their lot is far from being a happy one.

---

114 CCAMLR Conservation Measure 22–05 (2008) *Restrictions on the use of bottom trawling gear in high-seas areas of the Covention Area.*

115 CCAMLR Members are: Argentina, Australia, Belgium, Brazil, Chile, European Community, France, Germany, India, Italy, Japan, Republic of Korea, Namibia, New Zealand, Norway, Poland, Russian Federation, South Africa, Spain, Sweden, Ukraine, United Kingdom, USA and Uruguay. The Non-Member State Parties are: Bulgaria, Canada, Finland, Greece, Mauritius, The Netherlands, Peru and Vanuatu. See http://www.ccamlr.org/pu/E/ms/contacts.htm.

Any review of the literature surrounding the issue of flags of convenience, from press clippings to articles in legal journals to governmental pronouncements may, in many cases, lead the reviewer to words such as 'pirates' and 'piracy'. Firstly, there is an in-built inaccuracy in the use of such words – traditionally, of course, pirate vessels flew no flag and were registered to no port, rather than ports of convenience. Secondly, the use of such terms may instil in the reader a misguided sense of romanticism. When one thinks of pirates perhaps one could be forgiven if one's mind turns to bands of swashbuckling buccaneers plundering treasures to be buried and later shared, and generally having a wonderful time on their ill-gotten gains. The life of the modern day pirate, if we must use that term, could not be further from the romanticised and carefree ideal evoked by Byron's homage to the gallant and noble life of the pirates whose "souls are free."[116] Perhaps the modern day pirate may still enjoy this ethereal freedom, although if he does it is likely to be one of his very few liberties. As the International Tribunal for the Law of the Sea acknowledged in the *Camouco Case*, the life of a crewman aboard a pirate vessel, especially those engaged in fisheries, is more akin to that other mariner of a thankfully bygone age – the slave. Thus for over 60 years the International Transport Worker's Federation's campaign against flags of convenience has been driven in large part, although not exclusively, by its opposition to the conditions of employment of flag of convenience crew.

Unprotected by an effective trade union and hidden away from the scrutiny of inspectors, thousands of mariners currently crew ancient,[117] unsafe and unregulated "floating coffins"[118] where "a sub-standard ship is the norm rather than the exception."[119] These mariners are caught in an industry in which the spiral in the decline in standards of welfare, conditions and safety is ensured

[116] Lord Byron, *The Corsair*, 1814.

[117] The State of World Fisheries 2004, at p. 25, 28% of the global fishing fleet is over 30 years old. Although this figure includes vessels from all States, non-FOCs and FOCs alike, evidence suggests that vessels registered to FOCs are disproportionately represented in the group of vessels aged between 20 to 30 years. For instance the average ages of vessels on certain traditional FOC registers are as follows: Belize – 22 years, Bolivia – 20 years, Cambodia – 20 years, Honduras 23 years, Mauritius – 28 years, Panama – 28 years. It should be noted, however, that only two of these traditional FOC States, Panama and Mauritius, have an average age older than the global average of 24 years. These figures relate to 2003 data compiled by Lloyd's Maritime Services and cited in Matthew Gianni and Walt Simpson, *Flags of Convenience, Transhipment, Re-Supply and At-Sea Infrastructure in Relation to IUU Fishing*, in *Fish Piracy: Combating Illegal, Unreported and Unregulated Fishing*, OECD, Paris, 2004, at pp. 81–85 (herein after "Gianni and Simpson (2004)").

[118] International Transport Workers' Federation, *What do FOCs Mean for Seafarers?* At http://www.itfglobal.org/flags-convenience/flags-convenien-184.cfm.

[119] William O'Niell, Secretary General of the International Maritime Organisation, *The Financial Times*, 5th December 2002.

by a new crop of flag States, each hoping to establish their registries as the preferred choice of lower-end vessel owners. When vessels fail to attain the standards required by the more discerning of FOCs, instead of facing the final trip to the vast maritime scrap yards of Pakistan, India and Bangladesh, many vessels simply continue to sail under the flags of less exacting, "super unregulated" States such as Cambodia and Equatorial Guinea.[120] Not only do these relatively new entrants to the flag market ensure a prolonged life for vessels which, by all reasonable and relative standards, should be confined to the ship breakers, they also ensure that the safety and conditions for crew members reach new lows.

A good illustration of the economic imperatives at play in this two-tiered system is provided by the example of one 27 year old Maltese registered tanker, the *Kristal*, doomed to sink with the loss of eleven lives in February 2001:

> Though the *Kristal* was well painted and regularly passed inspections, it was at least five years beyond ideal retirement age, and had grown decrepit and difficult to maintain. Its owners kept it sailing anyway, apparently with the intention of squeezing a final few years of profitability from the hull before selling it to other operators still lower down the food chain...They were unable to attract business from the major oil companies, most of which now try to apply stringent standards to the tankers they charter and generally shy away from vessels past the age of twenty because of the risk of break-up, and the expense and negative publicity caused by spills. Nonetheless, there were plenty of other, less exacting customers available, as long as the *Kristal* could transport their cargos at a low enough price.[121]

The example of the *Kristal* is by no means unique, in the same year of the *Kristal's* demise a further 454 vessels were reported to have been involved in serious or very serious incidents, leading to a total of 343 persons killed or missing[122] and a further 51 injured. Of these reported incidents 225 involved vessels registered to 18 of the 32 known flags of convenience.[123] Nor are these types of vessels confined to the tanker industry – the IMO's casualty list shows that whilst cargo, container and tanker ships predominate, fishing vessels, ferries, tugs, factory ships, dredgers and passenger ships were all involved in incidents of varying severity. Whenever unscrupulous owners persist in squeezing those "few final years of profitability" from unsafe vessels they will always require indifferent flag States to provide registration and to sign them off as safe. And

---

[120] Nik Winchester and Tony Alderton, *Flag State Audit 2003*, Seafarers International Research Centre, at http://www.sirc.cf.ac.uk/fsa.html.

[121] William Langewiesche, *The Outlaw Sea: Chaos and Crime on the World's Oceans*, Granta Books, London, 2004, at pp. 8–9.

[122] Including the 11 crewmen who died with the *Kristal*.

[123] All data from the International Maritime Organisation, *Casualty Statistics and Investigations: Very Serious and Serious Casualties for the Year 2001*, IMO/FSI3/Circ.4, 10th February 2004.

in the competitive flag market, States will compete against each other to attract the aging fleet by ensuring that they offer the least interference and regulation. Whether it is decrepit tankers such as the *Kristal* or fishing vessels, which, because of their age and outdated, unsophisticated gear, cannot compete with more modern and safer vessels, economics dictate that corners must be cut. Obviously when these corners are cut, crew safety and conditions are likely to be sacrificed. The race to the bottom generated by competition in the flag market allows these sacrifices and as we have already seen in Chapter Two, there are always States willing to register these vessels when others refuse.

3.5 *Conclusion*

All in all then, measured by any standard that places the environment, sustainability, human life and natural biodiversity above profit and neo-conservative market economies, flags of convenience pose a problem for the world. Traditional flag State controls on their excesses are undoubtedly a recipe for further disaster unless, as is extremely unlikely, all States undertake a paradigm shift of Copernican proportions in their economic policies. To prevent the sustained decline of standards and to protect the marine environment the international community faces a stark choice between the status quo and real and effective solutions. Proper initiatives are necessary in this regard and not simply more treaties and conventions that, by their very nature, will never attract the support of the States that matter – those States placing short term profit above all else. Asking those States to so do is, to be frank, like asking a turkey to vote for Christmas.

Thus, it is necessary to ask the question as to how this intolerable situation has arisen. What has gone so badly wrong with the machinations of international law-making that allows States to effectively opt-out of their responsibilities to protect the marine environment? And perhaps more importantly, what is the international community doing to rectify the problem. The next Chapters will, therefore, consider the historical and contemporary attempts to curb the most destructive elements of the flag of convenience industry. Chapter Four will consider the legal vacuum that allows this industry to flourish and analyse the method in which responsible law-makers have attempted to plug the gap, whilst Chapters Five and Six will move away from the generality of the flag of convenience issue to consider recent initiatives to deal with the specific fisheries harms caused by the IUU/FOC fleet.

Chapter Four

The Laws of the Sea: The Legal Vacuum that has Created the Flag of Convenience Industry

4.1 *Introduction*

The international law of the sea is as vast and multifarious as the oceans themselves. For every use man subjects the oceans to, there will almost certainly exist some international treaty or national legislative provision regulating the actions of states and individuals. Whether it is pleasure boating in tranquil coastal waters, or transhipping commodities across the vast open oceans, subsistence fishing within the shallows or bottom trawling the deepest oceans there will be an applicable law that participants in these activities could find themselves subjected to. Strange then, that when we consider the oceans our minds should conjure up images of the free seas and that one of the most basic principles of ocean usage is the freedom of the seas.

In order to reconcile the seemingly contradictory principles of freedom and ultra regulation it is necessary to trace the historical development of the laws of the sea. This analysis will show, that in line with international law generally, the law of the sea facilitates certain traditional freedoms and binds those States wishing to be bound into the arguably embryonic framework of regulations. Likewise, and again in common with 'ordinary' principles of international law, the law of the sea suffers from the inability to regulate *all activities at all times* due to the requirement that in order for international treaties to be effective States must demonstrate a commitment to an acceptance of, and an adherence to, those treaties. This requires two levels of commitment. First, States must accede to these laws by voluntary signature and/or ratification of the treaty in question. Secondly, once accession has taken place, States must give effect to these commitments by adopting the necessary laws and sanctions to ensure compliance by their nationals.

There are, therefore, a number of obvious ways in which international treaties can fail to adequately achieve their aims. These range from: a State's refusal to be bound by the treaties themselves; insufficiently detailed provisions within the treaty concerning the measures a State must take in order to fully implement its provisions; a State's ambivalence towards enacting the requisite national legislation; or the failure of a State to ensure compliance with its national laws which implement international obligations. As has been shown in earlier Chapters it is this type of State ambivalence towards, or in some cases, outright opposition to international treaties that fuel the flag of convenience industry. The question remains, however, as to why and how international law allows vessel owners to pick and choose States of registry.

This Chapter will therefore consider the historical evolution of the Law of the Sea and identify how the controls over international fisheries can be circumvented by States and private entities engaged in IUU and flag of convenience fisheries. It will, in *Exclusive Flag State Jurisdiction Over Vessels: Its Pedigree and Consequences*, consider the way in which the principle of the freedom of the seas ensures that, with only a few and notable exceptions, the only laws that ships on the high seas are subject to are those to which the State of registry has chosen to accede to and implement. At the heart of this Chapter, therefore, is the requirement of a genuine link between State and vessel. This issue is first alluded to in the section entitled *Vessel Registration: Can a Vessel Choose Which Flag to Fly?* which considers the ability of States to grant the protection of its flag (and, of course, subject its jurisdiction) to any vessel of its choosing. As this section will show, however, whilst the notion of the genuine link may be a fundamental theoretical aspect of the ability of States to grant nationality to ships, in practice this concept is both ill-defined and largely ignored by international law. Thus the Chapter moves to consider the evolution of the principle (*The Origins of the Genuine Link Between Vessel and State*) and the underpinnings of the principle itself (*What is a Genuine Link?*). The Chapter then discusses, in *A Dearth or the Death of the Genuine Link*, how this concept has been marginalised and rendered impotent by its interpretation by successive international tribunals when the issue has been raised for discussion. Nevertheless, as *The Resurgence of the Genuine Link?* shows, certain sections of the international law-making community occasionally demonstrates a willingness to persist with the notion by making the genuine link a central tenet of numerous agreements aimed at reducing the impacts of deleterious FOC activity.

Finally the Chapter concludes by considering the 'best case scenario.' Even if a robust definition could be agreed upon and, perhaps more importantly, implemented, would this finally curtail the activities of the global FOC fleet? Or would this pose no more than a minor irritation to the industry?

4.2 *Exclusive Flag State Jurisdiction over Vessels: its Pedigree and Consequences*

Although flags of convenience vessels are undoubtedly considered to be a major problem in the contemporary laws of the oceans, they are, it is contended, an inevitable result of the existing and historical law of the sea. In geographical areas beyond State jurisdiction, generally only flag States may exercise jurisdiction over their vessels.[1] Thus, this prescriptive jurisdiction means that on the high seas, other than within a handful of exceptions noted later herein, only those laws enacted by the State of registry have any application to and over their vessels. Likewise, and again subject to those few exceptional cases, it is only the flag State that is entitled to actively enforce these laws. Other States, unless specifically authorised by the flag State, cannot intervene.[2]

Rooted in the centuries old tradition of the freedom of the high seas, famously espoused by Hugo Grotius in his early 17th century work the *Mare Liberum*, the principle of exclusive flag State jurisdiction is deeply embedded in contemporary international law[3] and "one of the most important means by which public order is maintained at sea."[4] For Grotius, basing his principles upon the prevalent natural law of his time, the seas were free: do not the blowing winds, he asked, "sufficiently signify that nature hath granted a passage from all nations unto all?"[5] Expanding his philosophy, Grotius stated that what could not be taken into possession could not be taken into dominion and thus remained common for all of mankind. The sea, he claimed, was "so infinite that it cannot be possessed"[6] and, because the use of the sea for navigation and fishing could not threaten its further use by others for these purposes, the seas remained common to all men. Those things which belong to all men, he stated, "can no more be taken away by one from all than you may take away from me which is mine."[7]

Almost three hundred years later in the *Lotus* case the Permanent Court of Arbitration elaborated upon this point, stating that:

> ...[A]part from certain special cases which are defined by international law – vessels on the high seas are subject to no authority except that of the State whose flag they fly. In virtue of the principle of the freedom of the high seas, that is to say, in the absence of any territorial sovereignty upon the high seas, no State may exercise any kind of jurisdiction over foreign vessels upon them.[8]

---

1 UNCLOS Article 92.

2 This point is expanded upon in a later section in relation to specific regional treaties, such as CCAMLR, NAFO, etc. under which third party intervention is permitted.

3 Indeed, it has been stated that this principle is a "basic principle of customary international law." DJ Harris, *Cases and Materials on International Law*, 5th Ed., p. 430 (herein after "Harris").

4 Churchill and Lowe, *The Law of the Sea*, 3rd Ed., p. 257 (herein after "Churchill and Lowe").

5 Hugo Grotius, *Mar Liberum*, (1609) Reprinted by Liberty Fund, Indiana, 2004, translated by Richard Hakluyt, at p. 11 (herein after "Grotius").

6 Grotius, p. 25.

7 Grotius, p. 26.

8 France v Turkey (1927) PCIJ Reports, Series A, No 10.

The exceptions to the general rule of exclusive flag State jurisdiction – those "special cases" referred to in the *Lotus* case – would later be codified by the 1982 United Nations Convention on the Law of the Sea (UNCLOS) and include the obligation incumbent upon all States to take measures to repress piracy by the seizure and arrest of vessels and crew;[9] the duty to suppress the trade in narcotics;[10] the right for affected States to arrest persons or ships engaged in unauthorised broadcasting;[11] and the right to board foreign vessels when there are reasonable grounds to believe that the vessel is engaged in piracy, unauthorized broadcasting, or the slave trade.[12] Similarly, it has been suggested by Churchill and Lowe that where acts of major pollution seriously affect the shoreline of a coastal State then both treaty and customary international law allow for States to take action against the vessel responsible, in the high seas, regardless of the flag flown.[13] The basis for this assertion is the infamous *Torrey Canyon*[14] case which concerned the sinking of a stricken oil tanker by the United Kingdom. Floundering off England's south-western coast, but not within its contemporary coastal waters, the Liberian-registered, American-owned and Italian-crewed Torrey Canyon eventually spewed a total of 80,000 tonnes of oil into the seas around and, eventually onto, the beaches of the Cornish coast.[15] To stem this flow of oil – by incinerating it – the UK government took the ultimate interventionist step of sinking the abandoned vessel by instructing the Royal Air Force to bomb it with rockets and napalm.[16] Noting the questionable legality of this act, the UK government referred the matter to the International Maritime Organisation, under whose auspices the so-called Intervention Convention[17] was subsequently issued.[18] It is noteworthy that unlike the latterly adopted UNCLOS, where the threshold for non-flag State intervention is that of a reasonable belief in the mere existence of acts of piracy, unauthorised broadcasting, or the transport of slaves, irrespective of the levels of severity, the Intervention Convention only permits intervention under certain circumstances. For instance, the threat to the marine environment must

[9] UNCLOS Article 105.
[10] UNCLOS Article 108.
[11] UNCLOS Article 109.
[12] UNCLOS Article 110.
[13] Churchill and Lowe, p. 216.
[14] (1967) Cmnd. 3246.
[15] Nanda, *The "Torrey Canyon" Disaster: Some Legal Aspects*, (1967) 44 Denv. L.J. 400, pp. 400–401 (herein after "Nanda").
[16] *Ibid.*
[17] The 1969 International Convention Relating to Intervention on the High Seas in Cases of Oil Pollution Casualties, entered into force in May 1975.
[18] Churchill and Lowe, p. 354.

be both 'grave' and 'imminent'[19] and non-flag State measures can only be taken without consulting with the flag State in cases of 'extreme emergency'.[20]

Irrespective of the difference in threshold, it is clear, however, that under both UNCLOS and the Intervention Convention a degree of non-flag State jurisdiction is conferred on interested States. As Nanda notes, "[t]he international community has a common interest in keeping the oceans – the joint property of nations [...] – free from pollution."[21] Likewise, the non-flag State interventionist measures found in UNCLOS reflect the common interest of States in ensuring that the oceans are not used for universally harmful practices such as piracy *et al.* One might, at this point, legitimately ask whether violations of fisheries regulations also impinge universally on all States and represent offences against the common interests of the international community to such an extent that a degree of universal jurisdiction might be vested in all States in a comparable manner.

Violations of fisheries laws, however, do not confer universal non-flag State jurisdiction. Certain violations of fisheries laws do vest powers in individual States, of course, for exmaple when the alleged incident concerns violations of domestic fisheries regulations committed by foreign vessels and occurs in the territorial waters of a coastal State. In this situation the coastal State has the right, if not the obligation, and subject to the specific procedures found under Article 111 of UNCLOS, to pursue the vessel into the high seas to effect the arrest or seizure of the vessel.[22] This right of 'hot pursuit' has been famously asserted by Australia on a number of occasions. For instance, in August 2003 the Australian navy, with the assistance of South African and British vessels, pursued the Uruguayan registered *Viarsa 1* for 20 days in the Southern Oceans after it was spotted fishing illegally for Patagonian Toothfish in Australian waters.[23] Although the *Viarsa*-type case (or, indeed, any other assertion of

---

[19] The Intervention Convention, Article I.

[20] The Intervention Convention, Article III (d).

[21] Nanda, p. 405.

[22] UNCLOS Article 111 gives States the right to pursue vessels when there are reasonable grounds to believe that a foreign vessel has violated the laws of the coastal State. Among the several conditions imposed by Article 111 are those to the extent that the pursuit must commence when the violating vessel is within the waters of the offended State and must not be interrupted, (Art 111(1)). The pursuit shall cease when the offending vessel reaches the territorial sea of its own or a third State, (Art 111(3)).

[23] TRAFFIC International, *TRAFFIC Lauds Detention of Suspected 'Pirate' Toothfish Fishing Vessel*, see TRAFFIC International at http://www.traffic.org/news/pirate_toothfish.html. Similarly Australia has affected the arrest in the high seas of the *Volga* for similar offences, see Russian Federation v Australia (The *Volga* Case) Case 11 of the International Tribunal of the Law of the Sea. Likewise, in 2001 the lesser known case of the *South Tomi* ended after a chase of four thousand miles to the edge of South African waters, again following allegations of illegal Toothfish harvesting in Australian waters near the Heard Islands, see Australian Antarctic

coastal State rights under Article 111) does represent something of an exception to the principle of exclusive flag State jurisdiction, this exception should not be over-stated. Rather than being a representation of common-interest, Article 111 is more a manifestation of self-interest – only coastal States may engage in hot pursuit (although as the *Viarsa* shows, other States may be asked to assist), and only when there has been an infraction of their domestic laws. The right of hot pursuit cannot be invoked for violations of fisheries laws on the high seas, and cannot be invoked by States other than the affected coastal State.

Thus, other than these obligations imposed upon States to undertake measures to suppress the *erga omnes* international crimes, and the limited rights of States to defend their coastal waters, any interference with the ships of other States is viewed both as a violation of the principle of the freedom of high seas and an unlawful interference with the territory of another State. Even if a State may justifiably and reasonably claim victim-hood as a result of the acts or omissions of another State's ship, the victim State is precluded from any acts of seizure, arrest or sanction against that vessel. That is not to say, though, that an aggrieved State has no redress whatsoever: there are courses of action open to States.

First, a specific treaty between the two States in question may authorise the victim State to enforce certain limited rights against ships acting in a manner inconsistent with the aims of that treaty. An example of such specific authorisation can be found in a number of regional fisheries agreements. For instance Article XXIV of the Convention for the Conservation of Antarctic Marine Living Resources (CCAMLR), establishes the procedures for, and circumstances under which, the fishing and research vessels of contracting States may be boarded and inspected by designated CCAMLR inspectors from all contracting States.[24] The jurisdiction of second States is, however, limited to boarding and inspection, as any prosecution emanating from the evidence of malpractice unearthed by the inspectors can only be instigated by the flag State of the errant vessel,[25] and inspection vessels have no powers of arrest or detention of either vessels, equipment, master or crew and must confine their activities strictly to the gathering of evidence of unlawful activity.[26] Nevertheless, this does represent a significant

---

Division Newsletter, Issue 2, Spring 2001, *Another One That Didn't Get Away*, at http://www.aad.gov.au/default.asp?casid=2111.

[24] The Text of the Convention for the Conservation of Antarctic Marine Living Resources, Article XXIV(2)(b).

[25] The Text of the Convention for the Conservation of Antarctic Marine Living Resources, Article XXIV(2)(a); Text of the CCAMLR System of Inspection, Article XI.

[26] Text of the CCAMLR System of Inspection, Article VII states that: "If a vessel refuses to stop or otherwise facilitate transfer of an inspector, or if the master or crew of a vessel interferes with the authorised activities of an inspector, the inspector involved shall prepare a detailed report…".

ceding by flag States of their otherwise unfettered sovereignty, for the right to board foreign vessels, as previously noted, is strictly the right of warships acting in accordance with the provisions of Article 110 of UNCLOS.

Similarly, the Northwest Atlantic Fisheries Organisation (NAFO) operates an inspection system which allows for the surveillance, boarding and inspection of contracting party vessels in the NAFO region. Under the terms of the Joint Inspection and Surveillance Scheme,[27] inspectors[28] remain under the operational control of their assigning State but may not enforce the laws of their own State with regard to vessels under the jurisdiction of other Contracting States and all inspections must strictly comply with the agreed rules.[29] These rules govern, *inter alia*, the procedures for boarding,[30] the duties of the boarded vessel's master in facilitating the boarding and inspection,[31] and the procedures to deal with infringements[32] and serious infringements[33] of NAFO Conservation and Management Measures. When the infringement is not considered to be serious under the criteria established in Article 32(1) of the Scheme, inspectors may request that the fishing gear, or any part of it, causing the infringement is removed,[34] and must note the nature of the infringement on the inspection report to be sent to the flag State of the inspected vessel and the Executive Secretary in conjunction with the procedures contained within Article 30 of the Scheme.[35]

Following serious violations of NAFO Conservation and Management Measures, as defined by Article 32(1) of the Scheme, inspectors shall contact an

[27] NAFO Conservation and Enforcement Measures, Chapter IV, *Joint Inspection and Surveillance Scheme*, Article 24(1) (herein after "NAFO/JISS").

[28] "Inspectors" when so called in this section are deemed to be nationals of a Contracting State other than the flag State of the inspected vessel.

[29] NAFO/JISS, Article 26.

[30] NAFO/JISS, Article 28.

[31] NAFO/JISS, Article 29.

[32] NAFO/JISS, Article 31.

[33] NAFO/JISS, Article 32.

[34] There is no specific obligation incumbent upon the master to act upon this request in NAFO/JISS Article 29, but flag States are obliged to treat any resistance to an inspector or a failure to comply with any directions as comparable to resistance to or non-compliance with inspectors from the flag State itself, NAFO/JISS, Article 33(4). Whether or not the failure to comply with a request constitutes a failure to comply with directions is deemed to be resistance is, however, not specified.

[35] In cases of an infringement of NAFO Conservation and Management Measures a copy of the inspection report is to be sent to the flag State within 10 days, NAFO/JISS, Article 30(2). In tandem with the formal transmission of the full report flag States must be given advanced notice of any reported infringements within 24 hours of the infringement coming to light, NAFO/JISS, Article 30(3).

inspector of the flag State of the inspected vessel,[36] and flag State inspection should be undertaken within 72 hours of the initial inspection.[37] During the time prior to the arrival of the flag State inspector, the original inspector is entitled to remain on board the vessel[38] and is empowered to take such steps as are necessary to ensure the safety and continuity of evidence.[39] Like the aforementioned CCAMLR inspection scheme, however, judicial or administrative jurisdiction in terms of dealing with the violation or serious infringement is very much left with the flag State of the infringing vessel.[40] Any judicial or administrative actions invoked by the flag State must both correlate to the manner in which violations of domestic fisheries are treated[41] and "effectively deprive those responsible of the economic benefit of the infringement, or sanctions proportionate to the seriousness of such infringements, thus effectively discouraging future infringements."[42]

It must be noted, however, that both the above mentioned treaty arrangements in no way diminish the basis of the exclusive enforcement jurisdiction of the flag State: any action undertaken by the victim or inspecting State is done with the consent of the flag State as evidenced by the flag State ceding limited powers to foreign States under the terms of the treaty. In line with the general principles of the law of treaties any State may make a reservation to the extent that it will not cede its jurisdiction to another State at the time of its signature, ratification, acceptance or accession,[43] or it may withdraw its consent to be bound by the terms of that treaty at any time.[44]

In the absence of such specific treaty authorisation, aggrieved States may still request the flag State to act against any vessel. Obviously, without agreements authorising the inspection and boarding of foreign vessels the evidence supporting the aggrieved State's request may not be as solid. Under Article 94(6) of UNCLOS there is, however, the general right of third party States to report the

---

[36] NAFO/JISS, Article 32(2).

[37] NAFO/JISS, Article 32(3).

[38] NAFO/JISS, Article 32(5).

[39] NAFO/JISS, Article 32(4). This could include, as appropriate sealing the vessel's hold and requesting the master to cease fishing operations.

[40] NAFO/JISS, Article 33(1).

[41] NAFO/JISS, Article 33(1).

[42] NAFO/JISS, Article 33(5).

[43] Vienna Convention on the Law of Treaties, 1969, Articles 19–23. This is naturally dependent upon the reservation not undermining the object and purpose of the treaty, as per Article 19(c) (herein after "VCLT 1969").

[44] VCLT 1969, Article 54. There is, of course, the possibility that the principles contained within the treaty in question could be representative of customary international law, in which case the State seeking to withdraw from that treaty would still remain bound, not by the treaty itself, but by the principles represented therein, as there is no possibility of that State claiming to be a unbound by that rule of law as a persistent objector.

facts to the flag State, when that State has "clear grounds to believe that proper jurisdiction and control with respect to a ship have not been exercised." Upon receipt of such a report the flag State of the vessel is obliged to "investigate the matter and, if appropriate, take any necessary action to remedy the situation."[45] Obviously in terms of fishing disputes, and especially in relation to flag of convenience vessels whose flag States are not party to any regional or international conservation and management agreements, there is a clear problem of defining what constitutes a failure to exercise proper jurisdiction and control. In this regard it must be noted that Article 94 imposes a general obligation upon flag States to exercise its jurisdiction and control over administrative, technical and social matters over ships flying its flag. The particular measures contained further within Article 94 pertain to the specific administrative, technical and social measures necessary to achieve the aim of 'effective jurisdiction' as required by Article 94, and not to the application of the Convention as a whole. Therefore it would seem that aggrieved States cannot use Article 94(6) as a basis to complain about any lack of effective jurisdiction and control over fishing activities on the high seas due to such activities not pertaining to the listed administrative, technical and social measures. Consequently, on huge tracts of ocean space, and in relation to a seemingly infinite number of activities, international law is almost entirely reliant upon flag States to uphold international norms.

4.3 *Vessel Registration: Can Vessels Chose Which Flag to Fly?*

Whilst it is undoubtedly a pre-requisite that all vessels must sail under the flag of a State to enjoy the protection of that State under international law, and in order to enjoy the freedoms of the seas vessels must only sail under the flag of one State,[46] it is for States to decide which vessels to allow on to their

---

45 UNCLOS Article 94(6).

46 UNCLOS Article 92. Any vessel sailing under the flag of more than one State will be treated as a vessel without nationality and thus debarred from enjoying the freedoms of the sea. UNCLOS Article 87 states that the high seas are open to all *States*, thus a vessel flying no flag or registered in no State will similarly be deemed a vessel without nationality and precluded from the freedoms of the high seas. It should be noted, however, that there is no *de facto* prohibition on flying no flag or having no State of registry, but without the protection of a State any vessel is in a particularly precarious position, as the Judicial Committee of the Privy Council noted following the seizure of the vessel the *Aysa* by a British warship on the high seas 100 miles of the Palestinian coast. Concurring with Oppenheim's International Law (6th Ed) Lord Simmons stated that "In the interest of order on the open sea, a vessel not sailing under the maritime flag of a State enjoys no protection whatever, for the freedom of navigation on the open sea is freedom for such vessels only as sail under the flag of a State." *Naim Molvan, Owner of Motor Vessel "Asya" v Attorney-General for Palestine* [1948] A.C. 351, at p. 370.

registries. Other than the requirement that a "genuine link" must exist between State and vessels, States are given the freedom to "fix the conditions for the grant of nationality to ships, for the registration of ships, and for the right to fly its flag."[47] The concept of the "genuine link" between the flag State and the vessels found in its registry has proven to be a widely and diversely interpreted one, and arguably the very basis under which the flag of convenience industry has flourished and expanded. International law has struggled, for over a century, and seemingly to no avail, to provide precise terms of reference as to what constitutes a genuine link, and similarly has failed to provide a definitive answer to the question of whether or not the genuine link is a pre-requisite for registration. This century of struggle was for some a century in which chaos ultimately replaced order as the over-riding principle of the sea. Liberated from the confines of nationality, and hidden from scrutiny by shadowy and sham corporate paper-trails, an ever expanding number of ships of all sizes and functions now criss-cross the oceans undisturbed by any attempts at regulation.[48] Thus, in order to fully appreciate the machinations of the flag of convenience industry, it is necessary to examine the history and workings of the genuine link concept, its evolution, its many interpretations, and the reasons behind its ultimate failure to address the flag of convenience problem.

4.4 *The Origins of the Genuine Link between Vessel and State*

Whether or not they possessed the foresight to predict the gloomy outlook portrayed above, the jurists comprising the 1896 Venice session of the Institute of International Law could certainly be suspected of having a greater degree of prescience than many of their contemporaries, as they, at least, appear to have been cognisant of the potential difficulties in establishing a genuine link between vessel and State. The solution arrived at was to require that the vessel "was to be controlled by the nationals of the State of registry, and the corporations were to have their seat in that State."[49] Perhaps with hindsight it is unfortunate the IIL's explicit requirements were superseded less than a decade later by the 1905 *Muscat Dhows* case, in which the Permanent Court of Arbitration was obliged to rule on the legality of the granting of the right to fly the French flag to the citizens of Muscat.[50] In reaching its judgment the

[47] UNCLOS Art. 91.

[48] For an excellent, if pessimistic, analysis of the anarchic state of the oceans see William Langewiesche's *The Outlaw Sea – Chaos and Crime on the World's Oceans*, Granta Books, London, 2004.

[49] Vukas and Vidas, p. 54.

[50] 2 AJIL 921 (1908).

Court provided contemporary jurists with a clue to at least a part of the future law regarding the registration of ships, by stating that: "[g]enerally speaking it belongs to every sovereign to decide to whom he will accord the right to fly his flag and to prescribe the rules covering such grants."[51] This principle would later be reflected in international law concerning the granting of nationality to individuals, and for the next few decades these two seemingly disparate contexts became inexorably linked. For instance, Article 1 of the Hague Convention on Certain Questions Relating to the Conflict of Nationality Laws certainly echoed the sentiments of the decision in the *Muscat Dhows* by stating that "[i]t is for each State to determine under its own laws who are its nationals," and that "[t]his law shall be recognised by other States in so far as it is consistent with international conventions, international custom, and the principles of law generally recognised with regard to nationality."[52]

It is probably fair to assume that the laws of the seas were the last thing on the mind of Herr Friedrich Nottebohm, born a German citizen, but resident of Guatemala, as he filed his application for citizenship with authorities in Lichtenstein on October 9, 1939.[53] Although Herr Nottebohm's case concerned his attempts to find a State of convenience for his business and personal interests, these interests had precious little to do with ocean governance.[54] Nevertheless the issues raised by Herr Nottebohm's attempts to evade Guatemalan laws concerning the expulsion and refusal to readmit German citizens under war measures, would have a tangible impact on later laws of the sea. Although the substantive claim (that Guatemala's actions in "arresting, detaining, expelling and refusing to re-admit Mr Nottebohm and in seizing and retaining his property without compensation" was a breach of international law) was never adjudicated upon, the procedural aspect of the case proved to be of extreme significance. The preliminary question for the ICJ was simply whether or not Lichtenstein's granting of citizenship to Herr Nottebohm was sufficient to create the necessary nexus between citizen and State so as avail him of the protection of Lichtenstein in international law.

In his dissenting opinion Judge Read followed the traditional line, basing his opinion that Nottebohm could be afforded the protection of Lichtenstein on the basis of the *Muscat Dhows* and Hague Convention principle that it is for each State to determine under its own laws the conditions of nationality. In response to the requirement under Article 1 of the Hague Convention that the domestic rules should be compatible with international conventions and

[51] 2 AJIL 921 (1908), p. 924.

[52] 1930, 179 LNTS 89.

[53] Lichtenstein v Guatemala, (*The Nottebohm Case*), 1955, ICJ 4.

[54] Nottebohm's business interests, said the ICJ, were in fact, "commerce, banking and plantations."

customs, Judge Read found no inconsistency and no international norms to the contrary. The majority, however, took a slightly different view. Whilst it was perfectly permitted for any State to affix the rules of nationality itself in the domestic context, in order for that nationality to provide State protection for citizens in international law, the State's conditions and rules must be consistent with international law. And, said the ICJ "[i]n order to appraise... the international effect [of a citizen's naturalisation], it is impossible to disregard the circumstances in which it was conferred, the serious character which attaches to it, the real and effective and not merely the verbal preference of the individual seeking it for the country which grants it to him."[55] In view of the facts of Nottebohm's naturalisation by Lichtenstein – his long standing ties to Guatemala, his "extremely tenuous" connection with Lichtenstein and his motivation in seeking citizenship, which were "lacking in the genuineness requisite to an act of such importance" ensured that Lichtenstein could not extend its protection to Nottebohm *vis-à-vis* Guatemala.

Within three years of the judgment in *Nottebohm* the widely held interpretation of it, i.e. that "where a State claimed to exercise diplomatic protection in respect of one of its nationals... nationality should be the legal reflection of a factual link – a 'genuine link' – between the individual and the State",[56] had become the prerequisite for vessel registration under the 1958 High Seas Convention.[57] Other than the requirement that "the State must effectively exercise its jurisdiction and control in administrative, technical and social matters over ships flying its flag" Article 5 of the High Seas Convention is replicated in its entirety by Article 91 of UNCLOS, which it will be recalled, states:

1. Every State shall fix the conditions for the grant of its nationality to ships, for the registration of ships in its territory, and for the right to fly its flag. Ships have the nationality of the State whose flag they are entitled to fly. There must exist a genuine link between the State and the ship; and
2. Every State shall issue to ships to which it has granted the right to fly its flag documents to that effect.

4.5 *What is a Genuine Link?*

Whilst Article 91, with its origins in both *Muscat Dhows* and *Nottebohm*, has a clear pedigree in its evolution and as such has been accepted as codifying a

[55] The *Nottebohm* Case, p. 24.

[56] Churchill and Lowe, p. 258.

[57] The influence of *Nottebohm* on the High Seas Convention has been noted by, *inter alia*, Churchill and Lowe, p. 258 and Harris, p. 424.

"well-established general rule of international law",[58] its substance is far from exacting. The explicit requirements of the 1896 Vienna Conference's Regulations which required the control of vessels to be exercised by nationals of the flag State and that the corporation owning the vessel should have its seat in the State in order to legitimately fly the flag of that State are but a distant memory. Consequently modern jurists must confront the very real question of what exactly constitutes a genuine link. Indeed Article 91 is arguably less clear than Article 5 of the High Seas Convention on what constitutes a genuine link due to the removal of the conditional phrase from the final 1982 draft:

> the State must effectively exercise its jurisdiction and control in administrative, technical and social matters over ships flying its flag.

Certainly prior to UNCLOS it could have been reasonably stated that in order to be genuinely linked to a vessel any State must be able to exercise effective jurisdiction and control over that vessel, as effective control is a component of the genuine link and thus a pre-requisite for registration, but post-UNCLOS this is not necessarily the case. UNCLOS does, of course, retain and build upon the requirement of effective control and jurisdiction, listing in Article 94 the measures which should be undertaken by flag States. The duties imposed upon States under Art 94 UNCLOS are, however, all on-going duties[59] none of which (with the exception of Art 94(4)(a))[60] relate to the granting of registration. The breach of Art 94 obligations therefore appears to relate to a failure to exercise on-going control and not as evidence of a lack of a genuine link between vessel and State for the purposes of its registration under Article 91.[61] The divergence

---

[58] The *M/V Saiga (No 2)* Case, St Vincent and the Grenadines v Guinea, The International Tribunal for the Law of the Sea, Case 2, Judgment of 1st July 1999, at para. 63.

[59] States shall, for instance, maintain a register of ships (Art 94(2)(a)); assume jurisdiction under its internal law over each ship flying its flag, its master, officers and crew in respect of administrative, technical and social matters concerning the ship (Art 94(2)(b)); take such measures as are necessary to ensure the safety of the ship at sea (Art 94(3)(a)(b)(c)).

[60] States shall ensure that each ship, *before registration* and thereafter at appropriate levels, is surveyed by a qualified surveyor of ships, and has on board such charts, nautical publications and navigational equipment and instruments as are appropriate for the safe navigation of the ship, (emphasis added). The fact that Art 94(4)(a) alone explicitly requires certain duties prior to registration can be read to reach the conclusion the other duties found in Art 94 do not have to undertaken prior to registration.

[61] Vukas and Vidas also point out in relation to this point the significance of the titles given to the UNCLOS Articles: Article 91 is headed "Nationality of Ships" whilst Article 94 is headed "Duties of the Flag State". Vukas and Vidas state in relation to the transfer of the requirement of effective control and jurisdiction from Article 5 of the High Seas Convention to the duties incumbent upon flag States change the scope of this requirement from "elements necessary for the *existence* of the genuine link" to being "merely duties of a State that had *already granted* its nationality to a ship." Vukas and Vidas, p. 60. Rayfuse (2004), at pp. 27–28 notes similarly

in substance and form between the 1958 Convention and UNCLOS is significant in two respects. Firstly, as Churchill notes, for a limited number of States the 1958 Convention is the treaty that applies to their conduct on the High Seas. Certain significant sea-going States such as the USA, amongst others, have yet to sign or ratify UNCLOS but are parties to the 1958 Convention.[62] Secondly, and on a more abstract level, the divergence may be evidence of a watering down of the requirement of a genuine link between vessel and State in the quarter of a century separating the two treaties. Nevertheless, whilst the differences between the two Articles may be open to interpretation, the principles behind their identical requirement that there should be a genuine link between vessel and State of registry remain largely un-stated. In order to identify these principles it may be necessary to return to *Nottebohm.*

Given that the genuine link requirements in Article 91 of UNCLOS and Article 5 of the 1958 High Seas Convention have directly evolved from *Nottebohm*, that case should provide at least a starting point. Unfortunately for ease and expediency an important caveat must be inserted to this. Whilst the ICJ subjected Herr Nottebohm's conduct prior to, during and after his naturalisation to a fairly rigorous examination in order to find against Lichtenstein's claim of protection, they went no further than was immediately necessary to resolve the case before them. Consequently, only illustrative examples of behaviour deemed to be demonstrative of the absence of a genuine link can be taken from this case.[63]

Nevertheless, on the basis of *Nottebohm* the following principles should be of relevance in gauging the manner in which the genuine link is interpreted in relation to ship registration, and whether *Nottebohm* is, in substance and in law, genuinely linked to Article 91 or is merely a case of conveniently borrowed phraseology.[64] These principles are:

---

that "[i]t is generally accepted that the genuine link in Article 91 – whatever it is – is a condition to be met before registration while Article 94 deals with the separate and consequential issue of effective control." See also, the Opinion of Advocate General Léger in *Commission v Netherlands*, Case C-299/02 (EC), Unreported, 27th May 2004, which states, at para 54, that "the requirement that there be a genuine link between the ship and its flag States relates to the implementation of the duties to be discharged by the flag State rather than to a necessary precondition for the registration of the ship."

[62] Robin Churchill, *The Meaning of the 'Genuine Link' Requirement in Relation to the Nationality of Ships*, A Study Prepared for the International Transport Workers' Federation, October 2000, at p. 10 (herein after "Churchill ITF Paper").

[63] The Court explicitly acknowledged its own limitations in this regard by stating that "The Court does not propose to go beyond the limited scope of the question which it has to decide..."

[64] The comments made by Churchill regarding the very limited expediency of using *Nottebohm* as a template for establishing the criteria under which the genuine link between vessel and registry can be found are duly noted, (Churchill, ITF Paper, p. 23). The purpose of the use

1. Internationally recognisable naturalisation will not be found when the subject of that naturalisation has a closer bond to another State than that of the bond between the subject and the adopting State. Clearly in *Nottebohm* the bond between Herr Nottebohm and Guatemala, based upon his long-standing residency and the fact that that State was the centre of his interests, was a strong one;
2. Internationally recognisable naturalisation will not be found when the subject has no close connection to the adopting State. At the time of his naturalisation Herr Nottebohm had no settled abode and no prolonged residency in Lichtenstein. Similarly, in the years following the granting of his naturalisation by Lichtenstein Nottebohm visited only sporadically and for all intents and purposes wished to remain a resident of Guatemala;
3. The payment of taxes and fees levied at the time of naturalisation is not a factor that should be considered when a Court is called upon to decide the legitimacy of a claim of internationally recognised naturalisation. Herr Nottebohm may have paid the necessary naturalisation fee, but in the ICJ's opinion it was unnecessary to attach much importance to this; and
4. The fact that no economic interests or business interests are, or are intended to be, incorporated or transferred into the adopting State will provide evidence of the lack of a genuine link between the subject of naturalisation and the adopting State. Herr Nottebohm had not transferred any of his interests, business or otherwise, to Lichtenstein but had instead chosen that all his business interests remained in Guatemala.

Clearly then when we apply the above as an illustrative example of, and not as a strict criteria for, the registration of ships then it is undoubtedly the case that, despite some initial hegemony, State practice has allowed for a marked divergence between the granting of internationally acceptable nationality for individuals and the granting of internationally acceptable nationality for ships. The case of the stern trawler the *Likos* starkly evidences this point.

For most of its working life the *Likos* was fairly undistinguished.[65] Built in 1983, named the *Birakan* and registered in the Soviet Union, it was owned,

of *Nottebohm* in the present regard is to highlight the disparity between the application of a genuine link test as between ships and individuals, and to provide the reader with an example of how the two applications differ.

[65] The case of the *Likos* is certainly not unique. Any analysis of the commercial history of vessels known to Lloyd's Register of Ships, as was undertaken in the preparation of this book, will reveal thousands of vessels with a similar history. The *Likos* was chosen for this example due to the distinguishing feature of its known registered owner, operator and management company throughout its working life. For many vessels showing similar movements between registries Lloyd's simply list ownership, management and operation as unknown for long periods of the vessel's history.

operated and managed by the Soviet, and later the Russian, conglomerate Dalryba (Far Eastern Shipping) based in Vladivostok. In 1998 the *Birakan's* ownership passed to another Russian entity, Gessar Fisheries, also of Vladivostok.[66] Both Dalryba and Gessar operate the majority of their vessels from the Primorye region of the far Eastern coast of the Russian Federation, making their vessels ideally placed to exploit the riches of the Sea of Japan, the Sea of Okhotsk and the Bering Sea. Whilst no specific data is available to ascertain the precise whereabouts and activities of the *Birakan* during this time it seems unlikely to have deviated from the pattern of similar vessels in this region at this time.[67] Throughout this period in its history the *Birakan* was a model of the genuine link by whatever yardstick used to measure the requirement. It operated from Russian ports, and contributed to the Russian economy, it had undergone the formalities of registration, and was owned by Soviet and Russian interests, that is to say – *genuine* Russian interests as both Dalryba and Gessar Fisheries are well established, fully incorporated Russian companies, both of which have their headquarters in Vladivostok. Nevertheless, in the late 1990s the *Birakan*, like many Russian owned and registered vessels lowered its Russian flag and severed its ties with Russia.[68]

Like many of its contemporaries the *Birakan* joined the Belizean register,[69] and although its beneficial owners were unknown during its two year association with Belize, the *Birakan's* registered owner, operator and manager was the Panamanian based Pandamore Shipping. This posed no problem under Belizean law as according to the Merchant Shipping Act of 1989 (as amended in 1996) any body corporate, whether established in Belize or elsewhere, may, upon application and the payment of the necessary fees, be granted Belizean registration for its vessel.[70] Other than the mere act of registration the only requisite link between the vessel and Belize was the appointment by Pandamore Shipping of a Belizean shipping agent. Either an attorney, accountant, Belizean registered company or "any person designated for the purpose" by the Attorney General would satisfy this requirement.[71]

---

[66] Lloyd's Registry of Ships.

[67] Clarence G Pautzke, *Russian Far East Fisheries Management*, Report to Congress of the North Pacific Fisheries Management Council, September 30th 1997, available at www.fakr.noaa.gov/npfmc/summary_reports/rfe-all.htm. See also: Gessar Fishery Company Ltd, at http://www.gessar.ru/about/eindex.htm.

[68] The UNFAO estimates that in the period 1994–2004 the Russian fishing fleet shrank in size by 40%. See http://www.fao.org/fi/fcp/en/RUS/profile.htm.

[69] Lloyd's Registry of Ships.

[70] Section 5(1) Merchant Shipping Act of Belize, 1989.

[71] Section 17(1) Merchant Shipping Act of Belize, 1989.

Following the clean up of the Belizean register initiated in 2001[72] the *Birakan* began the next stage of its career. Deregistered in Belize and renamed the *Likos*, its new registered owners – its beneficial owners remaining an unknown entity – transferred the vessel to Georgia.[73] Like Belize, and all the States operating open registries, Georgia has no requirement that vessels are crewed, operated or managed by Georgian citizens or corporations.[74] Fortunately for the registered owners, management and operating company – the Liberian "Ridley Holdings International SA" and the Greek "Cabochen Marine Inc." respectively, the international law of shipping registration does not, it seems, operate upon quite as stringent requirements for nationality as the ICJ in *Nottebohm*. Whilst the *Likos* may have the protection of the Georgian flag it is clearly not a Georgian vessel when analysed against *Nottebohm*: its ties with that State are not deeply embedded or long-standing, it has no business connections with Georgia other than for the purpose of vessel registration, and the payment of the required taxes and levies to facilitate that registration are not evidence of any genuine link between vessel and State. Thus, it may be safe to assume that the *Likos* – like Herr Nottebohm – assumed the nationality of another State "with the sole aim of thus coming under the protection of... [that State]... but not of becoming wedded to its traditions, its interests, its way of life or of assuming the obligations... and exercising the rights pertaining to the status thus acquired."[75] In short, the *Likos'* Georgian ties, like Herr Nottebohm's to Lichtenstein, are "lacking in the genuineness requisite to an act of such importance."

Even on this simple analysis, and cognisant of the aforementioned cautionary note regarding the use of that case as a template, it would appear that the requirement of a genuine link between shipping vessel and State bears no resemblance to the *Nottebohm* criteria, other than in terms of the language used. In shipping cases something much different, and much less exacting, is required and in 1960 the ICJ was given an almost immediate opportunity to differentiate between the requirements for the internationally recognisable grant of nationality for citizens and ships.

Freed from the necessarily self-imposed constraints of the narrow terms of reference in *Nottebohm*, in the *Constitution of the Maritime Safety Committee of IMCO* case[76] the ICJ was given the opportunity to spell out its vision of what the genuine link concept precisely consisted of. In the *IMCO* case the ICJ was

[72] See Chapter Two.

[73] Lloyd's Registry of Ships.

[74] No precise Georgian legislation is available at this time, but as a marketing tool Georgia is stated to have no restriction or limitations as to local ownership or participation in ownership of vessels on its registry: see http://www.flagsofconvenience.com/pdf_files/Georgia.pdf.

[75] The *Nottebohm* Case, ICJ.

[76] Advisory Opinion of 8th June 1960, ICJ Rep. 1960, p. 150.

asked to furnish the Inter-Governmental Maritime Consultative Organisation[77] with an answer to the question of whether or not the Organisation's Maritime Safety Committee was constituted in accordance with the IMCO Convention. Article 28(a) of the Convention required that the Maritime Safety Council should comprise of eight of the largest shipping nations. Both Panama and Liberia had been denied the opportunity to sit on the Council despite the fact that both States were in the top eight shipping nations in terms of registered tonnage. The IMCO, however, contended that the term "the largest shipping nations" referred not to registered tonnage but beneficially owned tonnage. Thus, the Court was presented with the opportunity to adjudicate on the question of whether or not registration alone was sufficient to link vessel to State. Perhaps it is unfortunate then, as Harris points out, that the ICJ side stepped the opportunity presented and instead, as it did in *Nottebohm*, "limited itself to the particular issue of treaty interpretation before it and did not consider the question of the nationality of ships and flags of convenience generally"[78] and found that by the IMCO's own procedures, and not as a matter of international law generally, registered tonnage was the criteria for establishing the link between vessel and State.

Unfortunately, the ICJ's avoidance of the issue was not the last missed opportunity for law-makers and those charged with interpreting international law to clarify what constitutes a genuine link. The latter half of the 20th century has witnessed one attempt after another to bring this contentious issue to a close, and it is almost certainly the very contentious nature of the subject matter, and not any lack of endeavour, that has resulted in the impasse.

4.6 *A Dearth or the Death of the Genuine Link?*

The UN Convention on the Conditions for Registration of Ships of February 1986 (UNCCRS) was perhaps the best opportunity for the international community to agree upon the precise criteria under which to grant nationality to ships. Although some of the provisions of the 1986 Convention correspond to both the 1958 High Seas Convention and UNCLOS by stating in Article 4(1) that all States are entitled to sail the high seas;[79] in Article 4(2) that ships have the nationality of the State whose flag they fly;[80] and, under Article 4(3)(4)(5)

[77] The IMCO was later to become the International Maritime Organisation.
[78] Harris, p. 426.
[79] UNCLOS Article 90; High Seas Convention Article 4.
[80] UNCLOS Article 91; High Seas Convention Article 5. It will be recalled that UNCLOS and the High Seas Convention specify the relative requirements for the conditions of granting nationality to ships in each individual Article. UNCCRS, on the other hand, does not specify at this juncture the specific requirements for the granting of nationality.

that ships shall have only one flag and shall not change this flag during a voyage or while in a port of call unless there has been a real transfer of ownership,[81] the UNCCRS goes much further than either the 1958 Convention or UNCLOS in terms of laying down the precise rules as to when nationality may be granted. Thus, UNCCRS boldly states as its objectives the strengthening of the genuine link between a State and ships flying its flag, and the effective exercise and jurisdiction and control over ships.[82] To achieve this objective UNCCRS lists numerous responsibilities incumbent upon States, including national manning requirements[83] and territoriality requirements of ship-owning companies[84] or their representatives.[85]

Whilst the provisions of UNCCRS may be far more comprehensive than either of the general provisions of the 1958 Convention or UNCLOS the Convention itself has neither entered into force, nor 20 years after its opening for signature is ever likely to so do. Requiring 40 States, (the combined tonnage of which amounts to at least one quarter of the world's fleet) to either sign, ratify or accede, the Convention currently languishes, not in force, with a mere 28 States having either signed or ratified or acceded.[86] The failure of the international community to embrace the rigorous principles contained within UNCCRS may never be overtly explained but clearly the requirements of the genuine link as interpreted by the Convention appear to have been a step too far for many States, including those crucial flag of convenience States at whom the measures were aimed.

To further evidence the point that any meaningful or robust definition of a genuine link might be self-defeating (in that very few States will actually subjugate themselves to any international agreement that might, in fact, spell out what a genuine link is) we should, at this juncture, briefly consider the process under which the FAO Agreement to Promote Compliance with International Conservation and Management Measures by Fishing Vessels on the High Seas (the "Compliance Agreement") came into existence.

Originally charged with the deterrence of re-flagging so as to avoid regulatory norms,[87] the initial draft of the Compliance Agreement contained a 'fleshed out' genuine link requirement which stated, in Article IV, that:

---

81 UNCLOS Article 92; High Sea Convention Article 6.

82 UNCCRS Article 1.

83 UNCCRS Article 9.

84 UNCCRS Article 10(1).

85 UNCCRS Article 10(2).

86 See UN Conference on Trade and Development, at http://r0.unctad.org/ttl/docs-legal/unc-cml/status/Registration%20of%20Ships%201986.pdf.

87 Churchill and Lowe, p. 260; Gerald Moore, *The Food and Agriculture Organisation of the United Nations Compliance Agreement*, 10 International Journal of Marine and Coastal Law (1995), at p. 412 (herein after "Moore").

1. No Party shall accord any fishing vessel to which the Agreement applies the right to fly its flag unless it is satisfied, in accordance with its own national legislation, that there exists a genuine link between the vessel and the Party concerned.
2. in determining whether or not there exists a genuine link for the purposes of paragraph 1, each Party shall give due weight to all relevant factors, including in particular:
   (i) the nationality or the permanent residence of the beneficial owner or owners of the vessel in accordance with their national law;
   (ii) where the effective control over activities of the vessel is exercised.[88]

When the final version of the Compliance Agreement was published, however, this particular Article, and specifically the comparatively strict requirements of Article IV(2)(a)(i) (when compared against the open-ended provisions of UNCLOS, for example) would prove to be a definition too far for most States. Thus, to avoid what Moore described as "a legal quagmire that would bog down the whole agreement initiative indefinitely",[89] the requirement of a 'genuine' genuine link – whereby the nationality or permanent residence of the vessel's owners should be factored in to the decision whether or not to grant the right to fly a State's flag – was abandoned.[90]

It is no great surprise then that international and regional tribunals do not refer to the principles contained within either the UNCCRS or specific criteria such as that found within the early draft of the Compliance Agreement when considering the issue of the genuine link. Instead they have consistently referred to either the High Seas Convention or UNCLOS whenever the issue has been raised. What may be surprising, however, is the manner in which even the watered down (when compared to UNCCRS) requirements of these Conventions have faired under judicial scrutiny, as on the few occasions when the genuine link question has been called into question the judiciary charged with the principle's interpretation has consistently shied away from adopting a robust meaning and has, on occasion, found that any interpretation going beyond a very basic administrative exercise by flag States may violate regional free trade laws.

The International Tribunal for the Law of the Sea, for instance, in the *M/V Saiga (No. 2)* case[91] considered the granting of nationality to ships under Article 91 UNCLOS as being merely an administrative exercise on behalf of the flag State, and in a manner echoing the *Muscat Dhows* attitude of years gone by, stated that:

[88] 9 International Organisations and International Law, Documentary Yearbook 639 (1993).
[89] Moore, at p. 413.
[90] See, for further, Moore, at p. 413; Churchill and Lowe, at p. 261; Vukas and Vidas, at pp. 64–65.
[91] *St. Vincent & the Grenadines v Guinea*, judgment of 1st July 1999.

> [u]nder this article, it is for Saint Vincent and the Grenadines to fix the conditions for the grant of its nationality to ships, for the registration of ships in its territory and for the right to fly its flag. These matters are regulated by a State in its domestic law[92]

The Tribunal did concede, however, that such decisions could be challenged by other States, and as such the legality of the granting of nationality to ships should "be determined on the basis of the evidence adduced by the parties."[93] The evidence required to support St Vincent & the Grenadines' claim of sovereignty over the Saiga was, to be frank, fairly scant. For the Tribunal the nationality of the Saiga could be established not by any reference to the duties of the flag State found under Article 94 UNCLOS but merely by the existence of certain indications such as the inscription "Kingstown" as the port of registry on the vessel's stern, documentation issued to the vessel by the Vincentian authorities, and the conduct of the Vincentian government in support of the vessel before the Tribunal. Guinea, by way of contrast, had produced little or no evidence to discharge its burden of proof to establish that the Saiga was not properly registered in St Vincent & the Grenadines.[94]

Having established that the Saiga was of Vincentian nationality the Tribunal then moved on to consider the principle of the genuine link which, according to Guinea was a prerequisite in order to afford the Saiga the protection of St Vincent & the Grenadines in international law. Thus the Tribunal was compelled to consider two questions:

> 1. whether the absence of a genuine link between a flag State and a ship entitles another State to refuse to recognise the nationality of the ship; and
> 2. whether or not a genuine link existed between the Saiga and St Vincent & the Grenadines at the time of the incident.[95]

Perhaps it is unfortunate that the Tribunal, when answering the above questions, focussed its attention almost exclusively upon the first: what the genuine link does and not what a genuine link actually is. With regards to what the genuine link does the Tribunal's analysis was entirely unremarkable and, as already noted earlier in this Chapter, considered the genuine link not to be a necessary precondition for the granting of nationality but as part of the ongoing duty to secure effective implementation of the duties incumbent upon flag States under Article 94 UNCLOS. As Article 94(6) states, when a State has "clear grounds to believe that proper jurisdiction and control... have not been exercised", ergo there is no genuine link between vessel and flag State, then all that that State may do is report the facts to the flag State and request an

[92] At para. 63.
[93] At paras. 65–66.
[94] At paras. 67–73.
[95] At para. 79.

investigation. Therefore the absence of a genuine link between vessel and flag State did not provide a basis for other States to challenge or refuse to recognise the nationality of that vessel.[96]

As regards the second question – perhaps the key question in this area of law – what is a genuine link? – the Tribunal's ruling offered absolutely no guidance whatsoever. Simply stating that Guinea had failed to adduce evidence in support of its assertion that no genuine link existed between the Saiga and St Vincent & the Grenadines, the Tribunal did not feel compelled to elaborate any further on this point.[97]

Like judgments of the ICJ, judgments of the European Court of Justice cannot be considered binding as a source of international law beyond the immediate confines of the case at hand. Instead these decisions act as persuasive authority.[98] Nevertheless the manner in which regional or even domestic courts have treated the requirement of a genuine link between vessel and State can be indicative as to how, in practice, this principle is interpreted.[99] This next section will, therefore, analyse the genuine link concept as adjudicated upon before the ECJ in two ways. First, what does the ECJ consider to be the elements of the registration of ships in order to find a genuine link between vessel and State, and secondly, in terms of EU law, are any national requirements exceeding these requirements compatible with EU restrictions on barriers to trade and the freedom of establishment.[100]

---

[96] At paras. 81–84.

[97] At para. 87.

[98] Article 38(1)(d) of the Statute of the ICJ states that the Court shall apply "...judicial decisions... as subsidiary means for the determination of rules of law". In the context of the ECJ no such formalised principle exists, although according to Zander there has been a noticeable trend in recent years whereby the ECJ has begun to consider itself bound by its own decisions, see Michael Zander, *The Law Making Process*, 6th Edition, Cambridge University Press, 2004, at p. 262. It is also the case that decisions of some courts are more persuasive than others, and the ECJ often appears to sit atop of the pile in this regard: see the MOX Plant litigation where the Arbitral Tribunal ceded jurisdiction to the ECJ on the basis that it would be "inappropriate for it to proceed further..." when there was a chance that the matter could be dealt with under the auspices of EC law (Permanent Court of Arbitration, *The MOX Plant Case*, Ireland v United Kingdom, Order No 3: Suspension of Proceedings on Jurisdiction and Merits, and Request for Further Provisional Measures, at paras 20–28.

[99] The European Union is, of course, as an entity, a signatory of UNCLOS and thus bound to give effect to the provision of that treaty.

[100] It is not the author's intention to devote too much time on this particular subject as the majority of EU anti-trust legislation is beyond the scope of the present analysis. Given the status of the EU in terms of its membership of many different RFMOs and the fact that many of its member States are significantly represented in the global fisheries industry, it is, however, necessary to briefly discuss certain national interpretations of the genuine link in relation to EU law.

The first element of this analysis – what does the ECJ consider to constitute a genuine link – can, it is contended be quickly dealt with. On any review of the occasions that the ECJ has been called upon to adjudicate upon the matter it is difficult to disagree with Churchill's assessment that for the ECJ, "registration alone is sufficient to establish nationality and that nothing further is required to constitute a genuine link."[101] Certainly on the evidence presented by Churchill regarding the assessment by the ECJ of the adequacy of measures adopted by Member States of the EU so as to comply with the genuine link requirement under both UNCLOS and the 1958 Convention, a contrary conclusion is difficult to justify.[102]

So, if the European Union, like ITLOS in *M/V Saiga*, considers that a genuine link can be established between vessel and State by registration alone, what of national measures applying a more stringent requirement? If, for instance, an EU member State applied as a pre-requisite for registration criteria as exacting as those envisaged by the 1896 Venice meeting of the Institute of International Law, would such requirements conflict with EU law? The answer to this question can be found explicitly stated in the *Factortame*[103] litigation.

The United Kingdom's Merchant Shipping Act 1988 and its related Merchant Shipping (Registration of Fishing Vessels) Regulations 1988[104] were, as noted by the ECJ in *Factortame*, specifically enacted to counter the problem of "...'quota hopping' whereby... [United Kingdom]... fishing quotas are 'plundered' by vessels flying the British flag but lacking any genuine link with the United Kingdom."[105] Thus the Merchant Shipping Act, s.14(1) required that in order to be eligible for entry on the UK register:

> a) the vessel is British owned; and
> b) the vessel is managed, and its operations are directed and controlled, from within the United Kingdom...

To qualify as "British owned" under s.14(1) the legal title of the vessel must be vested wholly in one or more British citizens (who must be resident and domiciled in the UK) or British owned companies.[106] The vessel must also be

---

[101] Churchill, ITF Paper, pp. 32–33.

[102] Churchill highlights a number of occasions when the ECJ has ruled upon issues surrounding the genuine link and its compatibility with European Law and includes in the list of considered cases *Factortame* and *Commission v Netherlands*, see below.

[103] *R v Secretary of State for Transport, ex parte Factortame Ltd and Others (No 3)* ECR (1991) I-3905, Case C-221/89.

[104] SI 1988 No 1926.

[105] *Ex parte Factortame*, at para. 4.

[106] British owned companies are referred to as "qualified companies" in the Merchant Shipping Act and defined, by s.14(7), as a company "incorporated in the United Kingdom and having its principle place of business there, at least 75% of its shares being owned by one or more

beneficially owned by one or more British owned companies, or at least 75% beneficially owned by a British citizen.[107] Therefore the certified questions for the ECJ were, *inter alia*:

> Question 1 – Does Community law affect the conditions under which a Member State lays down rules for determining which vessels are entitled to register in that State, to fly its flag and carry its nationality?

And:

> Question 2 – In light of the provisions and principles of Community law…is a Member State entitled to stipulate that in order to be registered in and entitled to fly the flag of that Member State, a fishing vessel:
>
> a) must have its legal title vested as to 100% in citizens of that Member State, resident and domiciled therein, or vested in a company at least 75% of the shares [of] which are legally and beneficially owned by such persons and of which at least 75% of the directors are such persons (herein after called a 'qualified company'); and
> b) must be beneficially owned as to at least 75% by citizens of that Member State resident and domiciled therein, or as to 100% by one or more qualified companies…; and
> c) must be managed and its operations directed and controlled from within that Member State; and
> d) must have as its charterer, manager or operator, a citizen of that Member State, resident and domiciled therein, or a qualified company…

The ECJ tersely responded to these certified questions by stating, in relation to Question 1, that it was for Member States to affix any conditions for the registration of ships in line with the ordinary principles of international law. The principles invoked by the United Kingdom – s.5(1) of the Geneva Convention on the High Seas – were not themselves in conflict with the relevant EU law, but, stated the ECJ, States must ensure compatibility between domestic provisions and Community law when exercising the powers vested in them for affixing conditions for registration.[108] Thus, moving on to the more important second question, whether or not the provisions of the United Kingdom's Merchant Shipping Act were compatible with Community law the ECJ was equally terse in its answer, stating that conditions of the types imposed by the Act were not compatible with Article 52 of the EC Treaty which allowed for the freedom of establishment free from discrimination on the grounds of nationality.[109]

---

qualified persons or companies, and at least 75% of its directors being qualified persons". The Act defines "qualified persons" in s.14(7) as "a British citizen resident and domiciled in the United Kingdom".

[107] UK Merchant Shipping Act 1988, ss.14(2), 14(7).

[108] *Factortame*, at para. 17.

[109] *Factortame*, at paras. 26–30.

Whilst it is perhaps noteworthy that the *Factortame* decision predated the coming into force of UNCLOS and solely concerned the relationship between Community law and the 1958 High Seas Convention, with its arguably more rigid requirement of a genuine link than UNCLOS, it is therefore not surprising that subsequent post-UNCLOS case law has not departed from the *Factortame* line of authority. For instance in *Commission v Netherlands*[110] the First Chamber of the ECJ, when called upon to assess the validity of certain Dutch measures on the conditions for the registration of ships under Community law, stated the Dutch requirements of EU nationality for the owners and operators of Dutch flagged vessels were in violation of European principles of the freedom of establishment, and went "beyond what was necessary to attain" the objectives of "effective control."[111] For the ECJ the crucial issue was not whether the Dutch measures ensured that effective control could be exercised over the vessels in question but whether or not the measures were the least burdensome for companies,[112] and the objective of effective control could be achieved, suggested the Court, irrespective of any requirements of citizenship.[113]

4.7 *The Resurgence of the Genuine Link?*

The above analysis shows, it is contended, that despite a century of efforts the genuine link concept can provide no real answer to the problem of flags of convenience vessels. Throughout this century it has become increasingly apparent that first there is absolutely no consensus as to what a genuine link actually is – whether it be international agreements such as UNCCRS which are ignored by the international community or judicial responses which at best remain silent (*M/V Saiga*) or at worst find any meaningful genuine link requirement unlawful (*Factortame, Commission v Netherlands*). Secondly even if a suitable definition could be arrived at it is clear from ITLOS' judgment in *M/V Saiga* that the most any State suspecting that a vessel is not genuinely linked to its flag State may do is request the flag State to investigate, and clearly does not render the vessel Stateless. Furthermore, the *M/V Saiga* judgment also fails to specify and elaborate upon a number of important issues regarding any flag State's investigation conducted under Article 94(6) UNCLOS. How rigorous should this investigation be and what appropriate action must be taken by the flag State? Does it require, for instance, that any vessel not conforming to domestic requirements be de-registered? Must any domestic legislation and its

[110] Case C-299/02, Unreported, 14th October 2004.

[111] *Commission v Netherlands*, at para. 20.

[112] *Commission v Netherlands*, at paras. 18–19.

[113] *Commission v Netherlands*, at para. 26.

implementation which contain loop-holes which ensure that jurisdiction cannot be properly exercised be replaced with a more effective regime? Given the deference to flag State competency shown by international tribunals in the last century it is doubted that ITLOS, if ever requested to adjudicate on these maters, would depart from the norm and instead revert to type – that is, that it is for the flag State to affix not just the conditions of first registry but those of ongoing registry too.

Despite the obvious failure of the genuine link concept, however, even the most up-to-date Conventions, International Plans of Action and Declarations persist with calls for there to be a genuine link between vessel and State.

For instance, the UNFAO Rome Declaration on IUU Fishing of 2005 calls for a "genuine link" between vessel and State.[114] Similarly, the Communication from the Commission of the EU recognises the current "vacuum" and the lack of an adequate definition of the "genuine link" required under Art. 91 of UNCLOS and calls for "the adoption of criteria of defining what is meant by a substantive link…"[115] Likewise the FAO Agreement to Promote Compliance with International Conservation and Management Measures by Fishing Vessels on the High Seas (the "Compliance Agreement") requires that flag States are able to effectively exercise responsibility over vessels "taking into account the links that exist between…[the flag State]…and the vessel concerned."[116] Similarly, whilst not expressly using the term "genuine link" the UNFAO Code of Conduct for Responsible Fisheries (the "Code of Conduct") requires that "States authorizing fishing and fishing support vessels to fly their flags should exercise effective control over those vessels…"[117] Thus, if certain members of the international community maintain a course of action which calls for a genuine link between vessel and State it is therefore worth considering the best case scenario. What if, for instance, a sufficiently meaningful definition of the genuine link could be found and implemented in a manner conferring real proscriptive powers upon aggrieved States?

Under those above listed Conventions and Agreements dealing specifically with the fisheries context, there is a clear consequence as to the lack of effective control – both the Compliance Agreement and its umbrella Code of Conduct do anticipate that without effective control no vessel shall be authorised to fish on the high seas[118] and although neither specify that *ex post facto* authorisation should be rescinded in light of breaches of the obligations imposed by the

[114] Article 5.

[115] Community Action Plan for the Eradication of Illegal, Unreported and Unregulated Fishing, Brussels, 28.05.2002, COM(2002) 180 Final, esp. at para. 4.3.

[116] UNFAO Compliance Agreement, Article III(3).

[117] Code of Conduct, Article 6.11.

[118] Compliance Agreement, Article III(2)(3); Code of Conduct, Article 6.11.

Agreement and Code, it is reasonable to assume that both measures anticipate this to be the case.[119] Clearly then this would represent somewhat of a blow to the IUU/FOC fleet, but it is suggested that it would not be a mortal one, because unfortunately the problem is that both the Compliance Agreement and the Code of Conduct have little, if any, current meaningful application in international law, as although the Compliance Agreement has entered into force only one recognised flag of convenience State (Georgia) is a contracting party.[120]

4.8 *Conclusion*

Notwithstanding the important practical hurdle noted above to be overcome, in concluding this Chapter consideration must be given to a best case scenario: if, despite the apparent evidence to the contrary, there could be an agreed, accepted and binding definition of a genuine link what would the consequences be for the flag of convenience industry? Would this effectively eradicate the problem? It is tentatively suggested that even in the best case scenario this would only be a partial, albeit important, step. Whilst the phenomenon of flag hopping would be made more time-consuming and difficult it would not make it impossible. Seats of business *can* be moved to a more attractive State if need be, and as previous Chapters have shown, even if in the unlikely event of there being a mandatory requirement that vessels are crewed by citizens of the State of registry, crews are expendable and transferable commodities. In principle there is nothing to stop vessel owners re-crewing their vessels with the requisite number of State nationals to fulfil any requirements. Likewise States *could*, if so inclined, offer nationality to any crew members deemed necessary for the ongoing registration of any given vessel.

It is thus contended that any continued search for the genuine link may one day prove beneficial in terms of making vessel movements between registries more difficult, it is also suggested that the marine wildlife and habitation currently threatened by IUU fishing simply may not have the time this search might need. To hope that the international community would re-write a century of jurisprudence regarding the laws of the sea simply so as to respond to a pressing, but discrete problem within the fisheries sector may be seen by many States as a disproportionate response to a relatively minor problem. After all,

[119] Indeed, as Rayfuse (2004) points out, at pp. 39–40, that the very reason behind the Code of Conduct and the Compliance Agreement is to deter re-flagging by reinforcing the notions of both the genuine link and effective control.

[120] See the UNFAO Treaty Database for a list of Contracting Parties to the Compliance Agreement, available at http://www.fao.org/legal/treaties/012s-e.htm.

what are a few albatrosses, dolphins, sea turtles or corals when compared to the benefits to be had for mankind as a result of the free market global merchant fleet?

The next Chapters will therefore move on to consider this notion of markets and certain problem-specific solutions to the issues of IUU/FOC fishing, focussing upon the manner in which inter-State trade can play a role in the regulation of the fisheries sector, and consider how denying unlawful fishing vessels a market place for their harvests can be one way by which the IUU/FOC fishermen are disincentivised. Chapter Five will focus upon regional fisheries agreements, their inherent handicaps and the way in which they can complement globally agreed measures. Chapter Six will consider the role that the Washington Convention on the International Trade in Endangered Species (CITES) could play in expanding coverage of any regional schemes and consider the manner in which CITES could provide an example of best practice in this regard.

Chapter Five

The Growing Use of Market Denial Strategies by Regional Fisheries Management Organisations

5.1 *Introduction*

The focus of this Chapter is to show how the rules of international law are evolving so as to control IUU fishing. The structure of the Chapter will be to show how, although UNCLOS could be described as fairly vague as regards to high seas fishing, the principles espoused by the Convention are by no means the last word on the subject. Following UNCLOS a plethora of international instruments have been negotiated. Whilst these instruments vary in terms of acceptance by the international community and the severity of the obligations imposed upon States, they can have a role in the management and regulation of the fisheries sector. The Chapter will therefore begin, in *The Basis for Regional Co-operation*, by contextualising the relationship between these international instruments (beginning with *The UN Convention on the Law of the Sea*, then *The UNFAO Compliance Agreement* and finally *The UN Fish Stocks Agreement*) and evaluate some of the key aspects of each instrument, insofar as they pertain to IUU/FOC fishing.

As this Chapter will show, increasing reliance is being placed under international law upon regional fisheries management organisations (RFMOs). Thus, in the section entitled *Regional Attempts to Tackle IUU Activities*, consideration will be given to the various attempts by these regional organisations to implement the overarching principles of the laws of the sea, and in so doing effectively deal with IUU activity and flags of convenience. In this regard much attention will be paid to how the principle of market denial can act in tandem with 'traditional' control mechanisms utilised by RFMOs such as the allocation of fishing rights, the denial of port State facilities (port State Measures)[1] and monitoring, control and surveillance.

---

[1] Despite having the similar goals, 'Port State measures' and 'market denial' differ both in their scope and application. Port State measures involve not just the denial of landing rights to IUU vessels but effectively deny all back up facilities to these vessels. Although these measures have a far-reaching scope their application is severely stymied by ports of convenience (discussed in part 4.5.2 "How Port State Measures are Undermined by Ports of Convenience"). Market

The Chapter will demonstrate that these RFMOs are all permitted to take certain measures to conserve and manage fish stocks under international law and will thus begin with an assessment of the regulatory powers invested in RFMOs through UNCLOS and its progeny. In this regard specific attention will be paid to the duty of States to co-operate, the ends that should be achieved by this co-operation, and the possible ways in which these ends should be achieved. Thus the Chapter takes note of what could be considered 'best practice' and, in *The 'General Principles' of Ocean Governance: The Code of Conduct for Responsible Fishing* considers the goals RFMOs should attempt to attain.

Although there are subtle differences in the manner in which RFMOs might tackle the problem of IUU/FOC vessels, the principle of port and trade-related denial through negative/positive listing of fishing vessels appears to have been firmly established among regional organisations. As will be shown by *Regional Implementation of the Code*, there is, as yet, no concerted effort by many of these RFMOs to apply port or market-based measures to activities other than the 'direct' harms caused by IUU/FOC vessels. For instance, not all RFMOs can prohibit catch landings when flag of convenience vessels are engaged in environmental degradation of the type evidenced in Chapter Three. Thus it has been necessary to scrutinise the mandates of many RFMOs in *RFMO Mandates: Which Regional Bodies Have the Competence to Regulate the Wider Marine Environment?*

In *How Certain Regional Measures can be Undermined by Ports of Convenience*, the Chapter will also recognise the inherent weakness of RFMO measures which rely upon 'traditional' port State measures alone to implement their management goals. Not only are such measures not always implemented when the breach of regulations pertain to wider environmental harms associated with fishing activities, but there is also an inherent problem of 'ports of convenience' which undermine conservation and management measures.

Because the principle of market denial is central to the remainder of the Chapter, it is only wise to test, at this juncture, the potential efficacy and legality of such measures. Therefore, the section entitled *Market Related Deterrents to IUU/FOC Activities* will consider, albeit briefly, the notional basis under which this tool operates. So as to identify best practice, the Chapter will consider in the next section, *CCAMLR's Catch Documentation Scheme*, one of the best regarded schemes aimed at denying market access to IUU/FOC vessels – the Catch Documentation Scheme, as adopted by the Commission for the Conservation of Antarctic Marine Living Resources (CCAMLR). This analysis will

---

denial, on the other and as discussed in part 4.6 "Market Related Deterrents to IUU/FOC Activities", concentrates on a chain of legitimacy between the fishing vessel and consumer – only when it can be proved that a catch has been legitimately harvested can *any* ongoing trade be permitted.

show that it is possible to apply non-discriminatory market measures against vessels that undermine the effectiveness of regional conservation measures – whether these measures have been enacted for the purposes of conserving target stocks or the protection of the wider marine environment.

5.2 *The Basis for Regional Co-operation*

As well as the limited duties incumbent upon States listed in Chapters Two and Four to regulate their ocean going vessels, a number of additional requirements, specific to the fisheries context, are laid out in UNCLOS and numerous other international and regional agreements, voluntary codes of conduct and international plans of action. This section will therefore list and analyse the various international agreements in 'pyramidical' form. The mandatory, albeit vague, requirements of UNCLOS will be fleshed out by considering the UNFAO Compliance Agreement and the UN Fish Stocks Agreement. Once the basis for co-operation has been established under these agreements, the Chapter will then move to consider the way RFMOs put this duty of co-operation in to effect.

5.2.1 *The UN Convention on the Law of the Sea*

Despite the enormity of the Convention itself, insofar as fisheries are concerned the duties found under UNCLOS could be described as rather vague and providing a framework only. For instance, in the context of high seas fisheries, the duties under UNCLOS have been succinctly described by Rayfuse as duties merely to "co-operate and conserve."[2] This, it is contended, is a fairly accurate description. All States, whether coastal or landlocked, are entitled to engage in high seas fishing, provided that those States ensure that their vessels have due regard for the rights of other States and those UNCLOS provisions governing, albeit in a relatively general manner, the freedom of high seas fishing.[3]

Thus, Article 116 reaffirms the rights and duties of States and builds slightly upon the general obligations provided in Article 87 by stating that:

> All States have the right for their nationals to engage in fishing on the high seas subject to:
>
> a) their treaty obligations;
> b) the rights and duties as well as the interests of coastal States provided, *inter alia*, in Article 63, paragraph 2, and Articles 64 to 67; and
> c) the provisions of this section

[2] Rayfuse (2004), at pp. 31–32.
[3] UNCLOS, Article 87(1)(e); Article 87(2).

The specific obligations referred to above in Article 116(b) pertain to straddling stocks,[4] highly migratory species, marine mammals and anadromous[5] and catadromous[6] species. In relation to straddling stocks Article 63(2) imposes an obligation upon fishing States to "seek...to agree upon measures necessary for the conservation" with affected coastal States.[7] For highly migratory species, Article 64 obliges co-operation between fishing States and coastal States "directly or through appropriate international organisations" to ensure conservation and to promote optimum utilization of the species.[8] Likewise, similar co-operative obligations exist in relation to the conservation of marine mammals under Article 65, anadromous stocks under Article 66 and catadromous stocks under Article 67. It should be noted that by virtue of UNCLOS Article 67 (2) the harvest of catadromous stocks is not permitted in the high seas.

Article 116(c) then, it will be noted, subjects all high seas fishing activities to the provisions of UNCLOS Part VII, Section 2, which goes on to slightly elaborate upon the earlier duties under Article 87, again with the emphasis on co-operation and conservation.[9] The term "co-operation" is further defined by Article 118 as the entering into of "negotiations with a view to taking the measures necessary for the conservation of the living resources concerned...[and States]...shall co-operate to establish sub-regional or regional fisheries organisations to this end." This former, rather open-ended obligation, does not, however, go beyond what might be described as encouraging States to begin a courtship: whilst States are obliged to embark upon negotiations they are not compelled to satisfactorily conclude them. The latter obligation, that of co-operating in the establishment of fisheries management organisations, does, however, seem to anticipate the creation of such organisations, but does not explicitly require ongoing co-operation post-creation.

---

4 Defined by UNCLOS Article 63(2) as "stocks or stocks of associated species occur[ing] both within the exclusive economic zone and in an area beyond and adjacent to the zone".

5 Those stocks spawned in inland waters but which will migrate to the oceans for large parts of their life cycles.

6 Those stocks spawned at sea but spending the majority of their life cycle in inland fresh waters.

7 Although, like Article 118 (discussed *infra*), there is no explicit requirement that any measures are actually agreed upon, merely that States *seek* to agree. The requirements of co-operation under Articles 64–67 do appear more obligatory, however, due to the use of the phrase 'shall agree' in these Articles.

8 Where no "appropriate international organisations" exist to facilitate this level of co-operation States are obliged to "co-operate to establish such an organisation and participate in its work", UNCLOS Article 64.

9 UNCLOS Article 117: "All States have the duty to take, *or to co-operate with other States in taking*, such measures...as may be necessary for the conservation of the living resources of the high seas" (emphasis added).

What constitutes "conservation" for the purposes of high seas fishing is defined, in rather general terms, under Article 119, which states that States shall "take measures which are designed, on the best scientific evidence available...to maintain or restore populations of harvested species..." The notion of co-operation is enhanced by the fact that conservation measures should conform to internationally agreed minimum standards, whether the standards are "sub-regional, regional or global."[10] To ensure further co-operation, Article 119 requires that all relevant and available scientific data regarding catch and effort, etc., shall be communicated to other interested States via competent international organisations.[11] Finally Article 119(3) reinforces the notion of equal access to the high seas for all States by requiring that any conservation measures adopted shall not "discriminate in form or fact against the fishermen of any State."

Whilst the relevant sections of UNCLOS clearly anticipate inter-State co-operation and spell out some of the minimum requirements, the Convention itself clearly falls short of prescribing the exact and exacting requirements of "conservation" and "co-operation". To elaborate upon these concepts it is necessary to consider the UN Fish Stocks Agreement (UNFSA)[12] and the UNFAO Compliance Agreement.[13]

5.2.2 *The UNFAO Compliance Agreement*

The UNFAO Compliance Agreement, as has been noted in Chapter Four, forms an integral part of the UNFAO's Code of Conduct for Responsible Fisheries, and has as its primary goals the deterrence of re-flagging and the strengthening of flag State responsibility.[14] Whilst these are clearly laudable aims, it is suggested that while the Compliance Agreement remains languishing with relatively little participation in terms of State ratifications and accessions, there is little chance that its biting provisions can have a great deal of impact upon the IUU/FOC industry other than to drive the vessels into the registries

[10] UNCLOS Article 119(1)(a).

[11] UNCLOS Article 119(1)(b).

[12] UN Agreement for the Implementation of the Provisions of the UN Convention on the Law of the Sea of 10th December 1982 Relating to the Conservation and Management of Straddling Stocks and Highly Migratory Fish Stocks, 34 I.L.M. 1542; (1995).

[13] UNFAO Agreement to Promote Compliance With International Conservation and Management Measures by Fishing Vessels on the High Seas, 33 I.L.M. 968; (1994).

[14] As noted in Chapter Four the Compliance Agreement operates in a manner which strengthens the concept of the genuine link by requiring that flag States to "exercise effectively its responsibilities" under the Agreement.

of States that are not party to the Agreement.[15] This is, of course, unfortunate because the Compliance Agreement does contain some particularly effective provisions, that if fully implemented[16] could have a significant impact upon the IUU/FOC fleet.

For instance, as well as the duty to co-operate with other States, discussed below, the aforementioned strengthening of flag State responsibility, as found in Article III, requires that a State party takes such measures as are necessary to ensure that all fishing vessels flying its flag do not "undermine the effectiveness of international conservation and management measures"[17] by ensuring that those vessels fish in accordance with the terms of the authorisation granted by the flag State.[18] Any authorisation so given must take into account the ability of the State to exercise effectively its responsibilities under the Compliance Agreement.[19] Furthermore, in order to prevent State parties from becoming havens for IUU vessels, the Compliance Agreement mandates that no States shall grant authorisation to fish to vessels, having previously engaged in IUU activity,[20] unless there has been a genuine change of ownership[21] or in circumstances when the State party has determined that the granting of authorisation will not result in the fishing vessel being used for a purpose that would undermine the purpose of the Compliance Agreement itself.[22] As well as obliging all vessels maintained

[15] Apparently cognisant of this failing, Article VIII of the Compliance Agreement urges all Parties to "encourage any State not party to this Agreement to accept this Agreement and shall encourage any non Party to adopt laws and regulations consistent with the provisions of this Agreement".

[16] The term 'if fully implemented' used at this juncture is, admittedly, considering a 'best-case scenario' as for certain of the provisions discussed throughout the following section of the Chapter any degree of objectively definable 'full implementation' can never be guaranteed due to the discretion given to States. This issue is discussed slightly further in relation to the individual Articles of the Agreement, below.

[17] Compliance Agreement, Article III(1)(a).

[18] Compliance Agreement, Article III(2).

[19] Compliance Agreement, Article III(3).

[20] Unless any period of suspension of has been served or the authorisation has not withdrawn within 3 years, Compliance Agreement, Article III(5)(a).

[21] I.e. when the new owner can provide evidence that the previous owner has no further legal, beneficial or financial interest in, or control over, the vessel, Compliance Agreement, Article III(5)(c).

[22] Compliance Agreement, Article III(5)(d). This provision could, of course, be utilised by less discriminating States to by-pass the requirements of Article III(5)(a) due to the lack of any meaningful level of scrutiny to which a vessel's previous history must be subject in order to authorise high seas fishing to a vessel previously de-registered by another (perhaps more discriminating) State. Article III(5)(d) simply requires that the proposed State of re-registry, in these circumstances, 'takes account of all relevant fact, including the circumstances in which the fishing authorization has been withdrawn…'.

on a State's register to be entered into a record of registration[23] and readily identified,[24] and to provide the State with accurate information about its fishing activities,[25] one of the key aspects of Article III is the obligation placed upon States to take proper enforcement measures in respect of any violations of the Compliance Agreement's principles, such as the withdrawal of authorisation to fish on the high seas.[26] This, however, does rest on a finding by the State of registry of an undefined "serious offence" having taken place by the vessel. For all other offences, presumably those deemed by the State of registry as not serious, sanctions should simply be of "sufficient gravity as to be effective in securing compliance" with the Agreement and should "deprive the offenders of the benefits accruing from their illegal activities."[27] The lack of any definition within the Agreement itself as to what constitutes an offence of sufficient severity so that authorisation to fish must be withdrawn could, of course, be seen as a brake on the overall efficacy of Article III(8) due to the fact that certain States, perhaps those wishing to pay lip service to the Agreement, might set the threshold of a "serious offence" as being so high that no vessel would ever have its authorisation withdrawn.

Article V requires States to co-operate so that information on the activities of fishing vessels is exchanged so that flag States may properly penalise any suspected IUU fishing vessels.[28] The principle of co-operation also extends to the initiation of consensual port State inspections, where any State, other than the flag State, has reasonable grounds to believe that a vessel in its port has engaged in IUU fishing.[29] When the vessel is not in the port of a State party, but at sea and that port State has reasonable grounds to believe that the Compliance Agreement's provisions are being undermined by the vessel's activities, at sea boarding is not permitted. Instead non-flag States should inform both the flag State of the vessel suspected and the FAO. Only when the flag State has had

---

23 See also, Compliance Agreement, Article IV. This record should include information such as the vessel's name, previous flag, international radio call sign, the name and address of the owner, where and when the vessel was built, the vessel's type and length (Compliance Agreement, Article VI(1)). This information should be made available to the UNFAO, as should any of the listed change of circumstances or any withdrawal of authorisation to fish (Article VI(5)).

24 Compliance Agreement, Article III(6), the identification of the vessel must be in line with "generally accepted standards, such as the FAO Standard Specifications for the Marking and Identification of Fishing Vessels. These standards generally relate to the visibility of the vessel's name, port of registry and international radio call sign.

25 Compliance Agreement, Article III(7).

26 Compliance Agreement, Article III(8).

27 *Ibid.*

28 Compliance Agreement, Article V(1).

29 Compliance Agreement, Article V(2).

the opportunity to comment on the allegations may the FAO circulate details of the infractions.[30]

5.2.3 *The UN Fish Stocks Agreement*

The UN Fish Stocks Agreement attempts to build upon the flag State obligations imposed by UNCLOS by spelling out in detail precisely what all flag States must do to control their vessels fishing on the high seas for fish stocks covered by the Agreement's provisions.[31] In a manner not dissimilar to the obligations found under the Compliance Agreement, the duties imposed by the Fish Stocks Agreement include the overarching obligation not to allow registered vessels to undermine the effectiveness of conservation and management measures, and oblige States to only authorise fishing vessels when effective jurisdiction may be exercised.[32] Although some of the Compliance Agreement's provisions are replicated almost verbatim[33] the UNFSA goes slightly further than the earlier drafted Compliance Agreement by detailing the precise requirements of catch[34] and position[35] certification and the monitoring, control and surveillance of vessels to be carried out by flag States.[36]

As its full title suggests the Fish Stocks Agreement builds upon and implements the rather vague obligations found under UNCLOS, and does so by

---

[30] Compliance Agreement, Article VI(8).

[31] In spite of its full title it has, been suggested that the provisions of the UNFSA also applies to high seas discrete fish stocks and not simply straddling and highly migratory stocks, on the basis that "if we consider the UNFSA as an instrument that gives effect to and elaborates upon the principles that were already inherent in the 1982 Convention as part of that general duty, then it follows that the principles for conservation and management that UNFSA elaborates, including the basic obligations to conserve biological diversity and to apply the precautionary approach , should be applied to discrete high seas stocks as well as to straddling and highly migratory fish stocks." See Michael W. Lodge and Satya N. Nandan, *Some Suggestions Towards Better Implementation of the United Nations Agreement on Straddling Fish Stocks and Highly Migratory Fish Stocks of 1995*, International Journal of Marine and Coastal Law, Vol. 20, (2005), Nos. 3–4, at p. 371 (herein after "Lodge and Nandan"). Likewise, Willock and Lack suggest that "there is increasing consensus that the principles of the UNFSA should also apply . . . to discrete fish stocks in the high seas, see: A. Willock and M. Lack, *Follow the Leader: Learning From Experience and Best Practice in Regional Fisheries Management Organisations*, WWF International and TRAFFIC International, 2006, at p. 16 (herein after "Willock and Lack").

[32] UNFSA Article 18(1) and (2).

[33] For instance the requirement that a national record of vessels is maintained (UNFSA, Article 18(3)(c)); that vessels are readily identified in accordance with international standards (UNFSA, Article 18(3)(d)).

[34] UNFSA, Article 18(3)(f).

[35] UNFSA, Article 18(3)(e).

[36] UNFSA, Article 18(3)(g).

defining precisely the requirements of conservation and co-operation in a manner that is transparent[37] and meaningful.[38] The relevant principles of conservation are to be found throughout the UNFSA but most specifically in Article 7, which states that all State parties must ensure that any conservation measures adopted are compatible with coastal State measures adopted under Article 61 UNCLOS[39] and any pre-existing measures adopted by interested States, independently or directly[40] or in the form of regional or sub-regional arrangements.[41] Furthermore, any conservation measures must take into account factors such as "the biological unity and the other biological characteristics of the stocks,"[42] the dependence on those stocks of coastal and fishing States,[43] and ensure that any measures "do not result in harmful impact on the living marine resources as a whole."[44] It is worthwhile noting at this juncture that the UNFSA incorporates the precautionary principle of environmental management throughout.[45]

To achieve the necessary co-operation for the Fish Stock Agreement's efficacy, Article 8 builds upon the rather aspirational statements of UNCLOS or the Preamble to the Compliance Agreement which simply call for States to co-operate in the formation of regional fisheries organisations.[46] Instead the UNFSA mandates and institutionalises co-operation by placing competency for conservation and management measures with regional fisheries management organisations (RFMO)[47] and compels interested States to either become

[37] UNFSA Article 12 requires that all decisions arrived at by States acting as part of regional or sub-regional fisheries management organisations shall be transparent by allowing for observation by appropriate third parties organisations, and by ensuring that all relevant records and reports are made available to such organisations.

[38] Unlike the requirement of co-operation under UNCLOS the Fish Stocks Agreement states, in Article 7(3), that "[i]n giving effect to their duty to co-operate, States shall make every effort to agree on compatible conservation and management measures within a reasonable period of time" and, under Article 7(4) that "[i]f no agreement can be reached within a reasonable period of time, any State concerned may invoke the procedures for the settlement of disputes provided for in Part VIII [of the agreement]".

[39] UNFSA Article 7(2)(a).

[40] UNFSA Article 7(2)(b).

[41] UNFSA Article 7(2)(c).

[42] UNFSA Article 7(2)(d).

[43] UNFSA Article 7(2)(e).

[44] UNFSA Article 7(2)(f).

[45] UNFSA Article 6. Whilst Article 6, in tandem with Annex II of the Agreement, defines the precise technical elements of precaution to be applied throughout the Agreement, the basic definition of precaution – that "the absence of adequate scientific information shall not be used as a reason for postponing or failing to take conservation and management measures" – underpins these precise elements and is explicitly referred to in Article 6(2).

[46] UNCLOS Article 118. Compliance Agreement, Preamble, 7th Recital.

[47] For present purposes no distinction will be drawn between regional fisheries management "organisations", or "arrangements", or "bodies": however, a distinction does exist and is

members or participants of the RFMO or to agree to abide by the RFMO's decided conservation and management stratagem.[48] A failure by any State party to adhere to the requirements of co-operation debars that State from engaging in the fisheries to which the management measures apply. In short, the UNFSA challenges the hitherto unfettered freedom to engage in high seas fishing by stating that only members of the RFMO or States implementing the RFMO's management and conservation measures may participate in the fishery.[49] This challenge to the freedom of the high seas is perhaps reiterated by the provisions allowing for the non-flag State apprehension of illegitimate vessels by virtue of Article 21 – although as noted in Chapter Four this yielding of sovereignty is by no means imposed and only occurs with the express permission of the flag State of the vessel in question.

Because of its reliance upon RFMOs it is not surprising that the Agreement provides the terms of reference and minimum requirements of what each RFMO should do. For instance, Article 9 of the Agreement requires States to agree upon the stocks to which the organisation shall be concerned,[50] the geographical limits to the organisation's competence,[51] the relationship between the organisation and other relevant RFMOs,[52] and how the organisation will obtain the necessary scientific advice regarding its conservation and management measures.[53] Similarly Article 10 of the Agreement spells out, in detail, the functions of any RFMO. As well as putting into place conservation and management measures these functions should include, *inter alia*, agreeing upon participatory rights in the relevant fisheries for new and existing participants,[54] applying "any generally recommended international minimum standards for the responsible conduct of fishing operations,"[55] collating and disseminating data regarding the status of fish stocks and non-target species,[56] and implementing control, monitoring, surveillance and enforcement mechanisms.[57]

---

recognised by the Agreement. For further see Tore Henriksen, Geir Hønneland and Are Sydnes, *Law and Politics in Ocean Governance: The UN Fish Stocks Agreement and Regional Fisheries Management Regimes*, Martinus Nijhoff Publishers, Leiden, 2006, pp. 16–17, (herein after "Henriksen *et al.*").

48 UNFSA Article 8(3).

49 UNFSA Article 8(4). See also Sands (2003), at p. 577, who refers to Article 8(4) as a "far reaching provision [which] has the consequence, in effect, of departing from traditional principles reflecting absolute rights of high seas fisheries freedoms…".

50 UNFSA Article 9(1)(a).

51 UNFSA Article 9(1)(b).

52 UNFSA Article 9(1)(c).

53 UNFSA Article 9(1)(d).

54 UNFSA Article 10(b)(i); Article 11.

55 UNFSA Article 10(c); Article 14.

56 UNFSA Article 10(d)(e)(f)(g).

57 UNFSA Article 10(h).

Whilst the principles of co-operation and conservation enunciated by the Agreement may expand upon and flesh out the provisions of UNCLOS in a manner that adds real meaning to the many "inadequate" management structures in place prior to the Agreement's creation, and seeks to address these deficiencies identified by the UNCED,[58] these principles may be seen as the natural progressive development of the law of the sea post-UNCLOS. Indeed in view of the fact that the Agreement acts as an implementing agreement for UNCLOS it is to be expected that the Agreement would attempt to operationalise and institutionalise the Convention.[59]

Perhaps of greater significance, however, is the manner in which the Fish Stocks Agreement attempts to bind non-participant States to its provisions and encourage participation by non-member States. In this regard the Agreement adopts a carrot and stick methodology,[60] with this being best exemplified by Article 33 which obliges States parties to both encourage non-parties to join with the UNFSA,[61] and to deter the activities of non-party registered vessels.[62] This principle can be seen to have been applied several times in recent years by RFMOs in relation to several non-party States, such as Belize, Honduras, Cambodia, *et al.* when diplomatic pressure has been successfully exerted by the International Commission for the Conservation of Atlantic Tuna in order to bring about greater participation with conservation and management measures by those States.[63] As already noted Article 8(4) seeks to ensure that "only those who play by the rules may fish"[64] by requiring either participation in regional organisations or adherence to rules created by those organisations. Likewise, Article 17 expands upon this principle by reminding non-participant States of the obligations under UNCLOS and the Agreement itself by stating that a failure to adhere to agreed conservation and management measures does not discharge that State of its obligation to co-operate[65] and that the State in question

---

58 The 5th Recital of the Preamble to the UNFSA states that the its function is that of "Seeking to address in particular the problems identified in Chapter 17, programme area C, of Agenda 21 adopted by the United Nations Conference on Environment and Development, namely that the management of high seas fisheries is inadequate in many areas…".

59 Alan Boyle, *Further Development of the Law of the Sea Convention: Mechanisms for Change*, International and Comparative Law Quarterly (June 2005) 54.3(563), at pp. 563–564 (herein after "Boyle (2005)"); Rayfuse (2004), at p. 43.

60 This terminology was first used by Satya N Nandan, in a speech to the International Seabed Authority's Conference on the Governance of High Seas Fisheries and the United Nations Fish Agreement, Newfoundland and Labrador, May 2005, transcript available at http://www.dfo-mpo.gc.ca/fgc-cgp/documents/presentations/nandan_e.pdf.

61 UNFSA Article 33(1).

62 UNFSA Article 33(2).

63 See Chapter Two.

64 Rayfuse (2004), at p. 44.

65 UNFSA Article 17(1).

must not authorise vessels flying its flag to engage in fishing operations for straddling or highly migratory stocks that are subject to regional conservation measures.[66] Where vessels do engage in proscribed activities RFMO participants must co-operate in the exchange of information about those vessels and take the necessary action, in line with international law, to deter those activities.[67]

It is to this point that the remainder of this Chapter will now turn its attention, because, as has been recognised on numerous occasions, any problems there may be with the UNFSA are not due to its content but rather due to the failure of States to embrace its provisions:[68] although it entered into force in 2001 following the 30th ratification or accession,[69] the number of Contracting Parties, whilst favourable compared to the Compliance Agreement, for instance, still number only 78 as of July 2011.[70]

5.3 *Regional Attempts to Tackle IUU Activities*

A common method of implementing the principles espoused by UNFSA Article 17(4), and to tackle the problem of "free-riders"[71] was the creation of so-called "vessel negative lists". These negative lists, whilst ranging in scope and threshold between RFMOs, operate essentially to deny the fishermen of non-compliant States (and the fishermen of State parties to the RFMO engaged in illegal fishing)[72] access to ports and the denial of access to markets.

This action may be justified under numerous international conventions ranging from the permissive UNCLOS Article 25(2) which recognises the right of States to deny entry to ports, to the obligatory UNFSA Article 23 and UNFAO 2001 International Plan of Action to Prevent, Deter and Eliminate Illegal,

[66] UNFSA Article 17(2).

[67] UNFSA Article 17(4).

[68] Lodge and Nandan at pp. 352–353.

[69] In line with UNFSA, Article 40.

[70] Despite entering into force in 2003 the Compliance Agreement has, as of June 2007, only 35 contracting parties. See http://www.fao.org/legal/treaties/012s-e.htm.

[71] A "free rider" is a State whose vessels fish in an area under the jurisdictional competence of a regional management organisation, but which is not a participant in that RFMO. Such States are of course obliged to co-operate with the RFMO *if* they are signatories of the UNFSA, but in all other cases there is no obligation for the State to adhere to the rules prescribed by the RFMO. According to Lodge and Nandan, at p. 354, "the UNFSA cannot attain its full potential unless and until the most important coastal, fishing and flag States become parties to it and comply with its obligations".

[72] The vast majority of RFMO negative lists do not differentiate between the different types of IUU fishing and simply act as a repository for the names of all vessels deemed to have engaged in any IUU activities.

Unreported and Unregulated Fishing (IPOA-IUU).[73] Although voluntary in application the IPAO-IUU has been embraced, in principle, by the majority of RFMOs,[74] with the majority of negative lists taking as their justification the IPOA-IUU's requirement that "the identification of vessels carrying out illegal, unreported and unregulated fishing activities should follow agreed procedures and be applied in an equitable, transparent and non-discriminatory way."[75]

The negative listing procedures referred to are relatively straightforward, and, insofar as the negative list procedures followed by IATTC, ICCAT, IOTC, WCPFC and SEAFO are concerned all that is initially required to be placed upon the "draft negative list" is the presentation of evidence by a Contracting Party or Co-operating non-Contracting Party that the vessel in question has engaged in activities proscribed by the RFMO's conservation and management measures. Typically these activities will be fishing for stocks governed by the RFMO by vessels not registered on the RFMO's authorised vessel list; or vessels whose flag State is not given quotas to fish in the region; the false or non-existent reporting of catches; the harvest of undersized fish; fishing during closed seasons; the use of prohibited gear; participating in joint operations with known IUU vessels; the unlicensed harvest of stocks in the waters under the jurisdiction of a coastal State; vessels without nationality; and, as a catch-all provision, vessels which "engage in activities contrary to any other conservation

73 UNFAO, Rome, 2001 Port State measures are governed by Articles 52–64. Further trade-related measures take their justification from Articles 65–76.

74 This section by no means offers a comprehensive overview of all RFMOs, instead selected RFMOs have been utilised in order to demonstrate the synergy of the provisions adopted under international agreements.

75 IPOA-IUU, Article 66, as applied by: Inter-American Tropical Tuna Commission (IATTC) Resolution C-05-07, *Resolution to Establish a List of Vessels Presumed to Have Carried Out Illegal, Unreported and Unregulated Fishing Activities in the Eastern Pacific Ocean*, Preamble, First Recital (herein after "IATTC Negative list Resolution"); International Commission for the Conservation of the Atlantic Tunas (ICCAT) recommendation 02-23, *Recommendation by ICCAT to Establish a List of Vessels Presumed to Have Carried Out Illegal, Unreported and Unregulated Fishing Activities in the ICCAT Convention Area*, Preamble, First Recital (herein after "ICCAT Negative list Recommendation"); Indian Ocean Tuna Commission (IOTC) Resolution 06/01, *On Establishing a List of Vessels Presumed to Have Carried Out Illegal, Unreported and Unregulated Fishing in the IOTC Area*, Preamble, First Recital (herein after "IOTC Negative list Resolution"); Western and Central Pacific Fisheries Commission (WCPFC) Conservation Measure 2010-06 *to Establish a List of Vessels Presumed to Have Carried Out Illegal, Unregulated and Unreported Fishing Activities in the Western and Central Pacific Ocean*, Preamble, First Recital (herein after "WCPFC Negative list Measure"); South-East Atlantic Fisheries Organisation (SEAFO), *Conservation Measure 08/06 Establishing a List of Vessels Presumed To Have Carried Out Illegal, Unreported and Unregulated Fishing Activities in the SEAFO Convention Area*, (herein after "SEAFO Negative list Measure").

and management measure."[76] This final catch-all provision could presumably be utilised in order to take action against vessels engaged in non-target depletion or related environmental harm if the relevant RFMO has adopted such measures in respect of participant States.[77]

Whilst many of the RFMO's requirements of activities deemed to fall within the definition of IUU fishing are clearly spelled out in the relevant negative list Resolutions/Recommendations the threshold requirements are vaguely worded, as certain draft negative lists simply require the "presentation of evidence" of wrongdoing, (ICCAT, IOTC, IATTC, for instance) but do not further stipulate what form this evidence should take. Other RFMO's negative list criteria do, however, elaborate upon the type of evidence required. For instance, both SEAFO and WCPFC specify that the identification of vessels engaged in IUU activity should be documented upon reports from contracting parties, reliable and verifiable trade statistics, and "suitably documented" information gathered from ports and fishing grounds.[78] A less stringent evidential threshold is adopted by NAFO. For the presumption of IUU activity to be raised within the NAFO sphere of competence, and thus warranting inclusion on the NAFO Provisional Negative list, all that is required is that a vessel of a non-Contracting Party has been "sighted or by other means identified…as engaging in fishing activities in the Regulatory Area."[79] The CCAMLR non-Contracting Party Negative list draws upon elements of both NAFO's scheme and of that utilised by WCPFC and SEAFO by requiring that the identification of vessels presumed to have engaged in IUU activities will be based upon similar criteria to that of WCFPC and SEAFO, with the additional criteria of the presumption being raised when a vessel registered with a non-Contracting Party has either: "been sighted engaging in fishing activities in the Convention Area or which has been denied port access, landing or transhipment,"[80] or participated in fishing operations with

[76] IATTC Negative list Resolution, Article 1; ICCAT Negative list Recommendation, Article 1; IOTC Negative list Resolution, Article 1; WCPFC Negative list Measure, Article 3; SEAFO Negative list Measure, Article 3.

[77] Whilst this provision exists in many RFMO negative list criteria, whether or not any RFMO's conservation strategy contains provisions for the protection of the wider marine environment is by no means certain. This topics is expanded upon later in this Chapter.

[78] WCPFC Negative list Measure, Article 2; SEAFO Negative list Measure, Article 2.

[79] Northwest Atlantic Fisheries Organisation (NAFO), Conservation and Enforcement Measures, (NAFO FC Doc. 07/1, Serial No. N5335), Article 44(1), (herein after "NAFO Blacklist Measure").

[80] Convention for the Conservation of Antarctic Marine Living Resources (CCAMLR), Conservation Measure 10-07(2006), *Scheme to Promote Compliance by Non-Contracting Party Vessels With CCAMLR Conservation Measures*, Articles 1–4 and Article 9 (herein after "CCAMLR Negative list Measure").

known IUU vessels, or engaged in fisheries operations in a manner that undermines the attainment of the Convention's objectives.[81]

Once evidence of a vessel's activities has been satisfactorily amassed, under the various threshold requirements of the authorising measure, it is generally the case that the vessel is then presumed to be engaged in IUU fishing. The vessel's details and evidence of its infractions are then communicated to the relevant Secretariat or Directorate who will place the vessel on a draft negative list, pending further enquiries and comments from member and participant States, as well as the flag State of the suspected vessel. At this point in time the evidence presented against the vessel may be rebutted by the flag State of the vessel, and additional evidence may be provided by Contracting Parties as to the activities of the vessel.[82] During this time most of the RFMOs germane to this study monitor the ongoing conduct of the suspected vessel "in order to determine their activities and possible changes of name, flag and/or registered owner."[83]

The final decision to name the vessel on the final published negative list is usually taken by the Commission of the RFMO during its annual session on the basis of any recommendations made by the RFMO's own management and compliance body.[84] At this point, in keeping with the "transparency" provisions of UNFSA (which it will be recalled oblige States to "provide for transparency in the decision-making process and other activities of sub-regional and regional fisheries management organisations and arrangements")[85] any evidence against the vessels, as well as any evidence to refute the charges against it, should be open to scrutiny.[86] Subject to the voting procedures of each individual RFMO the vessel will now be entered into the RFMO's vessel negative list.

---

81 CCAMLR Negative list Measures, Article 9 (i)–(vi).

82 NAFO Negative list Measure, Articles 44(4) and 48; CCAMLR Negative list Measures, Articles 10–11; IOTC Negative list Resolution, Articles 4–6; WCPFC Negative list Measures, Articles 5–8; SEAFO Negative list Measures, Articles 5–8; ICCAT Negative list Recommendation, Article 3, IATTC Negative list Resolution, Article 3.

83 IATTC Negative list Resolution, Article 3. Because of the near identical provisions of the IATTC measures with those of ICCAT, IOTC, WCPFC and SEAFO henceforth all references to IATTC should also be taken to refer to all, unless otherwise stated. NAFO and CCAMLR's measures, whilst similar, are slightly at variance and so shall remain discrete for the purposes of referencing.

84 In terms of IATTC this management and compliance body is the Joint Working Group on Fishing by Non-Parties, whose terms of reference are defined in ICCAT/AIDCP Document JWG Terms of Reference of October 2004.

85 UNFSA, Article 12(1).

86 See, for instance, IATTC's Joint Working Group Communiqué to the Commission 05-05, adopted by the 74th Meeting of IATTC, Korea, June 2006, Section 8. In the case of other RFMOs, however, the information upon a listing was recommended to the Commission is much more difficult to come by.

Once the vessel has been listed and the flag State and owner of the vessel have been notified,[87] the RFMO authorising measures then define the possible sanctions which may be imposed upon the vessel. These generally include port State measures, such as a prohibition on catch landings in the ports of participating States, and a prohibition on commercial transactions of species covered by the relevant RFMO Convention in respect of the identified vessel.[88] States should encourage traders, importers and transporters to do likewise. Participant States are normally requested to also ensure that their vessels do not tranship with the listed vessel. Only following a genuine change of ownership may participant States grant their flags to listed vessels – and only when the flag State concerned is satisfied that the grant of registration shall not result in the commencement of IUU activity.[89]

Having noted the above procedures, it is possible that one might assume that the RFMO negative list mechanism leaves no way for IUU vessels to proceed with their trade. After all, a listed vessel should be effectively stranded at sea with no way to land or tranship their catches, and even if they were able to land or tranship them there would be no viable trade route for them to follow. Unfortunately, in practice this is not the case, because, as is often the case with attempts at regulating the unregulated IUU/FOC vessels, there are always flaws in the arrangements and loopholes to be exploited. The following section will therefore catalogue some of the ways in which the RFMO negative list system fails in its avowed purpose of eliminating IUU/FOC activity.

The first point of note is perhaps obvious but worth reiterating. Unless the flag State of the vessel is a participant in the RFMO or has ratified the UNFSA there can be no onboard inspection or apprehension of that vessel. Therefore, for IUU/FOC vessels no hands-on enforcement is permitted even in cases of the most flagrant breaches of regional fisheries regulations and long-standing on any IUU list.[90]

The second reason is the very practical matter of how long it takes for a vessel that is suspected of IUU activity in any given RFMO's area of competence to actually find itself subject to any form of sanction. As Rayfuse notes, the listing process can take many years, in which time the vessel is free to pursue its unregulated and destructive practices.[91] For example, under the IAATC proce-

[87] This notification process is designed to allow the flag State of the vessel to act first to ensure that the vessel ceases to engage in IUU activity – see, for instance, IATTC Negative list Measure, Article 8.

[88] UNFSA Article 23(3). These port State measures are analysed in more depth later in this Chapter.

[89] IATTC Negative list Measure, Article 9.

[90] Henriksen *et al.* p. 89, p. 124.

[91] Rosemary Rayfuse, *To Our Children's Children's Children: From Promoting to Achieving Compliance in High Seas Fisheries*, The International Journal of Marine and Coastal Law, Vol. 20, (November 2005), Nos. 3–4, at p. 524, (herein after "Rayfuse 2005").

dures, which are largely representative of the majority of RFMOs, the timescale is typically as follows. The vessel is to be suspected of engaging in activity that undermines the regional management and conservation measures as a result of either a chance sighting or through the analysis of trade data. Timescales now become a factor, as under the IAATC negative listing procedures States suspecting non-participant State's vessels of undermining regional measures must report these suspicions to the IAATC Director before February 1st in a given year. The Director will then transmit the information to all participant States and the flag State of the vessel concerned within one month. Following consultations the Director shall draw up a provisional negative list at least two weeks prior to IATTC's annual conference, which generally takes place in late June of each year. Once the Commission has voted upon the inclusion of the vessel it will now enter the final negative list. In the very best of circumstances this can take a mere five months from evidence of IUU activity being introduced to the end of the negative listing process. Because of the highly migratory nature of many tuna species and their associated fisheries within the IAATC region, even in the best case scenario, by the time the listing process has been successfully completed the vessel may have moved on to another area beyond the jurisdiction of the RFMO, in which case there are numerous problems for the continuing identification of the vessel due to incomplete or non-existent exchange of information between certain RFMOs.[92] In the worst of circumstances the process may take years, either due to flag States contesting the evidence against the suspected vessel or because the RFMO annual meeting at which the decisions to list vessels are taken cannot achieve the necessary consensus to so do.

Even if a vessel is successfully listed and it avoids the temptation to decamp to any area beyond the RFMO in question this does not mean that the vessel's activities will necessarily be overly restricted by its negative listing as at this point a further two options are available to the shrewd vessel owner. Firstly they can simply change the vessel's name and registration details, and with a quick coat of paint it assumes an entirely new identity. This change of identity is easily facilitated in many cases due to the incomplete vessel details on many negative lists, which, often do not include either up-to-date ownership details or more importantly an IMO vessel registration number.[93] Thus when the vessel

[92] High Seas Task Force, *Closing the Net: Stopping Illegal Fishing on the High Seas*, Final Report of the Ministerial-led Task Force on IUU Fishing on the High Seas, Governments of Australia, Canada, Chile, Namibia, New Zealand and the United Kingdom, WWF, IUCN and the Earth Institute at Columbia University, HSTF, March 2006, at p. 44 (herein after "Closing the Net").

[93] Less than half of the vessel summaries on IATTC's Negative list database contain complete information, with typical omissions being IMO/Registration numbers, current flag and beneficial ownership. IOTC's vessel list is even more incomplete with only one of the five listed vessels being identified by its IMO/Registration number. On the other hand certain RFMO

once known and negative listed as the Belize registered *Reymar 6*, for instance, arrives in an IATTC member State port under its new unknown name and flag there is no means by which the port authority can identify the vessel as one which cannot unload its catch.[94, 95]

In response to the above noted loophole in the negative list procedure many RFMOs have embarked upon a positive listing program. Positive listings, or 'white lists' as they are often known, work in an opposite manner to negative lists because instead of prohibiting landings and facilities to known offenders they oblige participant States to only allow vessels deemed to be of "good standing" to land or tranship catches. Any vessel not deemed to have good standing will be automatically barred from any commercial activity within the area of the RFMO's competence. Thus it is crucial for all vessels wishing to conduct any form of activity in any RFMO area that they positively show compliance with measures adopted by that RFMO and can demonstrate that their activities do not undermine any conservation and management measures. In terms of non-contracting party vessels (which would obviously include the vast majority of FOC vessels) the presumption is that those vessels are undermining the effectiveness of conservation measures, and, as such, those vessels will be barred from any positive list and thus will be denied the benefits of port and trade facilities. To rebut this presumption it is necessary for the flag State of the vessel in question to demonstrate ongoing compliance with the RFMO's management measures.

An example of the positive list methodology is the scheme adopted by ICCAT in November 2002, which succinctly states that fishing vessels that are "not entered into the record [of ICCAT vessels] are deemed to be not authorised to fish for, retain on board, tranship or land tuna or tuna-like species."[96] In this respect it is for the flag State of the fishing vessel to both enter the vessel's records on to the central ICCAT list and to ensure that any vessels flying their flag are compliant with ICCAT conservation and management measures. The former obligation – to compile a list of vessels authorised to fish – goes beyond the requirements of UNCLOS Article 94(2)(b), which, it will be recalled obliges States to maintain a vessel register, by ensuring that ICCAT gives due publicity

negative lists do contain sufficient data to readily identify the vessel via its IMO/Registration number, see, for example, the negative lists of NAFO, NEAFC, CCAMLR and ICCAT.

94 See IATTC IUU Vessel list at http://www.iattc.org/VesselRegister/IUUENG.html.

95 For a further analysis of the way vessels avoid detection in this manner see: *Party to the Plunder: Illegal Fishing in Guinea and its Links to the EU*, Environmental Justice Foundation, London, 2005, (herein after "EJF: Party to the Plunder"), in which the EJF provide anecdotal evidence, at pp. 4–6, of many vessels operating under multiple names to avoid port State controls.

96 Recommendation 02-22 by ICCAT Concerning the Establishment of an ICCAT Record of Vessels Over 24 Meters Authorised to Operate in the Convention Area, Article 1, (herein after "ICCAT Positive list Recommendation").

to this list.[97] With regard to the latter requirement it is incumbent upon flag States to ensure that all vessels authorised to fish in the ICCAT region can be properly subject to the State's jurisdiction so that the State can fulfil its obligations under ICCAT conservation and management measures.[98] To achieve this aim the ICCAT Recommendation utilises the language of the genuine link, as found in the ill-fated UN Convention on the Conditions for the Registration of Ships, by requiring that the owners of any fishing vessel on the ICCAT record are "citizens or legal entities" within the flag State.[99] Flag States are also obliged to ensure that vessels flying their flag are not engaged in IUU fishing activities, either alone or in concert with other vessels not on the ICCAT Positive list.[100] Only when there has been a real change of ownership may ex-IUU vessels be authorised to fish in the ICCAT area.[101] Ongoing trade in any species of fish covered by ICCAT is regulated under the Positive list by requiring that all landings are accompanied by the relevant documentation, and the manner in which trade documentation is issued is generally governed centrally by ICCAT. For instance, if a vessel wishes to land its catch of bluefin tuna then this landing must be accompanied by validated documentation[102] and the documentation will only be validated by the relevant governmental authority when the vessel appears on the ICCAT Positive list.[103] Thus, so the theory goes, and barring any forged or erroneous documents,[104] only vessels with no record of IUU activity may trade or tranship catches of species covered by ICCAT.

97 ICCAT Positive list Recommendation, Article 4. The type of information pertinent to the vessel include its name and registration number, any previous names and flags, any history of deletion from other registries, its call sign, the vessel type, the gear used, its ownership details and the time period for which it is authorised to fish or tranship, see ICCAT Positive list Recommendation, Article 2.

98 ICCAT Positive list Recommendation, Article 5(a) and (b).

99 ICCAT Positive list Recommendation, Article 5(f). It will be recalled from Chapter Four that requirements obliging either citizenship or the seat of business being established in the flag State form part of the ill-fated UNCCRS, and have fallen foul of EU law.

100 ICCAT Positive list Recommendation, Article 5(e).

101 ICCAT Positive list Recommendation, Article 5(d), to demonstrate a real change of ownership vessel owners are obliged to "provide sufficient evidence demonstrating that the previous owners and operators have no legal, beneficial or financial interests in, or control over those vessels…".

102 ICCAT Recommendation 92-1, ICCAT Bluefin Tuna Statistical Document Program: Frozen Bluefin Products. It is not only frozen bluefin products that are covered by ICCAT's Statistical Document Program but also fresh bluefin (ICCAT Recommendation 93-3); bigeye tuna (ICCAT Recommendation 01-21); and swordfish (ICCAT Recommendation 01-22).

103 ICCAT Positive list Recommendation, Article 7(b).

104 In this regard ICCAT participants are strongly urged to co-operate to ensure that statistical documents are not forged or inaccurate, ICCAT Positive list Recommendation, Article 7(b)(iii).

On the basis of the seemingly successful model positive list program adopted by ICCAT a number of established RMFOs such as the Commission for the Conservation of Southern Bluefin Tuna (CCSBT) and "new entry" RFMOs such as SEAFO and WCPFC have embarked upon similar schemes.[105] Whilst these homogenised positive lists are clearly becoming the template by which many RFMOs are attempting to restrict IUU operations within their areas of competence, whether or not the positive list criteria can sufficiently tackle all the known consequences of IUU activity depends entirely upon the very purpose of the RFMO itself. In other words it is essential to consider whether or not any RFMO is mandated to go beyond the management of target species and is thus obliged to conserve and protect the wider marine environment and take into consideration the means by which the fishing is conducted. Contemporary thinking about the role of RFMOs is, it is submitted, indeed polarised, but as Lodge and Nandan note, this polarisation does not concern whether or not RFMOs are obliged to consider the wider marine environment but is more focussed upon whether the purpose of RFMOs is to conserve fish stocks or facilitate their optimum utilisation[106] and, according to one report, environmental considerations hardly trouble the majority of RFMOs at all, while they remain "fixated on the management of target stocks."[107]

To answer the above question it is necessary to consider both the underpinning principles behind the creation of any RFMO, as found, for instance in the UN Fish Stocks Agreement,[108] and, of course, the RFMO's own terms of reference. With regard to the UNFSA the answer is not entirely clear. The Agreement does, of course, oblige coastal States and States fishing on the high seas to:

> ... minimize pollution, waste, discards, catch by lost or abandoned gear, catch of non-target species, both fish and non-fish species,... and impacts on associated or dependent species, in particular endangered species, through measures including, to the extent practicable, the development and use of selective, environmentally safe and cost-effective fishing gear and techniques.[109]

Furthermore, the notion of ecosystem[110] conservation is expanded upon in relation to the precautionary principle in Article 6 which obliges States to apply

[105] The agreement establishing SEAFO entered into force in April 2003, see http://www.seafo.org/welcome.htm. The WCPFC Convention entered into force in June 2004, see http://www.wcpfc.int/.

[106] Lodge and Nandan, at p. 373.

[107] Willock and Lack, at p. v.

[108] There are, of course a number of RFMOs established prior to the UNFSA, for which the Agreement merely strengthens their mandate.

[109] UNFSA, Article 5(f).

[110] The use of the term ecosystem in the context of this Chapter does not connote any special meaning but instead is used as a synonym for the wider marine environment.

the principle in respect of the conservation and management of target species and the preservation of the marine environment, including the adoption of "plans which are necessary to ensure the conservation of such species and to protect habitats of special concern."[111] These duties are, however, imposed upon contracting States in their individual capacities, and not when giving effect to their duty to co-operate through sub-regional or regional fisheries management organisations. The only obligations imposed upon RFMOs in respect of ecosystem management under the Agreement are the rather vague requirements that co-operative arrangements should "adopt and apply any generally recommended international minimum standards for the responsible conduct of fishing operations"[112] and that they should "assess the impact of fishing on non-target and associated or dependent species."[113]

The "generally recommended international minimum standards for the responsible conduct of fishing operations" referred to in UNFSA, and indeed, UNCLOS,[114] are defined in neither the Agreement nor the Convention. It can, nonetheless, be safely stated that these generally accepted minimum standards are currently to be found in the "soft goals" of Chapter 17 of the UNCED's Agenda 21,[115] and UNFAO's Code of Conduct for Responsible Fishing ("the Code"),[116] of which the UNFOA Compliance Agreement forms an integral part. Thus, it is essential to note the provisions of these instruments insofar as they pertain to the duties of RFMOs to consider the wider marine environment. Prior to this analysis of the substance of the environmental mandate, it is worth, however, considering the extent to which the Code and Agenda 21 can be accurately described as "generally recommended international minimum standards for the responsible conduct of fishing operations."

5.4 *The 'General Principles' of Ocean Governance: The Code of Conduct for Responsible Fishing*

The Code of Conduct is, of course, exactly what it purports to be. It is simply a Code of Conduct and not a legally binding instrument. Nevertheless, the Code was voted for unanimously by 170 members of the UNFAO,[117] and thus it can be seen as representing the generally accepted standards of responsible fishing.

[111] UNFSA, Article 6(3)(d).
[112] UNFSA, Article 10(c).
[113] UNFSA, Article 10(d).
[114] UNCLOS, Article 119(1)(a).
[115] Birnie and Boyle, at p. 679.
[116] FAO Code of Conduct for Responsible Fisheries, Rome, FAO, 1995 (herein after "Code of Conduct").
[117] Sands (2003), at p. 577.

Likewise, Agenda 21 sets forth a number of targets to be achieved with regards to the fisheries sector, one of which, it will be recalled, was the convening of the conference leading to the formation of the UNFSA. To avoid tautologies, however, the present analysis of the general principles applicable to responsible fisheries will concern itself with only the Code of Conduct, for the simple reason that, as the Code itself explicitly acknowledges, it is against the backdrop of a variety of international instruments, including UNCLOS, UNFSA, the Compliance Agreement and Agenda 21, that the Code operates and many of the provisions of the earlier instruments are repeated in the Code.[118] Also explicitly acknowledged within the Code is its status in international fisheries governance, which is said to be to provide "principles and standards applicable to the conservation, management and development of all fisheries."[119]

The first thing that must be noted about the Code of Conduct is that it goes far beyond the environmental mandate of the present study and deals with an enormous number of fisheries related issues, many of which have previously been addressed in this Chapter in the context of UNFSA, the Compliance Agreement and the regulations governing RFMOs.[120] For this reason the present study of the Code will focus only upon the immediate issues of relevance to this section of the Chapter – that of the obligation to ensure that fisheries operations do not unreasonably impinge upon the wider marine environment.

The second noteworthy aspect of the Code is that, in terms of the present analysis, it does not specify any precise requirements in relation to explicit problems facing the marine environment resulting from harmful fishing practices. Instead the detailed requirements of exactly how to ensure compliance with the Code's overarching objectives are found in the numerous International Plans of Action "elaborated within the framework of the Code."[121] In terms of the Code's non-target species scope – or its wider environmental mandate – it merely states that one of its objectives is to "promote protection of living aquatic resources and their environments and coastal areas."[122] Likewise, in terms of the general principles underpinning the Code, Article 6.2 recognises that "[m]anagement measures should not only ensure the conservation of target species but also species belonging to the same ecosystem or associated with or

---

[118] Code of Conduct, Preface, at p. vi.

[119] Code of Conduct, Article 1.3.

[120] Especially, for instance, the duty of co-operation, the application of the precautionary principle, the maintenance of vessels registers, et cetera.

[121] UNFAO Fisheries and Aquaculture Department, *International Plans of* Action, available at: http://www.fao.org/fishery/ccrf/ipoa/en. It will be recalled from Chapter Four that the IPOA-Seabirds was initiated under the Code of Conduct, and this IPOA is typical of the various specific plans of action adopted under the Code to deal with the numerous harms caused by deleterious fishing practices.

[122] Code of Conduct, Article 2.

dependent upon the target species." To achieve this, and the other listed objectives of the Code, Article 6.6 (general principles) and Article 8.5 (fishing gear selectivity) require that selectivity in the use of gear and methods should be employed. It should be noted however, that even in the context of the Code, which is of course merely voluntary in application, the use of selective gear so as to minimise the environmental consequences of fishing operations is not an absolute and that minimising the use of such gear is only required "to the extent practicable."[123] States and industry should, nevertheless, work together in order to discourage discards and by-catch and the use of gear that increases the survival rates of escaping fish should be promoted,[124] as should methods of fishing which minimize the harmful impacts of lost or abandoned gear.[125]

The question that remains to be answered in relation to the protection of the marine environment is to what extent States and RFMOs are entitled to take action against vessels that do not conform to the general minimum standards of responsible fisheries. Although the Code does specify that States should, within the framework of regional bodies, ensure compliance with and enforcement of conservation and management measures,[126] ensure responsible fishing,[127] and deter the activities of vessels flying the flag of non-RFMO-participating States which undermine regional conservation and management measures,[128] to give these provisions real bite they must be interpreted in light of the binding requirements of the UNFSA. Taking the Code of Conduct in tandem with the UNFSA (with its requirement that RFMOs "adopt and apply any generally recommended international minimum standards for the responsible conduct of fishing operations")[129] the general principles of the Code of Conduct give RFMOs the provisional justification to adopt measures necessary for the protection of the wider marine environment.

5.5 *Regional Implementation of the Code and the International Plans of Action*

Despite the entitlement to take such measures it is apparent that for many RFMOs the protection of the marine environment and its non-target dependent species is not a priority, and, as the 10th Anniversary Review Conference

[123] Code of Conduct, Article 7.2.2(g), Article 7.6.9, Article 8.5.1.
[124] Code of Conduct, Article 8.4.5, Article 8.5.
[125] Code of Conduct, Article 8.4.6, Article 8.5.
[126] Code of Conduct, Article 6.10.
[127] Code of Conduct, Article 6.12.
[128] Code of Conduct, Article 7.7.5.
[129] UNFSA, Article 10(c).

of the UNFSA heard, RFMOs must do more to give effect to their obligations under UNFSA in a variety of ways, not least of which would involve States and regional bodies incorporating ecosystem considerations into fisheries management.[130]

How and why then are RFMOs failing to apply ecosystem principles into their management plans? To answer this question this Chapter will now consider a representative sample of RFMOs and the manner in which they address the issue of the protection of the marine environment and dependent species. This study will attempt to identify best and worst practice across the regional bodies considered, and begin by considering whether the RFMOs in question have, as one of their general principles the protection of the marine environment or whether their mandate is merely the optimum utilisation of stocks and the allocation of participatory rights amongst member States. An additional aspect of the analysis will be to note how each RFMO attempts to deal with transgressor vessels and States: do they, for instance, adopt any form of vessel listing system of the type noted earlier in this Chapter?

5.5.1 *RFMO Mandates – Which Regional Bodies Have Taken on the Competence to Regulate the Wider Marine Environment?*

As of summer 2011 there are over 40 regional fisheries bodies currently recognised by the UNFAO, 18 of which can be described as RFMOs proper – that is having a management mandate (as opposed to those organisations that act in a merely advisory capacity).[131] It is possible to further sub-divide the 18 RFMOs with a management mandate into those established for the conservation of single specific species (denoted below as 'SSS') and those established to conserve all fish stocks within a geographic location (denoted below as 'GL'). Omitted from this study are "closed RFMOs" such as the International Pacific Halibut Commission and the Pacific Salmon Commission which are, in fact, bilateral agreements between States. Likewise the International Whaling Commission, although classed as an RFMO by the UNFAO, does not form part of this study. Unless otherwise stated all of the RFMOs listed predate the Fish Stocks Agreement and thus have not been constituted under the terms of this Agreement. Likewise, unless otherwise stated, any RFMO measures enacted in relation to sharks, seabirds and turtles will have been done so as to comply with the various FAO International Plans of Action on these species.

---

[130] Summary of the UN Fish Stocks Agreement Review Conference, May 2006, *Earth Negotiations Bulletin*, International Institute for Sustainable Development, Vol. 7, No. 61, at p. 3.

[131] See UNFAO Fisheries and Aquaculture RFMO Factsheet, available at http://www.fao.org/fi/website/FISearch.do?dom=rfb#rfb_map.

The Commission for the Conservation and Management of Pollock Resources in the Central Bering Sea (SSS)

The Commission for the Conservation and Management of Pollock Resources in the Central Bering Sea takes its environmental mandate from its Convention, which stipulates, in Article II(4) that the organisation should "...provide, if the Parties agree, a forum in which to consider the establishment of necessary conservation and management measures for living marine resources other than pollock in the Convention Area as may be required in the future." To date no such additional management and conservation measures have been enacted, nor does the Commission operate any form of vessel or State sanctions. The Commission does not utilise either positive lists or negative lists.

The Commission for the Conservation of Southern Bluefin Tuna (SSS)

Although the Convention of the CCSBT does make mention of species other than bluefin tuna, the obligation imposed by the Convention is merely that data on 'ecologically related species'[132] is amassed and studied.[133] Other than this cursory nod in the direction of non-target species vulnerability (which, due to the required relationship between these and the target species, is largely a parasitic requirement) the Convention is entirely focused upon the conservation and management of bluefin tuna. The Commission has, however, gone beyond the Convention's original aims and since 1995 the Working Group on Ecologically Related Species has been in place. Primarily charged with data-collection and the provision of information,[134] the Working Group has, however, been instrumental in the enactment of CCSBT Recommendation to Mitigate the Impact on Ecologically Related Species of Fishing for Southern Bluefin Tuna.[135] As well as recommending the collection of data on the incidental mortality of various marine dependent species, such as sharks, turtles and seabirds, the Recommendation also urges compliance by contracting parties and co-operating non-members with the numerous FAO International Plans of Action on seabirds, sharks and turtles and any measures adopted by neighbouring RFMOs.[136]

132 Defined by Article 2(a) of the Convention as "living marine species which are associated with southern bluefin tuna, including but not restricted to both predators and prey of southern bluefin tuna".

133 CCSBT Convention, Articles 5(3), 8(1)(a) and 9(2)(c).

134 *Terms of Reference for the Working Group on Ecologically Related Species*, adopted at the Second Annual Meeting of the Commission for the Conservation of Southern Bluefin Tuna, September 1995.

135 Adopted at the Fifteenth Annual Meeting, October 2008.

136 Articles 1 and 2.

To ensure compliance with its conservation and management measures CCSBT adopts a positive vessel list.[137]

The Inter-American Tropical Tuna Commission (SSS)
One of the oldest RFMOs, IATTC was initially focused upon target species and achieving the maximum sustainable yield thereof, but since its inception in 1949 it has progressively moved towards a more ecological outlook. Although there is no mention of the wider marine environment in the 1949 IATTC Convention, the Commission has adopted numerous measures to deal with by-catch,[138] seabird mortality,[139] sharks,[140] and turtles.[141] IATTC has recently utilised both positive lists[142] and negative lists[143] to ensure compliance with its conservation and management measures.

The International Commission for the Conservation of Atlantic Tuna (SSS)
The Preamble to the ICCAT Convention states that the Commission's objective is to facilitate the co-operation of States in order to achieve the maximum sustainable yield of target stocks. Despite this, ICCAT has various measures in place to mitigate the impact of target fisheries on sharks,[144] seabirds[145] and sea turtles.[146] To ensure compliance with its management measures ICCAT operates both a positive list[147] and a negative list.[148]

---

137 *Resolution on Illegal, Unregulated and Unreported Fishing (IUU) and Establishment of a CCSBT Record of Vessels over 24 meters Authorized to Fish for Southern Bluefin Tuna*, adopted at the Fifteenth Annual Meeting, October 2008.

138 Resolution C 04-05 on Bycatch.

139 Resolution C 05-01 on the Incidental Mortality of Seabirds.

140 Resolution C 05-03 on the Conservation of Sharks Caught in Association with Fisheries in the Eastern Pacific Ocean.

141 Resolution C 04-7, revised by Resolution C 04-07 to Mitigate the Impact of Tuna Fishing Vessels on Sea Turtles.

142 Resolution C 03-07 on the Establishment of a List of Longline Vessels…Authorised to Operate in the Eastern Pacific Ocean.

143 Resolution C 05-07 to Establish a List of Vessels Presumed to Have Carried Out IUU Fishing Activities in the Eastern Pacific Ocean.

144 Resolution 03-10 on the Shark Fishery; Recommendation 04-10 Concerning the Conservation of Sharks Caught in Association with Fisheries Managed by ICCAT (amended by Recommendation 05-05); Supplementary Recommendation 06-10 Concerning the Conservation of Sharks Caught in Association with Fisheries Managed by ICCAT and Supplemental Recommendation 07-06 by ICCAT Concerning Sharks.

145 Recommendation 07-07 on Reducing Incidental By-Catch of Seabirds in Longline Fisheries.

146 Resolution 03-11 on sea turtles.

147 Recommendation 09-08 Concerning the Establishment of an ICCAT Record of Vessels over 20 m Authorized to Operate in the Convention Area.

148 Recommendation 09-10 to Establish a List of Vessels Presumed to have Carried Out Illegal, Unreported and Unregulated Fishing Activities in the ICCAT Convention Area.

The Indian Ocean Tuna Commission (SSS)
Like many of its pre-Fish Stocks Agreement contemporaries, the Indian Ocean Tuna Commission's Convention makes no reference to the ecological impacts of target fisheries. Again, however, like many of its contemporaries IOTC has, in line with the FAO International Plans of Action, adopted various measures to avoid or reduce the mortality of seabirds,[149] sharks[150] and turtles.[151] As will be, no doubt, a familiar refrain by now, IOTC utilises both positive[152] and negative[153] lists to ensure compliance with its management measures.

The North Atlantic Salmon Conservation Organisation (SSS)
The objective of NASCO, according to its Convention, is "to contribute through consultation and co-operation to the conservation, restoration, enhancement and rational management of salmon stocks subject to this Convention."[154] NASCO has not adopted any measures to guard against the incidental mortality of marine dependent wildlife, nor does it apply any form of listing procedure.

The North Pacific Anadromous Fisheries Commission (SSS)
The NAPAFC Convention prohibits the taking of anadromous species in the high seas area of the North Pacific. Although the Convention states that "the Commission may consider matters related to the conservation of ecologically related species in the Convention Area"[155] the taking of non-anadomous species in this area is not prohibited and nor are there any environmental measures in place. No listing procedures are utilised by NPAFC.

Commission for the Conservation of Antarctic Marine Living Resources (GL)
According to its constituting convention, CCAMLR's objective is the "rational use of all marine living resources... including finfish, molluscs, crustaceans and all other species of living organism" (other than whales and seals).[156] In recent years, however, and possibly because CCAMLR is concerned with all marine living resources in its area of competence, the Commission has applied a

[149] Resolution 10-06 on Reducing the Incidental Bycatch of Seabirds in Longline Fisheries.

[150] Resolution 05-05 Concerning the Conservation of Sharks Caught in Association with Fisheries Managed by IOTC.

[151] Resolution 09/06 on Marine Turtles.

[152] Resolution 07-02 Concerning the Establishment of an IOTC Record of Vessels Authorised to Operate in IOTC Area.

[153] Resolution 09-03 on Establishing a List of Vessels Presumed to have Carried Out Illegal, Unreported and Unregulated Fishing in the IOTC Area.

[154] NASCO Convention, Article 3(2).

[155] NPAFC Convention, Article VIII(3).

[156] CCAMLR Convention, Article 1(2).

"holistic ecosystem approach to the management of Antarctic resources"[157] and has adopted numerous measures to safeguard the wider marine environment. For instance, and as noted in Chapter Three, bottom trawling activities in the CCAMLR region are tightly controlled in most areas[158] or entirely prohibited in others.[159] Likewise, CCAMLR has implemented measures aimed at reducing the incidental mortality of a variety of species of marine wildlife, including sharks,[160] seabirds[161] and marine mammals.[162] As well as operating a list of authorised vessels and a negative list of IUU vessels, CCAMLR's measures are complemented by the use of its Catch Documentation Scheme (CDS) which prohibits all trade in target species unless accompanied by the relevant documentary evidence of compliance with CCAMLR conservation and management measures. The CDS will be discussed in greater depth later in this Chapter.

General Fisheries Commission for the Mediterranean (GL)
Another of the most established RFMOs – dating back to the late 1940s – the GFCM's mandate is "to promote the development, conservation, rational management and best utilization of living marine resources."[163] Despite this the GFCM has adopted measures to protect Vulnerable Marine Ecosystems,[164] dolphins[165] and sharks.[166] Only vessels on the GFCM list of authorised vessels may "fish for, retain on board, trans-ship or land species covered by the Commission."[167]

---

157 "CCAMLR's Management of the Antarctic" available at: http://www.ccamlr.org/pu/E/e_pubs/am/man-ant/p1.2.htm.
158 CCAMLR Conservation Measure 22-06 (2010), *Bottom Fishing in the Convention Area.*
159 CCAMLR Conservation Measure 42-01 (2010) *Limits on the fishery for* Champsocephalus gunnari *in Statistical Subarea 48.3 in the 2010/11 season.*
160 CCAMLR Conservation Measure 32-18 *Conservation of Sharks.*
161 CCAMLR Conservation Measure 25-02 *Minimising incidental seabird mortality*; CCAMLR Conservation Measure 24-02 *Longline weighting for seabird conservation.*
162 CCAMLR Conservation Measure 25-03 *Minimising incidental mortality of seabirds and marine mammals in the course of trawl fishing.*
163 GFCM Agreement, Article 3.
164 GFCM Recommendation 2006/03 *On the Establishment of Fisheries Restricted Areas in Order to Protect the Deep Sea Sensitive Habitats.*
165 GFCM Recommendation 2006/02 *On the Establishment of a Closed Season for the Dolphinfish Fisheries Based on Fishing Aggregation Devices.*
166 GFCM Recommendation 2006/08/B *Concerning the Conservation of Sharks Caught in Association with Fisheries Managed by ICCAT*; GFCM Recommendation 34/2010/4(c) *Concerning the Recommendation by ICCAT on the Conservation of Thresher Sharks Caught in Association with Fisheries in the ICCAT Convention Area.*
167 GFCM Recommendation 33/2009/6 *Concerning the Establishment of a GFCM Record of Vessels Over 15 Metres Authorized to Operate in the GFCM Area.*

Northwest Atlantic Fisheries Organisation (GL)
The Preamble to the NAFO Convention states that the Organisation's role is "...to promote the conservation and optimum utilization of the fishery resources..." NAFO's environmental measures include measures to reduce by-catch,[168] to conserve sharks,[169] and to regulate bottom fishing activities.[170] NAFO endeavours to ensure compliance with its management measures by utilising various measures against non-compliant vessels, including a negative list of IUU vessels.[171]

North East Atlantic Fisheries Commission (GL)
The 'New' NEAFC Convention was adopted in 2007. Being of the 'new era' the Convention explicitly 'recognises' the role of the UN Fish Stocks Agreement and the FAO Compliance Agreement, and 'takes into account' the FAO Code of Conduct. Consequently, NEAFC's role is "to promote the long term conservation and optimum utilisation of the fishery resources of the North-East Atlantic area, and in doing so to safeguard the marine ecosystems in which the resources occur..."[172] In attaining the primary objective of the Convention (the long term conservation and optimum utilisation of fisheries resources)[173] the Commission is bound to "...take due account of the impact of fisheries on other species and marine ecosystems, and in doing so adopt, where necessary, conservation and management measures that address the need to minimise harmful impacts on living marine resources and marine ecosystems; and...take due account of the need to conserve marine biological diversity."[174] Although the majority of NEAFC's environmental effort is directed to the regulation of bottom-trawling activities,[175] its Scheme of Control and Enforcement Measures does include requirements that lost fishing gear is retrieved.[176] Despite an acknowledgment by NEAFC that a degree of seabird, marine mammal and shark mortality occurs within its area of competence,[177] no species specific mitigation

168 NAFO Conservation and Enforcement Measures 2011, (NAFO FC Doc. 11/1 Serial No. N5867), Article 12.

169 *Ibid.*, Article 17.

170 *Ibid.*, Chapter I.

171 *Ibid.*, Chapter VI.

172 NEAFC Convention, Preamble.

173 NEAFC Convention, Article 2.

174 *Ibid.*, Article 4(2)(c)(d).

175 *Consolidated Text of all NEAFC Recommendations on Regulating Bottom Fishing*, available at: http://www.neafc.org/system/files/%252Fhome/neafc/drupal2_files/consolidated_bottomfishing_regulations.pdf.

176 NEAFC Scheme of Control and Enforcement, Article 7b, available at: http://www.neafc.org/scheme.

177 NEAFC Fishery Status Report 1998–2007, paragraph 7.12.3.

measures have been introduced. NEAFC operates a negative list system,[178] which is underpinned by numerous measures to prevent the refuelling and resupply of, and catch landings and imports from known IUU vessels.[179]

South East Atlantic Fisheries Organisation (GL)

Being a post-UNFSA organisation and being constituted in line with the principles of the Agreement, it is not surprising that SEAFO's Convention ensures that the organisation's primary purposes of "...ensur[ing] the long-term sustainable use of the fisheries resources in the Convention area"[180] is conducted so as to avoid environmentally harmful practices. Specifically, the Convention states that:

> In giving effect to the objective of this Convention, the Contracting Parties, where appropriate through the Organisation, shall, in particular: apply the provisions of this Convention relating to fishery resources, taking due account of the impact of fishing operations on ecologically related species such as seabirds, cetaceans, seals and marine turtles;
>
> adopt, where necessary, conservation and management measures for species belonging to the same ecosystem as, or associated with or dependent upon, the harvested fishery resources;
>
> ensure that fishery practices and management measures take due account of the need to minimise harmful impacts on living marine resources as a whole; and protect biodiversity in the marine environment.[181]

In order to meet the Convention's objectives and to implement the provisions of the various applicable FAO International Plans of Action and Guidelines, as well as the Code of Conduct for Responsible Fisheries, SEAFO has adopted management measures aimed at reducing the incidental mortality of seabirds,[182] turtles,[183] sharks[184] and to safeguard vulnerable marine ecosystems.[185] SEAFO's

---

178 NEAFC Scheme of Control and Enforcement, Article 44.

179 NEAFC Scheme of Control and Enforcement, Article 45.

180 SEAFO Convention, Article 2.

181 SEAFO Convention Article 3(c)–(f).

182 SEAFO Conservation Measure 15/09 *on Reducing Incidental By-catch of Seabirds in the SEAFO Convention Area.*

183 SEAFO Conservation Measure 14/09 *to Reduce Sea Turtle Mortality in SEAFO Fishing Operations.*

184 SEAFO Conservation Measure 04/06 *on the Conservation of Sharks Caught in Association with Fisheries Managed by SEAFO.*

185 SEAFO Conservation Measures 18/10 *on the Management of Vulnerable Deep Water Habitats and Ecosystems in the SEAFO Convention Area.*

negative listing process ensures that identified IUU/FOC vessels[186] cannot land or trans-ship catches, or refuel or resupply within the Convention area[187] or otherwise take advantage of SEAFO ports.[188] The responsibility for authorising vessels to fish within the SEAFO region lies with the (contracting) flag State of that vessel, and in granting such authorisation States must ensure that the vessels are subject to effective flag State jurisdiction and do not undermine any conservation measures.[189]

South Pacific Regional Fisheries Management Organisation (GL)
Although this particular RFMO's Convention has, as of July 2011, failed to come into force it is clear that the SPRFMO will, in time, operate in line with best post-UNFSA practice. As is increasingly common with newly convened RFMOs, the principles of UNFSA, the Compliance Agreement and the Code of Conduct are explicitly acknowledged in the Preamble to the Convention, and occasionally referred to throughout the Convention text. More important than this name-checking, however, is the way in which the Convention requires that the environmental principles enshrined within the above mentioned agreements are woven into the fabric of the SPRFMO's activities. For instance, all fishing activities within the Organisation's area of competence take into account their "impacts on non-target and dependent or associated species" and are consistent with "the general obligation to protect and preserve the marine environment."[190] Likewise, the Convention stipulates that vulnerable marine ecosystems must be protected[191] and the impacts on other species, due to pollution, abandoned gear etc, should be minimised.[192] The Convention also requires that the Commission adopts specific conservation and management measures that "protect the habitats and marine ecosystems in which fishery resources and non-target and associated or dependent species occur from the impacts of fishing."[193] Until longer-term and binding measures are adopted, the SPRFMO region is covered by certain non-binding voluntary interim measures, and although the majority of the interim measures concern the protocols for target fisheries it is noteworthy that controls over bottom trawling activities are already in place.[194]

---

186 SEAFO Conservation Measure 08/06 *Establishing A List Of Vessels Presumed To Have Carried Out Illegal, Unreported And Unregulated (IUU) Fishing Activities*, Article 3.
187 *Ibid.*, Article 17.
188 SEAFO Convention, Article 15.
189 SEAFO Convention, Article 14.
190 SPRMFO Convention, Article 3(1)(a)(ii).
191 *Ibid.*, Article 3(1)(a)(vii).
192 *Ibid.*, Article 3(1)(a)(x).
193 *Ibid.*, Article 20(1)(d).
194 The interim measures pertaining to bottom trawling will be discussed later in this Chapter.

Western Central Pacific Fisheries Commission (GL)

The WCPFC is another post-UNFSA organisation and is thus constituted in a UNFSA-compliant manner. Consequently all fishing activities in the Convention area shall only be undertaken after an assessment of "...the impacts of fishing, other human activities and environmental factors on target stocks, non-target species, and species belonging to the same ecosystem or dependent upon or associated with the target stocks." [195] Likewise the WCPFC Convention requires that members shall:

> adopt measures to minimize waste, discards, catch by lost or abandoned gear, pollution originating from fishing vessels, catch of non-target species, both fish and non-fish species, and impacts on associated or dependent species, in particular endangered species and promote the development and use of selective, environmentally safe and cost-effective fishing gear and techniques;
>
> protect biodiversity in the marine environment...[196]

Adhering to the principles enshrined in the FAO's International Plans of Action, and the Code of Conduct for Responsible Fisheries and putting the WCPFC Convention's aspirations into practice are a variety of conservation measures to reduce the incidental mortality of seabirds,[197] sharks[198] and turtles.[199] The use of large-scale driftnets in the Convention area is entirely prohibited.[200] Adopting a positive and negative listing procedure, the former requires that all contracting States effectively exercise flag State jurisdiction over their vessels so as to ensure compliance to WCPFC conservation and management measures.[201] As is the case with the majority of RFMO negative lists, identified IUU/FOC vessels[202] are debarred from all supply and port facilities.[203]

5.5.2 *Linking Environmental Measures with Market Denial*

As can be seen from the above, the majority of RFMOs do have measures in place to deal with IUU fishing and are either specifically mandated to take

---

[195] WCPFC Convention, Article 5 (d).

[196] *Ibid.*, Article 5 (e)(f).

[197] WCPFC Conservation and Management Measure 2007-04 *to Mitigate the Impact of Fishing for Highly Migratory Fish Stocks on Seabirds.*

[198] WCPFC Conservation and Management Measure 2010-07 *on Sharks.*

[199] WCPFC Conservation and Management Measure 2008-03 *Sea Turtles.*

[200] WCPFC Conservation and Management Measure 2008-04 *to Prohibit the Use of Large Scale Driftnets on the High Seas in the Convention Area.*

[201] WCPFC Conservation and Management Measure 2009-01 *Record of Fishing Vessels and Authorisation to Fish.*

[202] WCPFC Conservation and Management Measure 2010-06 *to Establish a List of Vessels Presumed to Have Carried Out IUU Fishing Activities in the WCPO*, Article 1(3).

[203] *Ibid.*, Article 22.

measures to protect the wider marine environment under their Conventions (CCAMLR, SEAFO, WCPFC) or have adopted Recommendations or Resolutions to put environmental protection measures into effect. For instance, as can be seen from the section above, many RFMOs have implemented many of the recommendations found in the various IPOAs on by-catch, seabirds, dolphins and turtles. The measures put in place by the RFMOs to implement the IPOAs are generally in the form of Resolutions which oblige all member States and non-contracting parties of the RFMO to abide by the provisions of the IPOA in question. Resolutions may also detail some of the specific measures to be taken so as to reduce the harmful impacts of fishing practices on the marine environment and associated species.[204] The interaction between the measures adopted to combat IUU fishing and its harmful effects, whether they be negative lists, positive lists, Port State Controls, etc., and any measures adopted for the protection of the wider marine environment, should, in theory mean that whenever a fishing vessel does not abide by the environmental measures it will become subject to the IUU sanctions, in the same manner as any fishing vessel fishing without authorisation or in a manner that violates this authorisation.

Positive lists, in this respect, have the potential to severely stymie the activities of the IUU fleet if applied to all types of IUU fishing – including environmentally unsound practices. Under a positive list scheme the presumption is that all non-contracting party vessels are deemed to undermine conservation and management measures simply by virtue of their flag-Statehood. This presumption can only be rebutted when any individual vessel can demonstrate compliance with those management measures and has no history of IUU activity. In theory, therefore, to combat the IUU fleet globally it is easy to see how the linkage between the various IPOAs and RFMO positive lists could work. First an IPOA is issued under the auspices of the UNFOA's Code of Conduct for Responsible Fishing. Although, as noted earlier in this Chapter, this Code is not itself legally binding but does represent the "general principles of ocean governance" and when it is implemented by RFMOs through binding resolutions the provisions of the Code and its related IPOAs can take on legal effect. Thus when a vessel fails to demonstrate strict adherence to the principles enshrined in the Code and IPOAs (as implemented by the RFMO's own Resolutions) then the vessel is deemed to be engaging in IUU activity and, under the positive or negative list criteria, denied crucial transhipment, landing, re-supply and port facilities.

Thus, the next section of this Chapter will show in slightly greater detail than the above theoretical model how this methodology can work in practice. It will demonstrate how the general principles of ocean governance enshrined in the Code of Conduct and its progeny, the various IPOAs, can be turned into

[204] These specific IPOAs and how they are implemented by RFMOs are discussed below.

positive rules which must be adhered to by all fishing entities under RFMO systems of governance. Finally the analysis will show that a breach of these rules can have potentially grave implications for fishing vessels when positive lists (or, in fact, negative lists) are employed by RFMOs in granting crucial port facilities to fishing vessels.[205]

As noted earlier, as well as issuing the Code of Conduct for Responsible Fishing, the FAO have produced numerous International Plans of Action to put into place specific guidelines to deal with specific types of irresponsible fisheries. These IPOAs supplement the basic Code by providing the technical guidelines for implementing best practice in relation to all manner of fishing activities and form the basis for many of the environmental measures adopted by RFMOs.

The first IPOA in this context is the International Plan of Action to Prevent, Deter and Eliminate IUU Fishing (IPOA-IUU), which it will be recalled, mandates States and regional bodies to take firm, effective and non-discriminatory action against IUU vessels, including when appropriate, trade and market based sanctions. The IPOA-IUU, whilst chiefly focussed upon the primary harms of IUU activity (that is, stock depletion etc) does recognise that IUU fishing can cause harm to the wider environment, and as such calls upon States and regional bodies to take action against vessels which both undermine the long term conservation and sustainability of stocks and undermine the protection of the environment.[206] No specific environmental harms are referred to in the IPOA-IUU, however, and as such it is necessary to further consider the various other IPOAs that have been promulgated by the FAO which do address specific types of deleterious activities.

As noted in Chapter Three the FAO issued, in 1999, the IPOA on Seabirds, which, it will be recalled, listed numerous measures which States and RFMOs should adopt *vis-á-vis* their longlining fleets to reduce the incidence of seabird mortality. The IPOA-Seabirds does not prohibit the use of longlines nor make the use of mitigation devices mandatory. Instead the IPOA-Seabirds is more aspirational and simply requires States, alone or in concert with other States through RFMOs, to take action to invest in technologies which reduce the impact of longlines on seabird populations. This interpretation of the responsibilities imposed by the IPOA-Seabirds is, therefore, the preferred interpretation of those RFMOs undertaking to implement the IPOA and, as such, is reflected in any regional measures adopted. For instance, as can be seen from section 5.5.1 (above) IATTC, ICCAT, IOTC, SEAFO, WCPFC and CCAMLR all have in place measures pertaining to the incidental mortality of seabirds. The

205 The word 'potential' is stressed at this juncture, as the Chapter will go on to describe the way in which even this system can be undermined by unscrupulous vessel operators by the use of 'ports of convenience'.

206 IPOA-IUU, Article 9.4.

measures adopted by each RFMO vary vastly, and range from the obligatory use of mitigation measures such as the use of 'tori' poles, a prohibition on the dumping of offal and mandatory night setting of lines, [207] to merely encouraging participant States to implement the IPOA-Seabirds.[208]

Despite the fact that these mitigation measures are aimed at the vessels of participating States it is contended that they do have a role to play in the fight against the harmful effects of non-participant vessels because of the interplay between these measures and the positive list criteria. It will be remembered that in order to be make use of participant States' ports and facilities, to land catches, re-supply etc, vessels must be included on the RFMO positive list and only vessels which do not undermine conservation measures can be so included. Thus it is necessary for all non-participant States' vessels to show that they adhere to all measures adopted in order to conduct commercial transactions within the RFMO's area of competence. For instance, taking one of the new entry post-UNFSA RFMOs as an example, namely the Western Central Pacific Fisheries Commission, any vessels flagged to a non-contracting party to WCPFC which does not adhere to the requirements of WCPFC Conservation Measure 2007-04 to Mitigate the Impact of Fishing for Highly Migratory Stocks on Seabirds by, for example, failing to employ one or more of the mitigation methods enunciated in that Conservation Measure, will be "undermining the effects" of that Measure contrary to Article 32(1) of the WCPFC Convention.[209] Therefore, by further reference to Article 32(1) the Commission of the WCPFC may then empower member States to take such action as is necessary and consistent with international law to deter the activities of these vessels, which under WCPFC Convention Articles 25(12)[210] and 27(3)[211] can include the imposition of trade sanctions and prohibitions on landings and transhipments. Although as of May 2011 no sanctions had been put in place by WCPFC against States under the

---

207 CCAMLR Conservation Measure 25-02; SEAFO Conservation Measure 15/09 (Articles 3,5,6 and 7); WCPFC Conservation Measure 2007-04 (Articles 1 and 2).

208 IATTC Resolution C-05-01; ICATT Resolution 07-07; IOTC Resolution 05-09.

209 "Each member of the Commission shall take measures consistent with this Convention, the Agreement and international law to deter the activities of vessels flying the flags of non-parties to this Convention which undermine the effectiveness of conservation and management measures adopted by the Commission."

210 "The Commission, when necessary, shall develop procedures which allow for non-discriminatory trade measures to be taken, consistent with the international obligations of the members of the Commission, on any species regulated by the Commission, against any State or entity whose fishing vessels fish in a manner which undermines the effectiveness of the conservation and management measures adopted by the Commission".

211 "Members of the Commission may adopt regulations empowering the relevant national [port State] authorities to prohibit landings and transhipments where it has been established that the catch has been taken in a manner which undermines the effectiveness of conservation and management measures adopted by the Commission".

Convention, the Commission has demonstrated its willingness to impose measures against individual vessels whose activities are deemed to have undermined Conservation and Management Measures. This framework for action is implemented in practice by WCPFC Conservation and Management Measure 2010-06 to Establish a List of Vessels Presumed to Have Carried Out IUU Fishing Activities in the Western and Central Pacific Ocean. Although creating a negative list, and thus susceptible to the previously noted deficiencies of such lists, WCPFC Measure 2010-06 allows for trade and port related measures to be imposed against any vessel suspected to be engaged in IUU activity.[212] A vessel will be deemed to be engaging in IUU activity when it is either not a WCPFC authorised vessel or when that vessel is engaged in one of the many listed prohibited activities, which can of course include undermining the effectiveness of WCPFC conservation measures such as Conservation Measure 2007-04 to protect seabirds.[213] There are currently five individual vessels languishing on WCPFC's IUU list, all of which have been found to have been in violation of WCPFC Conservation Measures.[214]

For those RFMOs that have merely implemented the IPOA-Seabirds by encouraging member States to adopt measures consistent with the IPOA, as opposed to providing outright prohibitions of, or restrictions on certain types of gear, the availability of port/trade measures is not so expressly permitted. Thus, for the Indian Ocean Tuna Commission (IOTC), Inter-American Tropical Tuna Commission (IATTC) and the International Commission for the Conservation of Atlantic Tuna (ICCAT), for instance, it is unlikely that a failure of any vessel flagged to a non-participant State to adopt measures to mitigate against the consequences of irresponsible longlining will be a serious enough infraction of RFMO conservation and management measures to justify port/trade measures being instigated against individual vessels (either by "negative listing" the vessel or denying it access to any positive list). This is because, as things currently stand, the individual vessels of participating States are under no strict obligation to adopt those mitigation measures and to instigate port/trade measures against foreign flagged vessels would be to impose a stricter burden on those vessels than participant State vessels and as such may fall foul of both the RFMO's own prohibition on discriminatory treatment[215] and the corpus of international law which empowers them.

---

212 Article 22.

213 Conservation and Management Measure 2010-06, Article 3(i).

214 WCPFC IUU Vessel List 2011, available at: http://www.wcpfc.int/doc/wcpfc-iuu-vessel-list-2011.

215 For instance, in terms of the WCPFC Conservation and Management Measure 2010-06, Article 22, measures taken against foreign flagged vessels must be non-discriminatory. This

It will be recalled that under the UN Fish Stocks Agreement and the FAO Code of Conduct for Responsible Fishing non-discrimination is a key principle. For instance, under UNFSA States must not exercise the powers vested in them, through regional agreements, in a manner "which discriminates against any State or group of States having a real interest in the fisheries concerned."[216] Likewise both the UNFSA and the Code of Conduct specify that any port State measures adopted against IUU vessels should not discriminate in form or fact against the vessels of any other State.[217] Additionally, and arguably even more importantly, any discriminatory treatment may also violate World Trade Organisation rules to which RFMO trade measures are necessarily subject.[218] The highly important issue of WTO-consistency will be discussed in Chapter Seven.

Many RFMOs have a policy on the incidental capture of sea turtles, which reflects the FAO position on the need to protect these creatures from the harmful effects of fisheries operations[219] and whilst the majority of RFMOs examined in the present study have taken these measures on board, very little has currently been done to turn these guidelines into rules. For instance, IOTC's measures encourage the use of mitigation measures but contain no obligation for States to apply these measures in a mandatory manner.[220] Likewise, ICCAT's measures stipulate that participant States should "encourage the release of marine turtles accidentally caught…" but stops short of requiring States to penalise vessels which neglect to so do.[221] This quasi-voluntary methodology is replicated by IAAT, WCPFC and SEAFO, all of which have measures in place to reduce the incidental capture of marine turtles but which impose no obligations upon States or vessel owners to adhere to mitigation methods.[222] Furthermore, as noted by Willock and Lack, even if one particular RFMO did decide to take seriously the harms posed to sea turtles and did enact instruments making the

prohibition on discriminatory treatment replicates the text of the UNFAO IPOA-IUU which also forbids discriminatory treatment.

216 UNFSA, Article 8(3).

217 UNFSA, Article 23(1); Code of Conduct, Article 8.3.1.

218 Code of Conduct, Article 6.14, which states that 'International trade in fish and fishery products should be conducted in accordance with the principles, rights and obligations established in the World Trade Organization (WTO) Agreement…'; Likewise, numerous RFMOs explicitly state that the principles of the WTO Agreement should not be violated by any measures aimed at IUU vessels operating in the RFMO's area of competence. See, for example: ICCAT Recommendation 09-10, Preamble (Eighth Recital); IOTC Resolution 09/03, Preamble (Tenth Recital); IATTC Resolution C-05-07, Preamble (Seventh Recital).

219 "Guidelines to Reduce Sea Turtle Mortality in Fishing Operations" FAO Committee of Fisheries, Twenty-sixth Session, March 2005.

220 IOTC Recommendation 09/06.

221 ICCAT Resolution 03-11.

222 IATTC Resolution C-04-07; WCFPC Resolution 2008-03; SEAFO Resolution 14/09.

use of mitigation measures mandatory then, because of the trans-jurisdictional nature of these highly migratory species, the instruments adopted may "be rendered virtually ineffective by inaction...by another [RFMO]."[223]

In respect of high seas bottom trawling a slightly different picture emerges. This picture is influenced to a lesser extent by the politics and policies of RFMOs but instead by geography. Only a few regional bodies have competence to regulate those areas blighted by this method of fishing due to the fact most RFMOs have competence to manage stocks that straddle EEZs and the high seas where very little bottom trawling is conducted. Of those RFMOs affected by this activity it is relatively clear that proscriptive measures are being implemented and these proscriptions can be made to apply to both the vessels of contracting or participating States and flag of convenience vessels operating in the vicinity.

For instance, the South Pacific Regional Fisheries Management Organisation (SPRFMO),[224] introduced interim measures to prohibit bottom trawling activities in the particularly vulnerable central southern Pacific high seas.[225] These measures, whilst voluntary in application pending full incorporation of the RFMO, include obligations upon States to identify areas of vulnerable marine ecosystems[226] – which are so defined as to include "seamounts, hydrothermal vents, cold water corals and sponge fields"[227] – and to prohibit participant State flagged vessels from engaging in bottom trawling within at least 5 miles of all known vulnerable marine ecosystems, unless it can be ascertained that bottom trawling activities will not have adverse impacts upon that area, or that any fishing activity will be conducted in a manner so as not to cause such impacts.[228]

In order for these measures to have any impact upon flag of convenience vessels, it is necessary, of course, for them to work in tandem with measures such as the aforementioned negative list/positive list prohibitions upon participant States assisting, directly or otherwise, in the landings, transhipment, refuelling or re-supplying of the foreign flagged vessels. As of April 2011 no such explicit negative list/positive list measures exist within the context of the SPRFMO, for reasons best explained by that particular body's recent inception. The SPRFMO Convention does, however, anticipate and warrant the use of positive/negative list procedures and does authorise market denial for

223 Willock and Lack, p. 9.

224 The SPRFMO has yet to become fully operation as of September 2008 and is still in the process of establishment.

225 SPRFMO, Interim Measures, May 2007. For text see: http://www.southpacificrfmo.org/assets/Third%20International%20Meeting/SPRFMO%20Interim%20Measures_Final.doc (herein after "SPRMO Interim Measures").

226 SPRFMO Interim Measures, *Management of Bottom Fishing*, Article 5.

227 SPRFMO Interim Measures, *Management of Bottom Fishing*, Footnote 3.

228 SPRFMO Interim Measures, *Management of Bottom Fisheries*, Articles 6 and 7.

both vessels and States whose activities undermine SPRFMO conservation and management measures.[229]

Perhaps cognisant of the flaws in stand-alone port State measures, explored below, the SPRMFO Convention also allows for further trade related measures to be introduced through the establishment of "appropriate market-related measures to monitor trans-shipments, landings and trade to prevent, deter and eliminate IUU fishing."[230] These measures may include the instigation of a catch documentation scheme (CDS) similar to the sort currently operated by CCAMLR and one of the main aims behind any CDS is, as SPRFMO Article 27 notes, to monitor and control the entire fishery from catch to market. This is largely because port State measures, whilst clearly helpful in assisting in the fight against IUU/FOC fisheries, have one fatal flaw, or weak link[231] – which can be exploited by irresponsible fishing entities – ports of convenience.

To highlight this problem let us briefly take stock of the various RFMO measures available so as to ascertain the "best case scenario". Assuming that the RFMO has competence to manage the marine environment, it can either adopt a negative list of vessels with which participant States are prohibited from trading, or a positive list of vessels with which participant States are authorised to trade. Again, provided that the RFMO's rules so allow, participating States should adopt port measures to deny landings etc to negative listed/non-positive listed vessels, and these prohibitions may be provisionally justified by a presumption that the vessel is either undermining the RFMO's own allocation rights or, in certain circumstances, undermining measures aimed at environmental protection. At this point in time the alleged IUU vessel cannot land or tranship its catch, refuel or take on board supplies from any State that is party to or co-operating with the RFMO's regulatory instruments. Thus it will attempt to find a port of convenience.

5.5.3 *How Certain Regional Measures can be Undermined by Ports of Convenience*

Ports of convenience operate in much the same manner as flags of convenience in that they provide a regulatory free haven for the unloading and transhipment of catches,[232] and, in the context of RFMOs, as noted by Fabra *et al.*, "...a

[229] SPRFMO Convention, Article 27(2).

[230] SPRFMO Convention, Article 27(1)(d).

[231] EJF: Party to the Plunder, at p. 9.

[232] Erik Jaap Molenaar, *Port State Jurisdiction: Towards Mandatory and Comprehensive Use*, in Freestone, Barnes and Ong, at p. 193, (herein after "Molenaar") in which Molenaar notes the incentives for operators to become of ports of convenience. The incentives noted by Molenaar are remarkably similar to those incentives of the flag of convenience industry as noted in Chapter Two. They may be a fiscal nature for the port (in terms of the payment of port fees

coastal State can become an important port for the landings of fish species managed by an RFMO to which the State is not a member…"[233] Simply stated, all that the owner of any vessel (including any transhipment vessel servicing the IUU/FOC fishing boat), denied port facilities by States pursuant to obligations imposed under RFMO prohibitions must do to take advantage of port facilities, is to find a port unbound by these RFMO measures. At this point the vessel may refuel and re-supply and land its catch. The catch now has the potential to enter international trade through the back door, so to speak, as the prohibitions on landings apply to first landings by vessels and not any subsequent imports from States and more often than not the shipment simply vanishes, mixed into the legitimate harvest.

If no geographically convenient port of convenience proper (that is, a purely unregulated port) exists for the IUU/FOC vessel, practice shows that this should pose no problem due to the failure of many 'regulated' ports to implement any obligations under international law. One such 'port of non-enforcement' has historically been Las Palmas de Gran Canaria in the Canary Islands, which has recently played hospitable host by providing landing, refuelling and re-supply services to numerous well known IUU vessels and as such has played a significant part in the route into the lucrative European market for all manner of IUU fish.[234] To compound this Las Palmas, being part of the Kingdom of Spain, is in fact regulated by several international agreements on the conservation of the marine environment which put into place port State controls.[235] That being the case it is therefore questionable as to how the unlawful catches managed to evade the scrutiny of customs officials, supposedly implementing these obligations. The EJF Report, unfortunately, does not provide an answer to this question, but it is widely accepted elsewhere that the failure of port States to properly implement any controls on IUU landings comes down to two key factors: a lack of capacity and a lack of willingness due to the high financial gains to be had by those operating ports of convenience.[236] And even if no

---

and the use of port services) and advantageous to the vessel because internationally agreed standards are simply not enforced. See also, Communication From the Commission of the European Communities, *Community Action Plan for the Eradication of Illegal, Unreported and Unregulated Fishing*, COM(2002) 180 Final, at paragraph 4.4.

233 Adriana Fabra, Virginia Gascón and Rodolfo Werner, *The Use of Port State Measures to Improve Fisheries Compliance*, National Environment Trust Paper, November 2006, available at: http://www.illegal-fishing.info/item_single.php?item=document&item_id=154&approach_id=13.

234 EJF: Party to the Plunder, at pp. 9–10.

235 Spain is party to UNCLOS, UNFSA and through its membership of the EU it is party to the FAO Compliance Agreement, as well as numerous RFMOs, such as ICCAT.

236 Judith Swan, *Port State Control: International Developments*, Paper prepared for UNFAO/FFA Regional Workshop to Promote the Full and Effective Implementation of Port State Measures to Combat IUU Fishing, Fiji, August/September 2006, at p. 3 (herein after "Swan (2006)");

geographically contiguous port of convenience can be readily found by the IUU/FOC vessel operator, this too does not pose a significant problem as evidence shows that ports thousands of miles from the area of harvest can attract the operators of IUU vessels to launder their unregulated catches.[237]

The problem of ports of convenience, whilst difficult to quantify in terms of their impact on the fisheries sector, should not be underestimated as a continuing challenge for the conservation and management of fish stocks and associated environmental harms. If parallels are drawn between the way that the flag of convenience fishing industry evolved from the flag of convenience fleet of merchant vessels, the fisheries port of convenience phenomenon could easily follow the current ports of convenience model as applied to the wider ocean going fleet. Reflecting much of the rhetoric of its earlier anti-flag of convenience campaign the International Transport Workers' Federation embarked, in 2006, upon a campaign against these ports.[238] Scrutinising many of the ITF's objections, it is easy to see the parallels between the ports of convenience and flags of convenience as the factors currently driving the general port of convenience sector are those which historically drove the flag of convenience industry. Indeed the ITF deliberately draws attention to the linkage between the two[239] and both, according to the ITF reflect "a general lowering of standards for commercial gain."[240] Given these parallels it is perhaps not too fanciful to suggest that port authorities currently turning a blind eye to breaches of, or choosing to remain unhindered by, international norms regarding human welfare and safety standards, should not be too concerned about the impacts of their ports on marine conservation.

Cognisant of this the UNFAO has reacted swiftly by drafting, initially, guidelines as to the best practice to be adopted by port States involved in the fisheries sector[241] and later promulgating its not-yet-in-force 2009 Agreement on Port State Measures to Prevent, Deter and Eliminate Illegal, Unreported

---

David J. Doulman, *Role of the Port State in Combating IUU Fishing and Promoting Long-Term Sustainability in Fisheries*, also prepared for UNFAO/FFA Regional Workshop, at p. 3 (herein after "Doulman"). Both available at ftp://ftp. fao.org/FI/DOCUMENT/tc-psm/Reg_Workshop_2006/Default.htm.

237 Willock and Lack, at p. 28, in which the authors note that despite the relatively stringent trade related measures adopted by ICCAT in respect of Atlantic caught bigeye tuna, IUU vessels simply decamp to the Pacific and Indian Oceans to launder their catches in less well policed ports.

238 International Transport Workers' Federation, 41st Congress, Durban, August 2006.

239 *TI Briefing: The Ports of Convenience*, Transport International Magazine, Issue 25, October 2006, at p. 25 (herein after "ITF: Ports of Convenience").

240 ITF: Ports of Convenience, at p. 25.

241 UNFAO Model Scheme on Port State Measures to Combat Illegal, Unreported and Unregulated Fishing, Rome, 2007 (herein after "UNFAO Port State Measures").

and Unregulated Fishing.[242] The first thing to be noted about the UNFAO Port State Measures and the Agreement is that, in a manner consistent with the many RFMO positive list models referred to earlier in this Chapter, both require that port States effectively withdraw all port[243] facilities to IUU vessels.[244] The precise designation of IUU vessels does vary between the Measures and the Agreement but, in essence, the principle remains the same. For instance, under the Port State Measures vessels which are not flagged to RFMO participant States will be denied access to port facilities – except in cases of *force majeure*[245] – unless the vessel operator can establish that the catch was taken in a manner consistent with the relevant regional conservation and management regulations.[246] Likewise, and reflecting the various negative lists adopted by RFMOs, ports States should deny access to port facilities to fishing vessels when there is evidence that it has engaged in IUU activity.[247] Even when no such evidence exists and vessels are flagged to RFMO-participating States, the Port

---

[242] Under Article 29 of the Agreement it shall come into force 30 days after the deposit of the 24th instrument of ratification, acceptance, approval or accession. At the time of writing, May 2011 (several months after the November 2010 date of closure of the Agreement) only 23 States had signed it (none of which have lodged their documents of ratification, acceptance or approval), with only a further 2 States having acceded to it.

[243] The term "ports" as used throughout the Port State Measures and the Port State Agreement also includes "off-shore terminals and other installations", UNFAO Port State Measures, Article 1.1; Port State Agreement, Article 1(g).

[244] The Measures also apply to transport and supply vessels as well as the obvious direct fishing vessels, UNFAO Port State Measures, Article 1.2. Under the Port State Agreement the vessels covered are those that are used for, in intended to be used for fishing and related activities and equipped to so do, Port State Agreement, Article 1(j).

[245] UNFAO Port State Measures, Article 9; Port State Agreement, Article 10. This caveat is replicated in the measures adopted by a variety of RFMOs which have adopted port State controls.

[246] UNFAO Port State Measures, Article 2.5. It should be noted that deference is given to RFMOs, by the UNFAO Port State Measures, to set their own conservation and management regulations and no minimum requirements are enunciated by the Measures themselves. Under the Port State Regulations, taken in the context of the Code of Conduct, of which the Port State Measures form a part, it is to be assumed that any regional regulations should be consistent with the Code.

[247] UNFAO Port State Measures, Articles 2.5, 2.6 and 2.7. Lobach points out, however, the difference between the measures to be invoked under Article 2.5 (non-participant State vessels engaged in IUU activities in RFMO waters), Article 2.6 (all IUU activity beyond areas of RFMO competence) and Article 2.7 (negative listed or non-positive listed vessels). Under Articles 2.5 and 2.7 ports States may only deny landing and transhipment facilities, whereas under Article 2.6 allows for the denial of all port facilities, such as landing and transhipping catches and refuelling and re-supply. Lobach does concede that this may simply be a case of inconsistent drafting as there appears to be no explicit justification for applying these different standards. Terje Lobach, *Port State Measures to Combat IUU Fishing: The FAO Model Scheme on Port State Measures*, Paper prepared for FOA/FFA Regional Worksop, at p. 3 (herein after

State Measures require numerous actions to be undertaken to ensure that IUU catches are not landed and include the obligation that port States should require advanced notice prior to entering any port,[248] and that only certain designated, competent ports should provide facilities for foreign flagged vessels.[249] Once in port any vessel may be subject to inspection so as to ascertain the nature of the fishing and its compliance with any authorisation under the relevant RFMO conservation and management measures.[250] Any infractions unearthed by these non-discriminatory inspections should, at first instance, be reported to the flag State of the vessel concerned as well as the appropriate RFMO. Only following an inadequate response from the flag State of the vessel may the port State deny the vessel the opportunity to land or tranship its cargo.[251] The adequacy of the measures expected of the flag State are, unfortunately for clarity, not specified under the terms of the UNFAO Measures themselves, but it is to be presumed that the flag State response should be consistent with the requirements of relevant instruments such as UNFSA and the Compliance Agreement and be commensurate and proportionate with the infraction alleged.

Broadly similar to the principle enunciated in the Measures, the Port State Agreement empowers port States to decide, based on information received, if any vessel requesting access to one of its designated ports[252] falls into the category of an IUU vessel.[253]Even when a State has identified the vessel as being engaged in IUU activity the Agreement does not necessarily oblige them to deny the vessel access to ports or port facilities[254] and it is only in cases of 'known offenders' when States are required to close off their facilities.[255] When in port the port State may still deny facilities to the vessel if it transpires that the vessel is fishing without or beyond the terms of its licence or authorisation.[256] As is the case with the Port State Measures, under the Agreement all vessels may be subject to port State inspections, provided that the decision to inspect a vessel in port, and

"Lobach"). Available at ftp://ftp. fao.org/FI/DOCUMENT/tc-psm/Reg_Workshop_2006/ Default.htm.

248 UNFAO Port State Measures, Article 2.4.

249 UNFAO Port State Measures, Article 2.3.

250 UNFAO Port State Measures, Article 3.

251 UNFAO Port State Measures, Article 4.5.

252 Like the Port State Measures, the Port State Agreement requires States to designate ports that are open to foreign-flagged vessels.

253 Port State Agreement, Articles 8 and 9(1).

254 Port State Agreement, Article 9(1).

255 Port State Agreement, Article 9(4). Under Article 9(5) States may permit known IUU vessels entry into ports (but deny it port facilities) in order to carry out an inspection of the vessel.

256 Port State Agreement, Article 11(1).

the physical inspection itself, is conducted in an Agreement-compliant manner.[257] Following any inspection that has revealed evidence of IUU activity, port States should notify any relevant States and international organisations and bar the vessel from the use of all port facilities other than those which pertain to the health and safety of the crew or vessel.[258]

Although the vast majority of the principles enshrined in the Port State Agreement are, quite naturally, aimed at port States, the Agreement does extend its provisions to cover State parties that are also flag States. In this regard flag States should ensure that their vessels co-operate with port States and use only ports of States that act in accordance with the Agreement.[259] In cases of known or suspected IUU activity on behalf of its vessels, flag States should, where possible, request port States to carry out inspections of the vessel[260] and, conversely, when port States inspections (undertaken not at the behest of the flag State, but when the vessel voluntarily enters the port) reveal the existence of clear grounds to believe that the vessel has engaged in IUU activity, flag States are obliged to take enforcement action and report these actions to the relevant States and organisations.[261]

Whilst the UNFAO Port State Measures (if properly implemented) and the Port State Agreement (if it comes into force and is properly and widely implemented) should ensure that port States properly carry out their obligations under UNFSA and ensure that ports such as Las Palmas de Gran Canaria cease to act as convenient ports due to the laxness of the procedures implemented, the Measures and Agreement should not be seen as a panacea. Remaining untroubled by troublesome standards imposed are those port States which are not party to the Agreement or any regional agreements which oblige port State inspections of fishing vessels. These genuine ports of convenience, or to borrow the phraseology of the flag of convenience industry, ports of non-compliance,

[257] Part 4 of the Agreement dictates when and how and inspection should be undertaken, and, in Article 12(3) lists the factors to be considered by a port State when decided whether or not to inspect a vessel. These factors include any evidence of actual or suspected wrongdoing on the vessel's part (as evidenced by any previous refusal to grant port facilities or when there are clear grounds for suspecting IUU activity), or when a port State is requested to inspect by another State or RFMO. In terms of the 'how', Article 13 provides some guidance, which includes the requirements that, *inter alia*, the inspection are carried out by competent and identified persons, that the inspections are sufficiently thorough so as to verify compliance the relevant conservation and management measures but not overly burdensome so as to unduly delay, harass or discriminate against vessels.

[258] Port State Agreement, Article 18. The 'relevant' States are the vessel's flag State, relevant coastal States and the master of the vessel's State of nationality.

[259] Port State Agreement, Article 20(1)(3).

[260] Port State Agreement, Article 20(2).

[261] Port State Agreement, Article 20(4). The relevant States and organisations are Parties to the Agreement, relevant port States, RFMOs and the FAO.

remain entirely unregulated by international standards and, as a consequence, provide the critical point of entry for IUU products into the international market place.

As noted earlier in this Chapter this is precisely the problem that landings-based measures must confront and in so doing forward-looking RFMOs have reacted by implementing "catch to marketplace" documentation schemes so as to close this loophole, and one possible template to follow would be based upon the hitherto successful model utilised by CCAMLR for a number of years. Prior to this, however, it is perhaps worth noting in slightly greater detail what might at first glance be obvious – that by denying a market place to the IUU fisheries industry, this industry cannot continue.

5.6 *Market Related Deterrents to IUU/FOC Activities*

The principle of denial is well established in tackling IUU operations and has a proven track record in combating States and individuals engaged in IUU activities. As noted earlier in Chapter One, the denial of trading rights by RFMOs such as ICCAT to Belize in the late 1990s was instrumental in ensuring that that State attempted to bring in measures to purge its vessel registry of IUU fishing boats. Likewise, as noted by Stokke and Vidas, numerous examples of the strategy of denial can be demonstrated in the IUU/FOC context which show that simply denying IUU vessels the means to or rewards for going about their activities can ensure that those activities are made as difficult as possible, and if sufficient denial is exercised, ensure that the activities cease.[262] The term "sufficient denial" therefore is key: as Stokke and Vidas further note – "[t]he effectiveness of the denial strategy is obviously enhanced if the number of deniers, or more accurately their share of the object desired by the IUU operators, is high."[263] Denying a large market to IUU/FOC operators therefore could present a fatal blow to their ability to continue their operations, because whilst it might appear obvious, it is worth repeating that IUU/FOC fishing is conducted for the single purpose of money-making. Without a return on the investment in vessel, crew, fuel, bait, etc. there is no incentive for vessel owners to continue with IUU activities,[264] because, as one recent OECD report

[262] Olav Schram Stokke and Davor Vidas, *Regulating IUU Fishing or Combating IUU Operations?*, in *Fish Piracy: Combating Illegal, Unreported and Unregulated Fishing*, OECD, Paris, 2004, at pp. 31–34, (herein after "Stokke and Vidas"). The examples cited by Stokke and Vidas include landing rights, port State facilities, crews, fuel, etc.

[263] Stokke and Vidas, at p. 35.

[264] Agnew and Barnes, at p. 182, who define the incentive in the simplest of equations: "IUU incentive ~ Profit from IUU fishing = Benefit from IUU fishing – Cost of IUU fishing".

surmises: "the bottom line is clear; fish pirates pursue their activities because it is profitable, and will keep pursuing it as long as their revenue exceeds their costs,"[265] and that "[u]nder present conditions IUU fishing is a profitable undertaking, and hence the first step in combating such activities is to identify measures that render them unprofitable."[266] Similarly, in its Report of August 2005 the UNGA/Secretary General noted in equally clear language that "the most effective means of eliminating IUU fishing is to focus on ways to deny the owners and operators of IUU fishing vessels any financial reward... [T]he implementation of internationally agreed market measures that would prevent or at least make the sale of such fish more difficult should decrease the expected financial returns from IUU fishing, leading to its reduction."[267] These assertions do, however, rest on the assumption that IUU/FOC vessels rely upon international, as opposed to domestic markets, for their profits. Clearly market-related measures would not provide a solution if IUU catches did not enter the international market place, or were simply traded between non-RFMO members. Thus, prior to stating in absolute terms that measures would deny a sufficiently large portion of the market to IUU/FOC operators it is first essential to ascertain what the market for IUU/FOC catches actually is.

As will be recalled from Chapter Three, ascertaining the incidence of IUU/FOC, due to its inherently unreported and unmonitored nature, is no easy task. Consequently analysing the precise movements of IUU/FOC fish and fisheries products within the market place may present an even greater challenge – in fact, according to one report there is no reliable data on the overall international trade in IUU/FOC fish and fish products.[268] In relation to certain stocks – those generally attracting higher prices (and thus presenting more of an incentive to IUU/FOC vessel owners)[269] – a little more information is available. As noted in Chapter Three, the estimated incidence of IUU/FOC capture of species such as

Thus, if "Benefit" is less than "Cost" then "Incentive - Profit" becomes a negative value. If this negative value is consistent over a period of time and with no possibility of future profit then the simplest of economics dictates that the entity engaged in that activity will cease to be viable. And whilst Agnew and Barnes also point to certain social drivers of IUU fishing, it is contended here that whilst these factors are of relevance they are, in effect, merely aspects of the overall incentive of money making.

265 *The Economics of IUU Fishing*, at p. 13.

266 *The Economics of IUU Fishing*, at pp. 21–22.

267 United Nations General Assembly Report, *Sustainable Fisheries*, A/60/189, 2nd August 2005.

268 *Implementation of the International Plan of Action to Prevent, Deter and Eliminate Illegal, Unreported and Unregulated Fishing*, FAO Technical Guidelines for Responsible Fisheries. No. 9. Rome, FAO. 2002, at p. 47 (herein after "FAO Technical Guidelines No. 9").

269 FAO Technical Guidelines No. 9, at p. 47, acknowledges this stating that "a number of the fish species that figure most prominently in international trade, including tunas and swordfish, are also species known to be targeted by IUU fishers."

Patagonian toothfish,[270] bigeye tuna,[271] Southern bluefin tuna,[272] Indian Ocean species,[273] and redfish is vast.[274] Information on the international trade in IUU/FOC fisheries is, however, only available for redfish and toothfish, and it is estimated that 20% of the redfish currently traded internationally has been harvested in contravention of regional norms.[275] Projecting this information to all high value stocks would mean that an approximate working figure of 80% of IUU/FOC harvests end up in the international market place.[276] In other words IUU fishing activities may account for 18 000 tonnes of toothfish,[277] 20 000 tonnes of bigeye tuna, 3000 tonnes of Southern bluefin tuna, 20 000 tonnes of redfish, and a staggering 100 000 tonnes of Indian Ocean species of tuna. In terms of cost this level of trade is far from insignificant. For instance, Willock notes that wildlife smuggling (all species) is estimated to be worth between US$6 billion and US$10 billion per annum, and that fisheries account for around 25% of the total value of wildlife products in world trade.[278] Extrapolating these figures would show that the illegal trade in fisheries products could amount to between US$1.5 billion and US$2.5 billion per annum – a figure which is not that surprising when it is considered that many of the high value stocks targeted by IUU fishers achieve prices in excess of US$7 per kilo for

[270] It will be recalled from Chapter Three that estimates of IUU/FOC toothfish capture within the CCAMLR region range from 25% to 50% to 80% of the total harvest. The toothfish problem is exacerbated by a significant tonnage being harvested by IUU/FOC vessels beyond the CCAMLR zone, *The Economics of IUU Fishing*, at p. 132.

[271] In the ICCAT region estimated to be 10% of the overall catches, *The Economics of IUU Fishing*, at p. 128.

[272] In the region falling under the control of the CCSBT, IUU catches account for 33% of the overall, *The Economics of IUU Fishing*, at p. 130.

[273] For species in the IOTC region such as yellowfin, skipjack, marlin and swordfish, IUU activities account for 10% of the overall, *The Economics of IUU Fishing*, at p. 131.

[274] In the NEAFC area IUU catches account for 25%, *The Economics of IUU Fishing*, at p. 134.

[275] *The Economics of IUU Fishing*, at p. 134.

[276] The methodology being that if IUU catches amount to 25% of the overall harvest and IUU trade amounts to 20% then 80% of IUU harvests are internationally traded. This figure of 80%, however, is perhaps conservative when considered against the estimated 90% of IUU toothfish which enters the international market, see Anna Willock, *Uncharted Waters: Implementation Issues and Potential Benefits of Listing Toothfish in Appendix II of CITES*, TRAFFIC International, Cambridge, 2002, at p. 3 (herein after "Willock (2002)").

[277] Combined CCAMLR and non-CCAMLR statistics. When arriving at this figure the lower estimate of 25% of all CCAMLR catches was used and clearly the figure of 18 000 tonnes could be at least doubled in the higher estimates were an accurate reflection of the actual IUU toothfish harvest.

[278] Willock (2004), at p. 67.

high grade bigeye tuna or swordfish,[279] or an enormous US$24 for toothfish.[280] Nevertheless, even the projected figure of US$2.5 billion may itself be a conservative one, as one recent report suggested this figure to be the minimum and that the global value of all IUU activities could be as high as US$9.5 billion,[281] thus if even only 80% of this figure were to enter into the international market place then the international trade in IUU fisheries could be as high as US$7.5 billion.

5.7 *Case Study: CCAMLR's Catch Documentation Scheme*

CCAMLR's Catch Documentation Scheme (CDS), although currently pertaining to toothfish (*Dissostichus*) species, is in many ways, similar to ICCAT's Positive list/Statistical Document Program in that it attempts to develop a chain of evidence from harvest to final import, and requires that all harvests of fish caught in the CCAMLR area of competence are accompanied by validated documentation.[282] But unlike the majority of positive list/negative list schemes the CDS's role does not end at the point when the catch is first landed. Instead the CDS regulates both imports,[283] exports,[284] and re-exports[285] as well as landings[286] and transhipments[287] by subjecting all movements of fish to a procedure whereby unless the transaction is accompanied by the relevant documentation

[279] Forum Fisheries Agency, *Tuna Markets Annual Review 2005*, 26th May 2006, Issue 69.

[280] Sumaila, U.R., Alder J. and Keith H., *Global Scope and Economics of Illegal Fishing*, Marine Policy 30 (2006) 696–703, at p. 700.

[281] *IUU Fishing on the High Seas: Impacts on Ecosystems and Future Scientific Needs*, Marine Resources Assessment Group / United Kingdom Department for International Development, MRAG, London, August 2005 (herein after "MRAG August 2005").

[282] CCAMLR Conservation Measure 10-05 (2009), *Catch Documentation Scheme for* Dissostichus *spp.*, (herein after "CCAMLR CDS Measure").

[283] Defined by CCAMLR CDS Measure, Article 1 (iv) as "[t]he physical entering or bringing of a catch into any part of the geographical territory under the control of a State..." other than for purposes of landing or transporting the catch.

[284] Defined by CCAMLR CDS Measure, Article 1 (iii) as "[a]ny movement of a catch in its harvested of processed form from territory under the control of the State or free trade zone of landing...".

[285] Defined by CCAMLR CDS Measure, Article 1(v) as "[a]ny movement of a catch in its harvested or processed form from territory under the control of a State" other than that of first export.

[286] Defined by CCAMLR CDS Measure, Article 1(ii) as "[t]he initial transfer of catch in its harvested or processed form from a vessel to dockside or to another vessel in a port or free trade zone where the catch is certified by an authority of the port State as landed".

[287] Defined by CCAMLR CDS Measure, Article 1(vi) as "[t]he transfer of a catch in its harvested or processed form from one vessel to another vessel or means of transport...for the purpose of effecting its removal from... [the port]... State".

(the *Dissostichus* Catch Document (DCD)), no trade shall be permitted. The DCD is initially issued by the flag State – both contracting CCAMLR parties[288] and co-operating non-contracting parties[289] – of the vessels authorised to fish for toothfish species and contains all the information necessary for the port State and State of import/export to accurately trace the catch back to the point of harvest. In common with the positive list procedures adopted by other RFMOs the DCD contains data pertaining to the issuing authority,[290] the vessel,[291] its authorisation to fish,[292] the actual fishery engaged in,[293] and the time, place and recipient of any transhipment or landing.[294]

As noted above, DCD forms must only be issued to vessels when those vessels are authorised to fish for toothfish species, and in this regard an element of deference is given by the CCAMLR CDS Measure to State sovereignty by allowing this authorisation to take place "in accordance with... [domestic]... laws and regulations."[295] A loophole in the original CDS system existed as to under what criteria authorisation to fish shall be granted, as this is nowhere stated in the CDS Measure itself. Fortunately this loophole was closed in 2006 by CCAMLR Conservation Measure 10-02, which builds upon the rather vaguely worded obligations found under Article XXI of the CCAMLR Convention which requires contracting parties to ensure compliance with the CCAMLR Convention and any measures adopted pursuant to it. Conservation Measure 10-02 thus acts as the basis under which authorisation to fish in the CCAMLR region is to be granted, and also acts as CCAMLR's positive vessel list. To grant the necessary authorisation to fish in CCAMLR area contracting flag States must be "satisfied of its ability to exercise its responsibilities under the Convention and its conservation measures,"[296] and whenever a licence is granted the

[288] CCAMLR CDS Measure, Article 5.

[289] CCAMLR CDS Measure, Article 6.

[290] CCAMLR CDS Measure, Article 8(i).

[291] CCAMLR CDS Measure, Article 8(ii). This information shall include the vessel's name, home port, national registry number and cal sign, and any IMO/Lloyd's registration number.

[292] CCAMLR CDS Measure, Article 8(iii).

[293] CCAMLR CDS Measure, Article 8(iv)(v) – i.e. the weight of each species caught and where and when the catch took place.

[294] CCAMLR CDS Measure, Article 8(vi)(vii).

[295] CCAMLR CDS Measure, Article 5.

[296] CCAMLR Conservation Measure 10-02 (2006) (Rev 2010), *Licensing and Inspection Obligations of Contracting Parties with Regard to their Flag Vessels Operating in the Convention Area*, Article 2, (herein after "CM 10-02"). Numerous sub-criteria are listed under Article 2, relating to the manner in which State responsibility must be exercised, these include the requirement that the flag State can monitor the whereabouts of the vessel, reporting of catch data, and the use of Vessel Monitoring Systems. Furthermore Article 9 requires flag States to undertake periodic inspections of vessels to ensure compliance with the authorisation to fish and CCAMLR conservation measures.

flag State must promptly inform the CCAMLR Secretariat[297] who will then publish the list of authorised vessels on the CCAMLR website.[298]

Similar to the manner in which other RFMO positive lists operate, the presumption under CCAMLR Conservation Measure 10-07[299] is that of non-compliance by non-contracting party vessels.[300] This presumption is partially rebutted only when, following a port State inspection by a contracting party, it is ascertained that the harvest of toothfish species was not carried out in a manner so as to undermine CCAMLR conservation measures. If the vessel can show, to the satisfaction of the port authorities, that no conservation measures have been undermined it will be allowed to land or tranship its cargo.[301] If, on the other hand, the port authorities take the view that the vessel has undermined conservation measures then the negative-listing procedure of that vessel will begin.[302] For all those vessels not entered in to the CCAMLR negative list, however, the harvest of toothfish species may continue, and in many cases participation with the CDS permitted. The precise criteria under which vessels flagged to non-contracting parties are permitted to join with the CDS, and crucially have their catches entered into the international market-place, are enunciated in Annex C of the CCAMLR CDS measure.[303] It should be noted, however, that this procedure is for States and not individual vessels and so it is for the flag States of vessels engaged in fishing activity in the CCAMLR area to demonstrate that it can implement the provisions of the CDS Measure. In so doing it would appear that the same conservation standards and authorisation requirements as are applicable to contracting parties should also apply in this situation. Thus, when the non-contracting State cannot fulfil its obligations in a manner equivalent to those imposed upon contracting parties under Conservation Measure 10-02, then no authorisation to join with the CDS scheme will be granted.

---

297 CM 10-02, Article 3.

298 CM 10-02, Article 6.

299 CCAMLR Conservation Measure 10-07 (2009), *Scheme to Promote Compliance by Non-Contracting Party Vessels with CCAMLR Conservation Measures*, (herein after "CM 10-07").

300 CM 10-07, Article 4.

301 CM 10-07, Article 5.

302 CM 10-07, Article 6. The negative list utilised by CCAMLR differs to no meaningful extent in this regard to that of the majority of RFMO IUU vessel list, and so a full analysis of this procedure is perhaps unwarranted at this point.

303 *Procedure Regarding Co-operation with CCAMLR in the Implementation of the CDS by Non-Contracting Parties Involved in the Trade of* Dissostichus *spp.*

5.7.1 *Practical Considerations of the CDS*

To ascertain the veracity of the information provided by the master of the vessel on the DCD, the scheme is now making use of electronic vessel positioning data provided by systems such as vessel monitoring systems (VMS)[304] and port side inspections of the types of gear used. With regard to the former, VMS technology, it is worth noting that although this particular method of verifying vessel movements is not without problems due to the fact that VMS 'black-boxes' can be tampered with,[305] only in certain circumstances can port side inspections operate in such a way as to reduce this danger. This is because when the suspected IUU fishing is that of fishing without or beyond authorisation it is essential that port authorities know exactly where the fishing activity took place – for instance it may be alleged that the vessel took catches from a prohibited area within the CCAMLR area of jurisdiction, but, having tampered with the VMS system the master of the vessel may refute this charge and escape sanction. Similarly port inspections may prove inadequate where the vessel's authorisation to fish may permit the use of gear in certain areas but not others. For instance CCAMLR regularly closes off certain grounds to high seas bottom trawling but does not prohibit the use of bottom trawling gear. Thus port side inspections can easily identify the gear used as being potentially in violation of CCAMLR Conservation Measures but cannot prove that the gear was used in a prohibited area if the VMS system has been tampered with. When the suspected infraction pertains not to the nature of the target fishery but the use of unlawful gear such as longlines without seabird mortality mitigation devices, or purse seines without dolphin or turtle mortality mitigation devices then this infraction would become obvious by even the most cursory port side inspection. Nevertheless, it may still be an option for the master of the vessel to state that the fishery occurred outside the waters of CCAMLR's jurisdiction, and again fraudulent VMS data may support this assertion.[306]

304 CCAMLR Resolution 16/XIX, *Application of VMS in the Catch Documentation Scheme.*

305 In the well reported case of the *Viarsa*, there was absolutely no synergy between the actual location of the vessels at the time it was apprehended by the Australian authorities and that indicated to the Uruguayan flag State authorities 'tracking' it by VMS. See Rachel Baird, *CCAMLR Initiatives to Counter Flag State Non-Enforcement in Southern Ocean Fisheries*, Victoria University of Wellington Law Review, December 2005, 36 VUWLR 733 (2005), at p. 748.

306 Indeed this method of escaping the reaches of the CDS is currently the preferred option of the IUU vessel, with many catches being claimed to have been caught in UNFAO Statistical Area 51, beyond the area of CCAMLR's competence, see further Rachel J Baird, *Aspects of Illegal, Unregulated and Unreported Fishing in the Southern Ocean*, Springer Publishing, The Netherlands, 2006, at pp. 167–168 (herein after "Baird (2006)"). The vessels owners' claims are almost certainly incongruous due to the fact that no meaningful research has supported the claims that toothfish species are to be found in this particular ocean region – see Scientific

Likewise, there is the problem of at-sea transhipments to reefers, because whilst the CDS operates in such a way as to prohibit transhipments without a completed DCD, it is impossible for the master of the reefer to be able to ascertain that the catch that is being transhipped has been caught in an authorised manner and that the information supplied on the DCD is accurate.

To address these problems CCAMLR has taken a number of steps to build upon the CDS and to close the evidential loopholes left by the traditional 'paper' CDS. Chief of these reforms to the CDS is the recent introduction of the C-VMS[307] and E-CDS. The C-VMS operates in a manner similar to the 'ordinary' VMS system, that is, it allows remote viewing of the vessel's position by a satellite tracking device, but rather than the data being transmitted to just the flag State of the vessel (with all the inherent problems of flag State ambivalence or lack of resources which has lead to abuse of the system), under the C-VMS system the positioning data is also transmitted in real time to the CCAMLR Secretariat.[308] In a similar fashion to the VMS the CDS has also benefited from an electronic make-over. The 'real time' electronic E-CDS[309] was successfully piloted between 2003 and 2004 and so the latest incarnation of the CDS requires that all catch documents are completed and transmitted electronically.[310]

A further problem with the CDS, and one that has taken up a great deal of the CCAMLR Commission's time and effort is its jurisdictional scope. Clearly, as with any port or market based measure it is susceptible to States inadvertently or deliberately undermining its provisions, and although some of the problems of the CDS in this regard may be mitigated because of the manner in which it applies to all States of final import (most of which are CCAMLR participants), it has become obvious to the Commission that certain ports were being used to launder toothfish catches and thus enter international trade. This occurred for two main reasons: firstly certain CCAMLR member States were not applying the CDS sufficiently rigorously, and secondly non-contracting parties were acting as a haven for unregulated landings. To address the former problem the Commission reminded States of their obligations to promote the efficacy of the

Committee for the Conservation of Antarctic Marine Living Resources, *Report of the Twentieth Meeting of the Scientific Committee*, Hobart, Australia, October 2001 (SC-CCAMLR XX), at paras. 2.10–2.15.

[307] 'Centralised Vessel Monitoring System'.

[308] CCAMLR Conservation Measure 10-04 (2010), Article 10.

[309] A technical evaluation of the workings of the E-CDS is, of course, beyond the scope of this study, but suffice to note that the E-CDS is an internet-based, real time data submission program, specifically designed for CCAMLR which utilises a 128–bit secure socket layer (SSL) encryption so as to reduce the risk of security breaches, see Report of the Standing Committee on Implementation and Compliance (SCIC), CCAMLR 22nd Annual Meeting, 2003.

[310] CCAMLR CDS Measure, Article 5.

CDS and as such urged all CCAMLR participant States to ensure that when granting licences to vessels intending to fish for toothfish species in the CCAMLR region, that "as a condition of that licence, that the vessel should land catches only in States that are fully implementing the CDS..."[311] Similarly, the problem of non-contracting parties undermining the provisions of the CDS are dealt with, after a fashion, by urging all non-contracting parties not participating in the CDS to do so.[312] To exert the necessary pressure on certain identified non-contracting parties, CCAMLR Commission members were requested to "make appropriate representations..." to those States not implementing the CDS.[313] Two key States identified in this process were Namibia and Mauritius, both of which had allowed their ports (Walvis Bay and Port Louis, respectively) to be used for the laundering of tens of thousands of tonnes of toothfish at the turn of the millennium. By 2004, however, sufficient diplomatic pressure had been exerted by CCAMLR Commission members so that both States had agreed to implement the CDS in an appropriate manner.[314]

5.7.2 *The CDS and Environmental Harms*

Even with the above noted glitches, the CCAMLR CDS has had an enormous impact on IUU activity in the southern oceans, because although IUU fishing still continues in the CCAMLR area, the reduction in terms of landed tonnage is dramatic in the post CDS era – falling from an estimated IUU annual landing of 68,000 tonnes in 1997 to a mere 8,000 tonnes at the turn of the millennium[315] to a figure of approximately 3,000 tonnes in 2006,[316] to a figure of 1700 tonnes in 2010.[317] Clearly then, on the basis of these figures, the CDS works to control the IUU fishing of target toothfish species. Whether this reduction in target species poaching correlates to a decline in the incidence of by-catch, non-target mortality and the destruction of the seabed, does require

---

[311] CCAMLR Resolution 15/XXII, *Use of Ports Not Implementing the Catch Documentation Scheme for* Dissostichus *spp.*

[312] CCAMLR Resolution 14/XIX, *Catch Documentation Scheme: Implementation by Acceding States and Non-Contracting Parties*, Article 1.

[313] *Ibid.*, Article 3.

[314] Baird (2006), at pp. 164–165.

[315] The Economics of IUU Fishing, at p. 132.

[316] Report of the 25th Meeting of the CCAMLR Commission, Hobart, November 2006, at paragraph 9.1.

[317] Report of the 29th Meeting of the CCAMLR Scientific Committee, Hobart. October 2010, at paragraph 6.1. It should be noted, however, that while the figure of 1700 tonnes is a mere fraction of the pre-CDS era there has been a slight rise in IUU incidence between 2008/09 and 2010/11. According to the Scientific Committee much of this rise might be explained by a handful of vessels engaged in illegal gillnet fishing in CCAMLR waters.

further investigation. Prior to this investigation it is worth noting the environmental mandate under which CCAMLR works.

It will be recalled from earlier in this Chapter that CCAMLR has both an environmental mandate which includes "the rational use of all marine living resources" and the managerial capacity to put measures into effect to carry out this mandate.[318] These measures include, *inter alia*, a prohibition on certain bottom trawling activities,[319] the conservation of sharks,[320] and various instruments to guard against the incidental mortality of seabirds and marine mammals.[321] For these measures to have any real bite against IUU/FOC activities, however, it is essential that these environmental measures work in tandem with the CDS, and whether or not this is the case in relation to each Conservation Measure depends entirely upon the content of each measure and its ability to interact with the CDS. Thus, we shall now consider each of the above noted environmental measures individually to analyse precisely whether or not a breach of the obligations imposed under their provisions constitutes the necessary "undermining of CCAMLR conservation measures" so as to prevent any non-contracting party vessel from taking advantage of market access through the use of the CDS. This is particularly important in the context of CCAMLR, of course, due to the fact that any presumption of wrong-doing by non-contracting party vessels may be rebutted by evidence that no conservation measures are being undermined, and that non-contracting party vessels are not barred from the CDS automatically as a matter of course.

The first thing to be noted about the CCAMLR Conservation Measures relating to the incidental mortality of seabirds is that they do not prohibit the use of longlines. Instead fisheries are subject to procedures whereby any harmful effects should be reduced and governed by numerous Conservation Measures, the majority of which could be described as technical guidelines. For instance Conservation Measure 25-03 encourages vessels "to develop gear configurations that will minimise the chance of seabirds encountering the parts of the net to which they are most vulnerable"[322] and certain practices associated with trawl

[318] CCAMLR Convention, Article 1(2).

[319] CCAMLR Conservation Measure 22-05 (2008), *Interim Restrictions on the Use of Bottom Trawling Gear* (herein after "CM 22-05").

[320] CCAMLR Conservation Measure 32-18 (2006), *Conservation of Sharks* (herein after "CM 32-18").

[321] CCAMLR Conservation Measure 25-03 (2009), *Minimising Incidental Mortality of Seabirds and Marine Mammals in the Course of Trawl Fishing* (herein after "CM 25-03"); CCAMLR Conservation Measure 25-02 (2009), *Minimising Seabird Mortality* (herein after "CM 25-02"); CCAMLR Conservation 24-02 (2008), *Longline Weighting for Seabird Conservation* (herein after "CM 24-02").

[322] CM 25-03, Article 6.

fishing are subject to an outright prohibition.[323] Similarly Conservation Measure 25-02 provides the technical specifications for the use of longlines so as to mitigate against their harmful impacts upon seabird populations.[324] Likewise Conservation Measure 24-02 obliges vessel owners, prior to the granting of any fishing licence and annually thereafter, to fully satisfy an appointed scientific observer as to the sink rate of the longline so as to reduce the time when the lines pose a threat to seabirds.

In relation to high seas bottom trawling activities CCAMLR does not impose an absolute prohibition on all bottom trawling at all times, but instead subjects this activity to rigorous controls. Thus, as was noted in Chapter Three, CCAMLR Conservation Measure 22-06 (2010) permits vessels to engage in bottom trawling only when so authorised by the CCAMLR Commission[325] and authorisation will only be granted following a risk assessment as to the potential dangers posed by the trawling.[326] In certain geographical areas (CCAMLR statistical sub-area 48.3, for instance) bottom trawling is entirely prohibited.[327] A similar picture emerges in relation to sharks, by virtue of the prohibition on the direct taking of sharks in all CCAMLR waters imposed by Conservation Measure 32-18.[328]

Clearly then, because of the positive obligations created by the above noted Conservation Measures, CCAMLR does have the means to regulate or prohibit many of the deleterious consequences associated with target fisheries in its region of competence. Simply because many of the obligations imposed by the Measures are of a technical nature should not take anything away from the fact that, unlike many of the rhetorical measures adopted by other RFMOs in

---

323 CM 25-03, Article 1 prohibits the use of net monitor cables. For further on the manner in which these devices increase the incidence of seabird mortality in relation to trawl fishing, see Leigh S. Bull, *Reducing Seabird Bycatch in Longline, Trawl and Gillnet Fisheries*, Fish and Fisheries, Vol. 8, 2007, at pp. 44–45 (herein after "Bull"). Similarly, under Article 3 the discharge of offal is prohibited during the time that the trawl nets are shot or hauled. Again for an overview of the problems associated with this practice see Bull at p. 35.

324 The preamble to CM 25-02 makes it clear that the technical measures contained within are mandatory and must be applied by all vessels engaged in longlining activities in the CCAMLR region. Space precludes any in-depth analysis of these technical measures but suffice to say that CM 24-02 and its Appendix incorporate many of the best practices as enunciated by the UNFAO IPOA-Seabirds.

325 CCAMLR Conservation Measure 22-06 (2010), *Bottom Fishing in the Convention Area*, Article 6.

326 *Ibid.*, Article 7.

327 CCAMLR Conservation Measure 42-01 (2010) *Limits on the fishery for* Champsocephalus gunnari *in Statistical Subarea 48.3 in the 2010/11 season*. Although subject to annual review, this measure has been in place, in various guises, since at 2001.

328 Like the above noted CM 22-05 on bottom trawling, the prohibition on the taking of sharks is qualified to the extent that fisheries for the purpose of scientific research is permitted.

respect of environmental harms, the CCAMLR Measures can act as a sufficient justification to bring to bear consequences on those vessels or States undermining their provisions. Taking these Conservation Measures in conjunction with the restrictions imposed by the CDS they can have an enormous and non-discriminatory impact upon the abilities of IUU/FOC operators to enter their wares into the international market place. Or so the theory goes.

Other than those problems associated with ascertaining the veracity of the information contained within the document referred to at the start of this section of the Chapter there are, however, a couple of further caveats to be added to statement that the CDS can limit the ability of IUU/FOC fishermen to profit from their activities.

The first noteworthy limitation to the CDS is that at present it simply applies to toothfish species and does not encompass other species found within the CCAMLR region. Consequently the *de facto* prohibition on bottom trawling cannot be further implemented under the CDS Measure as the target species of bottom trawling activities are not toothfish. Unless and until CCAMLR extends the CDS to all species found in its area of competence it is impossible to apply the market-related measures applicable to toothfish to unlawfully taken *Champsocephalus gunnari*, for example. Likewise, although the CDS may restrict the trade in toothfish when the harvest of that toothfish has had an adverse impact upon seabird populations (contrary to the Conservation Measures in place to regulate longlining and trawling activities) when the traded species is tuna, for instance, the CDS is impotent in terms of denying market access to IUU/FOC operators even when the most blatant evidence of undermining CCAMLR seabird measures exists – although it should be noted, of course, that CCAMLR's 'ordinary' negative listing procedures can apply in circumstances where non-toothfish fishing activities undermine CCAMLR Conservation measures: it is simply the catch-to-market place procedures of the CDS that are species specific. There is, of course, no incontrovertible reason why the CDS cannot be extended to cover all species within the CCAMLR region, and so it is suggested that if the present CDS were to be extended in terms of its coverage then this first loophole may be filled.

Likewise, on an abstract level at least, the second practical loophole potentially exploited by the IUU/FOC fleet – the number of States currently implementing the scheme – can also be closed off. As with all RFMOs the obligations imposed by CCAMLR extend only to those States that are either members or co-operating non-contracting parties. Thus, as the earlier analysis of market-related measures shows, if only a few States implement the CDS then the efficacy of the scheme will be severely undermined. Thus, despite the fact that the majority of the main recipient States of toothfish are those major economies such as the USA, Europe, Japan and Australia – all of whom are existing CCAMLR members – for greater, or even total, control over access to the marketplace it is necessary that as many States as possible embrace the CDS's principles. This issue shall form the subject matter of the following Chapter.

5.8 *Conclusion*

As this Chapter has shown, RFMOs are very much the key to the future management of fish stocks and the wider marine environment. How these bodies interpret their responsibilities under international instruments such as the UNFSA and the Code of Conduct are crucial to the future stability of many target and non-target species. It is conceded, of course, that the UNFSA, for instance, does not bind those RFMOs created prior to its coming into force, or those RFMOs whose membership does not include any UNFSA contracting parties. Likewise it is recognised that the Code of Conduct is merely soft law and does not bind all States to its provisions. Nevertheless, it is suggested that these instruments represent the benchmark by which RFMO performance should be measured and, as many RFMOs note, the Code of Conduct is representative of the general minimum standards applicable to fisheries.

Thus, it is suggested that if RFMOs are serious about tackling *all* the consequences of IUU/FOC every effort should be made to close off markets to their wares. Clearly this is not beyond the competence of regional managers, because, as has been shown, RFMOs already have in place market-related measures such as negative and positive lists of vessels and the ability to deny port facilities to these vessels. For the majority of RFMOs, however, it is essential that they clarify how and under what circumstances vessels will be denied access to markets. When, for instance, can a vessel be denied landing rights when that vessel does not conform to minimum gear specifications?

Likewise RFMOs must ensure that any port measures are adequately implemented and expansive enough in their coverage to close off any potential ports of convenience. It is suggested that CCAMLR's CDS, by tracking fish from line or net to market place, can act as a model scheme in this regard, and whilst the CDS may have its deficiencies, its success in ridding IUU/FOC from the southern oceans cannot reasonably be questioned. If such a success can be replicated and the CDS expanded to cover more States, or more species then there is the real possibility that IUU/FOC vessels could have almost insurmountable hurdles to overcome in getting their wares to market. Thus it is suggested that if all newly incorporated RFMOs follow the precedent set by the SPRFMO and adopt a CCAMLR-type scheme then this can only be a positive move. Likewise, if existing RFMOs can incorporate the principles found in CCAMLR's CDS into their own trade and market restrictive measures this would also be a move in the right direction. Of course, some RFMOs may claim that to factor in wider environmental considerations would run contrary to their mandates, because, it could be claimed it is not the purpose of certain RFMOs to manage and regulate the wider marine environment. This, it is submitted, ignores both the reality of the post-UNCLOS era and the principle that rights and responsibilities go hand in hand. Any RFMO which simply sees itself as a body which should only regulate catch and allocate rights to interested State parties is clearly ignoring the correlative of these rights.

Of course there is the possibility that the CCAMLR method of regulating the oceans is not the only way in which fisheries may be protected. The following Chapter will analyse the CCAMLR CDS from an alternative standpoint and review some recent proposals to regulate the harvest of toothfish via the use of the Washington Convention on the International Trade in Endangered Species (CITES). Additionally the Chapter will consider how the CDS has expanded its coverage to include the vast majority of the world's major trading States under the auspices of CITES.

Chapter Six

Multilateral Trade Measures: How CITES Could be Used in the Fight Against IUU Fishing

6.1 *Introduction*

To take stock of developments so far, it is possible to see that there is a significant move towards the use of regionally applied trade-related measures to combat all types of IUU activity. Unfortunately in terms of global coverage there is a major lacuna because of the manner in which regional regimes can be undermined by the use of ports of convenience and inadequate implementation in the regional and domestic context, specifically in the context of by-catch and environmental degradation. The following Chapter will consider how many of the problems highlighted in respect of regional measures are not unique to the management of fisheries and consider how one particular international agreement, the Washington Convention on the International Trade in Endangered Species (CITES), has risen to these types of challenge. The Chapter will demonstrate that it is possible for the international community to come together to create the necessary rules and infrastructure to prevent harmful practices and severely curtail international trade in 'living resources' on a global scale. As this Chapter will show, CITES *can* have a significant role to play in halting the decline of fish stocks and *could* be of importance in diminishing the harms of IUU/FOC fisheries. Thus the following Chapter will demonstrate how CITES can complement and augment existing fisheries management tools.

The Chapter will also consider the limits to this endeavour and highlight the ongoing challenges posed by synergising the two discrete regulatory frameworks of fisheries management and the trade in endangered species.

Consequently this Chapter will first, in the section entitled *The Workings of CITES*, concentrate upon the positives – what CITES can do and how it goes about securing its goals of preventing and regulating the international trade in endangered species. The next section, *CITES and Fish Stocks*, will consider recent initiatives attempting to ensure a greater role for CITES in the protection or conservation of commercially important fish stocks. Included in this section is an analysis of the ill-fated attempt to list Patagonian toothfish into the CITES Appendices, and how the initial proposal, whilst politically doomed, led to the agreement by which the CCAMLR CDS would be implemented by all CITES parties.

Paradoxically, however, the failed toothfish proposal has not seen the end of the debate under which CITES may be considered as an instrument by which the trade in commercially important fish may be regulated. The next section of the Chapter, *A Residual Role for CITES in Relation to Other Important Fish Stocks,* will chart some of the recent developments in relation to this matter and in the next section (*Continuing Issues – "Introduction From the Sea"*) consideration will be given to those issues still in need of resolution.

In concluding this section, the Chapter will then proceed to consider some of the negative aspects of the use of CITES in a fisheries context. In terms of the *Inherent and Practical Limits to CITES* the Chapter will demonstrate that it is by no means certain that the use of CITES can be used to prevent the environmental degradation associated with IUU/FOC fisheries. Nor is it axiomatic that CITES can, in all circumstances, tie all States to its provisions. The problem of "free-riders" under CITES will then be examined to see if the Convention has sufficient provisions to deal with this problem.

The Chapter will conclude by suggesting that if trade measures are to be invoked against States or vessels engaged in IUU/FOC activity then the CCAMLR CDS should be the template. Whilst CITES may have a role to play in terms of listing commercially important fish stocks, this role is yet to be defined and, as such, until the political wrangles which have beset the debate thus far have been reconciled, the international community should, perhaps through CITES, continue to work towards the greater homogenisation of CDS schemes. Put simply, if CITES can be utilised to increase participation in the CCAMLR CDS, can it not also have a role to play in relation to any other fisheries?

6.2 *The Workings of CITES*

Initially signed by 21 States in March 1973 in Washington, CITES came into force in 1975 following its 10th ratification.[1] Over the next two decades the Convention continued to attract new State parties so that as of summer 2011 the membership of CITES numbered 175 States,[2] and of the 20 or so States not

[1] Rosalind Reeve, *Policing International Trade in Endangered Species: The CITES Treaty and Compliance,* Earthscan/The Royal Institute of International Affairs, London, 2002, at p. 28 (herein after "Reeve").

[2] CITES website, at http://www.cites.org/eng/disc/parties/index.shtml.

currently members of CITES[3] perhaps only the Democratic People's Republic of Korea could be described as a significant actor on the world stage.[4] Nevertheless, it would be foolish in the extreme to ignore these States in terms of their membership of CITES. Whilst it is certainly true that none of the 17 non-party States are major global trading entities,[5] a number of them are of significance in the IUU/FOC debate due to their status as flags of convenience and as such could pose a not insignificant practical difficulty in implementing CITES' provisions to deal with IUU/FOC fishing.[6] Nevertheless, in general terms CITES is undoubtedly one of the most important Multilateral Environmental Agreements currently in place and as well as having a significant membership of trading States, it attempts to achieve its aims by rigorous, if simply defined, provisions within the Treaty itself and an admirable infrastructure, compliance and enforcement mechanisms.[7]

---

[3] At the time of writing the UN recognises 192 States, see http://www.un.org/Overview/unmember.html.

[4] The other States not party to CITES are Andorra, Angola, Bahrain, Haiti, Iraq, Kiribati, Lebanon, the Maldives, the Marshall Islands, the Federation of Micronesia, Nauru, Tajikistan, Timor-Leste, Tonga, Turkmenistan, and Tuvalu.

[5] According to GDP none of the aforementioned States are ranked in the top 50 global economies, with only Iraq (64th), Angola (66th), Lebanon (87th) and North Korea (98th) falling into the top 100. As a further point of reference, nine of the non-CITES member States rank below the Channel Island of Jersey in terms of GDP, see CIA World Factbook at: https://www.cia.gov/library/publications/the-world-factbook/rankorder/2001rank.html. Likewise a similar pattern emerges when considering these States as major exporting nations, with no representation in the top 50 export nation-entities, with only Angola (52nd), Iraq (55th), Bahrain (75th) and Turkmenistan (89th) found in the top 100. And again as a point of reference, nine States are ranked below the West Bank (165th) by export, see CIA World Factbook at https://www.cia.gov/library/publications/the-world-factbook/rankorder/2078rank.html.

[6] The States falling within the category of flags of convenience and non-CITES membership are the Marshall Islands, North Korea and Tonga, see International Transport Workers' Federation list of flag of convenience States at http://www.itfglobal.org/flags-convenience/flags-convenien-183.cfm.

[7] Juan Carlos Vasquez, *Compliance and Enforcement Mechanisms of CITES,* in Sara Oldfield (ed), *The Trade in Wildlife: Regulation for Conservation,* Earthscan Publications, London, 2003, at p. 63 (herein after "Vasquez"). Likewise Birnie and Boyle, at p. 625, describe CITES as "unique and remarkable" due, *inter alia,* to its status as "one of the most effective regulatory structures". These glowing references are by no means universally attested: Hutton and Dickson, for instance, are overtly damning in their assessment, frequently using terms such "failure", "weakness", "ineffective regulation" etc. to describe the Convention, Jon Hutton and Barnabas Dickson (eds), *Endangered Specie, Threatened Convention: The Past, Present and Future of CITES,* Earthscan, London, 2000, at pp. xv–xx (herein after "Hutton and Dickson").

6.2.1 *CITES as a Convention*

Although, as subsequent discussion will show, CITES as an administrative body possesses a sophisticated and mature infrastructure, CITES as an international Convention is a relatively straightforward document with a relatively straightforward purpose. What the Convention itself does is to place restrictions and conditions upon the international trade in many thousands of plant and animal species.[8] What the Convention does not do is overtly prohibit such trade.[9] Instead, for those species deemed the most endangered or threatened with extinction the Convention proceeds upon the basis that trade in such species must be "subject to particularly strict regulation...and only authorised in exceptional circumstances."[10] These most endangered species are listed in Appendix I to the Convention and include apparently obviously endangered creatures such as the Giant Panda (*Ailuropoda melanoleuca*) and Californian Condors (*Gymnogyps californianus*) as well as hundreds of less obviously endangered species ranging from rats to whales and all in between.

The precise criteria for establishing that a species is deemed to be "threatened with extinction" and therefore meriting the protection of Appendix I were defined at the 1st Conference of the Parties in Berne in November 1976 and eponymously referred to as the "Berne Criteria". These criteria proved controversial due, as Sands notes, to their "protectionist requirements" and thus in 1994 at the 9th COP Conference Resolution 9.24 detailed the latest formulation, based on the Precautionary Principle,[11] stating that a species will be threatened with extinction if the wild population is small and "characterised" by a number of essential sub-criteria.[12] Populations which are not "small" may still be listed in Appendix I if that species is found in a "restricted area of distribution" and

[8] Unless otherwise specified, in this Chapter the term "trade" refers to "international trade": nothing in CITES affects the domestic trade in listed species and its rules only apply when specimens are traded between State parties.

[9] Although under CITES Article XIV(1)(a) States are entitled to adopt national measures completely prohibiting trade in listed species they are not obliged to do so. Likewise, as will be discussed later in this section, under certain circumstances trade embargos may be imposed against State parties for a failure to fully implement the Convention's provisions. In neither case, however, does the Convention itself operate as a prohibition on species specific trade.

[10] CITES Article II(1).

[11] Sands (2003), at pp. 509–510; Conf. Res. 9.24 (Rev CoP 15), Preamble and Annex 4.

[12] These sub-criteria, as specified by Conf. Res. 9.24 (Rev Cop 15), Annex 1(A)(i–v) include "an observed, inferred or projected decline in the numbers of individuals or the area and quality of habitat"; or where sub-populations are small: or where the majority of individuals are "geographically concentrated during on or more life-cycle phases"; or prone to large short-term fluctuations in population size; or when a species can be characterised by a "high vulnerability to either intrinsic or extrinsic factors".

characterised by at least one of the additional specific criteria.[13] Finally, populations may fulfil the requirements for listing in Appendix I if there is "a marked decline in the population size in the wild, which has been either observed as ongoing or as having occurred in the past (but with a potential to resume)" or "inferred or projected".[14]

The methodology of the "strict regulation" referred to in Article II is further defined by Article III and it is under these circumstances that a *de facto* (rather than a *de jure*) prohibition on trade is enabled. For instance, in order for any Appendix I specimen[15] to be internationally traded, permission must be sought from the exporting State. This permission takes the form of an export permit which is granted by the competent domestic authorities.[16] This permit will be granted only when it can be established that the export of the specimen in question will not be detrimental to the survival of that species,[17] and the specimen was not obtained in contravention of domestic wildlife legislation.[18] It is also a requirement that prior to the issuing of export permits, the specimen in question will be transported in a manner so as to minimise the risk of injury, damage to health or cruel treatment[19] and that when the specimen arrives at its destination an import permit has already been granted by the competent authorities of the import State. The criteria for the granting of an import permit again depends upon the assessment, by the competent domestic authorities, that the import of the specimen will not be detrimental to the survival of the species,[20] and that the recipient of the specimen is able to house and care for it[21] and not use the specimen for primarily commercial purposes.[22] Where the

[13] Conf. Res. 9.24 (Rev CoP 15), Annex 1(B)(i–iv) requires "fragmentation or occurrence at very few locations"; or "large fluctuations in the area of distribution or the number of subpopulations"; or "a high vulnerability to either intrinsic or extrinsic factors"; or "an observed, inferred or projected decrease" in either "the area of distribution, the area of habitat, the number of subpopulations, the number of individuals, the quality of habitat, or recruitment".

[14] Conf. Res. 9.24 (Rev CoP 15), Annex 1(C)(i)(ii). An inferred or projected decline must be based upon either a decrease in area or quality of habitat, or levels or patterns of exploitation, a high vulnerability to either intrinsic or extrinsic factors, or a decreasing recruitment.

[15] As defined under CITES Article I(b)(i)(ii)(iii) as any animal or plant, whether alive or dead, or recognisable parts or derivative thereof.

[16] Competent domestic authorities are Management Authorities and Scientific Authorities established by each CITES State Party under CITES Article IX(1).

[17] CITES Article III(2)(a).

[18] CITES Article III(2)(b).

[19] CITES Article III(2)(c).

[20] CITES Article III(3)(a).

[21] CITES Article III(3)(b).

[22] CITES Article III(3)(c). The term "primarily commercial purpose" is not defined in the Convention itself but Conference Resolution 5.10 (Rev CoP 15) defines an activity as "commercial" if "its purpose is to obtain economic benefit, including profit (whether in cash or in kind)

specimen is to be re-exported the competent domestic authorities will refer to Article III(4) when issuing of re-export certificates. Similar to the criteria for 'first exports' (as governed by Article III(2)), Article III(4) requires that the re-exporting State ensures that the specimen in question will be transported in a manner so as to minimise the risk of injury, damage to health or cruel treatment.[23] In addition the re-exporting State must determine that the import of the specimen was conducted in a manner consistent with the provisions of CITES[24] and that the receiving State has also granted a valid import permit.[25] There is no requirement for the State of re-export to ascertain whether or not trade in any particular specimen would prove to be detrimental to the survival of the species, but this finding will, all things being equal, have already been made by the State of first export. Likewise the re-exporting State need not trouble itself to consider whether or not the eventual purpose of the specimen is primarily commercial as this will, again if all things are equal, be the role of the ultimate importing State.

When the specimen is 'introduced from the sea'[26] (a concept that will be covered in depth at a later stage of this Chapter) Article III(5) requires that the 'usual' criteria are met; e.g. that of a prior granting of the necessary certification which is based on criteria such as the by-now-familiar-sounding determination, by the 'introducing State' that "the introduction will not be detrimental to the survival of the species involved"[27] and that the ultimate use of the specimen will be non-commercial.[28] Finally, 'introducing States' are required, in a manner similar to the obligations to which importing States are subject under Article III(3)(b), to ensure that the proposed recipient of the specimen can adequately house and care for the specimen.[29]

Thus, for many species it is not any blanket prohibition on trade imposed by the Convention that renders international trade non-viable but the unwilling-

---

and is directed toward resale, exchange, provision of a service or other form of economic use or benefit" (Conf. Res. 5.10(2)). Furthermore the burden of proof falls upon the person or entity seeking to import specimens to demonstrate a contrary use and that State authorities should proceed upon the basis "that all uses whose non-commercial aspects do not clearly predominate shall be considered to be primarily commercial in nature" (Conf. Res. 5.10(3)).

23 CITES Article III(4)(b).

24 CITES Article III(4)(a).

25 CITES Article III(4)(c).

26 The term "introduction from the sea" is defined in Article I(e) as "transportation into a State of specimens of any species which were taken in the marine environment not under the jurisdiction of any State". Section 6.5 of this Chapter discusses the ongoing debate as to which State (either the flag State of the vessel actually taking the catch or the port State where the catch is first landed) is, in fact, the State of introduction.

27 CITES Article III(5)(a).

28 CITES Article III(5)(c).

29 CITES Article III(5)(b).

ness or inability of export and import States to grant the necessary documentation in all but the most extreme circumstances.

Appendix II listed specimens, however, can be more readily traded. Appendix II specimens are "not necessarily now threatened with extinction" but those which may become so unless trade in them "is subject to strict regulation in order to avoid utilisation incompatible with their survival"[30] or the trade in non-threatened species considered necessary so as to place the trade in listed species "under effective control."[31] Like Appendix I species, the strict regulation imposed for Appendix II species is further defined in the Convention and essentially comprises of the issuing of export permits,[32] and similar to the way in which export permits are granted for Appendix I species, it is for the competent domestic authorities of the exporting State to ascertain that the granting of permits will not be detrimental to the survival of the species, and that the specimen was not obtained in contravention of domestic legislation, and that transportation will minimise the risk of injury etc.[33] It is incumbent upon export States to monitor the trade in Appendix II listed species so that if trade volume exceeds that which is necessary for the maintenance of that species within "its role within the ecosystem in which it occurs" then the competent domestic authorities should adopt suitable measures to "limit the grant of export permits."[34]

Article IV(4) places only very limited responsibilities on importing States by simply requiring that a valid export or re-export certificate has been issued by

30 CITES Article II(2)(a). The more precise criteria for the placing of species on to Appendix II are governed by Conf. Res. 9.24 (Rev CoP 15), Annex 2 which states that "A species should be included in Appendix II when, on the basis of available trade data and information on the status and trends of the wild population(s), at least one of the following criteria is met: (A) it is known, or can be inferred or projected, that the regulation of trade in the species is necessary to avoid it becoming eligible for inclusion in Appendix I in the near future; or (B) it is known, or can be inferred or projected, that regulation of trade in the species is required to ensure that the harvest of specimens from the wild is not reducing the wild population to a level at which its survival might be threatened by continued harvesting or other influences."

31 CITES Article II(2)(b). This particular Article is often referred to as the "look-alike" provision whereby even if a certain species is not itself threatened the trade in that species may be restricted if legitimate trade in that species renders the restriction of trade in listed species ineffective: see Birnie and Boyle, at p. 628 and Conf. Res. 9.24 (Rev CoP 15), Annex 2b which states that "(A) The specimens of the species in the form in which they are traded resemble specimens of a species included in Appendix II under the provisions of Article II, paragraph 2 (a), or in Appendix I, such that enforcement officers who encounter specimens of CITES-listed species, are unlikely to be able to distinguish between them; or (B) There are compelling reasons other than those given in criterion A above to ensure that effective control of trade in currently listed species is achieved." This provision is discussed in greater depth below.

32 CITES Article IV(2).

33 CITES Article IV(2)(a)(b)(c).

34 CITES Article IV(3).

the exporting or re-exporting State. The relevant re-export criteria for Appendix II species are found in Article IV(5) of the Convention and differ only slightly to the requirements as per Appendix I species. Appendix II species may, for example, be re-exported when the species is imported "in accordance with the provisions of the... Convention"[35] and when it will be "prepared and shipped" in a way so as to "minimize the risk of injury, damage to health or cruel treatment".[36] Re-exporting States are not required, for Appendix II species, to ascertain if an import permit has been granted.

Appendix II species may be introduced from the sea when the fall-back criteria of non-detriment is met[37] and when the specimen in question will be handled in a way so as to "minimize the risk of injury, damage to health or cruel treatment."[38] There is no requirement for Appendix II species, when introduced from the sea, (unlike Appendix I species) that their ultimate use will be for primarily non-commercial purposes.

Appendix III species are those "which any Party identifies as being subject to regulation within its jurisdiction for the purpose of preventing or restricting exploitation, and as needing the co-operation of other Parties in the control of trade."[39] The regulation of the trade in Appendix III specimens is governed by Article V and is dependent upon the exporting State granting the necessary certification.[40] This certification shall only be granted when the Management Authority is satisfied that the specimen has been lawfully obtained[41] and that the transhipment of live specimens will be conducted in a way so as to minimise the risk of injury, damage to health or cruel treatment.[42] Other than in cases of re-export, imports of Appendix III listed species should only be permitted upon the prior presentation of the appropriate certificate of origin or export permit.[43]

---

[35] CITES Article IV(5)(a).

[36] CITES Article IV(5)(b).

[37] CITES Article IV(6)(a).

[38] CITES Article IV(6)(b).

[39] CITES Article II(3).

[40] CITES Article V(2).

[41] CITES Article V(2)(a).

[42] CITES Article V(2)(b).

[43] CITES Article V(3). In cases of re-export once the Management Authority of the re-exporting State has certified that the specimen was processed in that State or is being re-exported then this should suffice as evidence that the Convention's requirements have been met in respect of that specimen, CITES Article V(4).

6.2.2 *CITES as an Institution*

Whilst many practical and administrative decisions and actions are taken and acted upon by the numerous committees and the Secretariat established under its rules,[44] like any other international convention worth its salt, CITES' primary decision-making body is the Conference of Parties (COP). Nominally scheduled to convene "at least once every two years"[45] or extraordinarily at any time upon the written request of one third of the Parties,[46] the COP's function is to decide, *inter alia*, upon the adoption of provisions (financial or otherwise) necessary for the Secretariat to carry out its duties,[47] to consider and adopt amendments to the Appendices,[48] and to review the progress of measures adopted pertaining to the conservation and restoration of listed species.[49] When considering or adopting amendments to Appendices I and II (in other words, adding or removing species from these Appendices)[50] the COP is bound by the procedures laid down in Article XV. These procedures dictate that any proposed amendment must be communicated by the proposing Party to the Secretariat at least 150 days prior to the next meeting.[51] Following a consultation period the Secretariat is obliged to inform all Parties of any proposed amendment at least 30 days before the next meeting.[52] When voting upon any proposed amendments to Appendices I and II the COP adopts the procedures laid down in Article XV(1)(b) which states that proposed amendments will be adopted following a two-thirds majority vote in its favour by Parties present and voting.[53] Any amendment will enter into force 90 days after the meeting.

Between meetings the Parties may still consider amendments to the Appendices via the postal procedures set forth in Article XV(2) which generally mirror the voting procedures during meetings albeit with a modified timescale.[54]

---

44 As discussed below.

45 CITES, Article XI(2), although Reeve notes, at p. 38, that in practice the COP actual convenes once every two and a half years.

46 CITES, Article XI(2).

47 CITES Article XI(3)(a).

48 CITES Article XI(3)(b).

49 CITES Article XI(3)(c).

50 Appendix III, being more unilateral in nature, as discussed above, has its own particular rules regarding the listing of species, which for the purposes of this Chapter are not of the utmost relevance.

51 CITES Article XV(1)(a).

52 *Ibid.*

53 Abstaining Parties are not classified as being "present and voting" for the purposes of Article XV(1)(b).

54 In this regard the type of species under consideration is also of relevance: for marine species the Secretariat immediately communicates any proposed amendment to Parties and shall consult with relevant inter-governmental bodies "with a view to obtaining scientific data...and to

As well as considering Appendices amendments the COP can also adopt recommendations, typically taking the form of resolutions,[55] and deal with such diverse matters as the Secretariat's budget[56] to the establishment of specific committees and working groups.[57] These committees and working groups may be general and integral to the functioning of the Convention as a whole or *ad hoc* and dealing with specific issues. For instance the Animals, Plants and Nomenclature Committees are examples of the former, whilst the latter may be exemplified by the creation of committees such as the Bushmeat Working Group[58] the mandate of which was, *inter alia,* to "examine issues raised by the trade in bushmeat, with the aim of identifying solutions that can be willingly implemented by range States."[59] Additionally, so as to "circumvent the delay imposed by treaty amendments,"[60] the COP may from time to time vote upon "soft law" designed to further implement the provisions of CITES. Taking the form of "resolutions" or "revised resolutions" or "decisions" such soft law has radically altered the manner in which the Convention operates. To date the COP has adopted over 250 Conference Resolutions[61] ranging from the creation of rules essential to the efficacy of the Convention as a whole, such

ensuring coordination with any conservation measures enforced by such bodies." Upon receipt of such information the Secretariat shall "as soon as possible" communicate it, along with its own findings and recommendations to the Parties (Article XV(2)(b)). For non marine species there is no mandatory requirement to consult with any other body prior to the "immediate" communication of any proposed amendment to the Parties (Article XV(2)(c)). In either event all Parties must respond within 60 days of the Secretariat's initial communiqué (Article XV(2)(d)), and these responses should be circulated to all Parties as soon as is possible (Article XV(2)(e). If no objections have been raised within 30 days to the proposed amendment the amendment will enter into force 90 days later (Article XV(2)(f)). In the event of objections being lodged with the Secretariat within that period then the amendment is voted upon by Parties (Article XV(2)(g)). Postal ballots are regulated by Article XV(2)(h)(i)(j), which require at least half of the Parties to vote for a valid ballot to have occurred with a required two thirds majority of voting States voting in favour of the amendment for it to be carried forward. Upon an affirmative vote the amendment will enter into force 90 days after notification to the Parties. As with all CITES provisions, amendments are only valid insofar as States have not lodged a reservation in line with the specific provisions dictated by Article XV(3). In the event of the Secretariat receiving votes from less than half the Parties then the vote shall be carried forward to the next scheduled COP for further consideration (Article XV(2)(i)).

55 Reeve, at p. 40.

56 For instance see Res. Conf. 13.1, *Financing and Budgeting of the Secretariat and of Meetings of the COP.*

57 Sands (2003) at pp. 506–507.

58 Established at the 11th Conference of Parties in Kenya, see Decision 11.166.

59 Decision 11.166(a).

60 Reeve, at p. 41.

61 CITES website, at http://www.cites.org/eng/res/all/index.shtml.

as those found, for example, under Resolution 1.5 (as amended as COP 12) which governs the "Interpretation and Implementation of Certain Provisions of the Convention,"[62] to specific and particular rules dealing with such matters as the use of a "Universal Tagging System for the Identification of Crocodilian Skins,"[63] or the labelling of Vicuña cloth,[64] or requirements for ending the trade in Tibetan antelope.[65] Clearly then, whether it be the creation of Committees or the creation of general or specific rules and procedures the COP has an extensive remit and creates an extremely large legislative and logistical legacy after each and every meeting.[66]

Therefore, the Standing Committee, established in 1979, has gradually assumed the role of overseeing the implementation of COP decisions and acts as a *de facto* executive between Conferences. The task of ordering and administrating the vast body of work generated by Conferences and the Standing Committee falls largely on the shoulders of the CITES Secretariat.[67]

Whilst the majority of the "behind the scenes" work is undertaken by the Secretariat, and relevant decisions and policies concluded at the Conferences of the Parties, CITES itself does not possess its own implementation arm. Instead implementation and enforcement is left to State Parties themselves. As well as being obliged, as previously noted, to regulate the granting of import and export permits, through the creation of Scientific and Management Authorities, State parties are also under the general obligation imposed by Article II(4) to "not allow" the trade in species listed in the Appendices (except in accordance with the provisions of CITES).[68] Similarly, and couched in the same general terms, States are obliged, by virtue of Article VIII, to "penalize trade in, or possession of" specimens falling within the reach of the Convention,[69] and "provide for the confiscation or return to the State of export of such specimens."[70] Where lawful trade is undertaken States must, as far as is possible, ensure that this is

---

62 This particular Resolution prohibits State parties from placing species on to Appendix III when that same State has lodged a reservation to that same species being place on Appendices I or II.

63 Conf. Res. 11.12 (Rev CoP 15).

64 Conf. Res. 11.6 (Rev CoP 13) (Repealed CoP 13).

65 Conf. Res. 11.8 (Rev CoP 13).

66 These soft laws are voted upon in much the same way as Appendices amendments, that is to say, a successful vote in favour of any proposed Resolution requires a two-thirds majority of votes cast (abstentions not included), see Reeve, at p. 41.

67 CITES Article XII(2).

68 CITES Article II(4).

69 CITES Article VIII(1)(a).

70 CITES Article VIII(1)(b).

done in a prompt and expeditious manner, in a way which causes no, or rather minimal, harm to living specimens.[71]

Unfortunately, however, it is often claimed that many States fall woefully short of adequately implementing the Convention.[72] Consequently the National Legislation Project was initiated at the 8th Conference of the Parties.[73] Essentially a State audit, the National Legislation Project subjects the national measures adopted for the implementation of CITES to review by the Secretariat based on the core elements of CITES implementation. Thus, under Conference Resolution 8.4, the Secretariat was directed "to identify those Parties whose domestic measures do not provide them with the authority to designate at least one Management Authority and one Scientific Authority, prohibit trade in specimens in violation of the Convention, penalise such trade, or confiscate specimens illegally traded or possessed."[74] So as to order and rationalise the results of this audit State measures would be grouped into three categories so as to reflect the "apparent sufficiency in implementing the requirements of the Convention."[75] Category 1 States were those whose legislation was "believed to generally meet the requirements for CITES implementation."[76] Category 2 listed those States whose "legislation which is believed generally not to meet all requirements for the implementation of CITES"[77] and Category 3 contained those States whose domestic measures "believed generally not to meet the requirements for the implementation of CITES."[78]

---

[71] CITES Article VIII(3). The term "lawful trade" used above denotes that which falls within the scope of CITES and is undertaken in a manner consistent with its provisions: CITES does not place any restrictions upon the trade in wild animals or plants not found within its Appendices.

[72] See, for instance, Reeve, at p. 54; Vasquez, at p. 65, cites the statistic that "approximately 70% of the parties reviewed did not have the full range of national legislative and administrative measures needed to give effect to a aspects of the Convention." Likewise, Birnie and Boyle, at p. 629, point to "the practical difficulties of enforcement, which enable large numbers of species listed on all appendices to escape detection since enforcement is left to individual State parties, whose domestic wildlife laws, scrutiny and controls vary greatly in scope and stringency of enforcement."

[73] Kyoto, March 1992.

[74] Conf. Res. 8.4(a)(i–iv). Tellingly, and as noted by Reeve, at p. 252, although one of the core measures for CITES implementation is the prohibition of trade there is no requirement that States designate specific wildlife law enforcement agencies. When compared to the mandatory creation of Scientific and Management Authorities the lack of any obligation for States to so do does raise the question as to whether the focus of CITES is more to do with monitoring and surveillance than control and enforcement.

[75] CITES Doc. 10.31(Rev), at para 10.

[76] CITES Doc. 10.31(Rev), at para 11.

[77] CITES Doc. 10.31(Rev), at para 12. As Reeve clarifies, at p. 135, this Category concerns States whose measures "meet only some of the requirements".

[78] CITES Doc. 10.31(Rev), at para 13.

Significantly, the National Legislation Project was more than a mere paper exercise. At the Standing Committee's instructions the Secretariat has on numerous occasions had recourse to notify the Parties that trade with certain States should be suspended due to those States' failure to enact adequate domestic measures. Whilst in the majority of cases these sanctions were relatively short lived[79] there were, as of May 2011, three States subject to sanctions in respect of all commercial trade for non-implementation of CITES' provisions under the National Legislation Project.[80]

6.3 *CITES and Fish Stocks*

As the above analysis shows, despite its critics,[81] and whilst not being perfect, CITES can prove to be effective in providing a framework under which its aims of ensuring that "international co-operation... for the protection of certain species of wild fauna and flora against over-exploitation through international trade"[82] may be achieved. Thus it is little wonder that individuals, agencies and governments, also concerned to protect certain species of fish against over-exploitation, have begun to show an interest in what CITES could do to achieve this goal. Whilst any study of CITES will reveal that there are some marine species found on its Appendices it is also obvious that the Convention does not extend its protection to many varieties of commercially valuable fish stocks.[83] In the late 1990s, however, a growing body of opinion sought to

---

[79] For instance, under Notification to the Parties No. 2004/024 (30th April 2004) Parties were advised to suspend commercial trade in CITES-listed species with Mozambique and Panama. The sanctions were lifted against Panama by Notification to the Parties 2004/043 (24th May 2004) due to Panama's adoption of domestic regulations. Likewise the sanctions against Mozambique were lifted, for the same reason, by virtue of Notification to the Parties 2004/047 (16th June 2004). Similarly sanctions imposed under Notification to the Parties 2004/080 (22nd December 2004) pertaining to trade with India and Gambia were withdrawn due to those States' progress in implementing domestic measures by Notifications to the Parties 2005/011 (14th March 2005) and 2005/043 (8th August 2005) respectively.

[80] Djibouti (Notification to the Parties 2011/10); Mauritania and Somalia (Notification to the Parties 2004/055).

[81] Without wishing to over-generalise, those writers who criticise CITES tend to do so from an ideological point of view and could largely fall into the category of advocating free markets for flora and fauna. For example, see Hutton and Dickson, whose primary objection to CITES is that in order to achieve sustainable growth and conservation it is necessary to de-regulate the trade in wildlife, thus providing an incentive for those individuals at ground level to conserve wildlife populations.

[82] CITES Convention, Preamble.

[83] The marine species listed on the Appendices to CITES are: Queen conch (*Strombus gigas*, on Appendix II); over 20 different varieties of clams and mussels on Appendix I and a further 5

challenge the conception that CITES was not, and never was, a tool for the conservation of fish stocks or a regime under which the international trade in such stocks may be managed and regulated.[84] Chief among the organisations considering this point of view were the UN's Food and Agriculture Organisation, who, since the turn of the 21st century, has launched numerous consultations to evaluate CITES' potential as a fisheries trade regulating tool, as has TRAFFIC International – albeit in species specific terms rather than the general approach adopted by the UNFAO. Additionally the CITES infrastructure itself has produced a prodigious amount of literature on the subject. The next section of this Chapter will therefore appraise some of the major issues raised by these consultations, as well as trace the most important developments in the on-going debate.[85] As has been shown in Chapter Five, in the section entitled *Market Related Deterrents to IUU/FOC Activities,* market related measures can have an enormous impact on the ability of the IUU/FOC fleet to profit from their labours provided that the closed market is large enough. One of the key attractions of CITES in this situation is its membership – it will be recalled that

on Appendix II; 4 species of corals and sea anemones on Appendix II; basking sharks (*Cetorhinus maximus,* on Appendix II); great white sharks (*Carcharodon carcharias,* on Appendix II); whale sharks (*Rhincodon typus,* on Appendix II); all forms of sturgeon, and paddlefish (*acipenseriformes*) are listed on Appendix II, except short-nosed sturgeon and European (or Baltic) sturgeon (*Acipenser brevirostrum* and *Acipenser sturio*) which are listed on Appendix I; Asian arowanas (*Scleropages formosus,* on Appendix I); several species of carp (*Probarbus jullieni,* Appendix I and *Caecobarbus geertsi,* on Appendix II); Arapaima (*Arapaima gigs,* on Appendix II); sucker fish (*Chasmistes cujus,* on Appendix I); giant catfish (*Pangasianodon gigas,* on Appendix I); seahorses (*Hippocampus spp.* on Appendix II); hump-head wrasse (*Cheilinus undulates, on Appendix II*); totoaba (*Totoaba macdonaldi,* on Appendix I); two species of lungfish (*Latimeria* spp., on Appendix I and *Neoceratodus forsteri* on Appendix II); and Galapagos sea cumbers (*Isostichopus fuscus,* listed by Ecuador on Appendix III), see CITES website at http://www.cites.org/eng/app/appendices.shtml.

84 See, for instance, Anna Willock, *Uncharted Waters: Implementation Issues and Potential Benefits of Listing Toothfish in Appendix II of CITES,* TRAFFIC International, Cambridge, 2002, at p. 1 (herein after "Willock (2002)"); Erik Franckx, *The Protection of Biodiversity and Fisheries Management: Issues Raised by the Relationship between CITES and LOSC,* in Freestone, Barnes and Ong, *The Law of the Sea: Progress and Prospects,* Oxford University Press, Oxford, 2006, at p. 211–212, (herein after "Franckx (2006)"); UNFAO Fisheries Circular No. 954, *An Appraisal of the Suitability of the CITES Criteria for Listing Commercially Exploited Aquatic Species,* UNFAO, Rome 2000, at pp. 1–2 (herein after "Fisheries Circular No. 954"). The argument that CITES was not a suitable vehicle to address the issue of fish stock depletion is discussed elsewhere in this Chapter.

85 The purpose of this analysis is not to attempt a lay-person's evaluation of many of the complex scientific issues raised in many of the studies but simply to highlight the context in which these complex scientific issues are founded and to provide the reader with an overview of the action taken towards the listing of certain commercially important fish stocks on the Appendices of CITES.

the vast majority of the world's States are members of CITES and so *if* CITES could be used to regulate the trade in fish stocks then, other than any States lodging reservations to COP resolutions, the majority of markets would close to fishermen not adhering to the principles of the Convention as implemented by domestic legislation.

6.3.1 *Case Study on Patagonian Toothfish*

Irrespective of the real practical difficulties facing the concerned law-maker regarding the status of IUU/FOC vessels, perhaps the primary concern should be that of the apparent lack of political will and impetus to sustain the process of the inclusion of commercially important fish stocks on the CITES Appendices. Even if CITES were to be viewed as a practicable solution to both the general problem of over-fishing and the specific issue of IUU/FOC, the opposition of certain States may predicate that, at least for the foreseeable future, no great strides towards this goal may be made. Thus, to explain and evidence the lack of political momentum the next section of this Chapter will turn its attention to the hitherto ill-fated attempts, chiefly by Australia, to include the Patagonian toothfish (*Dissostichus eleginoides*)[86] and Antarctic toothfish (*Dissostichus mawsonii*)[87] on CITES' Appendix II. Given the failure of this Australian endeavour, the Chapter will then pose the question that if no progress can be made even in the most pressing and seemingly obvious case such as this, then what are the chances of achieving large-scale CITES inclusions in the fisheries sector?

The initial aspect of this study, however, will be to elaborate on the above mentioned terms of reference – that is to say, the description of the toothfish problem as being a "most pressing and seemingly obvious" case for inclusion onto the CITES Appendices. To facilitate this elaboration it is thus necessary to consider the characteristics of the toothfish and associated fishery patterns against the requirements of the CITES Appendices. If a compelling case can be made out for the inclusion of the toothfish onto either CITES Appendix due to the characteristics of the species and associated fishery, then it can only be assumed that any opposition to such an inclusion, by both States and other interested bodies, will not be pragmatic but principled. And of course any principled objection to the inclusion on CITES' Appendices of the toothfish, reflecting as it may a deeply entrenched opinion as to what CITES is actually

[86] To be listed in accordance with the procedures laid down in CITES Article II(2)(a): CITES Conference Proposal 12.39, 17th June 2002, made by Australia for the 12th Conference of the Parties, paragraph A (herein after "CITES Proposal 12.39").

[87] Under the look alike provision on Article II (2)(b) on the basis that "the species resembles *Dissostichus eleginoides* closely so that a non-expert with reasonable effort is unlikely to be able to distinguish between them." CITES Proposal 12.39, paragraph A.

for, may prove a more difficult argument to overcome than any pragmatic objection which may be countered or rebutted by the available evidence. With this in mind it is now necessary to consider this evidence.

It will be recalled from earlier in this Chapter that to be considered a candidate for inclusion onto Appendix II any species must fulfil the specific requirements laid down by Conference Resolution 9.24 (Rev CoP 15), which states that:

> A species should be included in Appendix II when, on the basis of available trade data and information on the status and trends of the wild population(s), at least one of the following criteria is met:
>
> (A) it is known, or can be inferred or projected, that the regulation of trade in the species is necessary to avoid it becoming eligible for inclusion in Appendix I in the near future; or
>
> (B) it is known, or can be inferred or projected, that regulation of trade in the species is required to ensure that the harvest of specimens from the wild is not reducing the wild population to a level at which its survival might be threatened by continued harvesting or other influences.[88]

The Australian toothfish proposal was unambiguous in this respect: IUU/FOC trade in toothfish species clearly has had and continues to have a detrimental effect on the long term sustainability of the Patagonian toothfish, by "making the annual harvest continually exceed the level that can be continued in perpetuity."[89] The Australian solution was, therefore, fairly simple and with a straightforward goal: to bind those non-CCAMLR member States whose vessels currently operate within the CCAMLR region and account for almost 50% of the catch to a set of international conservation standards. This goal would be achieved by the adoption of a two-fold strategy involving, first, the listing of both *dissostichus* species on Appendix II of CITES and secondly, for the vast majority of stocks under consideration, the utilisation of CCAMLR's Catch Documentation Scheme as the means of authenticating the legitimacy of any internationally traded toothfish.[90] Thus, so the Proposal claimed, the CDS would be dramatically improved in its efficacy, as at present the Scheme is "constrained by being binding only on the Contracting Parties to the CCAMLR Convention." The involvement of CITES would extend the coverage of CCAMLR trade regulations to all 159 [sic] CITES member States[91] including the flag States of those "IUU fishing vessels…flagged to non [CCAMLR] Contracting

[88] CITES Conf. Res. 9.24, Annex 2B.

[89] CITES Proposal 12.39, paragraph A.

[90] Whilst the incidence of toothfish harvest occurs throughout the Southern Ocean, CITES Proposal 12.39 recognises that 96% of toothfish capture occurs within the CCAMLR region itself or within the EEZs of CCAMLR members, see CITES Proposal 12.39 at p. 4 and p. 18.

[91] Now standing at 175 member States.

parties who are not bound by management regulations but are parties to the CITES Convention."[92]

Although Proposal 12.39 appeared to tick all the necessary boxes in terms of the immediate threat to Patagonian toothfish posed by IUU/FOC fishing and the ability of those stocks to recover,[93] the Proposal faced an early and ignominious demise, for reasons explained herein. It should be noted, however, that significant elements of the Proposal found new life in the alternative measures proposed by Chile which were adopted at CITES' 12th COP at Santiago, Chile in 2002.[94] Paradoxically, however, although the Australian Proposal centered entirely around the use of CCAMLR's best practice for the conservation of toothfish it was the opposition from within CCAMLR itself that led to Australia withdrawing its proposal before the CITES COP could deliberate upon it, with the objections being both principled and pragmatic. For instance Japan, along with Norway (being the most vociferous opponents of the Australian proposal) claimed, at the CCAMLR Commission meeting of October/November 2002, that one of the key aspects of the proposal – that of increasing the level of participation in the conservation of toothfish from the 31 CCAMLR member States to the much greater number of CITES members – was an entirely misconceived argument. The Japanese position was that the existing CCAMLR participating parties comprised 85% of the global population and all major toothfish importing States were already CCAMLR members and thus bound to implement the CDS – therefore any perceived necessity to extend the reach of the CDS was far from urgent.[95]

Whilst there is obvious validity to this point and Japan's mathematics are difficult to refute,[96] there is clearly something missing from the calculations: only half of all toothfish harvests entering the international market place in

---

[92] CITES Proposal 12.39, Paragraph B(6)(7).

[93] Due to its low level of fecundity and the long period of time taken to reach reproductive maturity, as well as the fragmented nature of its habitat, Patagonian toothfish are "particularly vulnerable" to over-fishing, CITES Proposal 12.39, at section 2.3.1.

[94] CITES Conf. Res 12.4, *Co-operation Between CITES and the Commission for the Conservation of Antarctic Marine Living Resources Regarding Trade in Toothfish.* Further analysis of the similarities and differences between the adopted Chilean Proposal and the withdrawn Austrailian Proposal will be conducted throughout this Chapter.

[95] CCAMLR, *Report of the Twenty First Meeting of the Commission,* Hobart, Australia, 21 October – 1 November 2002, at para. 10.5 (herein after "CCAMLR/CITES Response").

[96] In acknowledging the validity of the figures cited by Japan, Willock (2002) further states that a "more stringent application of the current CCAMLR conservation measures by...[the major importing States]...could potentially achieve the same result" as any measures which include CITES. Willock does, nonetheless, go on to note the Canadian position: Canada is both a major importing State and an Acceding Party to CCAMLR but for many years failed to fully implement the CDS, despite "repeated requests from CCAMLR members", Willock (2002). Canada has, however, begun the process of implementing the CDS – see, Report to

the four years prior to Proposal 12.39 were legally caught by the vessels of CCAMLR member States,[97] despite the CCCMLR CDS having been in operation between CCAMLR members for the majority of that time. Although showing clear signs of success in combating IUU/FOC activity, the CDS – as Proposal 12.39 acknowledged – was not perfect and even though IUU/FOC incidences have shown a marked decline since its introduction,[98] the level of unlawful or unregulated catch remained disproportionate to Japan's claim that the vast majority of players in the toothfish industry were already governed by the CDS.[99] Similarly Japan's response ignored the fact that although the majority of toothfish stocks are found within CCAMLR's area of competence, a significant harvest occurred, or more pertinently was claimed to occur by the vessel owners, beyond CCAMLR's delineated boundaries.

Of chief concern in this regard was UNFAO Statistical Area 51, a vast tract of the western Indian Ocean, extending from the Gulf of Oman in the north, down the east African coast and beyond to a latitude of 45°00S, then eastwards to a longitude of 80°00E, then northwards to the equator to intersect with the southern tip of India at a longitude of 77°00E.[100] Historically, Statistical Area 51 has, however, never been an area in which toothfish are found: according to the UNFAO's own data, as well as independent studies, there is no discernable toothfish population in Area 51 and any reports of harvests of toothfish in that area were "catches taken as a result of IUU fishing in other areas inside the Convention Area".[101] Of course, at the time of the toothfish proposal this was a very 'live' issue. Since that time the CCAMLR CDS has become more digitalised with the use of real-time VMS, as discussed in Chapter Five, a prerequisite for all legitimate toothfish operations. Thus, at the time of the proposal it is possible to see that the listing of toothfish in CITES Appendices

the 13th CITES Conference of the Parties, Bangkok, October 2004, Cop 13 Doc. 36 (Rev1), Annex, at footnote 5.

97 CITES Proposal 12.39, at paragraph B(5). This figure corresponds with studies conducted by TRAFFIC International, see M. Lack and G. Sant, *Patagonian Toothfish: Are Conservation and Trade Measures Working?* at p. 15, TRAFFIC International Bulletin Vol. 19, No. 1 (2001), (herein after "Lack and Sant"); and Willock (2002) at p. 11.

98 *The Economics of IUU Fishing,* at pp 132, which attributes the immediate decline in incidences of IUU/FOC trade in toothfish following the introduction of the CDS in 1999 to the existence of that scheme.

99 *The Economics of IUU Fishing,* at pp. 132–133, which described recent trade data for IUU toothfish harvests as being of "significant concern" and at a rate of 22 000 tonnes for a six month period in 2003.

100 Detailed map available at UNFAO Fisheries Global Information System, at: http://www.fao.org/figis/servlet/static?dom=area&xml=Area51.xml.

101 Scientific Committee for the Conservation of Antarctic Marine Living Resources, *Report of the Twentieth Meeting of the Scientific Committee,* Hobart, Australia, October 2001 (SC-CCAMLR XX), at paras.2.10–2.15.

may have had merit, because unless the exporting State (the flag State of the vessel in question) could satisfy the requirement that the harvest was taken lawfully under CITES Articles III and IV then no international trade would be possible. To contemporise this issue it is likely that the digitalised CCAMLR CDS has now gone some way to negating any further arguments put forward in support of any toothfish listing on the basis of catches purportedly taken beyond areas of CCAMLR jurisdiction such as Statistical Area 51.

A further argument against the Australian proposal, made by numerous States, including both Japan and Norway, as well as Russia and Chile, related to the necessity of any listing. The consensus of these States' position could be summed up by the Russian response, which was to claim that "the available scientific data on the status of toothfish stocks were inadequate to reach an unequivocal conclusion of the necessity for such a listing."[102] Whilst there is an obvious question to be posed as to whether there is any need for "unequivocal conclusions" to be arrived at under the precautionary principle, a principle applied by both CCAMLR[103] and CITES,[104] which essentially states that the lack of data should not be the basis for a failure to apply cost-efficient measures,[105] there is some truth in the further contention of both Russia[106] and Norway that "management decisions for marine species were normally made on the basis of stocks, rather than species… [and that]… generally speaking, one or more stocks of a species may be in difficult conditions whilst, at the same time, other stocks of the same species may be in good condition."[107] To reinforce this point Norway pointed out in its response that certain stocks of Patagonian toothfish were indeed "in good condition" and noted that CCAMLR's Scientific Committee had, at the time of the proposal, recommended an increase in the total allowable catch within one CCAMLR sub-area. In response to Norway's assertion it is, of course, possible to suggest that the split listing procedures, allowed for under CITES and discussed later in this Chapter, could be utilised so that only threatened stocks would be listed, with non-threatened stocks not subject

---

[102] CCAMLR/CITES Response, at para. 10.19.

[103] Whilst not explicitly recognised in the CCMLAR Convention the precautionary principle has "evolved to guide CCAMLR in carrying out its management responsibilities, namely: (i) Management strives to follow a 'precautionary' approach. This means that CCAMLR collects the data it can, then weighs up the extent and effect of the uncertainties and gaps in such data before making a management decision", see CCAMLR website at : http://www.ccamlr.org/pu/e/sc/eco-app-intro.htm.

[104] CITES Conf. Res. 9.24, Preamble, 15th Recital.

[105] For further on the Precautionary Principle see Sunkin, Ong and Wight, *Sourcebook on Environmental Law* 2nd Edition, Cavendish Publishing, London, 2002, at p. 45 (herein after "Sunkin *et al.*"), at pp. 50–52.

[106] CCAMLR/CITES Response, at para. 10.19.

[107] CCAMLR/CITES Response, at para. 10.11.

to any listing procedure. In view of the enforcement problems that the use of split lists can cause this point shall not be pursued at this juncture.

In the face of these objections Australia agreed to drop its proposal to list toothfish on the CITES Appendices, and whilst this could be seen as a set back in terms of conservation, positives can be taken from the process. At CITES COP 12 in Santiago, Chile, the host nation's proposed compromise suggested that instead of listing toothfish species in the CITES Appendices, CITES parties should adopt the CCAMLR *Dissostichus* Catch Document.[108] Approved at the Santiago Conference,[109] Resolution 12.4 could be seen as the first step towards a global implementation of the CDS. As well as obliging CITES parties to apply the CDS to all forms of trade in toothfish, that is all introductions (imports), exports and transits of toothfish species, Conference Resolution 12.4 further institutionalises the co-operation between the two organisations through the exchange of data on the trade in toothfish. To monitor the implementation of Conference Resolution 12.4 by CITES members, and to facilitate this exchange of information, the Santiago Conference also agreed a number of further Decisions. For instance Conference Decision 12.57 states that "Parties should, by the end of 2003, report to the Secretariat their use of the *Dissostichus* Catch Document used by CCAMLR, and their verification requirements for such Catch Documents."

Unfortunately, CITES Decision 12.57 did not have the desired effect as the only States taking it upon themselves to respond were existing CCAMLR participant States.[110] For CCAMLR this was of particular concern as CITES Resolution 12.4 had, by the time of CITES' 14th Conference of the Parties, in June 2007, at the Hague, failed in its avowed aim to expand the coverage of the CDS beyond the States already implementing its provisions.[111] Furthermore, as CCAMLR noted at the Hague Conference, several CITES member States (as well as some which were not CITES members) were undermining the efficacy of the CDS by acting as both flags and ports of convenience for the IUU toothfish industry.[112] Thus CCAMLR initially had planned to request that these

[108] CITES Conference of the Parties Doc. 16.1, *Co-operation Between CITES and the Commission for the Conservation of Antarctic Marine Living Resources (CCAMLR) Regarding Trade in Toothfish* (herein after "CITES CoP Doc. 16.1").

[109] CITES Conference Resolution 12.4, *Co-operation Between CITES and the Commission for the Conservation of Antarctic Marine Living Resources Regarding Trade in Toothfish* (herein after "CITES Conf. Res. 12.4").

[110] See, CITES' 13th Meeting of the Conference of the Parties, Bangkok, October 2004, CoP Doc. 36 (Rev.1), *Conservation of and trade in* Dissostichus *Species,* Annex.

[111] CITES, 14th Meeting of the Conference of the Parties, The Hague, June 2007, CoP 14 Doc. 61, *Toothfish: Report of CCAMLR,* at p. 4 (herein after "CoP 14 Doc. 61").

[112] CoP 14 Doc. 61, at pp. 3–4 and Table 1. The flag of convenience States undermining CCAMLR's CDS were identified as Togo and Equatorial Guinea. The ports of convenience

States adhere to the CDS and report their position regarding the implementation of Resolution 12.4 at the earliest opportunity after the conclusion of the Hague Conference.[113] A few days prior to the Hague Conference, however, this request was withdrawn so it is impossible to say whether or not those States so requested will provide the CITES Secretariat with any information. In view of the fact that these States, and many others, have already failed to fulfil their obligations under Resolution 12.4 for almost a decade, it is perhaps simply a question of wait and see.

6.3.2 *Case Study on Atlantic Bluefin Tuna*

If the treatment of toothfish by CITES hints of a lacklustre and half-hearted compromise, the manner in which the proposal by Monaco to list Atlantic bluefin tuna on Appendix 1 should provide proof positive that CITES (as an organisation) is not willing to countenance the possibility of the Convention being used as a vehicle to regulate the trade in commercially important fish stocks. Monaco's flagship proposal – trumpeted in a CITES press release prior to the Doha Conference of the Parties in 2010 as being "the main course of CITES world conference"[114] met a most ignominious demise amid allegations of voting misconduct.[115] When stripped of any political and diplomatic niceties Monaco's proposal was, in its most basic terms, a vote of no confidence in ICCAT's management of bluefin tuna in the west and east Atlantic. Despite ICCAT having had an obligation to conserve and manage these populations for over four decades, it had done this so poorly, said the Monacan proposal, that both eastern and western bluefin tuna populations were in almost terminal decline.[116]

Fortunately from the perspective of any non-scientist or statistician, one does not need to be particularly well versed in either discipline to understand precisely why the Monacan proposal failed. Although the proposal did contain some quite detailed studies on, for example, reductions in spawning stock biomass

were noted as being the Hong Kong Special Administrative Region, Indonesia, the People's Republic of China, and to a lesser extent, Singapore.

113 CoP 14 Doc. 61, at pp. 4–5. CCAMLR's suggested time scale for the reporting of progress towards implementing Resolution 12.4 was November 2007.

114 CITES Press Release, February 2010, available at: http://www.cites.org/eng/news/press/2010/20100205_cop15.shtml.

115 CITES, 15th Meeting of the Conference of the Parties, Doha (Qatar), March 2010, *Summary Record of the Eighth Session of Committee 1*, 18th March 2010, CoP15 Com.1 Rec (Rev.1), (herein after "Doha Committee 1 Record"), at p. 4.

116 CITES, 15th Meeting of the Conference of the Parties, Doha (Qatar), March 2010, *Proposal to include Atlantic Bluefin Tuna (*Thunnus thynnus *(Linnaeus, 1758)) on Appendix I of CITES in accordance with Article II(1) of the Convention*, (herein after "Monaco Bluefin Tuna Proposal"), at pp. 4–5.

decline, the fecundity and natural mortality of bluefin tuna and the ecological and environmental factors that might influence population declines, the opposition to the proposal was not, in any meaningful sense, led by any disagreement as to whether the criteria for inclusion on Appendix I were met. Instead the grounds of opposition echoed the principled, not pragmatic, dissents of the States opposed to the listing of toothfish a few years earlier: CITES, said opponents of Monaco's proposal, was not the appropriate mechanism under which commercially important fish stocks should be regulated. For instance, Canada (while drawing attention to its own role as a "model for sustainable management") claimed "ICCAT was the most appropriate body for [the] management" of bluefin tuna.[117] Japan, whose delegate was keen to stress at the outset that his country's opposition to the proposal was not driven by its enormous consumption of bluefin tuna, posited a number of objections. Like the Canadian delegate, the Japanese representative thought that any listing would benefit only developed States (whose 'domestic' tuna harvest would not be subject to any trade-based regulations under CITES) and thought that, in any event, ICCAT was best placed to manage the tuna stocks. With this latter statement, the delegates from Venezuela, Chile, Grenada, Indonesia and Tunisia agreed.[118] Japan also considered that the listing of bluefin tuna would potentially open the floodgates, whereby numerous other tuna or tuna-like species would require listing for "look-alike reasons."[119]

6.4 *A Residual Role for CITES in Relation to Other Important Fish Stocks*

Notwithstanding the above mentioned and ill-fated attempts to bring the CITES infrastructure into the fight against illicit fisheries trade, it should be noted that fisheries regulation has not entirely gone off CITES' agenda and still represents a "work in progress." Although the Australian toothfish proposal was roundly criticised by many States it is suggested that much of this criticism stemmed from the fact that toothfish are already a relatively well protected species by CCAMLR. Other species, however, such as those found beyond the reaches of any RFMO's jurisdictional competence, or not subject to such rigorous conservation measures as applied by CCAMLR – such as ICCAT, perhaps – may present a different challenge and pose a new set of questions. It was seemingly against the backdrop of the toothfish proposals that the 2007 Hague CITES Conference of the Parties considered the control of fisheries trade – suggesting that this issue was still very much on the agenda. Whilst far from being the

117 Doha Committee 1 Record, at p. 2.

118 *Ibid.*, at p. 3.

119 *Ibid.*, at pp. 2–3.

final word on the subject, the documents presented to the Hague Conference represent at the very least an indication of the state of play so far in ironing out some of the problems associated with any large-scale listing of commercially important fish stocks.

Thus the following sections will consider the key interpretational and implementational difficulties highlighted by this process and will be informed by the work of the UNFAO, which, in February 2000 embarked upon a period of consultation so as to establish the viability of listing commercially exploited aquatic species on CITES' Appendices. Whilst the UNFAO consultations did not focus specifically upon the IUU/FOC problem it did consider many of the practical issues surrounding the use of CITES as a general fish management or conservation tool, and many of these general issues will inexorably have a bearing upon the more discrete issue of IUU/FOC fisheries.

6.4.1 *The Technical Burden To Listing Commercially Exploited Aquatic Species*[120]

The immediate focus of the UNFAO's consultation was the suitability of the CITES criteria for listing commercially exploited aquatic species. To date two Technical Consultations[121] have been initiated upon this issue alone and have largely focussed on the ability of the listing criteria, as determined by CITES Conference Resolution 9.24, to extend to fish stocks. It will be recalled that for Appendix I species, Resolution 9.24 dictates that species may be determined as threatened with extinction based upon population or habitat decline, population sizes, population distribution, fluctuations in population sizes, vulnerability to intrinsic or extrinsic factors, or decreased recruitment.[122] Likewise, species may be listed on Appendix II when "...(A) it is known, or can be inferred or projected, that the regulation of trade in the species is necessary to avoid it becoming eligible for inclusion in Appendix I in the near future; or (B) it is known, or can be inferred or projected, that regulation of trade in the species is required to ensure that the harvest of specimens from the wild is not reducing the wild population to a level at which its survival might be threatened by continued harvesting or other influences." Thus in the case of both Appendix I and Appendix II it is essential that there is sufficient data on population sizes, habitats *et al.* to inform the decision to list species, and whilst with regards to terrestrial fauna this information may be known or knowable, the same cannot

---

120 The term "Commercially Exploited Aquatic Species" has been held to encompass "resources exploited by fisheries in marine and large freshwater bodies", see *Report of the Exert Consultation on Implementation Issues Associated With Listing Commercially Exploited Aquatic Species on CITES Appendices,* UNFAO Fisheries Report No. 741, Rome, 2004, at paragraph 11 (herein after "UNFAO Fisheries Report No. 741").

121 Rome, Italy 28–30 June 2000 and Windhoek, Namibia, 22–25 October 2001.

122 Conf. Res. 9.24, Annex 1(A).

necessarily be said for marine species. Therefore the first task undertaken by the UNFAO consultation was to establish, in light of the perception of a lack of sufficient data on fish populations and habitats *et al.* whether the existing listing criteria would need modification so as to bring commercially exploited fish stocks under the protection of CITES.

Drawing extensively from FOA Fisheries Circular No. 954[123] the first Technical Consultation into this problem took place in Rome in June 2000 and brought together representatives from 58 UNFAO Member States, as well as observers from numerous other organisations, with the mandate of reviewing the CITES listing criteria. Whilst not arriving at any concrete conclusions as to the appropriateness of the listing criteria under CITES for commercially exploited aquatic species, this first Technical Consultation did recognise that there were numerous issues to be resolved before CITES could be considered as a tool for the management of aquatic species and proposed further consultations.[124] Thus, the following year, the Technical Consultation resumed in Windhoek, Namibia. This Consultation did, however, make numerous concrete, if slightly technical, recommendations concerning the changes to the CITES listing, specifically referring to the measurement of rates of decline in population numbers[125] necessary to allow for the inclusion of commercially exploited aquatic species on to the CITES Appendices. These recommendations were endorsed first by the UNFAO Committee of Fisheries (COFI)[126] and then adopted by the CITES Parties at COP 13 to form the basis of the revised Conference Resolution 9.24.[127, 128]

At its 14th Conference of the Parties in June 2007, CITES further clarified this issue by restating the relationship between Conference Resolution 9.24 (Rev. CoP13) and its Annexes. The clarification document presented to the Conference noted that for commercially-exploited aquatic species different rate of decline factors may exist, as compared with other forms of taxa. Thus it

---

[123] *An Appraisal of the Suitability of the CITES Criteria for Listing Commercially Exploited Aquatic Species,* UNFAO Fisheries Circular No. 954, UNFAO, Rome, February 2000 (herein after "Fisheries Circular No. 954").

[124] *Report of the Technical Consultation on the Suitability of the CITES Criteria for Listing Commercially-Exploited Aquatic Species,* UNFAO Fisheries Report No. 629, Rome, June 2000.

[125] CITES Conf. Res. 9.24, Annex 5, footnote 2, *Application of Decline for Commercially Exploited Aquatic Species.*

[126] Eighth Session of the UNFAO Committee on Fisheries Sub-Committee on Fish Trade, Bremen, Germany, February 2002.

[127] *CITES Issues With Respect to International Fish Trade and the CITES/FAO MOU,* Tenth Session of the UNFAO Committee on Fisheries Sub-Committee on Fish Trade, Santiago de Compostela, May–June 2006, at p. 3.

[128] Herein after "Conf. Res. 9.24(Rev. CoP13)".

is essential that when considering the appropriateness of listing any aquatic species on either Appendix I or II, reference must always be had to the more detailed guidelines enunciated by Annex 5 of Resolution 9.24 (Rev. CoP13).[129] Clearly any appraisal of the precise and technical criteria adopted under Resolution 9.24 (Rev. CoP13) is beyond the scope of the present work and so no attempt is made to so do. Nevertheless it is noteworthy and telling that CITES is moving towards defining the criteria under which commercially important fish stocks may be listed on its Appendices. Thus the next section of this Chapter will consider some of the key legal aspects requiring resolution prior to this event occurring.

6.4.2 *Implementation and Legal Issues Surrounding CITES and Fish Stocks*

The next stage for the UNFAO, and of more relevance for this particular study, was then to move on to consider the legal and implementation issue surrounding CITES and commercially important fish stocks. The latter issue was the subject of a further Technical Consultation initiated by the UNFAO in May 2004 with the mandate of addressing specific aspects of CITES including potential problems arising from the "look alike" clause found under CITES Article II(2)(b), split listing and the inter-relationship of these two topics, and the administrative implications of listing and down-listing.[130]

The "Look Alike" Clause

As will be recalled from earlier in this Chapter the "look alike" clause found under CITES Article II(2)(b) (when read in conjunction with Conference Resolution 9.24, Annex 2(b)(A)) allows for certain non-threatened species to be listed on Appendix II so as to effectively control the trade in species that are threatened when "[t]he specimens of the species in the form in which they are traded resemble specimens of a species included in Appendix II under the provisions of Article II, paragraph 2 (a), or in Appendix I, such that enforcement officers who encounter specimens of CITES-listed species, are unlikely to be able to distinguish between them." Obviously, when dealing with processed fish

---

129 CITES 14th Meeting of the Conference of the Parties, The Hague, June 2007, CoP Inf.64, *The Interpretation of Annex 2a (Criteria for the Inclusion of Species in Appendix II in Accordance with Article II, Paragraph 2 (a), of the Convention) and Annex 5 (Annex 5 Definitions, Explanations and Guidelines) of Resolutions Con. 9.24 (Rev. CoP13) in Relation to Commercially-Exploited Aquatic Species.*

130 UNFAO Fisheries Report No. 741, *Background and Purpose of the Expert Consultation,* at p. 1. The Consultation also considered the implications of CITES listing of commercially exploited aquatic species in relation to the aquaculture industry and noted some concerns: these concerns are not immediately relevant to the present study.

products this could be a problem.[131] For instance, is it possible to adequately tell the difference between two similar looking fish when those fish have been processed or filleted? Linked to this would be the objection that some fish or fish stocks could be unnecessarily listed on Appendix II merely because of difficulties in differentiating between that non-threatened fish and the threatened one. Thus, all tuna fish, for example, could conceivably be listed simply because it is impossible to identify endangered southern bluefin. The UNFAO Technical Consultation addressed these issues by first acknowledging the problems that could be caused by an inability to differentiate between marine species and noting the concerns that some unnecessary listing may take place.

The solution offered by the FAO was a multi-faceted strategy: first customs officials already make extensive use of identification manuals so as to identify a number of marine species, and for a number of species potentially subject to a CITES listing these guides could be "extremely valuable".[132] In many cases visual identification would be impossible, and so, as already is the case with certain fish such as sturgeon, genetic testing may be required. Unfortunately, as the UNFAO study acknowledged, DNA testing is extremely expensive and would require a level of technical resources that render the genetic testing of large volumes of fish unfeasible. Thus DNA testing should only be used as a secondary means of identification.[133] Perhaps of more practical appeal is the use of labelling requirements. As recognised by the UNFAO, mandatory labelling is already required by many RFMOs, so that only legitimate catches may be traded. Any catches which cannot be properly evidenced as being lawful and caught within the regulations imposed by the RFMO will simply not be issued with the appropriate documentation. The UNFAO recognised the usefulness of these types of scheme, noting that "the ultimate goal of the fisheries sector is to have an international standard for traceability of fisheries products."[134] And as developments post the UNFAO Consultation regarding the use by CITES member States of CCAMLR's Catch Documentation Scheme have demonstrated this particular hurdle is well on the way to being overcome.

Split-Listing

A unified standard of traceability and the use of Catch Documentation Schemes could also be of great help in tackling the next of the UNFAO's concerns: that of so called "split-listing." Split-listing occurs when different sub-populations of species are listed in more than one Appendix, or when one sub-population is

[131] It will be recalled that Article I(b)(ii) defines "specimen" as relating to Appendix I and Appendix II as "in the case of an animal ... any readily recognisable part or derivative thereof".

[132] UNFAO Fisheries Report No. 741, at p. 10.

[133] UNFAO Fisheries Report No. 741, at p. 10.

[134] UNFAO Fisheries Report No. 741, at p. 11.

listed and others are not.[135] Split-listings, stated the UNFAO Technical Consultation, whilst a "valuable tool" should "generally be avoided because they create enforcement problems."[136] This could clearly pose a problem in using CITES' Appendices for commercially exploited fish stocks, because, as the Technical Consultation recognises, "[t]he concept of split-listing is a common one in a fisheries context, where procedures and regulations may vary according to the stock or geographic area concerned."[137] For example, closed areas and Marine Protected Areas are commonly used in the fishing sector when it is necessary to implement stock recovery programs. Unfortunately, as the example of the *Daisy Christiane,* a UK registered beam trawler demonstrates, not all fishing vessels respect such zones and will often attempt to pass off unlawfully taken catches from these zones as lawful ones taken from elsewhere.[138] In these cases the fish themselves are for all intents and purpose identical, with the only difference being the area in which they were captured with the result that the trade in stocks taken from one fisheries zone is prohibited or severely limited whilst no such restrictions or limitations are in place in another zone. This is the equivalent to a split-listing under CITES, and the enforcement problems are clear to see. How is it possible to tell if the traded species falls within the sub-population listed under Appendix I, Appendix II, or no Appendix at all? As a hypothetical example consider, as the UNFAO Technical Consultation did, if yellowfin tuna were to be listed. Some sub-populations, Eastern Pacific yellowfin – perhaps at risk of being over-harvested and subject to major habitat degradation – were listed under Appendix II. Other subpopulations – Western and Central Pacific yellowfin, perhaps being abundant and in no danger of extinction, and posing no risk to dolphins – were not listed at all under CITES. The customs official, at the time of import, cannot know for certain whether the tuna specimen before her is that which is listed on Appendix II (thus requiring an export permit) or no Appendix at all (and not subject to any

135 CITES Article I(a) explicitly recognises the need to occasionally differentiate between sub-populations and thus defines "species" as "any species, subspecies, or geographically separate population thereof".

136 UNFAO Fisheries Report No. 741, at p. 11. The reluctance of CITES itself to place too much reliance upon split-listing is evidenced by Conf. Res. 9.24, Annex 3 which emphasises that split-listing between Appendices should be avoided, and that split-listings "that place some populations of a species in the Appendices, and the rest outside the Appendices, should not normally be permitted".

137 UNFAO Fisheries Report No. 741, at p. 11.

138 Department of the Environment, Food and Rural Affairs/Marine Fisheries Agency news release, *UK Beam Trawler Fined for Fishing in Closed Area,* 27th June 2006, available at http://www.defra.gov.uk/news/2006/060627e.htm.

import/export requirements).[139] The same difficulties would present themselves if those same two sub-populations of yellowfin tuna were listed on two different Appendices – the customs official would not know if the specimen presented was subject to the export and import permit requirements of Appendix I or merely the export permit requirements of Appendix II. Thus, one method of avoiding the problem of enforcement created by split-listing is simple: all species of yellowfin tuna should be listed equally using the look-alike provisions of Article II(2)(b). This then creates problems for the optimum utilisation of fish stocks which lies at the very heart of the relevant provisions of UNCLOS and its progeny, as millions of tonnes of Western and Central Pacific tuna swim needlessly unmolested by purse seines and long-lines. To avoid such anomalies the UNFAO urges the use of "strong and effective monitoring, control and surveillance" so as to ensure that any documentary evidence could be corroborated and that "fish harvested from one stock were not transhipped and claimed as having been taken from the other stock."[140]

CITES itself is no stranger to these types of problem, and has on occasion overcome the problems of enforcement by utilising documentation and identification schemes. Notable examples of how such schemes may, when properly adopted, implemented and monitored, prove successful are to be found by reference to crocodile species. So impressive have the results been for certain crocodilian species that even CITES' most ardent and profligate critics are forced to concede, despite reservations as to whether the crocodile example actually fits with the greater vision of CITES as a protectionist strategy, that the regime imposed by CITES *vis-á-vis* crocodiles has been "an impressive demonstration of conservation through sustainable use."[141] In fact, "impressive" may be an understatement given that in the period between 1995 and 2000 no verified incidences of illegal crocodile trade were recorded.[142] At the risk of editorialising it may not be too bold a suggestion to state that if future critics of CITES are forced to concede a similar success regarding fish stocks then maybe a job has been well done.

As a general rule all Nile crocodiles (*crocodylus niloticus*) are listed on Appendix I of CITES, except the populations of Botswana, Ethiopia, Kenya, Madagascar, Malawi, Mozambique, Namibia, South Africa, Uganda, the United

139 Obviously there is a real risk of fraud in these situations, as the trader may claim that the imported tuna is not of the sub-population listed and have fraudulent documentation to that effect.

140 UNFAO Fisheries Report No. 741, at p. 12.

141 Henriette Kievit, *Conservation of the Nile Crocodile: Has CITES Helped or Hindered?,* in Hutton and Dickson, at p. 88.

142 John Hutton and Graham Webb, *Legal Trade Snaps Back,* in Sara Oldfield (ed), *The Trade in Wildlife: Regulation for Conservation,* Earthscan Publications, London, 2003, at p. 117 (herein after "Hutton and Webb").

Republic of Tanzania, Zambia and Zimbabwe, which are included in Appendix II.[143] Likewise the Australian salt water crocodile (*crocodylus porosus*) is listed as an Appendix I species except the sub-populations found in Australia, Indonesia and Papua New Guinea, which are included in Appendix II.[144] To overcome the problems of the identification of the various sub-populations the 11th CITES Conference of the Parties in Gigiri, Kenya adopted Conference Resolution 11.12 to implement a universal tagging system for the identification of crocodile skins.[145] Identification is crucial for such split-listed species, as Resolution 11.12 acknowledges by stating that "several crocodilian species may be subject to some levels of illegal trade" and that "the tagging of all crocodilian skins in international trade would be a fundamental step towards the effective regulation of international trade in crocodilians."[146] The basis for this assertion was that in the early 1990s the illegal trade in crocodile skins was flourishing with illegally captured wild crocodile skins being laundered through legitimate trade.[147] Conference Resolution 11.12 therefore requires that a number of technical and procedural measures are adopted by exporting and importing States to ensure that no unlawfully garnered skins enter the international market place. For instance, range States should not allow any crocodile skins to be internationally traded unless those skins are properly tagged[148] and no State may accept consignments or individual specimens of crocodile skins unless those skins are also properly tagged.[149, 150] A properly tagged crocodile skin will bear identification codes as to species, country of origin, year of capture, etc. and the tag itself should have numerous fail-safe characteristics.[151] Concerned at the possibility of fraud and other types of criminal misuse of the identifying tags, Resolution 11.12 further dictates that the manufacture of the tags should be co-ordinated

143 Despite its name the Nile crocodile is to be found on the majority of the sub-Saharan African continent and located in at least 40 States, see *Crocodilian Biology Database*, at http://www.flmnh.ufl.edu/cnhc/cbd.html.

144 Like the Nile crocodile, the geographical spread of the Australian salt water crocodile belies its name and sub-populations are located throughout Southern East Asia, also see *Crocodilian Biology Database*.

145 The crocodile identification process began in 1992: Conf. Res. 11.12 is merely the latest refinement of the procedures.

146 Conf. Res. 11.12, Preamble.

147 Hutton and Webb, at pp. 116–117.

148 Conf. Res. 11.12(a).

149 Conf. Res. 11.12(k).

150 Obviously it is also a prerequisite for international trade that each consignment or individual specimen is also accompanied by the relevant import/export permits which will only have been issued when the criteria under CITES Article III and Article IV.

151 Conf. Res. 11.12(c). These fail-safe characteristics include "a self-locking mechanism, heat resistance, inertia to chemical and mechanical processing, and alphanumeric information applied by permanent stamping".

through the Secretariat and any manufacturer of the tags will agree, in writing, that no tags shall be duplicated, and sold only to appropriate CITES recognised Management Agencies.[152]

As the above example shows, CITES has the ability and the will to adopt, implement and monitor proper identification and documentation schemes, and whilst there are obviously numerous practical differences between, for instance, a consignment of a dozen or so crocodile skins and a consignment of hundreds of tonnes of fish, procedurally the same issues exist in both cases. The success of the crocodile scheme shows that CITES can work, and if, as anticipated in the UNFAO Technical Consultation, RFMOs can be brought on-board and a standardised and universal CDS can be agreed upon and implemented then there is no reason to suggest why these two schemes cannot have a complementary role to ensure that unlawfully harvested fish stocks do not enter the international market place.

6.4.3 *Administrative, Economic and Social Implications*

The next endeavour of the UNFAO Consultation was to consider the administrative, economic and social implications of the use of CITES in managing aquatic species, and the consultation pointed out that more regulation equates to more administration which, in turn, equates to an increased financial burden. The question therefore remains who shall bear this burden. On this point the Consultation noted the existing practice in many CITES member States when implementing its Appendix listing obligations. Essentially, this can be described as the "user pays" principle. Under this principle administration costs, as well as the inevitable costs of stock assessment, and perhaps even on-going enforcement, are met by those seeking to trade in CITES listed species by the payment of a fee for any export and/or import permit granted.[153]

Whilst the above proposals on this point may be fairly straightforward and simple, the UNFAO study did acknowledge a number of significant implications that require further consideration. Drawing from previous experience it is apparent that in many States the start up costs of increased regulation in wildlife trade can have a detrimental effect upon legitimate trade as, when faced with the additional costs of compliance, many fishers have been forced to turn to poaching. The UNFAO Consultation did not, in this regard, make any concrete proposals, but did again rather state the obvious by recommending that "[p]arties should make every effort to mitigate any undesirable social and economic effects."[154]

---

[152] Conf. Res. 11.12, Annex 2.
[153] UNFAO Fisheries Report No. 741, at p. 16.
[154] UNFAO Fisheries Report No. 741, at p. 16.

6.5 *On-going Legal Aspects – "Introduction From the Sea"*

The types of problem thus far highlighted are, it is submitted, precisely the types of problem that the best Catch Documentation Schemes can help fisheries managers avoid, whether it be in the context of RFMOs or under the provisions of CITES. As the next stage of the Consultation explicitly acknowledged, however, the expansion of CITES' remit into the world of fisheries management may present the international community with numerous jurisdictional challenges pertaining to the relationship between CITES and the many existing treaties on the same subject matter. Thus, in the view of the Consultation, it was essential that any future role for CITES should focus upon the "synergies and complementarity between these regimes."[155] Drawing heavily from two reports prepared for the Consultation by Franckx, the first task of the consultation was to address the meaning of the term "introduction from the sea."[156] The term "introduction from the sea" is central to the workings of Articles III and IV of CITES, governing the trade in both Appendix I and Appendix II species respectively, with Article III(5) stating that "[t]he introduction from the sea of any specimen of a species included in Appendix I shall require the prior grant of a certificate from a Management Authority of the State of introduction…"; CITES Article IV(6) operates identically in as far as Appendix II species are concerned. Both Articles expand upon the primary obligation by stating the criteria for the granting of the necessary certification and for both Appendices the primary criteria is that the "Scientific Authority of the State of introduction advises that the introduction will not be detrimental to the survival of the species involved."[157] Clearly then the obligations of a non-detriment finding and the ongoing welfare of the specimens in question fall upon the Scientific

[155] *Report of the Expert Consultation on Legal Issues Related to CITES Commercially Exploited Aquatic Species,* UNFAO Fisheries Report No. 746, Rome, 2004, at p. 3 (herein after "UNFAO Fisheries Report No. 746").

[156] *Applications of the Term "Introduction from the Sea",* Eric Franckx, available from CITES at: www.cites.org/eng/news/meetings/ifs-05/term_IFS.pdf (herein after "Franckx, Introduction From the Sea"); *Legal and Institutional Implications of Listing Commercially-Exploited Aquatic Species,* Eric Franckx, also available from CITES at: www.cites.org/eng/news/meetings/ifs-05/IFS-05-implications.pdf (herein after "Franckx, Legal and Institutional Implications"). See also, Eric Franckx, *The Protection of Biodiversity and Fisheries Management: Issues Raised by the Relationship Between CITES and LOSC,* in Freestone, Barnes and Ong (eds.), *The Law of the Sea: Progress and Prospects,* Oxford University Press, Oxford, 2006, at p. 210 (herein after "Franckx, The Protection of Biodiversity").

[157] CITES Articles III(5)(a) and IV(6)(a). The further criteria oblige the Management Authorities of the State of introduction to satisfy themselves that the "proposed recipient of…[an Appendix I listed]…living specimen is suitably equipped to house and care for it" and that "the specimen is not to be used for primarily commercial purposes" (CITES Article III(5)(b)(c)). For Appendix II species the Management Authority of the State of introduction must be

Authority and Management Authority of the State of introduction. The question is, however, which State is "the State of introduction"? Is it the flag State of the vessel that takes the specimen on board or the port State where that fish is landed and cleared by customs?[158]

Little information can be gleaned on this matter from the Convention itself, as CITES simply defines an "introduction from the sea" as "transportation into a State of a specimen of any species which were taken in the marine environment not under the jurisdiction of any State."[159] Nevertheless both Franckx and the UNFAO Report considered that, in a manner "consistent with recent developments in international fisheries law," specimens should generally be considered "introduced" when they are landed in the port State.[160] To support this assertion Franckx cites numerous examples, ranging from the slightly irrelevant[161] to the eminently logical, the most logical of which being that "border controls constitute a quintessential element" of CITES.[162] Equally logical is the assertion that recent developments in international fisheries law have tended to introduce the principle of port State jurisdiction, evidenced by the UNFAO and Franckx by certain provisions of the UN Fish Stocks Agreement (UNFSA) such as Article 23 which empowers ports States to "take measures, in accordance with international law, to promote the effectiveness of sub-regional, regional and global conservation and management measures."[163] These measures may include the port State's right to "*inter alia*, inspect documents, fishing gear and catch on board fishing vessels, when such vessels are voluntarily in its ports or at its offshore terminals."[164]

From an enforcement point of view the role of port States appears entirely sensible, and given that neither Franckx nor the UNFAO advocate exclusivity in this regard, preferring "duality between flag and port state," the logic seems hard to fault. There are, however, two essential caveats, one practical and one legalistic, to be made at this stage. First, it must be cautioned that any over-reliance upon port States could exacerbate the phenomenon of "ports of convenience" whereby, particularly in the IUU context, vessel owners will simply land their catches in the ports of States that are not party to CITES, or in the

"satisfied that that any living specimen will be so handled as to minimise the risk of injury, damage to health or cruel treatment" (CITES Article IV(6)(b)).

158 UNFAO Fisheries Report No. 746, at p. 3.

159 CITES Article I(e).

160 UNFAO Fisheries Report No. 746, at pp. 3–4.

161 Citing CITES' current Secretary-General Willem Wijnstekers' "personal opinion" that "a specimen is only introduced from the sea when it is landed", Franckx, *Introduction From the Sea*, at p. 13.

162 Franckx, *Introduction From the Sea*, at p. 13.

163 UNFSA, Article 23(1).

164 UNFSA, Article 23(2).

ports of States whose CITES compliance mechanisms are less well managed or enforced than their peers. In the former case, catches would be deemed to be exports when transhipped to consumer States and reliant upon Scientific or Management Authorities (which may or may not exist) in non-Party States determining, *inter alia,* that the trade in that catch will not be detrimental to the survival of the species.[165] In the latter case IUU fishers may deliberately use the ports of State Parties whose track record is one of non-implementation of CITES' provisions due to the non-creation or inadequate performance of the requisite Scientific or Management Authorities.[166]

In the second of the two caveats to be inserted (also briefly recognised by Franckx), it is contended that more attention must be paid to the more substantial principle of flag State jurisdiction, found in both customary international law and the provisions of UNCLOS, so as to avoid any future conflict between CITES and the general body of international law. Although it is certainly true that the UNFSA allows for limited port State jurisdiction, in terms of fisheries law the UNFSA is a ground-breaking Agreement and hardly described as being widely accepted by the majority of the international community.[167] Similarly the UNFSA only allows for port State jurisdiction in very discreet circumstances and does not create a new category of general port State jurisdiction. Equally the UNFSA explicitly recognises its subservient role to UNCLOS by stating that "[n]othing in this Agreement shall prejudice the rights, jurisdiction and duties of States under the Convention. This Agreement shall be interpreted and applied in the context of and in a manner consistent with the Convention."[168] Further to this, and so as to avoid any future confusion, a number of States made interpretive Declarations upon ratification of or accession to the UNFSA reaffirming their belief in the principle of exclusive flag State control.[169]

---

165 CITES Article X covers trade with non-Parties and states that "[w]here export or re-export is to, or import is from, a State not Party to the present Convention, comparable documentation issued by the competent authorities in that State which substantially conforms to the requirements of the present Convention for permits and certificates may be accepted in lieu thereof by any Party".

166 It is of course acknowledged here that the very same problem could occur regarding flags of convenience if the flag State of the vessel on which the catch was brought aboard was the State in which the catch had been "introduced".

167 In terms of signatures, ratifications and accessions it is clear that the UNFSA has not been widely embraced by a significant number of States. Over a decade after it was open for signature only 78 States are currently members: whilst this is a respectable number of States it does mean, however, that there are 90 States that are party to UNCLOS and not the UNFSA, see UN Oceans and the Law of the Sea website at http://www.un.org/Depts/los/index.htm.

168 UNFSA, Article 4.

169 Whilst the majority of these Declarations concerned the "Stop and Search" provisions of Article 21 for vessels on the high seas these Declarations are evidence of the manner in which many States cling to the sanctity of exclusive flag State jurisdiction. See, for instance

Under the more widely accepted provisions of UNCLOS, port State jurisdiction is generally limited to the taking of action against vessels believed to have engaged in the pollution of the high seas.[170] Thus, although it is certainly true that under the UNFSA port States are given powers to promote the efficacy of fisheries agreements, as one UNFAO study conceded:

> Regimes on port State control are most effective if such regimes have common goals with the flag State and are initiatives that supplement and do not substitute flag State control. The principle of flag State responsibility over vessels continues to be the fundamental principle in international shipping.[171]

Nevertheless, and despite the clear precedence of flag State jurisdiction over port State jurisdiction in the general body of international law, it is necessary to further analyse the two principles in terms of sovereignty: after all, in relation to the immediate topic – that of the term "introduction from the sea" – sovereignty would appear to be key, and clearly the landing of a catch would seem to be the first time that the species are, in fact, subject to the sovereignty of a State.

Although international law has moved away from the once firmly held belief that flag State jurisdiction was based upon territoriality,[172] the same cannot so readily be said about sovereignty and the duties imposed upon States as a result of the exercise of this sovereignty. To separate the principle of flag State rights and flag State duties by an artificial construct such as the sort proposed by the UNFAO's tentative attempt to define "introduction from the sea" to mean when the catch is landed would, it is contended, run counter to all rational readings of UNCLOS. Under this Convention it is the flag State that is obliged to exercise the general duties of jurisdiction under Article 94 and it is to that State that nationality is affixed under Article 91. Of course it could be argued that simply because the vessel onto which the fish were taken is of a certain nationality it does not necessarily follow that anything aboard that vessel should also be nationalised in such a way – consider, for instance, the crew. Just because an Indonesian crew member, for example, serves on board a Panamanian fishing boat it does not mean that that crew member, although

the Interpretative Declarations by Austria, China, the European Community, France, Malta, Slovenia, Spain, the United Kingdom and Northern Ireland, and Uruguay.

170 UNCLOS Article 218.

171 Terje Lobach, *Port State Control of Foreign Fishing Vessels,* UNFAO Fisheries Circular No. 987, UNFAO, Rome, 2003, at section 2: *Justifications for a Harmonised System,* (herein after "Lobach").

172 See, for instance, Birnie and Boyle, at p. 376 who describe the principle as an "erroneous equation of ships with floating territory"; Rayfuse (2004), at p. 21, who states that the theory of territoriality of ships has been rejected as "an illogical, imprecise, inaccurate and inappropriate basis upon which to ground jurisdiction".

subject to Panamanian internal laws, becomes a nationalised Panamanian. The difference is, as Grotius would argue, one of dominion: the crew member being "previously owned" by his State of nationality cannot be taken into dominion and subject to the exclusive sovereignty of the flag State. The fish, on the other hand, when caught, are taken into the dominion of the flag State and thus the sovereign possessions of that State, and it is this sovereignty that facilitates the necessary exercise of jurisdiction as required by UNCLOS. Accordingly then, even though the UNFAO's proposals regarding port State dominion may be attractive in terms of enforcement, and whilst acknowledging that the UNFAO stops short of making an out-right recommendation that all catches should only be viewed as "introduced" when landed, it is contended that so as to arrive at the necessary consensus it may be necessary to give further thought to the sensitive matter of any reduction in real or perceived flag State competence.

Thus it is understandable that when CITES' 14th Conference of the Parties[173] undertook to scrutinise the issue of which State constitutes the "State of introduction" it was decided that further appraisal of the subject was required. Thus the Standing Committee was directed to convene a Working Group to clarify the term "State of Introduction" and asked to prepare a discussion paper and Draft Resolution in time for the 15th Conference of the Parties in Doha.[174] Unfortunately, the document presented to the 15th COP by the Working Group betrays only indecision on this issue: although the Doha Conference of the Parties did revise Conference Resolution 14.6, it was not given the opportunity to clarify which State would be the State of introduction because deleted from the Draft Revision to 14.6 was the phrase "Further agrees that 'the State of introduction' means the [port State] [flag State]."[175] Presumably, if the Conference had been given the opportunity to consider the issue of State of introduction then it would simply have been a case of "delete as appropriate." The endeavour of clarifying the State of introduction was subsequently postponed until the 16th CITES Conference of the Parties in March 2013.

One issue that has been clarified at CITES Conferences of the Parties, (and perhaps even more contentious and of greater practical significance than the term "introduction") was the second element of the UNFAO's initial consultation, that of what constitutes "the sea". From the wording of the CITES Convention it is obvious that "the sea" means "the marine environment not under the jurisdiction of any State,"[176] ergo the high seas. Slightly complicating this issue is the precise delineation of the high seas, not in solely geographic terms, but also in historic terms, because, as the UNFAO study notes, since

173 The Hague, June 2007.

174 CITES, Conf. Decision 14.48.

175 Draft Revision of Conference Resolution 14.6, CoP 15 Com. II 35.

176 CITES Article I(e).

1973 when CITES was concluded the high seas have undergone enormous changes, the practical importance of which, according to Franckx, "can hardly be overstated."[177] In other words, should the areas "not under the jurisdiction of any State" be construed so as to reflect the 1973 position whereby millions of square nautical miles remained "high seas" or the post-UNCLOS position whereby these same regions formed the Exclusive Economic Zones of coastal States? To answer this important question, it is necessary, as Franckx noted, to examine the doctrine of inter-temporal law, and for Franckx the logical and "basic point of reference in this domain" was the resolution adopted by the 11th Session of the *Institut de Droit International* held in Wiesbaden in August 1975,[178] the basic rule of which stated that:

> Unless otherwise indicated, the temporal sphere of application of any norm of public international law shall be determined in accordance with the general principle of law by which any fact, action or situation must be assessed in the light of the rules of law that are contemporaneous with it.[179]

To further complicate matters, CITES, like very many of its contemporary Treaties, aware of the preparatory work being undertaken for the Third UN Conference on the Law of the Sea (UNCLOS), seemed to pre-empt future developments by stating in Article XIV(6) that:

> Nothing in the present Convention shall prejudice the codification and development of the law of the sea by the United Nations Conference on the Law of the Sea convened... nor the present or future claims and legal views of any State concerning the law of the sea and the nature and extent of coastal and flag State jurisdiction.[180]

For the UNFAO Consultation, CITES Article XIV(6) nonetheless represented no more than a red herring, and rather than providing an "ongoing basis for clarifying the relationship between the 1982 Convention and CITES" this Article simply pertained to a statement by the CITES Parties that "nothing in CITES could have an influence, either positive or negative, on the development of the law of the sea."[181] Accordingly therefore, in the absence of any further

[177] Franckx, *Introduction From the Sea*, at p. 14.

[178] *Ibid.*, at p. 15.

[179] Le Problème Intertemporel en Droit International Public, Institut de Droit Internatioal, Wiesbaden, August 1975. The exact wording of the authoritative French text reads: A défaut d'une indication en sens contraire, le domaine d'application dans le temps d'une norme de droit international public est déterminé conformément au principe général de droit, d'après lequel tout fait, tout acte et toute situation doivent être appréciés à la lumière des règles de droit qui en sont contemporaines.

[180] This conflict clause was repeated verbatim in a further 7 international agreements contemporaneous to CITES, see Franckx, *Introduction From the Sea*, at p. 19.

[181] UNFAO Fisheries Report No. 746, at p. 4.

guidance or evidence to the contrary then the position should revert to the "default regime" of the *Institut de Droit International's* resolution. Fortunately for clarity, and indeed sanity, sufficient evidence does appear to exist in the form of State practice specific to the fisheries context under UNCLOS to avoid the situation under which CITES must operate under an entirely alien regime for the delineation of the ocean space. Therefore, so as to update and clarify CITES' interpretation of what constitutes "areas beyond any national jurisdiction" the 14th Conference of the Parties adopted, in Conference Resolution 14.6, the entirely rational definition of "the marine environment not under the jurisdiction of any State" to mean:

> ...those areas beyond the areas subject to the sovereignty or sovereign rights of a State consistent with international law, as reflected in the United Nations Convention on the Law of the Sea.[182]

The final aspect of the UNFAO's consultation concerned the thorny and complicated relationship between CITES and the general body of the law of the sea, as found under UNCLOS, and specific fisheries related agreements. Here again, the UNFAO utilised the work of Professor Franckx. The first point of note is, of course, that in order for substantive conflicts to arise between UNCLOS and CITES it is necessary that there is no synergy of the objectives of the two Treaties – this therefore, in the majority of cases envisaged, is obviously not the case as both Treaties would appear to aspire to the same thing: that of conserving and protecting the (oceanic) environment. Of course UNCLOS and CITES operate on entirely different levels and adopt radically different means of achieving their objectives: UNCLOS, of course, is entirely silent on the issue of international trade, and CITES clearly does not prohibit certain activities, rather it simply states that the fruits of any given activities cannot be internationally traded. Thus, considering the synergy of purpose and the polarised means of achieving this purpose it is difficult to envisage a scenario in the IUU/FOC context in which UNCLOS and CITES are drawn into substantive conflict.[183]

Nevertheless, it may be argued that under UNCLOS all States have a right to exploit the oceanic environment, regardless of whether this exploitation is carried out within the sovereign EEZ[184] or the high seas[185] provided that the

182 CITES Conf. Res. 14.6.

183 Indeed Fisheries Report No. 746 adopts this type of approach itself by stating, at p. 3, that "The Consultation...focussed on looking for synergies and complementarity between these regimes taking into account their respective strengths and weaknesses" and that the differences of approach, but synergy of aspiration, could "be easily used to strengthen instead of weaken the level of over-all conservation of commercially exploited aquatic species."

184 UNCLOS Article 56(1)(a).

185 UNCLOS Article 87(1)(e).

exploitation is carried out in a manner not inconsistent with the proprietary limits imposed by the Convention itself.[186] Therefore, so the argument could continue, any further restrictions imposed by CITES upon the manner in which States may exercise their rights and freedoms may be deemed to be inconsistent with UNCLOS. It is contended, however, that within the generality of scenarios there is no inconsistency here as any restrictions imposed by CITES do nothing to limit the rights of States under UNCLOS. CITES does not and cannot limit the rights of harvest and exploitation: at the very most it can only limit the international trade in the harvest, and there is nothing within the provisions of UNCLOS which guarantees access of States to the international market place. Nor does UNCLOS guarantee landing rights, and so even in the scenario envisaged by the UNFAO whereby a vessel may, in pursuit of its rights of fishing in the high seas enshrined under UNCLOS Article 116, be prevented from landing this catch in a port due to prohibitions imposed on imports under CITES, no contravention of UNCLOS would occur.[187] Nevertheless, for the sake of completeness if nothing else, it is probably worth considering the situation in the event of any hitherto unforeseen yet genuine conflict between UNCLOS and CITES.

Essentially UNCLOS appears to trump all. This is clear from both the perspective of CITES and UNCLOS, as from the CITES perspective it will be recalled from earlier in this Chapter that during the drafting of CITES a proprietary UNCLOS conflict clause, Article XIV(6), was inserted to the effect that CITES would not prejudice the codification and development of UNCLOS. Whilst not explicitly yielding to UNCLOS it is clear that the effect of CITES Article XIV(6) is to acknowledge the *lex specialis* of UNCLOS for all oceanic matters. A similar result ensues when the issue is considered from the point of view of UNCLOS itself, as UNCLOS Article 311(2) (although couched in positive terms) states that "[UNCLOS] shall not alter the rights and obligations of State Parties which arise from other agreements *compatible* with this Convention…"[188] This clearly indicates that in the absence of such compatibility then UNCLOS prevails. As Franckx notes, there is, however, the thorny but relevant issue of Article 311(5) to contend with before any absolute conclusions as to the supremacy of UNCLOS can be established.[189] Article 311(5) effectively allows for any international agreements "expressly permitted or preserved by other articles of [UNCLOS]" to remain not subject to the supremacy principle of Article 311(2). Of course, these international agreements are not specified by name within the provisions of UNCLOS, and CITES is therefore

186 UNCLOS Articles 61–62; UNCLOS Part VII, Section II.

187 Fisheries Report No. 746, at paragraph 38.

188 Emphasis added.

189 Franckx, *The Protection of Biodiversity*, at p. 220.

nowhere mentioned, but for Franckx, at least, Article 311(5) indicates that Article 311(2) is by no means absolute. Indeed, to evidence this point Franckx considers UNCLOS Article 237 which allows for derogations from the supremacy principle of UNCLOS Article 311(2) for all activities carried out under Part XII of UNCLOS, which allows for the protection of the marine environment from pollution, and states that UNCLOS, in this specific regard, operates "without prejudice to the specific obligations assumed by States under special conventions and agreements concluded previously..."

Furthermore, in regard to the specific fisheries context Franckx points to the fact that numerous UNCLOS Articles governing straddling stocks, anadromous stocks and catadromous stocks all operate on the basis that further international agreements are necessary and thus fall within the exception to the supremacy principle under Article 311(5).[190] Likewise, again as Franckx acknowledges, UNCLOS Article 116, which empowers all States to fish on the high seas, is governed not by UNCLOS Article 311(2) but its exception, UNCLOS Article 311(5). Again, it is difficult to imagine a scenario in which a genuine conflict could arise because although UNCLOS Part VII, Section II obliges States to factor in economic considerations – "including the special requirements of developing States"[191] in their calculations of the maximum sustainable yield, these calculations may also consider the long term stability of the stocks in question and associated stocks.[192] Thus, it is conceivable that CITES may allow for the setting of higher standards of conservation than explicitly allowed for under UNCLOS (due to the fact that under CITES there is no "developing State qualification"). Again the argument can be repeated to negate any suggestions of conflict – that is that CITES does not prohibit the harvest of these stocks, and so all States, irrespective of any prohibition on the international trade in certain fish products, may still legitimately exercise their rights of exploitation as enshrined under UNCLOS Article 116.

6.6 *The Inherent and Practical Limits to CITES*

Thus far this Chapter has concentrated upon the positive side to CITES and demonstrated that both CITES as a Convention and an infrastructure is particularly sophisticated and mature in its scope and coverage. The Chapter has demonstrated that *if* CITES were to be accepted by the international community as a fisheries management tool then the Convention and the infrastructure could have an important role to play in regulating the international

[190] Franckx, *the Protection of Biodiversity,* at p. 220.
[191] UNCLOS Article 119(1)(a).
[192] UNCLOS Article 119(1)(a)(b).

trade of commercially important fish stocks. Nonetheless, as Chapter Three has demonstrated, the problem posed by IUU/FOC vessels goes far beyond the depletion of fish stocks. Hence it is further necessary to ask whether it is possible for CITES to regulate international trade when it is not the traded commodity itself that is endangered but plant and animal species associated with the harvesting of the traded species.

At this stage it is worth recalling the principle enunciated in CITES Article II(2)(b) which states that "Appendix II shall include...other species which must be subject to regulation in order that trade in specimens of certain species referred to in sub-paragraph (a)[193] of this paragraph may be brought under effective control." This would seem to indicate that CITES is perfectly capable of "indirect" conservation – where, for instance, species 'A' is threatened by the harvest of species 'B' then limits may be imposed on the international trade in species 'B' irrespective of whether species 'B' is threatened provided that the trade in species 'A' needs to be "brought under effective control." Thus, in the next section of this Chapter we shall revisit some of the "indirect" environmental harms evidenced in Chapter Three to consider how CITES could operate to reduce the threats posed to the greater marine environment.

The first example of indirect harms, it will be recalled, concerned barbed and baited longlines on which a variety of seabirds meet their deaths. Unfortunately for the albatrosses, petrels, fulmars *et al.*, they cannot rely upon Article II(2)(b) to come to their aid as, whilst they may be threatened by extinction, they are not traded, and Article II(2)(b) may only be invoked when trade must be curtailed. Thus, there exists the rather bizarre situation by which the critically endangered short tailed albatross (*Diomedae Albatrus*), listed on Appendix I of CITES, may be doomed to die on Alaskan longlines,[194] with CITES currently powerless to prevent large numbers of their deaths.[195] Of course, in theory it is possible to offer a solution: the wording of Article II(2)(b) could be modified so as to include a phrase such as "Appendix II shall also include those species that must be subject to regulation in order to prevent the decline in populations of species listed in Appendix I" but politically this notion would seem to

---

[193] CITES Article II(2)(a) "all species which although not necessarily now threatened with extinction may become so..."

[194] The Ecologist Online, at http://www.theecologist.org/archive_detail.asp?content_id=292.

[195] This situation has been brought to the attention of the CITES COP on several occasions, not least by the US Government's submission to the 11th COP in Gigiri (Kenya) in 2000 that CITES and the UNFAO "should work co-operatively in the implementation of the FAO plans of action on seabirds, sharks, and fishing capacity management and in the upcoming review of CITES listing criteria," see Conf. Doc. 11.14. Likewise, see the Australian proposal regarding the listing of Patagonian tootfish on the CITES Appendices which recognised the terrible consequences for many albatrosses and petrels as a result of the IUU toothfish longline fleet operating within the extended CCAMLR region, see CITES Proposal No. 12.39.

be a non-starter,[196] and, of course, could only operate when or if commercially important fish stocks find their way onto the CITES lists themselves. This situation is not unique to albatrosses caught on longlines, either: it appears that all incidental environmental harms are beyond the scope of the currently phrased Article II(2)(b) – whether those harms concern CITES listed species such as *Diamedea Albatrus,* or the many species of coral crushed beneath the steel rollers of the high seas bottom trawler, or the dolphins drowning in purse seine nets.

One criticism frequently levelled at CITES is that it is not so much trade that threatens wildlife but habitat destruction and that CITES simply cannot combat this threat.[197] This would clearly pose a problem for the regulation of certain types of IUU/FOC fishing activities such as the high seas bottom trawling of sea-mounts and cold water corals. As indicated in Chapter Three, high seas bottom trawling is a particularly insidious crime against wildlife and one of the worst (or best) examples of short term gain being put before long term sustainability. The above mentioned short-coming of CITES is not, however, the only hurdle to be crossed when considering this Convention as a tool to combat IUU/FOC fishing.

As was noted earlier in this Chapter there is a very real and pressing practical difficulty in applying CITES' to deal with IUU/FOC fisheries due to the non-membership of CITES of 3 recognised flags of convenience States.[198] Whilst only two of these States, the Marshall Islands and Tonga, are held to be major IUU/FOC States by the ITF they can be joined by Tuvalu which is designated as such by the UNFAO.[199] Thus, although the numbers of vessels currently on these States' registries may be relatively small,[200] as has been shown in earlier Chapters, the lack of any obligation upon these States to comply with CITES

---

[196] When reacting to the USA's above mentioned proposal the CITES Secretariat tersely responded by stating that "though of importance with regard to conservation, [they] do not deal with international trade in CITES species. The Secretariat questions the appropriateness of adopting a statement about the importance of these [proposals]."

[197] Birnie and Boyle, at p. 630; Hutton and Dickson, at p. xvi; Morne A. du Plessis, *CITES and the Causes of Extinction,* in Hutton and Dickson, at p. 16.

[198] North Korea, the Marshall Islands and Tonga.

[199] Swan (2002), Appendix 1.

[200] As per data available in summer 2005 the Marshall Islands' FOC fleet comprised of a mere 0.6% of worldwide FOC vessels (1.2% if measured in Gross Tonnage, or 7 vessels), Gianni and Simpson (2005), at p. 14. Likewise Tonga demonstrated a similarly low figure of 9 fisheries capture vessels and 2 fisheries support vessels as per latest available data, see Swan (2002) Appendix 4. At present little is known about the number the of vessels on the Tuvaluan register, other than at the time of writing this State was not one of the top 14 States as identified by Gianni and Simpson and nor did it warrant sufficient attention to have been subject to the 2003 study conducted by Winchester and Alderton on behalf of the Seafarer's International Research Centre, see http://www.sirc.cf.ac.uk/fsa.htm. Nevertheless, as the notorious *Pong Su* incident testifies Tuvalu's open registry has clearly been open to abuse by unscrupulous vessel

practices can and almost certainly would, if past practice can be held to be indicative of future behaviour, operate as a significant attraction to vessel owners wishing to avoid troublesome regulation.

Exacerbating the problem of non-party States is the very real issue of reservations. This issue is, of course, not unique to CITES, because under the Vienna Convention on the Law of Treaties all States are permitted to lodge reservations to any treaty.[201] The limited exceptions to this are when reservations are not permitted under the terms of the treaty in question,[202] or when the treaty only allows reservations of limited scope[203] or when such a reservation would prove to be incompatible with the object and purpose of that treaty.[204] The text of CITES operates in such a way as to put into practice the provisions of the Vienna Convention by prohibiting 'general reservations' to the Convention,[205] whilst allowing for specific reservations in respect of species subject to inclusion on any of the Appendices.[206] Thus, it is clearly possible that if any given Conference of the Parties were to vote to include, for example, Patagonian toothfish on to Appendix II then States not wishing to subject themselves to the restrictions on toothfish trade imposed by such a listing would simply lodge a reservation in line with the dictats of Article XXIII.

Being 'unilateral' in scope – that is to say that such reservations do not require acceptance by other States,[207] and thus not capable of being formally objected to – these reservations have the effect of ensuring that reserving States are not bound by the provisions of the Treaty amendment to which they lodge a reservation. Clearly then this could pose a significant problem for any proposed listing of species, but especially so when one considers the previously discussed State antagonism towards the listing of commercially important fish stocks. It is not difficult to imagine that in the case of, for example, Patagonian toothfish that a plethora of States, for reasons of either ideology (because, for instance, they object to the use of CITES for such fish stocks) or practicality (because they might wish to benefit from a less regulated trading environment in that

owners. In this case North Korean heroine smugglers attempted to use the Tuvaluan registered *Pong Su* to import vast quantities of drugs into Australia, *The Times,* 2nd May 2003.

201 Vienna Convention, Article 19.

202 Vienna Convention, Article 19(a).

203 Vienna Convention, Article 19(b).

204 Vienna Convention, Article 19(c).

205 CITES Article XXIII(1).

206 CITES Article XXIII(2)(a). Reservations in respect of 'parts or derivatives' of Appendix III species are also permitted under Article XXIII(2)(b).

207 Vienna Convention, Article 20(1), which states that "A reservation expressly authorized by a treaty [as would be the case in a reservation lodged to a Conference Resolution to list a species in a CITES Appendix, per CITES Article XXIII(2)(a)] does not require any subsequent acceptance by the other contracting State unless the treaty so provides."

species), would promptly lodge reservations to the Resolution. In the event of such an occurrence then a significant weakening of the Resolution would occur whereby potentially significant import, export and re-export States (having lodged a reservation) might need to pay no heed to the Resolution. Although the reservation in question would undoubtedly operate between reserving States in a manner rendering CITES entirely inapplicable, fortunately the Convention text of CITES contains provisions that deal with the relations between reserving States and non-reserving States in the same way that relations between State parties and non-party States are dealt with.

In these former cases, and as noted by Kunich, "such reservations allow reserving parties to be treated as non-parties with regard to the trade in the applicable species…"[208] Thus the provisions of Article X will apply to both non-parties and reserving parties and require that member States should deal with non-member States (and, of course, reserving parties) in a comparable fashion as member States, by stating that:

> Where export or re-export is to, or import is from, a State not a Party to the present Convention, comparable documentation issued by the competent authorities in that State which substantially conforms with the requirements of the present Convention for permits and certificates may be accepted in lieu thereof by any Party.[209]

Thus, when a final consumer State imports fisheries products from a non-CITES State (flag of convenience or otherwise) it is essential that some form of documentation which "substantially conforms to the requirements" of CITES' import/export permits accompany the shipment. One such conforming document would, of course, be a valid RFMO catch or trade document. On this basis 'legitimate' vessels, registered to non-CITES parties, but conforming with regional conservation measures would not be denied access to the international marketplace. On the other hand those traditional IUU/FOC vessels which, as a result of undermining regional measures are not issued with the relevant permits to trade will not be able to provide the importing State with the requisite documentation.

6.7 *Conclusion*

To conclude this Chapter it is suggested that CITES can play a role in the management and regulation of the fisheries sector and this role can be of enormous

---

208 John Charles Kunich, *Killing Our Oceans: Dealing with the Mass Extinction of Marine Life*, Greenwood Publishing Group, Santa Barbara, 2006, at p. 92.

209 CITES, Article X.

significance in the fight against IUU/FOC vessels by restricting their access to consumer States. This role can be direct via listing commercially important fish stocks on the CITES Appendices or indirect via the adoption by CITES parties of regional schemes such as the CCAMLR CDS, or a combination of both. Nonetheless it is suggested that directly applying CITES' provisions to commercially important fish stocks is neither immediately likely nor necessary if schemes such as the CCAMLR CDS can be given global application via the auspices of CITES.

This, in the author's opinion, is the best case scenario. Unlike CITES, CCAMLR is best placed to regulate its own marine environment and has the infrastructure and explicit mandate to so do. Additionally the CCAMLR CDS can operate in a manner so as to deny market access to IUU/FOC vessels causing indirect harms to the wider marine environment in a way that CITES is entirely ill-equipped to do. As we have seen in Chapter Five it is possible that the CCAMLR CDS can prevent the trade in toothfish when the manner in which those fish are harvested undermines CCAMLR's conservation measures, and these conservation measures include prohibitions on the use of certain types of destructive fishing gear. CITES, in its present incarnation, cannot do this.

What is required, and what CITES – as an institution or infrastructure – can do is allow for the greater coverage of the CCAMLR CDS. Provided that this institution uses its powers to properly implement Conference Resolution 12.4 to compel those States not currently implementing the CCAMLR CDS to so do then it is suggested that the CDS can further its avowed aim of ridding the southern oceans of IUU toothfish vessels. The degree of necessary compulsion to be exercised by CITES to bring this situation about is not unprecedented because, as has been noted, this is already the type of action undertaken in the National Legislation Project with regard to State compliance with CITES measures. Admittedly any further National Legislation Project may have to be reconstituted with a mandate slightly different from the one convened at the 8th Conference of the Parties,[210] but this is clearly not beyond the scope of CITES.

Rather than expend its energies attempting to find and justify a direct role for CITES (which may or may not ever come to fruition) it is suggested that CITES should proceed on the course adopted at the Santiago Conference whereby CITES is given a complementary role to that of RFMOs such as CCAMLR. On the evidence of the vote in favour of this course of action at the Santiago Conference this would appear to be the more politically acceptable

[210] Which it will be recalled from earlier in this Chapter was to "to identify those Parties whose domestic measures do not provide them with the authority to designate at least one Management Authority and one Scientific Authority, prohibit trade in specimens in violation of the Convention, penalise such trade, or confiscate specimens illegally traded or possessed".

role for CITES. Thus it is suggested that CITES embarks upon two courses of action: first it must ensure full and proper compliance with Resolution 12.4 and secondly open up a dialogue with the many other RFMOs whose role could be complemented by CITES. If, for instance, a similar agreement could be reached between all those RFMOs currently applying trade and market based regulations against IUU/FOC vessels it is suggested that the major problem currently besetting their efforts – ports of convenience – can be negated.

Chapter Seven

International Trade Law: The WTO, GATT and Regional Free Trade

7.1 *Introduction*

Because much of the focus of previous Chapters has been on the denial of international markets it is necessary to briefly consider the relevant principles of international trade law writ large in agreements such as the General Agreement on Tariffs and Trade (GATT) as applied by the World Trade Organisation. In terms of the 'bottom line' it would not be overstating the case to say that State restrictions on international trade, unless serving some prescribed and laudable aim, are not permitted under international trade law and have, in the past, rendered certain State-invoked, 'environmentally justified' barriers to trade unlawful. Consequently, lurking in the corner of the present analysis, like a pair of (white) elephants in the room, are the *Tuna-Dolphin*[1] and *Shrimp-Turtle*[2] cases that have cast a disproportionately long shadow over the ability of States to enact trade restrictive environmental measures (TREMs).

It should be stated at the outset, however, that this Chapter will dispel any fears (if such fears exist) that RFMO measures, when properly enacted (that is, enacted under the mandate of the RFMO's own constitution, taking into consideration the requirements of openness, transparency and non-discrimination as required by the Fish Stocks Agreement, the Compliance Agreement and the Code of Conduct) will violate free trade principles. Indeed, recent developments have indicated that quite the opposite is true: for instance, at a regional level, the European Union (the primary mandate of which remains, of course, to facilitate free trade between member States) has warmly embraced RFMO strategies of market denial. While the WTO has not quite gone this far, the conclusion of this Chapter will be that while fisheries managers must be aware of the previous WTO decisions, these decisions do not impinge on the ability

---

[1] *United States – Restrictions on the Imports of Tuna (I)*, Report of the Panel, 30 ILM 1594 (1991); *United States – Restrictions on Imports of Tuna (II)*, Report of the Panel, 33 ILM 839 (1994).

[2] *US – Import Prohibition of Certain Shrimp and Shrimp Products*, Report of the Appellate Body, WT/DS58/AB/R (1998).

of managers to apply properly constituted strategies of market denial against those fishing entities that undermine conservation measures.

Perhaps it is worth indicting here at the outset, however, that this Chapter will not delve into the world of international trade beyond what is immediately necessary: as tempting as it might be for an indulgent author to devote half a Chapter to a reassessment or critique of, for instance, *Tuna-Dolphins*, this endeavour would serve little useful purpose in the context of RFMO measures. Likewise, although the *Shrimp-Turtle* decision has, as has been briefly noted in the Chapter, created some debate as to the interaction and ongoing application of certain of the General Exceptions found under Article XX of GATT, the author feels that there is little practical benefit in pursuing this debate beyond what is written herein. With these apologies delivered, the Chapter shall now – and for the benefit of any reader who might, as Sands notes, fall into the category of viewing international trade law "as a separate, self-contained field" and a discipline that environmental lawyers "traditionally had very little to do with"[3] – proceed by introducing the relevant institutions and agreements.

7.2 *The World Trade Organisation*

As part of the global rebuilding framework envisioned post-World War II, GATT's rationale at the time of inception in 1947 was to "complete the foundations of the new economic order by abolishing trade barriers" in conjunction with the newly established World Bank and the International Monetary Fund.[4] Initially a free-standing non-institutional agreement GATT's powers were strengthened in 1994 with the creation of the World Trade Organisation (WTO).[5] The WTO is responsible for the "implementation, administration, and operation" of numerous multilateral trade agreements (MTAs), chief of which is the restructured 1994 version of GATT.[6] These functions are facilitated by the various bodies. The Ministerial Conference takes place every two years and is the highest authority of the WTO and can take decisions on all matters relevant to the WTO.[7] The General Council is responsible for the day-

[3] Philippe Sands, *Principles of International Environmental Law,* 2nd Edition, Cambridge University Press, Cambridge, 2003, at p. 941, (herein after "Sands, 2003").

[4] Antonio Cassese, *International Law,* OUP, Oxford, 2001, p. 406 (herein after "Cassese (2001)").

[5] Cassese (2001), p. 408; Thomas J. Schoenbaum, *International Trade and Environmental Protection,* in Birnie and Boyle, *International Law and the Environment,* 2nd Edition, OUP, Oxford, 2002, p. 698 (herein after "Schoenbaum").

[6] Schoenbaum, pp. 698–699.

[7] *Understanding the WTO,* WTO Information and Media Relations Division, Geneva, 2005, p. 100 (herein after "Understanding the WTO").

to-day running of the Organisation and to so do it takes on a number of forms: the General Council *qua* the General Council "acts on behalf of the Ministerial Conference on all WTO affairs", whilst as the Trade Policy Review Body it analyzes members' trade policies and in its judicial capacity as the Dispute Settlement Body it oversees procedures for settling disputes between members.[8]

The Dispute Settlement Body (DSB), being as it is, the General Council by another name, does not act as a traditional court due to the sheer weight of numbers involved: currently there are in excess of 150 WTO members,[9] all of which are entitled to equal representation on the General Council and thus the DSB.[10] Consequently the precise method by which the Body reaches its decisions requires special consideration in Annex 2 of the WTO Agreement. This Annex covers the establishment of the DSB,[11] the capacity of the DSB to rule on disputes arising under the various trade agreements covered by the WTO,[12] and the general provisions and methodologies for so doing.[13] More specifically Article 6 of Annex 2 obliges the DSB, when so requested by a complaining State, to establish a proprietary DSB Panel, whose function it is "to examine... the matter referred to the DSB... and to make such findings as will assist the DSB in making recommendations or in giving rulings..."[14] These Panels generally comprise of three[15] independent[16] experts.[17] The recommendations of

---

[8] Understanding the WTO, p. 101.

[9] As of May 2011 the WTO had 153 members – see: http://www.wto.org/english/thewto_e/whatis_e/tif_e/org6_e.htm.

[10] Agreement Establishing the World Trade Organisation, Article IV (2)(4) (herein after "WTO Agreement").

[11] WTO Agreement, Annex 2, Article 2(1).

[12] WTO Agreement, Annex 2, Article 1.

[13] WTO Agreement, Annex 2, Article 3. These general provisions include, *inter alia,* the adherence by Member States to the rules and procedures of the DSB (Art. 3(1)); the role of the DSB in ensuring "security and predictability" in international trade by "preserving the rights and obligations of the Members under the covered agreements in accordance with customary rules of interpretation of public international law." In so doing the judicial capacity of the DSB is strictly interpretive – none of its rulings or recommendations can "add to or diminish the rights and obligations provided by the covered agreements." (Art. 3(2)). The DSB shall settle disputes in a "prompt" and "satisfactory" fashion (Arts. 3(3)(4)) consistent with the provisions of the agreement under scrutiny (Art. 3(5).

[14] WTO Agreement, Annex 2, Article 7(2).

[15] WTO Agreement, Annex 2, Article 8(5). Although at the request of the parties to the dispute the membership of the Panel may be increased to five Panellists.

[16] Unless otherwise decided by mutual agreement between the parties to the dispute, citizens of disputing States cannot sit on any Panel (Art. 8(3)). Additionally Panellists shall sit in their individual capacities and not as governmental representatives, or representatives of any organisation (Art. 8(9)).

[17] Panels should be comprised of "well-qualified... individuals" the precise criteria of which is governed by Article 8(1) of Annex 2.

the Panel may then be rejected or adopted by the DSB,[18] although the presumption is that Panel reports shall be adopted unless "a party to the dispute formally notifies the DSB of its decision to appeal or the DSB decides by consensus not to adopt the report."[19]

When a party to the dispute does formally notify the DSB of its intention to appeal the report this appeal is heard by a Standing Appellate Body established by the DSB under Article 17 of Annex 2 of the WTO Agreement. The Appellate Body's findings are final and shall be unconditionally accepted by the parties to the dispute and adopted by the DSB unless the DSB decides by consensus to reject the findings.[20] As well as adjudicating on the immediate issue before it the Appellate Body shall, after finding a State in violation of any covered agreement, recommend to that State ways in which the violating measures may be brought into conformity with the relevant laws,[21] and any measures undertaken as a result of a DSB finding may be subject to on-going surveillance by the DSB.[22]

7.3 *The General Agreement on Tariffs and Trade*

Whilst the WTO provides the institutional framework for the control and regulation of international trade, the substance remains, *inter alia,* the reformulated GATT of 1994.[23] The Chapter will now proceed to analyse each of the Articles of GATT that are of relevance to the imposition of trade-related measures aimed at protecting the (marine) environment. This analysis will first have regard to the limitations imposed upon States by GATT insofar as they may adopt trade restrictive measures, while the remainder of this section will consider the instances when these limitations may be qualified for the purposes of avoiding harm to humans, animals, plants and the environment.

7.3.1 *Article I: Most-favoured-nations*

One of the chief elements of GATT is the most-favoured-nation principle found in Article I. Essentially this means that no State may discriminate against any other in terms of trade barriers or incentives – in effect all members of

[18] WTO Agreement, Annex 2, Article 16.
[19] WTO Agreement, Annex 2, Article 16(4).
[20] WTO Agreement, Annex 2, Article 17(14).
[21] WTO Agreement, Annex 2, Article 19.
[22] WTO Agreement, Annex 2, Article 21.
[23] The other MTAs covered by the WTO are to be found listed in Annex 1 of the WTO Agreement and include such diverse Agreements as those relating to Agriculture, Textiles and Clothing, Technical Barriers to Trade, and Subsidies and Countervailing Measures. As the Chapter progresses the applicability of certain of these Agreements will also be considered.

GATT must be granted the same advantages, favours, privileges or immunities as any given State's most-favoured-nation. Thus, if one WTO member, France for instance, allows certain fish or fish products to be imported from another WTO member, Germany, without restrictions or under a preferential treatment regime then France must extend this facility to all other WTO members. If France, however, imposes additional burdens upon the imports of those same or like fish or fish products originating in, again for hypothetical example, Mexico, then France will be in violation of Article I unless it can be shown that the restriction was justified under Article XX (discussed below) as this will be inconsistent with the manner in which it trades with its most-favoured-nation (Germany).[24, 25]

7.3.2 *Article III: National Treatment*

Article III of GATT 1994 prohibits internal State measures implemented for the protection of domestic concerns, when such measures have a prejudicial effect upon trade between the implementing State and other WTO members.[26] This means that imported goods and products cannot be subject to any taxes or charges in excess of those levied upon "like" domestic goods,[27] nor can taxes or other charges be applied in a manner so as to afford protection to domestic production.[28] Likewise internal regulatory requirements may not be adopted so as to afford protection to domestic producers by subjecting imports to "less favourable treatment" than to "like" domestic goods.[29]

Clearly, insofar as measures enforced by importing or exporting States, there are avenues of ambiguity to be explored regarding what constitutes "like"

---

[24] This hypothetical example draws upon the slightly more in-depth analysis provided by Cassese at p. 406 in which the eminent Professor goes on to show how this principle, when applied by all member States on the basis of reciprocity *should* create an equal application of the most conducive trading conditions between the WTO members.

[25] The most favoured nation principle has two noteworthy exceptions. "Where regional trade agreements have been adopted then preferential tariffs may be established between the parties to these agreements... [and insofar as developing countries are concerned]... GATT allows members to apply preferential tariff rates, or zero tariff rates, to products coming from these countries while still having higher rates for like products from other countries." See *Environment and Trade: A Handbook,* 2nd Edition, United Nations Environmental Programme, Division of Technology, Industry and Economics, Economics and Trade Branch and the International Institute for Sustainable Development, UNEP/IISD, Winnipeg, 2005, at 3.4 (herein after "UNEP/IISD Handbook").

[26] GATT 1947 (as amended by GATT 1994), Article III(1) (herein after "GATT"). For the purposes of Article III, internal measures include those that are collected or enforced against imported goods at the point of importation, see, *Ad*-Article III in GATT Annex I.

[27] GATT, Article III(2), first sentence.

[28] GATT, Article III(2), second sentence.

[29] GATT, Article III(4).

products,[30] and as Matsushita points out, "because discrimination between unlike products is permissible, the determination as to whether products are 'like' is central to the administration of Article III."[31]

7.3.3 *"Like" Products and the Product/Process Distinction*

Giving "likeness" a particularly wide interpretation would not allow States to invoke measures aimed at restricting the trade in certain commodities without reliance upon the General Exceptions found in Article XX. Yellowfin tuna, for instance, are yellowfin tuna regardless of the manner of harvest, or its "production or processing method" (PPM) according to this interpretation. If any State were to prohibit the importation of yellowfin tuna harvested using techniques deemed by that State to be harmful to dolphins, whilst at the same time allowing imports from States whose vessels adopt dolphin-friendly methods of capture, or where domestic production involves dolphin-friendly harvesting, then, accordingly, the trade-restrictive measure could be deemed to fall under the conduct prohibited under Articles I and III. It would then be incumbent upon the restricting State to justify the restrictions under Article XX.

On the other hand, given a narrow interpretation of what constitutes a "like" product when determining the likeness of domestic goods the possibility of an offended State attempting to invoke the counter-protectionist measures of GATT may be severely curtailed. Clearly in this case yellowfin tuna would not necessarily all be the same and those harvested using dolphin-safe methods would not be "like" those harvested using non-dolphin safe techniques.

Thus the question essentially becomes whether or not the term "like" is given a narrow or wide interpretation under GATT jurisprudence. In other words does the method by which a product comes into existence or, in the case of marine life, is captured, have any bearing upon the character of that product so as to distinguish it from physically similar or identical products? During the 1990s much debate on this issues was engendered by the decisions of the WTO DSB in the infamous *Tuna-Dolphins* litigation[32] in which it was held

---

30 Whilst the term "product" is used extensively throughout this Chapter it is done so simply to reflect the language of GATT/WTO rules and jurisprudence under which "product" appears to relate not only to manufactured goods but also (once) living creatures and flora. Rather than devote any further attention to the fact that living creatures maybe captured and taken into possession they are never "produced", ergo products, it is probably more expedient for the purposes of this Chapter to utilise the established phraseology.

31 Matsuo Matsushita, Thomas J. Shoembaum and Petros C. Mavroidis, *The World Trade Organisation: Law, Practice and Policy,* Oxford University Press, Oxford, 2004, at p. 158, (herein after "Matsushita *et al.*").

32 *Tuna-Dolphin I,* Judgment of 3rd September 1991. Whilst the relevance of this case may be questioned in light of its non-adoption by the General Council at Mexico's request, and the

that US restrictions on the import of tuna and tuna products, due to the less-than-dolphin-friendly manner in which the tuna was harvested, constituted a violation of GATT Article XI which regulates the use of quantitative restrictions (see below). The DSB did not, however, sympathetically consider the US measures from the point of view of whether or not the non-dolphin friendly tuna that was subject to the prohibition on imports was 'unlike' the dolphin friendly tuna that was not subject to any such restrictions. Had the DSB done so then, according to some of the contemporary writings, a very different outcome would have ensued.[33]

Much of the debate surrounding the product/process distinction – and cognisant of the fact that most of this debate concerned a hypothetical notion of 'what if the DSB had considered it' – is largely academic given events since the 1990s. Certainly the decision of the WTO Appellate Panel's findings of the application of GATT Article XX ('General Exceptions') in *Shrimp-Turtle* (discussed below) means that rather than having to argue that the prohibition found in Articles I, III and XI do not apply – because the product subject to the import restrictions is 'unlike' those that are not subject to import restrictions, it is open to States (or RFMOs) in *Tuna-Dolphin* or *Shrimp-Turtle*-like cases to claim that the measures are justified under Article XX.

7.3.4 *Article XI: Quantitative Restrictions*

A further anti-protectionist measure found in the GATT is Article XI. This Article forbids quantitative restrictions on imports and exports and applies to all measures other than duties, taxes, or other charges.[34] Although prohibiting quotas and other restrictions, Article XI does not amount to an absolute

subsequent marginalisation of the *ratio* in following DSB Panel and Appellate Body reports (see below) it is nevertheless suggested that as a high-water-mark of possible interpretations of the terms "product" and "like" this case cannot be ignored. See also *United States – Restrictions on Imports of Tuna (II),* Report of the Panel (DS29/R), Judgment of 20th May 1994, ILM 839 (1994) (herein after "*Tuna-Dolphin II*") which concerned the EC's assertion that the MMPA's requirements insofar as they applied to intermediary nation imports of tuna also violated GATT/WTO. Whilst the Panel's reports in *Tuna-Dolphin I* and *Tuna-Dolphin II* are at variance on a number of issues the reasoning and final recommendations were broadly similar.

33 Marco C.E.J. Bronkers with Natalie McNelis, *Rethinking the 'Like Product' Definition in GATT 1994: Anti-Dumping and Environmental Protection,* in Marco C.E.J. Bronkers, *A Cross-Section of WTO Law,* Cameron May, London, 2000, at p. 38; Henry L. Thaggert, *A Closer Look at the Tuna Dolphin Case: 'Like Products' and Extra-jurisdictionality in the Trade and Environment Context,* in *Trade and the Environment: The Search for Balance,* Cameron, Demaret and Geradin (eds), Cameron & May, London, 1994, at p. 72.

34 Which should, by virtue of the previously discussed GATT Articles, be levied equally to all trading partner States under the MFN principle, and domestic produce under the equal treatment principle.

prohibition. Contained therein are a number of exceptions which allow for temporary measures to be applied to exports when the aim is to prevent or relieve shortages or foodstuffs or other essential commodities,[35] or measures necessary for the protection of standards, grading or marketing.[36] Moreover, the qualifications under Article XI(2) also allow for imports of agricultural and fisheries products to be restricted provided that any measure is necessary in the enforcement of governmental measures aimed at reducing consumption or surpluses.[37] For domestic measures such as those invoked by the USA in *Tuna-Dolphin* not falling within the scope of *Ad*-Article III,[38] Article XI could be described as a "catch all" provision and one that is very difficult to refute. In such cases rather than denying that the domestic measures fall beyond the scope of Article XI States will often attempt to justify their actions under the General exceptions found under Article XX.[39]

7.3.5 *Article XX: General Exceptions*

Any measure *prima facie* offensive to the restrictions imposed under Articles I, III, or XI may still be permitted provided that the measure in question pursues one of the legitimate aims listed in Article XX. In environmental spheres the most important of the General Exceptions are where the measures are necessary to protect human, animal or plant life or health,[40] or when the measures relate to the conservation of exhaustible natural resources and are made effective in conjunction with domestic production or consumption.[41] In this context it is important, however, to take note of the preamble, or *Chapeau,* to Article XX,

---

[35] GATT Article XI(2)(a).

[36] GATT Article XI(2)(b).

[37] GATT Article XI(2)(c).

[38] As noted by Matsushita *et al.*, at pp. 124–125; pp. 166–167, distinguishing between Article XI and *Ad*-Article III can occasionally be difficult. *Ad*-Article III, it will be recalled allows "measures enforced or collected... at the time or point of importation" to be classed as internal regulations. Thus, when a product reaches customs it is permissible to enforce internal regulations provided that these regulations are applied equally to imports and domestic goods. As a consequence imports not conforming to the relevant internal requirements may be turned away by customs officers. This does not necessarily mean, however, that simply by virtue of the fact that these internal regulations are implemented at the time and place of importation that the measures fall within the scope of the prohibitions under Article XI. In *Tuna-Dolphins,* however, because the domestic measure prohibiting the importation of Mexican tuna was not an internal measure enforced at the time or point of importation it became a quantitative restriction under Article XI.

[39] Matsushita *et al.,* at pp. 166–167, assert that "[if a measure] fails the tests of Article III, Article XI automatically applies and, unless it falls under the scope of one of the narrow exceptions in that Article, it will fail the Article XI test".

[40] GATT Article XX(b).

[41] GATT Article XX(g).

which states that no measures may be "applied in a manner which would constitute a means of arbitrary or unjustifiable discrimination between countries where the same conditions prevail, or a disguised restriction on international trade." Clearly this necessitates multiple levels of inquiry: first the measure undertaken must fall within the scope of the General Exceptions under Article XX (the so-called "provisional justification"[42]) and following this stage the actual application of the measure will be scrutinised (the "final justification."[43]).

Prior to discussing the core provisions of each sub-Article in relation to the aforementioned environmental harms it may be helpful to first acknowledge the similarities and differences between the Article XX(b) and Article XX(g). Both sub-Articles may serve to justify trade restrictive environmental measures (TREMS) and at a superficial level both sub-Articles could be interpreted as serving the same ends: whilst Article XX(b) "protects," Article XX(g) "conserves." Article XX(b) deals with human, animal or plant life or health whereas Article XX(g) focuses upon "exhaustible natural resources." States may invoke either Article XX(b) or Article XX(g) depending upon suitability of each sub-Article invoked in respect of the harm to be avoided. Given that the Appellate Body has interpreted the term "exhaustible natural resources" to refer not just to commodities such as oil, gas and minerals but also "living resources" such as, for instance, sea turtles, it *could* appear that Article XX(g) has a sufficiently broad remit as to render the words "plants" and "animals" in Article XX(b) inutile. This is especially so when it is considered that the "necessity" requirement, as found in Article XX(b) is not replicated in Article XX(g), for which the provisional justification is simply "relating to the conservation of…" These terms – both threshold requirements relating to the "provisional justification" – are not, however, synonymous.[44] Hence under these circumstances any State wishing to defend *any* living-resource based TREM would clearly choose to utilise Article XX(g). In such cases the domestic measure could fall within the scope of that sub-Article without having to be justified under the higher threshold of "necessary" but simply by demonstrating that the measure invoked was "relating to the conservation of exhaustible natural resources" and are "made effective in conjunction with restrictions on domestic production or consumption."[45]

---

42 UNEP/IISD Handbook, at p. 35.

43 UNEP/IISD Handbook, at p. 35.

44 *United States – Standards for Reformulated Gasoline,* WTO Appellate Body Report, WT/DS2/AB/R, Judgment April 1996, at pp. 16–17 where the AB stated that "it does not seem reasonable to suppose that the WTO Members intended to require, in respect of each and every category [Article XX (a)–(j)], the same kind or degree of connection or relationship between the measure under appraisal and the state interest or policy sought to be promoted or realized" (herein after "*US Gasoline*").

45 Indeed, the requirement that the measure must be "made effective in conjunction with restrictions on domestic production or consumption" could also be viewed a tautologous due to the

7.4 Shrimp-Turtle: *Clarity in the Face of Defeat*

The first thing to note about *Shrimp-Turtle* is that "exhaustible natural resources" are deemed now not simply to include oil, gas, etc but also sea turtles, and indeed any other living creature, which might reasonably include any species threatened by deleterious practices.[46] Secondly, even when these measures have an extra-territorial application, that is to say, when they have the practical effect of modifying practices beyond the territory of the enacting State, they can still be successfully invoked.[47]

To recap the issue in *Shrimp-Turtle*, the complainant States – India, Malaysia, Pakistan and Thailand – alleged that US measures imposing restrictions upon imports of shrimp and shrimp products which had not been harvested in a manner so as to minimise the risk of death or injury to sea-turtles should be prohibited. Once it had been established that the USA's measures violated Article XI(1)[48] it was therefore necessary for the USA to justify the prohibition under Article XX. Thus, the argument put forward in support of the complainant States was that the attempt by the USA to rely upon Article XX violated the principles of State sovereignty and autonomy enshrined in international law: in short the complaining States said that the unilateral US measures "infringed

requirement in the *Chapeau* of Article XX that measures cannot be applied in a discriminatory or arbitrary manner.

46 Report of the Appellate Body, at paragraphs 128–133. Birnie and Boyle note, at p. 709, that the AB's finding in *Shrimp-Turtle* may have been a 'generous' one on this point. Whether this reading of Article XX(g) is too generous and, as has been claimed, has rendered Article XX(b) (measures "necessary to protect human, animal or plant life or health") inutile is a matter of much further debate and beyond the scope of the present analysis. For further on this point, however, see Arthur E. Appleton, *Shrimp-Turtle: Untangling the Nets,* Journal of International Economic Law (1999) 477, at Part 1, in which the author claims that the Appellate Body's decision renders Article XX(b) "virtually insignificant"; Bradley J. Condon, *GATT Article XX and Proximity of Interest: Determining the Subject Matter of Paragraphs (b) and (g),* 9 UCLA Journal of International Law and Foreign Affairs, No. 2 (Fall/Winter 2004). Condon argues that the differentiating factor between the two sub-Articles is the proximity of relationship between enacting State and the harm to be avoided.

47 Birnie and Boyle, at p. 710.

48 As was found in the earlier judgment of the WTO Dispute Resolution Body, see *United States – Import Prohibition of Certain Shrimp and Shrimp Products,* Report of the Panel, WT/DS58/R (1998) (herein after "*Shrimp Turtle*, Panel Report"). GATT Article XI(1) states that "No prohibitions or restrictions other than duties, taxes or other charges, whether made effective through quotas, import or export licences or other measures, shall be instituted or maintained by any contracting party on the importation of any product of the territory of any other contracting party or on the exportation or sale for export of any product destined for the territory of any other contracting party." This particular finding was not appealed by the USA, which instead focussed its efforts on persuading the Appellate Body that the domestic measures invoked could be justified under Article XX.

upon... [the]... sovereign right to formulate its own environmental and conservation policies".[49] The USA countered by claiming, *inter alia,* that because of the highly migratory nature of many of the sea-turtles under threat from trawling these turtles were a shared global resource, and thus the USA had "an interest and a right to impose the measures at issue."[50] The first judgment, given by the Dispute Settlement Body (DSB) Panel, disagreed and stated that even if sea-turtles were a shared global resource, and thus representative of a common interest between States, then the manner in which these should be protected or conserved should be through international co-operation and not unilateral measures such as those invoked by the USA.[51]

On this point the Appellate Body's judgment diverged from that of the DSB Panel. Whilst it did not subject the USA's measure to the utmost scrutiny on this issue, the Appellate Body did offer its thoughts on the matter:

> Neither the appellant nor any of the appellees claims any rights of exclusive ownership over the sea turtles, at least while they are swimming freely in their natural habitat – the oceans. We do not pass upon the question of whether there is an implied jurisdictional limitation in Article XX(g), and if so, the nature or extent of that limitation. We note only that in the specific circumstances of the case before us, there is a sufficient nexus between the migratory and endangered marine populations involved and the United States for the purposes of Article XX(g).[52]

On the basis of the above statement it is clear that whilst no precise criteria were laid out for what constitutes a "sufficient nexus" between State and resource, it is equally clear that such a nexus must exist. In the immediate case the evidence of such a nexus was the fact that many of the populations of sea-turtles under threat regularly migrated through US waters throughout their life cycle.[53]

With regard to RFMOs it is almost trite therefore that any measure adopted by an RFMO (within its sphere of competence) will not fall foul of any extra-territorial limitations imposed by Article XX(g). RFMOs have not only the right to co-operate and regulate within their jurisdictions but also the obligation to do so under the variety of international agreements, as considered in previous Chapters. Even based upon the more draconian parameters devised by the DSB Panel regarding the sufficiency of any nexus, it is clear that RFMOs attain the requisite standard of international co-operation, which, as will be recalled, was the suggested way in which the DSB thought that shared global resources should be regulated.[54]

---

49 *Shrimp-Turtle,* Panel Report (Part I), at paragraph 32.
50 *Shrimp-Turtle,* Panel Report (Part II), at paragraph 7.53.
51 *Shrimp-Turtle,* Panel Report (Part II), at paragraph 7.55.
52 *Shrimp-Turtle,* Report of the Appellate Body, at paragraph 133.
53 *Shrimp-Turtle,* Report of the Appellate Body, at paragraph 133.
54 *Shrimp-Turtle,* Panel Report (Part II), at paragraph 7.55.

The primary brake on the use of Article XX as a justification for the use of TREMs, and what constituted a hurdle too far for the USA's restrictions on shrimp in the immediate litigation, is the *Chapeau* attached to Article XX, which states that:

> Subject to the requirement that such measures are not applied in a manner which would constitute a means of arbitrary or unjustifiable discrimination between countries where the same conditions prevail, or a disguised restriction on international trade, nothing in this Agreement shall be construed to prevent the adoption or enforcement by any contracting party of measures.

One of the reasons for the failure of the US case in *Shrimp-Turtle* was that the US measures were not applied in a non-arbitrary and non-discriminatory manner. TREMs can be justified under Article XX provided that the measures are 'provisionally justified' by falling within one of the specified exceptions under Article XX *and* not arbitrarily or discriminatorily applied: States must apply TREMs fairly with due regard to the rights of WTO members and must not misuse the general exceptions found in Article XX.

In terms of GATT jurisprudence the WTO's Analytical Index proves to be extremely helpful in this regard by providing examples from case law of practices deemed to be discriminatory.[55] A note of caution should be exercised at this point, however. Because of the case sensitive nature of applying the *Chapeau,* it is suggested that very few concrete conclusions as to the nature of discriminatory practices can be drawn merely by an analysis of previous cases. As Bhala notes: "[t]he language of Article XX(b) and (g), and in the *Chapeau,* is inherently malleable. It invites the Appellate Body to consider each case, on its merits, and weigh economic and environmental concerns."[56]

Nevertheless, *some* information may be gleaned from the case law as to what type of practice is arbitrarily discriminatory and it is to this case law that our attention should now turn.

In the *Shrimp-Turtle* litigation it will be recalled that certain Caribbean States were given a "phasing-in period" to implement the requirements of the US measures whilst the complaining States were not.[57] Similarly the USA had engaged in serious dialogue with numerous States under the auspices of the Inter-American Agreement but no such negotiations had been initiated with the complaining States.[58] Such action was clearly in violation of the *Chapeau* to Article XX, which states that any measures seeking to rely upon that Article

---

55 Available at: http://www.wto.org/english/res_e/booksp_e/analytic_index_e/gatt1994_07_e.htm#article20.

56 Raj Bhala, *Modern GATT Law: A Treatise on the General Agreement on Tariffs and Trade,* Thompson – Sweet & Maxwell, London, 2005, at p. 634.

57 *Shrimp-Turtle,* Report of the Appellate Body, at paragraph 173.

58 *Shrimp-Turtle,* Report of the Appellate Body, at paragraphs 166–172.

must be applied in an even-handed manner and must not be "applied in a manner which would constitute a means of arbitrary or unjustifiable discrimination between countries where the same conditions prevail, or a disguised restriction on international trade."

It is suggested that, subject to one qualification to be dealt with shortly, in the context of RFMOs no such discrimination should take place if that RFMO follows the requirements of its own terms of reference or the UNFSA. As was noted earlier in Chapter Five, in order to give effect to the provisions of the UNFSA, all RFMOs are required to ensure that all interested States are given participatory rights and are not excluded from the decision-making process of that RFMO. Likewise, under positive or negative listing procedures, again as demonstrated in Chapter Five, flag States have a right to hear and respond to allegations made against their vessels. It is only when, in the absence of any concerted attempt by these States to fulfil their obligations of effective control and once a response from the flag State has been solicited, that State sanctions or exclusions from any RFMO positive list may be undertaken. Thus, unlike the complaining States in *Shrimp-Turtle*, recipient States of RFMO measures cannot claim that they have been excluded from the market place arbitrarily[59] unless that State has been treated differently from a State, also in flagrant breach of RFMO rules, *in which similar conditions apply*.

In the final aspect of this discussion it is necessary to expand upon the above emphasised key phrase of "in which similar conditions apply." Discrimination under GATT rules can, of course, be avoided by treating like cases alike but more, however, is required. What is abundantly clear from *Shrimp-Turtle* is that unlike cases must be treated differently. For example, it may not be sufficient for RFMOs to simply offer the opportunity to avoid sanctions by requiring all States to adopt equal criteria: these criteria must be equitable and must "allow for... [an]... enquiry into the appropriateness of the regulatory program for the conditions prevailing in those exporting countries."[60] In a recent set of guidelines the UNFAO has re-emphasised this point, stating that developing countries – as many FOC States are – should be given time and assistance in order to adequately implement regional measures.[61] Thus, only when RFMOs properly consult, act in good faith and allow for a phasing in period that recognises the ability of States to comply with regulatory measures, may 'GATT safe' TREMs be invoked.

59 Indeed the Appellate Body in the *Shrimp-Turtle* litigation recognised the inherent flaws in the USA's measures and noted that there existed "... no formal opportunity for an applicant country to be heard, or respond to any arguments that may be made against it...".

60 *Shrimp-Turtle*, Report of the Appellate Body, at paragraph 165.

61 UNFAO Technical Guidelines for Responsible Fisheries 11, *Responsible Fish Trade*, UNFAO, Rome, 2009, at paragraphs 56 and 69.

7.5 *The Agreement on Technical Barriers to Trade*

The WTO's Agreement on Technical Barriers to Trade (TBT) was enacted in 1995 to further the objectives of GATT,[62] and in essence it fills in any gaps left by the latter agreement. Where, for instance, regulations or standards exist that do not act as quantitative restrictions (contrary to Article XI of GATT), or an internal charge (contrary to Article III of GATT) but nevertheless restrict access to markets then those regulations or standards must be compliant with the TBT. In a fashion similar to that of GATT, the requirements under the TBT Agreement are essentially those of fair dealing: that is, the measures must be necessary and proportionate,[63] equitable[64] and non-discriminatory[65] and must pursue one of the listed legitimate aims.[66] Also, and where appropriate, any measures – whether they be mandatory 'regulations'[67] or voluntary 'standards'[68] – adopted by States or a group of States should conform with any internationally applied standard.[69]

While the requirements under the TBT Agreement that pertain to fair dealing loosely mirror those of GATT, the TBT Agreement does demonstrate some appreciable differences. For instance, in the determination of 'like' products (again, like GATT, the TBT only prohibits measures applied to 'like' products) the TBT does appear to allow for the process or production method to be taken into account. For instance, the term 'technical regulation' is defined in Article 1 of Annex I as being "[a] document which lays down product characteristics *or their related processes and production methods*... [which]... may also include... terminology, symbols, packaging, marking or labelling requirements

62 The Agreement on Technical Barriers to Trade, Preamble, 2nd Recital (herein after "TBT Agreement").

63 TBT Agreement, Article 2.2. "... technical regulations are not prepared, adopted or applied with a view to or with the effect of creating unnecessary obstacles to international trade... technical regulations shall not be more trade-restrictive than necessary to fulfil a legitimate objective...".

64 WTO members should be cognisant of the special development, trade and financial needs of developing countries and adapt any technical regulations accordingly: TBT Agreement, Article 12.

65 TBT Agreement, Article 2.1. "... products imported from the territory of any Member shall be accorded no less favourable than that accorded to like products of national origin or to like products originating in any other country."

66 TBT Agreement, Article 2.2. The listed legitimate aims are, "*inter alia*, national security requirements; the prevention of deceptive practices; protection of human health or safety, animal or plant life or health, or the environment.

67 TBT Agreement, Annex 1, Article 1.

68 TBT Agreement, Annex 1, Article 2.

69 TBT Agreement, Article 2.4.

as they apply to the product, *process or production method*" (emphasis added).[70] The significance of the recognition of processing methods being of relevance to the TBT Agreement should not, however, be over-emphasised – it is, after all, only a recognition that technical regulations and standards might pertain to the process by which a product came into existence. The TBT Agreement does not explicitly state that this recognition should translate into a reason to distinguish between products that are ostensibly 'alike.' Again, however, one might question why a State might quibble over whether a product is 'like' or 'unlike' any other if the measure in question is a serious attempt to prevent or reduce the impacts of a genuine harm.

In these types of case the State should, instead, justify its actions by reference to exceptions found in the Agreement. For instance, even if a technical regulation or standard is put in place that does violate the fair dealing requirements of the TBT Agreement the measure may still be justified in that it pursues a legitimate aim of, for instance, "the protection of…animal or plant life or health, or the environment."[71] Unfortunately, given the paucity of reported cases concerning the application of these exceptions very little can be stated with any certainty as to what any State or group of States wishing to avail themselves of the exceptions must actually show.

Most germane for present purposes is the requirement under the TBT Agreement that conformity assessment procedures – such as Catch Documentation Schemes, for instance – operate in an open and non-discriminatory manner, subject to the provisions of Article 5. Thus, "any procedures used, directly or indirectly, to determine that relevant requirements in technical regulations or standards"[72] are applied subject to the "no less favourable treatment"[73] provisos of the Agreement and are enacted no more strictly than is necessary to assure conformity with the technical regulation or standard in issue.[74] Where RFMO measures have a distinct advantage over purely domestic measures is that the Agreement stipulates that where possible conformity assessment procedures should adhere to any recommendations issued by international or regional systems.[75] Thus, being both the regional standard setting organisation, and, in many cases, the body implementing international standards (such as the Code of Conduct for Responsible Fishing, for instance), RFMOs are well placed to

[70] A similar turn of phrase is used in Article 2 of Annex I in relation to the definition of 'standard'.

[71] TBT Agreement Article 2.2.

[72] TBT Agreement, Annex I, Article 3.

[73] TBT Agreement, Article 5.1.1.

[74] TBT Agreement, Article 5.1.2.

[75] TBT Agreement, Article 9.

enact measures, subject to the aforementioned 'fair dealing' requirements that do not offend the principles of the TBT Agreement.

7.6 *The Applicability of WTO Rules to Multilateral Environmental Agreements*

To date, no RFMO has found itself brought before the WTO's Appellate Body and charged with a violation of the principles found in any of the covered agreements. Indeed, no group of States – working under the auspices of any Multilateral Environmental Agreement (MEA) – has found itself in violation of WTO jurisprudence.[76] Does this mean that there is a *de facto* and *de jure* injunction against bringing cases against MEAs? In short, the answer is no. Indeed, as the WTO recognises, the potential for conflict between MEA measures (often being restrictions on trade) and WTO measures (which prohibit restrictions on trade) very much exists:

> a multilateral agreement could authorize trade in a specific product between its parties, but ban trade in the same product with countries that have not signed the agreement.
>
> This could be found to be incompatible with WTO's non-discrimination principle known as "most favoured nation treatment", which requires countries to grant equivalent treatment to the same (or "like") products imported from any WTO member country.[77]

To reduce the potential for conflict, the Doha Ministerial Declaration of 2001, at paragraph 31, stated that WTO members would "agree to negotiations" on this issue[78] and a decade later, in April 2011, the Chair of the Trade Negotiations Committee introduced the Draft Ministerial Decision on Trade and the Environment.[79] Despite being a decade in the making, this seemingly-hurriedly put together document is, to be frank, rather disappointing and a long way off a finished product. In fact there is very little in the document's content or its aspirations that would appear to indicate that the issue of trade versus environment is any closer to resolution than at the close of the *Shrimp-Turtle* litigation. Indeed, if one wished to glean any clues as to the compatibility of TREMs with WTO principle then, rather than looking forward to any finalised Ministerial

76 *Doha Development Agenda: Relationship Between WTO and MEA Rules,* available at: http://www.wto.org/english/tratop_e/envir_e/envir_neg_mea_e.htm.

77 *Ibid.*

78 Doha Ministerial Declaration, November 2001, Doc WT/Min (01)/Dec/01, paragraph 31 (herein after "Doha Declaration").

79 *Report by the Chairman of the Trade Negotiations Committee,* Committee on Trade and Environment, April 2011, Doc 11–2083.

Decision, perhaps one should look back to *Shrimp-Turtle* instead. Of course, given that *Shrimp-Turtle* concerned a single State initiative, rather than a multilateral measure and considering the fact that the jurisprudence of the WTO's Appellate Bodies are not binding on subsequent tribunals, using this case as the sole set of parameters in the determination of the WTO compatibility of any RFMO measure is clearly not best practice. And further, as Eckersley suggests, the temptation to view *Shrimp-Turtle* as the dawn of a "green era" in international trade brings with it its own set of problems: *Shrimp-Turtle* does not, for instance, rule out any challenge against MEA or RFMO measures as offensive to WTO rules – certainly the political impasse since the case is not suggestive of the WTO's judicial Appellate Body and its political overlords being particularly synergised in their outlook. [80] Nor does *Shrimp-Turtle* in any way address the conception that "environmental measures must be compatible with free trade" rather than vice versa: although some of the preambular language of the 2011 draft Ministerial Decision hints at a spirit of mutual compatibility and lacking in a hierarchy,[81] the Doha Declaration's instruction to the drafters of the Decision were not, in fact, to consider the impact of free trade on the environment but to "give particular attention to…the effect of environmental measures on market access."[82]

7.7 *EC Council Regulation 1005/2008*

Although the European Union's attempt to recognise the "instrumental role" of multilateral environmental agreements within the context of the WTO[83] might be doomed to failure due to the WTO's inability to agree any sort of coherent policy in a timely fashion, the EU's own commitment to MEAs and, in particular trade restrictive environmental measures, cannot be doubted. Insofar as the imports of fish and fish products into the 27 EU member States are concerned, TREMs are not only permitted, but, subject to certain provisos, mandatory and representative of the Community's international commitments:

80 Robyn Eckersley, *The Big Chill: the WTO and Multilateral Environmental Agreements*, Global Environmental Politics 4:2, May 2004, pp. 35–36.

81 In particular the inserted draft recitals of Switzerland and the European Union, which read, respectively, that the Ministers are "*Committed* to ensure coherence between international trade and environmental law in a mutually supportive way in order to continue to improve the architecture of international law to better cope with future challenges in an ever more interlinked world" and that the Ministers "*Reaffirm […]* that MEAs constitute the response of the international community to environmental problems and play an instrumental role in reinforcing the individual and collective actions of all Members".

82 Doha Declaration, paragraph 32(i).

83 *Supra*, n. 81.

> As the world's largest market for, and importer of fisheries products, the Community has a specific responsibility in making sure that the fisheries products imported into its territory do not originate from IUU fishing. A new regime should therefore be introduced to ensure a proper control of the supply chain for fishery products imported into the Community.[84]

Council Regulation 1005/2008 purports to do exactly what its full title suggests it should: it "establishes a Community system to prevent, deter and eliminate illegal, unreported and unregulated fishing" and aims to do so almost exclusively by adopting a strategy of market denial. Nowhere mentioned in the Regulation's 57 Articles and numerous annexes are any aspirational calls for member States to implement vaguely worded policies or guidelines, and nowhere in the Regulation is the oft-utilised tool of monitoring, control and surveillance specified. Tellingly, the Regulation makes no reference to any form of genuine link being required between vessel and State, and nor is there an enormous reliance upon flag State jurisdiction.[85] Instead the bottom line, for Regulation 1005/2008, is thus: if a vessel (or a State) is engaged in IUU fishing it will not be permitted access to the millions of consumers in the European market.

The determination of a vessel as being engaged in IUU activity is quite a straightforward process under the Regulation: a vessel will be adjudged to have engaged in IUU[86] activity when it has committed one of the 12 listed offences under Article 3 or when allegations of such activity have not been refuted, or when the presumption of IUU fishing is not rebutted.[87] While many of the offences listed are obviously important, they are rather "run-of-the-mill" and include most of those offences that one might expect to find in any serious attempt to tackle IUU activity.[88] For our immediate purposes the most pressing provisions are those that deal with the relationship between the EU and RFMOs and those measures that deny access to markets.[89]

---

[84] Council Regulation (EC) No. 1005/2008 of September 2008, Preamble, 9th Recital, (herein after "EU/IUU Regulation").

[85] Although, under the Regulation flag States do, of course, have a role to play (for instance in regard to the issuing and validation of catch documents (see below)) their role is of a comparatively secondary nature to that of the market State.

[86] The definition of 'IUU' under the Regulation is, for all intents and purposes, a replication of the FAO's 'original' definition found in the International Plan of Action of 1993.

[87] EU/IUU Regulation, Articles 25 and 26. The factors that give rise to allegations and presumptions of IUU activity are dealt with later in this section of the Chapter.

[88] The offences include: fishing without a licence; the non-recording of catch data; fishing beyond quota or in a closed area or season; fishing for prohibited stock; the use of prohibited or non-compliant gear; the falsification of identifying markers; the tampering, concealment or disposal of evidence relating to investigations; the obstruction of investigations; the possession of undersized fish; participating in joint enterprises with known IUU offenders; and fishing by vessels without nationality.

[89] For a fuller analysis of each of the provisions of the Regulation see, for instance, Tsamenyi, Palma, Milligan and Mfodwo, *The European Council Regulation on Illegal, Unreported and*

The first thing of note in this regard is the quite remarkable presumptive prohibition of market access[90] and port services to all 'third party' (i.e. non-EU States) vessels. Only when third party vessels can demonstrate compliance with the provisions of the Regulation can they, except in cases of *force majeure*, enter and land catches in EU designated ports.[91] To evidence compliance with the Regulation, masters of third party vessels are required to produce a validated catch document which either conforms to the template specifications of Annex II of the Regulation, or has been issued by a compliant RFMO.[92] As has been noted in Chapter 5, however, port State measures alone cannot always effectively close off markets: often IUU products may circumvent port and first landing measures by passing through third (or fourth, or fifth) party States, where the catch is often mixed with legitimate catches and enters the market through the back door. Regulation 1005/2008 deals with this problem by requiring that all indirect imports are accompanied by both a valid catch document and documentary evidence that the catch or transhipment was not laundered in any way.[93]

As part of its strategy of market denial, the Regulation creates a Community IUU vessel list[94] and this list will include the details of both 'EU/IUU' vessels and those identified as such by RFMOs.[95] In terms of the former – that is EU/IUU vessels – the criteria for inclusion are helpfully listed in the Regulation itself[96] and are based on the analysis of information gleaned during port inspections; information taken from catch documents (or the lack thereof); the perceived non-compliance of the flag State with Community, regional or international laws; vessel sightings; or data exchange with other interested parties.[97] In the event of a vessel being placed upon the Community IUU vessel list it is, for all intents and purposes, *non grata* within the European Union and cannot be authorised to fish, cannot be refuelled, resupplied or transhipped from, cannot access port facilities (except in cases of *force majeure* or when the master of the vessel agrees to surrender any catches or prohibited gear onboard) and cannot engage in any trade with EU States.[98]

As well as targeting IUU vessels and prohibiting access to the European market for them, another key feature of Regulation 1005/2008 is the manner in

Unregulated Fishing: An International Perspective, the International Journal of Marine and Coastal Law, Vol. 25, No. 1, 2010, pp. 5–31 (herein after "Tsamenyi *et al.*").

90 EU/IUU Regulation, Article 12(1).

91 EU/IUU Regulation, Article 4(2) and Article 5(2).

92 EU/IUU Regulation, Article 13(1).

93 EU/IUU Regulation, Article 14(1)(a)(b).

94 EU/IUU Regulation, Article 27(1).

95 EU/IUU Regulation, Article 30(1).

96 EU/IUU Regulation, Article 25(1).

97 EU/IUU Regulation, Article 25(1)(a)(b).

98 EU/IUU Regulation, Article 37.

which it addresses IUU haven States. Non-co-operating third countries, as the Regulation calls these States,[99] are those States that, *inter alia*, have poor records of compliance[100] or those States that are not party to international agreements (such as UNCLOS, UNFSA or the Compliance Agreement) or are not members of any applicable RFMO.[101] In other words, 'non-co-operating third countries' are typical flag of non-compliance States.

Once identified as such, non-co-operating third countries are subject to a process of what might be best described as notification and persuasion. This process requires the Commission of the European Union to promptly inform the third country of the charges against it,[102] coupled with a request to take action to ensure the cessation of the IUU activities in question.[103] Following this notification and request to cease, non-co-operating countries are given an 'adequate' and 'reasonable' period of time to respond and remedy the situation.[104] Subject to this State failing to respond or rectify the situation it will then be placed on the Community's "list of non-co-operating third countries" and thus subject to the measures prescribed by Article 38 of the Regulation. Thus, all imports of fishery products from identified States will be prohibited,[105] as will numerous 'fisheries-related' commercial activities, such as vessel sales, reflagging, chartering agreements, vessel export agreements, private trade arrangements and joint fishing ventures.[106] Significantly – and a measure that could have an enormous deterrent impact given the huge sums of money paid annually for such arrangements – the EU Commission may refuse to enter into any new bilateral fishing arrangements, or seek the termination of existing arrangements with non-co-operating States.[107]

---

[99] EU/IUU Regulation, Article 31.

[100] EU/IUU Regulation, Article 31(5).

[101] EU/IUU Regulation, Article 31(6).

[102] EU/IUU Regulation, Article 32(1).

[103] EU/IUU Regulation, Article 32(2).

[104] EU/IUU Regulation, Article 32(4).

[105] If, however, the IUU activity that gave rise to the listing procedure noted above concerns a State's failure to properly regulate catches of only certain stocks, then only these stocks will be subject to the import prohibition: see EU/IUU Regulation, Article 38(1).

[106] EU/IUU Regulation, Article 38(2)–(7).

[107] EU/IUU Regulation, Article 38(8)(9). According to the OECD "Fisheries activities by European Union countries in the seas of West Africa contribute EUR 120 million annually in government revenues. A part of the contribution is dedicated for the support of national fisheries policy to promote sustainable fishery resource management. For some of the poorest countries under these agreements, such as Guinea-Bissau, the EU payments represent a significant part of government revenues." *Natural Resources and Pro-Poor Growth: The Economics and Politics,* OECD, 2008.

7.7.1 *Regulation 1005/2008 and Environmental Harms*

Although the EU IUU Regulation has tremendous potential to deny market access to those fishing entities that do not play by the rules, a hitherto undiscussed issue is that of what – precisely – constitutes the 'rules' when the Regulation is viewed from the environmental perspective underpinning the present study. In short, can the Regulations exclude from the European market fish or fish products when the methods of capture are of the environmentally destructive type referred to in Chapter Two? In principle the answer is that there is no reason why they should not: indeed, the preambular language of the Regulations does note that "Community action should be targeted primarily at behaviour…which causes the most serious damage to the marine environment"[108] and that IUU fishing is activity that "jeopardises…the conservation of the marine environment."[109] In practice, however, the answer is slightly less straightforward.

It will be recalled that under the Regulations no imports are permitted unless accompanied by a valid catch document and that a valid catch document may either be one issued by a recognised RFMO[110] or a validated 'EU model' catch document. In the former case, when any RFMO requires, as a condition of any catch document being issued, compliance with specified conservation measures on, for example, gear type or methods of capture then it is almost axiomatic that Regulation 1005/2008 would allow for market denial when those conditions have not been met. When, however, the 'EU model' catch document is used in substitution of an RFMO catch document, does this necessarily require compliance with any particular environmental measures? Although placing the burden of proof on flag States of the vessel, the answer appears to be 'yes': Article 12(3) of the Regulation requires that any catch document must certify that the catch has taken in conformity "applicable laws, regulations and international conservation and management measures." Obviously, it is necessary for flag States to firstly identify the relevant applicable laws and international conservation measures – including any regional requirements concerning, say, the methods of capture – prior to certifying conformity, and so the burden imposed cannot be underestimated. This burden is not, however, one that flag States must carry simply to satisfy the requirements of Regulation 1005/2008: it is, after all, incumbent upon all States to ensure, under UNCLOS, that effective jurisdiction is exercised over flagged vessels. And provided that States do what they are required to – that is, ensure that vessels flying their flags adhere to the rules – Regulation 1005/2008 should not present an insurmountable challenge.

---

108 EU/IUU Regulation, Preamble, 6th Recital.

109 EU/IUU Regulation, Preamble, 41st Recital.

110 EU/IUU Regulation, Article 13(1).

7.8 *Conclusion*

Because it has only been in force for a relatively short amount of time[111] it might be a little too early to make any claims about the success of Regulation 1005/2008.[112] Indeed, there are, perhaps, a few teething problems to be sorted out prior to an exact evaluation of the measure's efficacy can be accurately gauged: for instance, the inclusion of the vessel *Marta Lucia R* on the EU/IUU list on the basis of that vessel's inclusion on the IAATC IUU list has been subject to challenge by the vessel's owners on the basis that the IAATC procedures were flawed and discriminatory.[113] Likewise Tsamenyi et al note that in certain circumstances[114] a coastal State's ability to enter the EU market depends on the ability or will of the flag State (over which the coastal State may not exercise a great degree of control) to adequately validate catch documents.[115] The above may, of course, be legitimate concerns and it may be the case that certain of the Regulation's provisions may require a degree of interpretation by the European Court of Justice. Nevertheless, the fact that the Regulation has, at its very heart, the notion of trade restrictive measures is a most positive step forward. Putting many of the principles, guidelines and plans of action discussed throughout this book into action the Regulation is a legally binding document that subjects the world's main fisheries product consumer-bloc to its provisions. While CITES has struggled to find a way to properly apply the provisions of regional catch documents to its many members, the EU Regulation should not face so many of the implementational problems highlighted in the previous Chapter. And while CITES member States might struggle to see a role for the Convention in the protection of the marine environment, or the WTO might wish to cling on to the notion that free trade trumps all, the European Commission has had no such qualms.

---

[111] Despite its titular nomenclature the Regulation only came into force in January 2010.

[112] For instance, despite the requirement, under Article 35, that the list of non-co-operating third countries is published, this has not yet been done.

[113] See *Seatech International and Others v Council and Commission,* Case T-337/10. At the time of writing the judgment of the court in this case has not yet been issued.

[114] When, for instance, a foreign-flagged vessel is fishing within the coastal waters.

[115] Tsamenyi *et al.*, p. 25.

Chapter Eight

Conclusions

In concluding this study it is worth, at the outset, reaffirming a point made in the Introduction. What this book intended to do was to provide a framework for the imposition trade-related measures, justified under the corpus of international law, that could have a major impact against the most harmful aspects of IUU/FOC fishing. Thus, a framework by which the international community could, through regional and global bodies such as RFMOs and CITES, effectively deny IUU/FOC vessels access to the international marketplace was posited. The framework envisaged did, of course, require certain assumptions to be borne out in practice. In order to justify the imposition of trade-related measures at both a regional and international level it was first essential to demonstrate that these measures are proportionate, necessary and efficacious.

The proportionality of any measures considered, it is suggested, must bear in mind the reality of the FOC industry as a whole. As suggested in Chapter Two it would be easy, at least on an abstract level, for the international community to rid the oceans of the worldwide FOC merchant fleet. This would of course not only be met with such political and fiscal opposition so as to make this solution unworkable, but would also render any law imposed deeply susceptible to claims of disproportionality. As Chapter Two noted, flags of convenience, for better or for worse, are an essential part of the global trading economy. Thus any measures enacted against any specific threats posed by the worst aspects of the FOC fleet must have as their aim the lessening of that precise threat.

Therefore Chapter Three demonstrated precisely what the nature of the threat was, and, by the same token demonstrated the necessity that *some* positive action should be taken. It is hoped that Chapter Three gave the reader an additional insight into the consequences of IUU/FOC activity which goes beyond the traditional portrayal of the IUU/FOC as merely a problem for target species. When read in conjunction with the example of Belize given in Chapter Two it is suggested that when an issue of concern is drawn to the attention of the international community and regulations begin to be promulgated – either through hard or soft law, or when political pressure begins to mount – then the vessel owners will have no hesitation in moving on to a new State of refuge so as to avoid domestic legislation giving effect to these regulations. This is not to say, of course, that the regulations contained in the various Plans of Action or Codes of Conduct cited in Chapter Two should be ignored – for the many responsible vessel owners and States that put the principles into action these soft laws are invaluable tools in maintaining a healthy marine environment. For the IUU/FOC industry, however, they just move the problem elsewhere.

So, what is the solution? As Chapter Four has demonstrated the answer may not be arrived at even with another century of attempting to define a workable and acceptable "genuine link" between vessel and State of registry. Whilst the entrenched principles of exclusive flag State jurisdiction and a State's freedom to affix terms and conditions for registration remain, the search for the genuine link is, in the author's opinion, not the most pressing of issues when one considers the degradation of the marine environment that is currently taking place. Although UNCLOS has left room for a further definition of the genuine link concept, given the rejection by international tribunals of any notion of "genuineness" that extends beyond the most cursory and passing acknowledgement of a connection between vessel and State, it is contended that the solution does not lie in the further search for a genuine link.

Instead, as Chapter Five demonstrates, UNCLOS can suggest an alternative, more piecemeal solution. By requiring States to work together under the auspices of RFMOs, and when coupled with the more specific obligations imposed upon, and powers granted to, these organisations by the Fish Stocks Agreement and the UN Code of Conduct, States are empowered in the fight against IUU/FOC operations. Obviously RFMOs must embrace these powers and obligations, and as Chapter Five also shows, there is a divergence of practice among many RFMOs. Although those organisations adopting trade restrictive measures such as positive and negative lists have demonstrated a willingness to take some of these obligations seriously, it is not necessarily the case that trade-restrictive measures are always adopted in response to all perceived problems. Many RFMOs have, of course, indicated a readiness to embrace trade-restrictive measures when the stocks under their management jurisdictions are threatened, but it is not necessarily the case when the threat is to the wider marine environment.

Of course some RFMOs may cite the justification that under their terms of reference or constitutions – which may pre-date UNCLOS, the Fish Stocks Agreement and the Code of Conduct – that the wider marine environment is not within their area of competence. Indeed this may be true as certain of the older RFMOs may have been established with the single purpose of managing fish stocks and allocating quotas. Post-UNCLOS and its progeny, however, the reality is that only these organisations have the infrastructure and membership to prevent the destruction of the oceanic environment, and despite the relatively ambiguous terminology employed in UNCLOS it is clear that all signatory States are obliged to co-operate in the management and conservation of the marine environment.

Thus, despite any prior commitments to the singular terms of reference of RFMOs' management functions, the imperatives of the provisions of UNCLOS to which the vast majority of States have acceded ensure that these States are granted the power to adapt the mandate of any regional body to include a wider maritime agenda. And for those older RFMOs if a template of reform were needed they should look no further than the CCAMLR CDS. Clearly recently established RFMOs, such as SEAFO, WCPFC and SPRFMO are embracing environmental concerns into their terms of reference and doing so in a way that allows effective trade-restrictive measures to be utilised in a manner very similar to that of the CCAMLR CDS. It is important, however, to restate at this point that to be effective these trade-restrictive measures track the IUU catch beyond first landing. As many RFMOs have realised to their detriment, ports of convenience are a serious problem, and so it is essential that any trade-restrictive measures must operate from "catch to market place".

Obviously such inroads into international trade may not be possible for RFMOs acting alone and to ensure that unlawful harvests are not laundered through non-RFMO States these type of scheme require truly international coverage and an infrastructure that is well-equipped to regulate the international trade in wildlife. In other words what RFMO schemes need is an international umbrella organisation that can ensure compliance with any agreed measures.

As Chapter Six is at pains to stress, this is what CITES can offer. CITES has the infrastructure, membership and capability to regulate the international trade in threatened species and therefore it is little wonder that concerned fisheries managers looked upon CITES in the 1990s as a potential solution to the problem of unlawful international fisheries trade. The problem, as has been highlighted in Chapter Six, is that CITES is not a fisheries management convention. The solution offered in this study therefore recognises that CITES can have a role to play in a way that does not derogate from its current purpose. Using CITES in a complementary fashion, rather than incorporating the management of commercially important fisheries into the Appendices of CITES, has two major benefits, other than the important issue of expanding State coverage.

First, the political opposition mounted to the proposal to list Patagonian toothfish has been negated by the acceptance of CITES parties of the proposal to adopt the CCAMLR CDS by all CITES member States at the Santiago conference of 2007. Secondly, the complementary role of CITES, as an infrastructure, could allow for trade-restrictions to be applied even when there is no direct threat to target species, in a way that would not be permitted via the use of the CITES Appendices.

Of course there are problems of a logistical nature to proposed joint initiatives between CITES and RFMO schemes such as the CCAMLR CDS that should not be underestimated. Nor should these problems be overestimated. These logistical problems – the recognition and identification of flora and fauna, in particular, are what any CITES regime encounters on a daily basis. In terms of expertise, for domestic customs officials – upon whom the majority of the burden would fall, there would be challenges. It is worth emphasising again, however, that these are no different in principle from the challenges faced by those same officials when presented with other types of flora and fauna.

The crucial aspect, nonetheless, is the fact that such joint ventures would allow customs officials in all States that are party to CITES to confiscate consignments of fish products that do not conform to the regulatory requirements of any CDS scheme. Thus, significant markets would be closed off to any vessel operator that could not produce the necessary documentary evidence that their catch was lawfully harvested in line with regional requirements. With no market to peddle their illicit wares in, so the theory goes, there will be no incentive to take part in the destructive practices associated with IUU fishing.

Thus, the Council of the European Union's Regulation on Illegal, Unreported and Unregulated Fishing is an extremely welcome and valuable move towards denying the IUU fishing fleet a large market. And this is good for the legitimate fishing industry, seabirds, turtles, sharks and the very seas themselves, as well as being a proportionate, necessary and efficacious solution to a pressing problem.

Appendix One

Vessels Registration Movements to and from Belize between 2001–2005

Current name	IMO	Current flag state	Intermediate flag states
Adi Bahari I	7801520	Indonesia	Japan, Belize (97–01)
Akademik Khokhlov	7826128	Russia	USSR, Latvia, Cyprus, Malta, Belize (03)
Al Yakada	7920170	Unknown	Japan, Panama (94–99), Belize (99–02)
Alana I	7302627	Unknown	Japan, Panama, St Vincent, Belize (02)
Ameranus 1	8844907	Indonesia	Japan, Belize (03–04)
Amoria	7221536	Unknown	Netherlands, UK, South Africa, St Vincent, Belize (01–02)
Amorinn	7036345	Togo	Japan, Panama, Ghana, Honduras (94–98), Belize (98–03)
Antares I	7733620	Unknown	USSR, Estonia, Russia, Belize (01–03)
Appollo-I	7627730	Unknown	USSR, Russia, Belize (00–01)
Apuokas	7042409	Lithuania	USSR, Russia, Belize (99–01)
Aqua Reefer	6718805	Tonga	Panama (67–91), Honduras (91–98), Belize (98–01)
Aroa	7639977	Sao Tome	Guatemala, South Korea, Belize (99–01)
Arowana No. 8	9038402	Unknown	Japan, Belize (02), Vanuatu
Artyk	8403947	Russia	Japan, Belize (04–05)
Asamo	8313491	Broken Up	Japan, Thailand, Belize (02–05), Russia, Cambodia (09)
Assos	7114367	Cambodia	Japan, Pakistan, Honduras (90–96), Belize (96–03)
Atlantic Preserver	9137480	Canada	Russia, Belize (04), Russia
Atlantic Protector	9137507	Canada	Russia, Belize (04), Russia
Australio	7719519	Panama	Spain, China, Belize (93–01), Uruguay, (Panama (05))
Badminton	6909650	Togo	UK, Belize (98–02)
Baek Yang No. 29	7380198	South Korea	Japan, Ghana, Panama (89–93), Belize (93–95), South Korea, Belize (00–05)

(*cont.*)

Current name	IMO	Current flag state	Intermediate flag states
Basani	8817916	South Africa	Morocco, Belize (00–01)
Belgie 103	8950691	Unknown	Belize (87–02)
Belgie 111	8950706	Unknown	Belize (86–02)
Bermeotarrak Cuatro	7817309	Belize	Spain, Belize (92–03), Ghana (03–09)
Blue Ocean	7731309	Indonesia	USA, Belize (98–02)
Borealis	7208948	Panama	Japan, St Vincent, Honduras (91–92), S Leone, Belize (96–01), Togo, Uruguay
Borey	7720001	Russia	Norway, Belize (02), Russia, Belize (06)
Bouzon	7705659	Seychelles	Honduras (88–98), Belize (98–01)
Bugsy	8723725	Russia	USSR, Lithuania, Belize (01–02), Georgia (02–10)
Cabo De Hornos	7404372	Chile	Spain, Falkland Islands, Belize (04)
Cadiz	8610100	Cambodia	Japan, Russia, Belize (98–01), Russia
Calvin	8008199	Panama	Netherlands, Belize (02–03), Unknown, (Panama (06))
Carmen Reefer	7420766	Unknown	Cuba, Belize (02–04)
Castro No. 168	8017762	Philippines	Japan, Belize (99–01), Panama (01–02)
Catching Tuna	8950718	Unknown	Belize (88–02)
Celta De Vigo	7622663	Unknown	Netherlands, Panama (97–98), Honduras (98–99), Belize (99–06)
Cevita	5225851	Norway	Norway, Vanuatu, Belize (99–02), Faeroe Islands
Chang An 668	8951827	Unknown	Belize (99–02)
Chang An 998	8951839	Unknown	Belize (99–02)
Chang Yi No. 212	8619259	Unknown	South Korea, Honduras, Belize, St Vincent
Chen Chieh No. 888	8947242	Chinese Taipei	Belize (98–03), Georgia (03)
Chen Fa No. 1	8947254	Unknown	Belize (97–02)
Chi Fung No. 10	7416430	Unknown	Costa Rica, Belize (02)
Chi Hung No. 6	8951451	Unknown	Belize (93–02)
Chi Yang No. 1	7416430	Unknown	Costa Rica, Belize (95–02)
Chien Chung No. 307	8430237	Unknown	Honduras (90–99), Belize (99–02)
Chieng Chung No. 301	8430201	Unknown	Honduras (92–99), Belize (98–02)
Chin Cheng Pong	7921095	Unknown	Japan, St Vincent, Belize, Eq Guinea, Belize (98–02)
Chong Un San 2	6803088	North Korea	Panama (89–03), Honduras (93–00), Cambodia, Belize (01–02), Cambodia

(*cont.*)

Current name	IMO	Current flag state	Intermediate flag states
Chun Fa	8957431	Unknown	Honduras (97–00), Belize (00–02)
Chun I No. 307	8947503	Philippines	Belize (98 – 03?), Seychelles, Vanuatu
Chun I No. 316	8947515	Philippines	Belize (98–03), Seychelles, Vanuatu
Chun Ying No. 202	8947163	Vanuatu	Belize (98–03)
Chun Ying No. 777	8947101	Vanuatu	Belize (97–03)
Columbo IV	6604248	Unknown	Panama (66–93), Belize (93–02)
Conta Dora I	7385409	Panama	France, St Vincent & the Grenadines, Belize (98–02)
Cusmaan Geedi Raage	7929009	Somalia	Somalia, Belize (98–04)
Dai Ho	8947527	Unknown	Belize (97–03)
Daniela	9020742	Panama	Japan, Belize (03), (Panama (03))
De Li No. 1	8963856	Cambodia	China, Belize (03–05)
Der Wei No. 676	7106358	Unknown	China, Belize (01–02)
Develop Tuna	8950720	Unknown	Belize (88–02)
Dmitriy Pokramovich	8015922	Belize	USSR, Russia, Belize (00–04), Russia, (Belize (09))
Ekvator	8606692	Russia	USSR, Latvia, Honduras (95), Panama (96–98), Belize (98–03)
El Marquez	7515652	Panama	USA, Belize (98–99), Honduras (99–02), Bolivia, Equador, Belize (03), (Panama (03))
Elvira	7830442	Unknown	South Korea, Belize (00–02)
Eridan	8606939	Russia	USSR, Lithuania, Belize (98–01), Russia, Belize (03–04)
Espadeiro	7238515	Unknown	Japan, Honduras (89–98), Belize (98–01)
Fanee	6706462	Unknown	Japan, Nigeria, Honduras, Belize (93–03), Bolivia (04)
Feng Hai 2	7810698	China	Japan, Belize (01–04)
Feng Ya No. 11	8947266	Unknown	Belize (98–02)
Fish Islands	7387952	Unknown	Cuba, Belize (96–04)
Fish Marine	7122091	Unknown	Brunei, Malaysia, Panama, Belize (97–02)
Flipper 1	8417156	Comoros	USSR, Estonia, Belize (95–05)
Flipper 4	8522092	Comoros	USSR, Ukraine, Ghana, Belize (02)
Fong Kuo No. 16	8947292	Unknown	Belize (97–02)
Fong Kuo No. 3	8947278	Unknown	Belize (97–02)
Fong Kuo No. 33	8947307	Unknown	Belize (98–02?)
Fong Kuo No. 36	8947319	Unknown	Belize (98–02)
Fong Kuo No. 6	8947280	Unknown	Belize (97–02)
Fortuna	8114106	Eq Guinea	Japan, Belize (98–05)
Fortuna Star	7914078	Unknown	Japan, Belize (94–02)
Fox	8312382	Cambodia	Japan, Belize (02–07)
Fu Yuan No. 11	8950768	Unknown	Belize (86–01)

(*cont.*)

Current name	IMO	Current flag state	Intermediate flag states
Fu Yuan No. 3	8950756	Unknown	Belize (87–00)
Fu Yuan No. 66	8947204	Philippines	Chinese Taipei, Belize (99–03)
Fulling Tuna	8950732	Unknown	Belize (85–02)
Gata	8723701	Unknown	USSR, Lithuania, Mozambique, Belize (01–04), Georgia (04–08)
Geminis	7514945	Unknown	USSR, Ukraine, Belize (97–02)
Genny No. 8	8947321	Unknown	Belize (96–02)
Gloria Del Mar 1	7410292	Mexico	South Korea, Belize (98–01), Panama (01)
Glory	8015362	South Korea	Japan, Sierra Leone, South Korea, Belize (00–02)
Golden Rich	7394838	Unknown	South Korea, Honduras, Belize (00–01)
Golden Tuna	8950744	Belize	Belize (85–02)
Golden Tuna No. 1	7217327	Unknown	Japan, Panama (91–95), Belize (94–02)
Golta	7218591	Unknown	USSR, Lithuania, Belize (98–04)
Graciela	8613956	Unknown	Japan, Belize (03), Panama (03–10)
Grant	7903940	Cambodia	Japan, Belize (94–06)
Green Star I	7815038	Unknown	Japan, Cambodia, Honduras (90–02), Belize (02–05), Vanuatu (05–08)
Guan Xiang 3	8974996	Cambodia	China, Belize (03–04), Tuvalu
Havour 3	7385411	Iran	Cayman Islands, Malta, Belize (92–04)
Haw Hua	8130150	Unknown	Japan, Ecuador, Belize (01)
Hemao	8217142	Cambodia	Japan, St Vincent, Belize (03), (Cambodia (09))
Hsiang Lai Fa	8910964	Unknown	Japan, Belize (98–06)
Hsiang Yuan No. 102	8014552	Unknown	Japan, Honduras (97–01), Belize (01), Honduras (01–04), Vanuatu
Hsieh Yung No. 636	8947357	Unknown	Belize (97–02)
Hsien Hua No. 106	9225756	Unknown	Belize (00–03)
Hsien Hua No. 107	9225768	Unknown	Belize (00–03)
Hsing Yang	7900405	Unknown	Japan, Mauritius, Honduras, Eq Guinea, Belize (98–02)
Huang Hai Yu Len 3	8951463	Unknown	Belize (93–02)
Hui Fa	8947498	Vanuatu	Belize (98–03)
Hung Chia 202	8947369	Unknown	Belize (97–02)
Hwa Chih No. 212	8947539	Unknown	Belize (97–02)
Hwa Chin No. 202	8947541	Unknown	Belize (97–02)
Hwa Shan No. 301	9219836	Unknown	Belize (00–02)
Ice Tulip	7213125	Unknown	Panama (72–95), Liberia, Panama (95–99), Belize (99–02)

(*cont.*)

Current name	IMO	Current flag state	Intermediate flag states
Iel 505	6525650	Broken up	Taiwan, Panama (91–98), Belize (98–03), Maldive Islands
Inter Seven	7118832	Unknown	Senegal, Ghana, Belize (98–02)
Isla Gorriti	7918270	Mauritius	Japan, Belize (97–01), Uruguay
Jain Yung No. 202	8947187	Unknown	Belize (97–02)
Jeffrey No. 168	8947553	Unknown	Belize (97–02)
Jeng Yu	8942838	Unknown	Belize (98–04)
Jessica S II	7313353	Unknown	Japan, Belize (93–02)
Jetmark 102	7927257	Unknown	Japan, Mauritius, Honduras (95–00), Belize (00–03)
Jetmark No. 8	9038402	Philippines	Japan, Belize (02), Vanuatu, Mongolia
John-Loren	7404798	UK	UK, Belize (00–02)
Ju Ying No. 666	8947113	Unknown	Belize (97–02)
Jupiter	7700116	Russia	Cyprus, Lithuania, Belize (03)
Kao Fong No. 1	8947371	Unknown	Belize (97–02)
Katco 3	8708309	Unknown	Japan, Belize (02), Honduras (02–06)
Katran	7506924	Unknown	USSR, Latvia, Belize (98–01)
King Bora	8033297	Belize	USSR, Russia, Belize (98–02), Namibia, (Belize (04))
Kormoran 1	8820353	Seychelles	Somalia, Belize (98–01)
Kotoyarvi	7002368	Russia	Faeroe Islands, Vanuatu, Belize (99–03)
Koufuku	8618542	Cambodia	Japan, Panama (03), Belize (04), (Cambodia (08))
Kristina Logos	7618014	Unknown	Canada, Panama (92), Canada, Iceland, Belize (99–03), Unknown, Estonia
Kurilskoye Ozero	9183037	Russia	Russia, Belize (03–05), Unknown, Cambodia (07–08)
Lanzardo	8137164	Unknown	USSR, Estonia, Ghana, Latvia, St Vincent, Belize (01–04)
Lelilia	8950770	Unknown	Belize (89–02)
Leonid Yelkin	7703948	Russia	USSR, Russia, Belize (98–01)
Lian Horng No. 777	8947383	Unknown	Belize (98–02)
Lian Xing Hai	7817452	Unknown	Poland, Ukraine, Cambodia (01–05), Unknown, Cambodia (06), Belize (06)
Liao Chang Long 2	8843939	Unknown	China, Belize (00–01)
Lien Tai	7921100	Bolivia	Japan, Belize (93–04)
Likos	8136570	Georgia	USSR, Russia, Belize (02–04)
Lis I	7238448	Unknown	Japan, Honduras (89–98), Belize (98–01)

(*cont.*)

Current name	IMO	Current flag state	Intermediate flag states
Lucky 101	8831431	Sierra Leone	China, Belize (01–04), Panama (04–09)
Mahi No. 1	7013408	Guinea	Panama (70–95), Sierra Leone, Belize (98–02)
Mar De Bens	7527423	UK	Panama (88–96), Belize (98–01), Unknown
Marianne	6700171	Unknown	Canada, Belize (94–02)
Marine Ocean	7806702	Unknown	USSR, Panama, Belize (99–04)
Marsopa	7809388	Panama	Vanuatu, Belize (99–05)
Martin	8713263	Cambodia	Japan, Belize (06), (Cambodia (06))
Masai	7410216	Togo	Sierra Leone, Honduras (95–99), Belize (99–04)
Matritsa	8810451	Russia	Japan, Belize (03)
Maya V	8882818	Unknown	India, Panama (95–99), Belize (99–01), Panama (01–03), Uruguay, Panama (05–09)
Mekhanik Noskov	8868032	Russia	Russia, Belize (99–02)
Melian Reefer	5098595	Unknown	St Vincent, Belize (91–95), Ghana, Belize (97–01)
Melilla No. 203	8514930	South Korea	Japan, Belize (04–06)
Meng Fa No. 368	9216884	Unknown	Belize (99–06)
Meng Wen Fa No. 666	9229518	Unknown	Belize (00–06)
Mercury	8947125	Vanuatu	Belize (98–03)
Ming Shun No. 3	8944525	Indonesia	Belize (98–03)
Missy	8415562	Unknown	USSR, Russia, Marshall Islands, Belize (02)
Mitzi	6710944	Unknown	Canada, Panama (92–94), Belize (94–02)
Monterrey	9044358	Russia	USSR, Russia, Panama (92–94), Cyprus, Russia, Belize (04)
More Rich	9254991	Vanuatu	Belize (01–03)
Munsu	7626126	Georgia	North Korea, Belize (96–07)
Mys Rubikon	8921614	Russia	Japan, Belize (03)
Nadezhda	7809106	Russia	Liberia, Portugal, Antigua & Barbuda, Cyprus, Ukraine, Belize (04), Cambodia (05–10), Belize (10)
Nam San 6	7238412	North Korea	Japan, Belize (98–02)
Nardel	7033692	Philippines	Japan, Belize (94–01)
Neptune No. 301	8011055	Unknown	Japan, Malaysia, Honduras (92–96), South Korea, Belize (00–06)

(*cont.*)

Current name	IMO	Current flag state	Intermediate flag states
Night Ray	8403832	Cambodia	Japan, Panama (99–02), Russia, Cambodia (05), Russia, Belize (06), (Cambodia (08))
Nine Lucky No. 1	8947400	Unknown	Belize (98–01), Vanuatu
Nine Lucky No. 6	8947412	Vanuatu	Belize (98–03)
Nordic-1	8106707	Panama	Japan, Belize (02–04), Unknown, (Panama (06))
Northern Challenger	7404425	Unknown	Japan, Vanuatu, Australia, Vanuatu, Belize (98–02)
Notlar	7945522	Unknown	USSR, Russia, Belize (99–01), Russia
Ocean Age	8960799	Unknown	Panama (00–02), Seychelles, Belize (03)
Ocean Conquest	7826283	Unknown	USSR, Panama, Belize (99–01)
Ocean Glory	7826233	Equatorial Guinea	USSR, Russia, Liberia, Panama (95), Unknown, Belize (99), Maldive Islands
Ocean King	7950618	Guyana	Japan, Taiwan, Belize (95–03)
Ocean No. 5	7381403	South Korea	Panama (74–95), South Korea, Belize (99–01), Unknown
Ocean Pride Marine	7826245	Maldive Islands	USSR, Russia, Panama (95), Unknown, Belize (99–03)
Ocean Tempest	7114056	Unknown	USA, Russia, Belize (02–06)
Orion	7920546	Russia	Antigua & Barbuda, Panama (96), Lithuania, Belize (06)
Orion III	8128315	Unknown	Netherlands, Belize (01–06)
Oscar	7322990	Togo	United Arab Emirates, Honduras (88–94), Panama (94–99), Belize (99–03)
Osiris	6818942	France	Spain, Panama (89–93), Belize (93–01), Seychelles
Ostrov Russkiy	7048714	Sierra Leone	USA, Russia, Belize (02–04), Unknown
Pacific 8	7104831	Sierra Leone	South Korea, Russia, Belize (03), Panama (03–10)
Pardela-1	7928990	Unknown	Somalia, Belize (99–01)
Peche No. 211	8950794	Unknown	Belize (87–02)
Pei Sheng No. 1	9278416	Chinese Taipei	Belize (02)
Perekat	6521173	Unknown	USSA, Russia, Belize (94–01)
Pervorechensk	7630361	Unknown	USSR, Russia, Unknown, Belize (05)
Pescamex I	6903826	Unknown	Panama (80–92), Belize (92–02)

(*cont.*)

Current name	IMO	Current flag state	Intermediate flag states
Pescatero	7529550	Unknown	Spain, Chile, Argentina, Belize (98–02)
Peter No. 617	7916167	Unknown	Japan, Unknown, Belize (95–01)
Pilgrim	6602252	Unknown	USA, Belize (94–01)
Ping Shin 201	8947424	Unknown	Belize (96–01)
Ping Yuan 201	8947436	Unknown	Belize (97–02)
Polartraal	7913531	Uruguay	Canada, Norway, Russia, Belize (03)
Printon I	7373808	Ghana	Panama (74–92), Honduras (92–98), Belize (98–03)
Queen	7424621	Sierra Leone	Honduras (74–90), South Korea, Belize (96–05), Unknown, Cambodia (05–07), Panama (07–10)
Radishev	8928167	Georgia	Australia, Belize (00–05)
Reham	6813966	Georgia	Cyprus, Honduras (92–99), Belize (99–01), Panama (01), Honduras (01), Bolivia
Rex	6818930	Unknown	Spain, Panama (89–93), Belize (93–01), Seychelles, Belize (03), Togo
Rolmar	8029404	Namibia	Japan, Indonesia, Panama (94–97), Belize (97–02)
Rolmar Dos	7314668	Namibia	Iceland, Belize (99–03)
Rondys	7308255	Unknown	USA, Russia, Belize (02–06)
Rossana L	7930735	Ecuador	Mexico, Belize (01–03)
Rueca-1	7928988	Unknown	Somalia, Belize (99–02)
Rustavi	7102039	Unknown	USSR, Russia, Panama (00–04), Belize (05), Georgia, Russia
Rybolov-1	8723880	Ukraine	USSR, Estonia, Russia, Unknown, Belize (01–03), Latvia, Georgia
Salus	7030054	Unknown	USSR, Latvia, Belize (98–03)
Sam	8008840	Panama	Cuba, Belize (01), Spain, (Panama (03))
San Antonio	8811663	Russia	USSR, Panama (91–95), Cyprus, Belize (04)
San Tong 3	8426937	China	China, Belize (98–01), China, Cambodia (01–03)
Santa Joana	6923424	Unknown	Panama, Belize (92–02)
Sargal	7828748	Russia	USSR, Russia, Belize (03)
Sea Green Star	9101259	Vanuatu	Russia, Belize (97–03)
Sea Idol	8017750	Cambodia	Japan, Panama (96), Russia, Belize (03), Russia, (Cambodia (09))
Sea Producer	6510930	Russia	USA, Russia, Belize (02)
Seawind I	8721143	Russia	USSR, Russia, Belize (98–01), Cambodia (01–02)
Seljevaer	9188960	Norway (NIS)	Norway, St Vincent, Belize (04), French AT, Belize (06–07)

(*cont.*)

Current name	IMO	Current flag state	Intermediate flag states
Seo Dong 3	6808909	Unknown	Panama (80–96), Sierra Leone, Belize (98–02)
Seven	8615019	Cambodia	Japan, Honduras (99), Russia, Belize (03), Bolivia, (Cambodia (05))
Shang Yun	8319299	Unknown	Japan, Belize (98–02)
Shelikhov	7728637	Russia	USA, Russia, Belize (02–04)
Shin Lung No. 216	8947474	Unknown	Taiwan, Belize (96–02)
Shinn Mann No. 11	8947228	Vanuatu	Belize (97–03)
Shinn Mann No. 21	8947565	Vanuatu	Belize (98–03)
Shiva	7045451	Unknown	USSR, Russia, Honduras (95–97), Belize (97–01)
Shkval	8225589	Unknown	USSR, Russia, Belize (98–04)
Shun Kuo No. 2	7825306	Unknown	Japan, Belize (97), Eq Guinea, Belize (98–02)
Shye Sin 1	8947448	Unknown	Belize (97–02)
Si Hong No. 128	8974532	Chinese Taipei	Belize (98–03)
Si Tai No. 326	8947450	Unknown	Belize (98–03)
Silver Ice	7819759	Comoros	Cyprus, Belize (00–05)
Sipa 212	8951671	Unknown	Belize (97–02)
Sivuch	7723027	Russia	Fiji, Liberia, Belize (01), Bolivia, Cambodia (05), Panama (06–09)
Sobolevo	8859897	Russia	Russia, Belize (98–01), Russia, Unknown
Somang	7900481	Panama	Vietnam, Vanuatu, Honduras (96–02), Belize (02–06)
Southern Star No. 888	8971762	Unknown	Belize (01–02)
Sun No. 11	7629764	Unknown	South Korea, Belize (97–02)
Sun Warm No. 1	8950782	Philippines	Belize (87–02)
Sung Hui	8947462	Vanuatu	Belize (97–03)
Sung Jin 3	7327419	North Korea	Japan, Belize (92–02), Unknown
Sur Este No. 502	7904451	Unknown	Japan, Panama, Belize (97–01)
Svesda Maru	7908627	Unknown	Japan, Ecuador, Belize (99–01), Unknown, Sierra Leone
Tai Hu	7815521	Unknown	Japan, Thailand, Honduras (97–99), Belize (99–03)
Teresamar	5283554	Unknown	Portugal, Belize (99–02)
Thai Union 1	8919427	Thailand	Liberia, Panama (97–02), Belize (02–05), Comoros, Eq Guinea, Thailand, Eq Guinea
Thai Union 2	8919403	Thailand	Liberia, Panama (97–02), Belize (02–05), Comoros, Eq Guinea, Thailand, Eq Guinea

(*cont.*)

Current name	IMO	Current flag state	Intermediate flag states
Thai Union 3	8919415	Thailand	Liberia, Panama (97–05), Belize (05), Eq Guinea, Thailand, Eq Guinea
Thai Union Star	9223227	Thailand	Belize (00–05), Comoros, Eq Guinea, Thailand, Eq Guinea, El Salvador
Tian Li	7824077	Unknown	USSR, Russia, China, Belize (99–01), Cambodia (01–03)
Tian Yuan	8614895	Unknown	Japan, Belize (99), South Korea, Belize (00–06)
Torin	8899744	Russia	Russia, Australia, Belize (00–04), Ghana, Panama (05)
Trans Caribbean 111	8943741	Unknown	Belize (86–02)
Trans Caribbean 116	8943753	Unknown	Belize (87–02)
Trans Caribbean 126	8430196	Unknown	Honduras (87–94), Belize (94–02)
Trans Caribbean 127	8943765	Unknown	Belize (87–02)
Trans Caribbean 132	8943777	Unknown	Belize (87–02)
Trans Caribbean 137	8943789	Unknown	Belize (87–02)
Trans Caribbean 203	8943791	Unknown	Belize (89–02)
Trans Caribbean 21	8943806	Unknown	Belize (86–02)
Trans Caribbean 231	8943818	Unknown	Belize (88–02)
Trans Caribbean 237	8943820	Unknown	Belize (88–02)
Trans Caribbean 301	8943832	Unknown	Belize (89–02)
Trans Caribbean 302	8943844	Unknown	Belize (90–02)
Trans Caribbean 66	8943856	Unknown	Belize (86–02)
Trans Caribbean 701	8943868	Unknown	Belize (90–02)
True Love	7029861	Unknown	USA, Belize (96–02)
Tunamar	7409138	Panama	Spain, Belize (94–01), Unknown, (Panama (03))
Tung Yuang No. 168	7322823	Unknown	Unknown, Cayman Islands, Japan, Belize (02–04)
Tung Yuang No. 88	8951877	Unknown	Belize (90–04)
Typhoon I	6905408	Togo	Faeroe Islands, UK, St Vincent, Seychelles, Belize (03)
Uchumi	7901356	Unknown	Kenya, Belize (97–02)
Ulovistyy	9213923	Russia	Belize (99–03), Seychelles
Urgull	8810190	Honduras	Somalia, Belize (97–05), Panama (05), (Honduras (06))
Urpeco Uno	6712643	Panama	France, St Vincent, Belize (95–05)
Vany	8522016	Unknown	USSR, Russia, Marshall Islands, Belize (02–04)
Vasco da Gama	7904449	Namibia	Japan, Panama (96), Belize (97–03)
Veles	8845676	Panama	USSR, Russia, Belize (01–04), Cambodia (05)
Venicento-V	7337971	Unknown	USSR, Lithuania, Belize (01)

(*cont.*)

Current name	IMO	Current flag state	Intermediate flag states
Venus I	8721193	St Vincent	USSR, Latvia, Belize (97–01)
Viarsa	8001335	Uruguay	Japan, St Vincent, Sierra Leone, Panama, Belize (99–02)
Victoria No. 11	8914867	Unknown	Japan, Belize (05)
Viola	6711479	South Africa	Iceland, Belize (93–02), Uruguay
Voditel	7045085	Unknown	USSR, Russia, Belize (05)
Volk Arktiki	8024002	Russia	Faeroe, Islands, Cyprus, Norway, Greenland, Belize (04)
Wen Sheng No. 116	8947486	Unknown	Belize (85–02)
Win Far No. 828	9219537	Unknown	Belize (99–03)
Win Far No. 868	9215945	Unknown	Belize (99–02)
Win Far No. 878	9219549	Unknown	Belize (99–03)
Wing Sang 108	8955017	Unknown	China, Belize (00–02)
Xing Da	8978734	China	China, Belize (04), Cambodia (05)
Yat Tung	5323665	Unknown	Taiwan, Belize (93–02)
Yes Sir	6825452	Panama	Netherlands, St Vincent, Belize (98–01)
Yong Yi	6421555	Unknown	USSR, Russia, Belize (93–01)
Young Bok	7042497	Ghana	USA, Philippines, Panama (91–99), Belize (99–05)
Yuan Lee	7507526	Unknown	South Korea, Belize (94–96), Panama (96), Honduras (96–01), Belize (01–03)
Yue Chao 5	8519540	China	Japan, Belize (01–04)
Yugo Vostok No. 1	8001969	Russia	Japan, New Zealand, Belize (02)
Yugo-Vostok 3	8509870	Russia	Japan, Belize (03–05)
Zarqa Al Yamama	8911671	Libya	Panama (91), Liberia, Unknown, Belize (99–01)
Zhong No. 1	8941810	Unknown	China, Eq Guinea, Belize (00–02)
Zhou Yu No. 5	8708294	China	Japan, Belize (02–05), Sierra Leone
Zhou Yu No. 6	8911047	China	Japan, Belize (02–05), Sierra Leone

Primary Source Referencing Materials

Global Treaties

International Organisations and their Proprietary Legislation

Regional Conventions and Legislation

Domestic Legislation

- IMMARBE Fishing Vessel Circular 2009/01, *Guidelines for Vessels which Carry Out Transhipment Activities* 35

United Kingdom
- Abolition of Slavery Act 1833 12n.4
- Merchant Shipping Act 1988 97–98
- Merchant Shipping (Registration of Shipping) Regulations 1988 97

United States
- 18th Amendment to the Constitution (1919) 13, 14n.10
- Neutrality Act (1939), 22 United States Code, § 441 14
- Marine Mammal Protection Act (1972), 16 United States Code, § 1371 58–59, 60
- Lacey Act Amendments (1981), 16 United States Code, § 3371 7–8
- Dolphin Protection Consumer Information Act (1990), 16 United States Code, § 1385 60
- International Dolphin Conservation Act (1992), 16 United States Code § 1411 60

Table of Cases

Behring Fur Seal Arbitration, Moore's International Arbitration Awards, I (1898) 811, Arbitral Tribunal, Paris 26–27

Commission of the European Union v Netherlands, Case C-299/02 (EC), Unreported, May 2004, European Court of Justice 88, 99

Committee for Humane Legislation Inc v Elliot L Richardson et al., 540 F.2d 1141 (D.C. Cir. 1976), United States 59

Constitution of the Maritime Safety Committee of IMCO Case [1960] ICJ Rep 150, International Court of Justice 91–92

France v Great Britain (*Muscat Dhows Case*) (1908) 2 AJIL 921, Permanent Court of Arbitration 84, 94

France v Turkey (*The Lotus Case*), (1927) PCIJ Reports, Series A, No 10, Permanent Court of International Justice 77

Ireland v United Kingdom (*The MOX Plant case*), Order Number 3, 2003, Permanent Court of Arbitration 96

Bibliography

Agnew, David J. and Barnes Colin T., *Economic Aspects and Drivers of IUU Fishing: Building a Framework,* in *Fish Piracy: Combating Illegal, Unreported and Unregulated Fishing,* OECD, Paris, 2004

Alderton, Tony and Winchester, Nik, *Regulation, Representation and the Flag Market,* Journal of Marine Research, September 2002

Anderson, H. Edwin, *The Nationality of Ships and Flags of Convenience: Economics, Politics and Alternatives,* 21 Mar. Law. 139

Appleton, Arthur E., *Shrimp-Turtle: Untangling the Nets,* Journal of International Economic Law (1999) 477

Australian Antarctic Division Newsletter, Issue 2, Spring 2001, *Another One That Didn't Get Away*

Baird, Rachel J., *Aspects of Illegal, Unregulated and Unreported Fishing in the Southern Ocean,* Springer Publishing, The Netherlands, 2006

Baird, Rachel J., *CCAMLR Initiatives to Counter Flag State Non-Enforcement in Southern Ocean Fisheries,* Victoria University of Wellington Law Review, December 2005, 36 VUWLR 733

Balton, David A., *The Bering Sea Doughnut Hole Convention,* in *Governing Highs Fisheries: The Interplay of Global and Regional Regimes,* Olav Scram Stokke (ed.), Oxford University Press, Oxford, 2001

Bhala, Raj, *Modern GATT Law: A Treatise on the General Agreement on Tariffs and Trade,* Thompson – Sweet & Maxwell, London, 2005

Birnie, Patricia and Boyle, Alan, *International Law and the Environment, 2nd Edition,* Oxford University Press, Oxford, 2002

Boczek, Boleslaw Adam, *Flags of Convenience: An International Legal Study,* Harvard University Press, Cambridge, Massachusetts, 1962

Boyle, Alan, *Further Development of the Law of the Sea Convention: Mechanisms for Change,* International and Comparative Law Quarterly (June 2005) 54.3(563)

Bronkers and McNelis, *Rethinking the 'Like Product' Definition in GATT 1994: Anti-Dumping and Environmental Protection,* in Marco C.E.J. Bronkers, *A Cross-Section of WTO Law,* Cameron May, London, 2000

Bull, Leigh S., *Reducing Seabird Bycatch in Longline, Trawl and Gillnet Fisheries,* Fish and Fisheries, Vol. 8, 2007

Cassese, Antonio, *International Law,* Oxford University Press, Oxford, 2001

CCAMLR, *Report of the Twenty First Meeting of the Commission,* Hobart, Australia, 21 October–1 November 2002

Churchill, Robin and Lowe, Vaughan, *The Law of the Sea,* 3rd Ed. Manchester University Press, Manchester, 1999

Churchill, Robin, *The Meaning of the 'Genuine Link' Requirement in Relation to the Nationality of Ships,* A Study Prepared for the International Transport Workers' Federation, October 2000

CITES Conference of the Parties Doc. 16.1, *Co-operation Between CITES and the Commission for the Conservation of Antarctic Marine Living Resources (CCAMLR) Regarding Trade in Toothfish*

Communication From the Commission of the European Communities, *Community Action Plan for the Eradication of Illegal, Unreported and Unregulated Fishing,* COM(2002) 180 Final

Condon, Bradley J., *GATT Article XX and Proximity of Interest: Determining the Subject Matter of Paragraphs (b) and (g),* 9 UCLA Journal of International Law and Foreign Affairs, No. 2 (Fall/Winter 2004)

DeSombre, Elizabeth R., *Convenient Fishing: Participation in International Fishery Management,* Paper for presentation at the International Studies Association Annual Meeting, March 2002, New Orleans

du Plessis, Morne A., *CITES and the Causes of Extinction,* in Jon Hutton and Barnabas Dickson (eds), *Endangered Specie, Threatened Convention: The Past, Present and Future of CITES,* Earthscan, London, 2000

Eason, Henry, Journal, U.S. sloop-of-war of *Marion,* 1858–60, Log 902, G.W. Blunt White

Eckersley, Robyn, *The Big Chill: the WTO and Multilateral Environmental Agreements,* Global Environmental Politics 4:2, May 2004

Environmental Justice Foundation, *Party to the Plunder: Illegal Fishing in Guinea and its Links to the EU,* Environmental Justice Foundation, London, 2005

Ferrell, Jessica K., *Controlling Flags of Convenience: One Measure to Stop Over-fishing of Collapsing Fish Stocks,* 35 Envtl. L. 323

Flewwelling, Cullinan, Balton, Sautter and Reynolds, *Recent Trends in Monitoring, Control and Surveillance Systems for Capture Fisheries,* UNFAO Fisheries Technical Paper 415, UNFAO, Rome, 2002

Flewwelling, P., *An Introduction to Monitoring, Control and Surveillance Systems for Capture Fisheries,* UNFAO Technical Paper 338, UNFAO, Rome, 2004

Forum Fisheries Agency, *Tuna Markets Annual Review 2005,* 26th May 2006, Issue 69

Franckx, Eric, *The Protection of Biodiversity and Fisheries Management: Issues Raised by the Relationship Between CITES and LOSC,* in Freestone, Barnes and Ong (eds.), *The Law of the Sea: Progress and Prospects,* Oxford University Press, Oxford, 2006

Gianni, Matthew and Simpson, Walter, *Flags of Convenience, Transhipment, Re-Supply and At-Sea Infrastructure in Relation to IUU Fishing,* in *Fish Piracy: Combating Illegal, Unreported and Unregulated Fishing,* OECD, Paris, 2004

Gianni, Matthew and Simpson, Walter, *The Changing Nature of High Seas Fishing: How Flags of Convenience Provide Cover for Illegal, Unreported and Unregulated Fishing,* Australian Department of Agriculture, Fisheries and Forestry, International Transport Workers' Federation, and WWF International, 2005

Gianni, Matthew, *High Seas Bottom Fisheries and Their Impacts on the Biodiversity of Vulnerable Deep Sea Ecosystems,* IUCN, Gland, Switzerland, 2004

Grotius, Hugo, *Mar Liberum,*(1609) Reprinted by Liberty Fund, Indiana, 2004, translated by Richard Hakluyt

Hampton, Rachel C., *Of Dolphins and Tuna: The Evolution of an International Agreement,* 10 Fordham Envtl. Law J. 99

Harris, D.J., *Cases and Materials on International Law,* 5th Ed. Sweet and Maxwell, London, 1998

Henriksen, Tore, Hønneland, Geir and Sydnes, Are, *Law and Politics in Ocean Governance: The UN Fish Stocks Agreement and Regional Fisheries Management Regimes,* Martinus Nijhoff Publishers, Leiden, 2006

High Seas Task Force, *Closing the Net: Stopping Illegal Fishing on the High Seas,* Final Report of the Ministerial-led Task Force on IUU Fishing on the High Seas, Governments of Australia, Canada, Chile, Namibia, New Zealand and the United Kingdom, WWF, IUCN and the Earth Institute at Columbia University, HSTF, March 2006

Hinckley, Robert, *How Corporate Law Inhibits Social Responsibility*, Business Ethics: Corporate Social Responsibility Report, January/February 2002

Hordal, Kjartan, *IUU Fishing in the NEAFC Area: How Big is the Problem and What Have We Done?*, in *Fish Piracy: Combating Illegal, Unreported and Unregulated Fishing*, OECD, Paris, 2004

Hummels, David, *Have International Transportation Costs Declined?* Journal of International Economics, Volume 54 (1)

Hutton, Jon and Dickson, Barnabas (eds), *Endangered Specie, Threatened Convention: The Past, Present and Future of CITES*, Earthscan, London, 2000

Hutton, Jon and Webb, Graham, *Legal Trade Snaps Back*, in Sara Oldfield (ed), *The Trade in Wildlife: Regulation for Conservation*, Earthscan Publications, London, 2003

International Council for the Exploration of the Seas, *Report of the Working Group on the Ecosystem Effects of Fishing Activities*, ICES CM 2002, ACE;03

International Dolphin Conservation Program and the Inter American Tropical Tuna Commission, Report of the Joint Working Group on Fishing by Non-Parties, 2nd Annual General Meeting, Antigua (Guatemala), June 2003, JWG 02/06 FAO/IUU/IPOA

International Maritime Organisation, *Casualty Statistics and Investigations: Very Serious and Serious Casualties for the Year 2001*, IMO/FSI3/Circ. 4, 10th February 2004

International Transport Workers' Federation, Annual Report 2004, *ITF Campaign Against Flag of Convenience and Sub-Standard Shipping*, 2004, ITF, London

International Transport Workers' Federation, *More Troubled Waters: Fishing, Pollution and Flags of Convenience*, Major Group Submission to the 2002 World Summit on Sustainable Development in Johannesburg, August 2002, ITF, London, 2002

International Transport Workers' Federation, *Steering the Right Course: Towards an Era of Responsible Flag State and Effective International Governance of Oceans and Seas*, ITF, 2003

Joseph, James, *The Tuna-Dolphin Controversy in the Eastern Pacific Ocean: Biological, Economic and Political Impacts*, 25 Ocean Devel. and Int'l L. 1, 21 (1994)

Joyner, Christopher C., *Canadian activism in the Grand Banks*, in *Governing Highs Fisheries: The Interplay of Global and Regional Regimes*, Olav Scram Stokke (ed.), Oxford University Press, Oxford, 2001

Kievit, Henriette, *Conservation of the Nile Crocodile: Has CITES Helped or Hindered?*, in Jon Hutton and Barnabas Dickson (eds), *Endangered Specie, Threatened Convention: The Past, Present and Future of CITES*, Earthscan, London, 2000

Klop and Lubbers, *Natural Resources and Pro-Poor Growth: The Economics and Politics*, OECD Publishing, Paris, 2008

Komatsu, Masayuki, *The Importance of Taking Co-operative Action Against Specific Fishing Vessels That Are Diminishing Effectiveness of Tuna Conservation and Management Measures*, Expert Consultation Paper on IUU Fishing, prepared for the Government of Australia and the UNFAO, May 2000, Document AUS:IUU/2000/5. 2000

Kunich, John Charles, *Killing Our Oceans: Dealing with the Mass Extinction of Marine Life*, Greenwood Publishing Group, Santa Barbara, 2006

Lack M. and Sant G., *Patagonian Toothfish: Are Conservation and Trade Measures Working?* TRAFFIC International Bulletin Vol. 19, No. 1 (2001)

Lack, Mary, *Continuing CCAMLR's Fight Against IUU Fishing for Toothfish*, WWF Australia and Traffic International, Cambridge, 2008

Langewiesche, William, *The Outlaw Sea: Chaos and Crime on the World's Oceans*, Granta Books, London, 2004

Lobach, Terje, *Port State Control of Foreign Fishing Vessels*, UNFAO Fisheries Circular No. 987, UNFAO, Rome, 2003

Lodge Michael W., and Nandan, Satya N., *Some Suggestions Towards Better Implementation of the United Nations Agreement on Straddling Fish Stocks and Highly Migratory Fish Stocks of 1995,* International Journal of Marine and Coastal Law, Vol. 20, (2005), Nos. 3–4

MacFadyen, Huntington and Cappell, *Abandoned, Lost or Otherwise Discarded Fishing Gear,* FAO/United Nations Environment Programme, Rome, 2009

Marine Resources Assessment Group, *Implementation of the International Plan of Action to Prevent, Deter and IUU Fishing on the High Seas: Impacts on Ecosystems and Future Scientific Needs,* Marine Resources Assessment Group/ United Kingdom Department for International Development, MRAG, London, August 2005

Marine Resources Assessment Group, *Review of the Impacts of Illegal. Unreported and Unregulated Fishing on Developing Countries,* July 2005, MRAG, London

Matsushita, Shoembaum and Mavroidis, *The World Trade Organisation: Law, Practice and Policy,* Oxford University Press, Oxford, 2004

McDiarmid, Bunny, Gotje, Martini and Sack, Karen, *The Northwest Atlantic Fisheries Organisation: A Case Study in How RFMOs Regularly Fail to Manage Our Oceans,* Greenpeace, June 2005

McGrath, Deirdre, *Writing Different Lyrics to the Same Old Tune: The New (and Improved) 1997 Amendments to the Marine Mammal Protection Act,* 7 Minnesota Journal of Global Trade 431, Summer 1998

Miller, Denzil G.M., *Patagonian Toothfish: The Storm Gathers,* in *Fish Piracy: Combating Illegal, Unreported and Unregulated Fishing,* OECD, Paris, 2004

Molenaar, Erik Jaap, *Port State Jurisdiction: Towards Mandatory and Comprehensive Use,* in Freestone, Barnes and Ong (eds), *The Law of the Sea: Progress and Prospects*

Moore, Gerald, *The Food and Agriculture Organisation of the United Nations Compliance Agreement,* 10 International Journal of Marine and Coastal Law (1995)

Nanda, Ved, *The "Torrey Canyon" Disaster: Some Legal Aspects,* 44 Denver Law Journal, 400, 1967

Oceana, *European Trawlers are Destroying the Oceans,* Oceana, Madrid, 2004

OECD Secretariat, *Economics of IUU Fishing Activities,* in *Why Fish Piracy Persists: The Economics of Illegal, Unreported and Unregulated Fishing,* OECD, Paris, 2005

Oppenheim, Adrienne J., *The Plight of the Patagonian Toothfish: Lessons From the Volga Case,* 30 Brooklyn J Int'l L. 293

Ouzumi, Yuji and Ota, Shingo, *Problems in the Fisheries Management of International Tuna Fisheries and its Relation With Fishery Subsidies,* paper presented to UNEP Fisheries Workshop, Geneva, February 2001, Oxford University Press, Oxford, 2006

Özçayir, Z. Oya , *Flags of Convenience and the Need for International Co-operation,* International Maritime Law, Vol. 7, Issue 4, May 2000

Ramach, Jennifer, *Dolphin Safe Tuna Labelling: Are the Dolphins Finally Safe?* (1996) 15 Va. Envtl LJ 743

Rayfuse, Rosemary, *Non-Flag State Enforcement in High Sea Fisheries,* Martinus Nijhoff Publishers, Lieden, 2004

Rayfuse, Rosemary, *To Our Children's Children's Children: From Promoting to Achieving Compliance in High Seas Fisheries,* The International Journal of Marine and Coastal Law, Vol. 20, (November 2005), Nos. 3–4

Reeve, Rosalind, *Policing International Trade in Endangered Species: The CITES Treaty and Compliance,* Earthscan/The Royal Institute of International Affairs, London, 2002

Roheim, Cathy A. and Sutinen, Jon G., *Trade and Market Related Instruments to Reinforce Fisheries Management Measures to Promote Sustainable Fishing Practices,* Report for the International Centre for Trade and Sustainable Development and OECD-High Seas Force, March 2006

Sands, Philippe, *Principles of International Environmental Law,* Cambridge University Press, Cambridge, 2003

Scientific Committee for the Conservation of Antarctic Marine Living Resources, *Report of the Twentieth Meeting of the Scientific Committee,* Hobart, Australia, October 2001

Sedley, Stephen, *Ashes and Sparks: Essays on Law and Justice,* Cambridge University Press, Cambridge, 2011

Stokke, Olav Schram and Vidas, Davor, *Regulating IUU Fishing or Combating IUU Operations?,* in *Fish Piracy: Combating Illegal, Unreported and Unregulated Fishing,* OECD, Paris, 2004

Sumaila, U.R., Alder J. and Keith H., *Global Scope and Economics of Illegal Fishing,* Marine Policy 30 (2006) 696–703

Summary of the UN Fish Stocks Agreement Review Conference, May 2006, *Earth Negotiations Bulletin,* International Institute for Sustainable Development, Vol. 7, No. 61

Sunkin, Maurice, Ong, David and Wight, Robert, *Sourcebook on Environmental Law* 2nd Edition, Cavendish Publishing, London, 2002

Swan, Judith, *Fishing Vessels Operating Under Open Registries and the Exercise of Flag State Responsibilities – Information and Options,* Fisheries Circular No. 90, FIPP/C980, UNFAO, Rome, 2002

Thaggert, Henry L., *A Closer Look at the Tuna Dolphin Case: 'Like Products' and Extra-jurisdictionality in the Trade and Environment Context,* in *Trade and the Environment: The Search for Balance,* Cameron, Demaret and Geradin (eds), Cameron & May, London, 1994

The Royal Commission on Environmental Pollution, *Turning the Tide: Addressing the Impact of Fisheries on the Marine Environment,* December 2004, Cm 6392

TI Briefing: The Ports of Convenience, Transport International Magazine, Issue 25, October 2006

Tolofari, S.R., *Open Registry Shipping: A Comparative Study in Costs and Freight Rates,* Gordon and Breach Science Publishers, London, 1989

Tsamenyi, Palma, Milligan and Mfodwo, *The European Council Regulation on Illegal, Unreported and Unregulated Fishing: An International Perspective,* the International Journal of Marine and Coastal Law, Vol. 25, No 1, 2010

UN Convention on Biological Diversity, 7th COP, Kuala Lumpur, February 2004, Working Paper prepared by the Subsidiary Body on Scientific, Technical and Technological Advice, *Management of Risks to the Biodiversity of Seamounts and Cold-Water Coral Communities Beyond National Jurisdiction,* UNEP/CBD/COP/7/INF/25

UNFAO Fisheries Circular No. 954, *An Appraisal of the Suitability of the CITES Criteria for Listing Commercially Exploited Aquatic Species,* UNFAO, Rome 2000

UNFAO Fisheries Department, *The State of World Fisheries and Aquaculture 2004,* UNFAO, Rome, 2004

UNFAO Fisheries and Aquaculture Department, *The State of World Fisheries and Aquaculture 2010,* UNFAO, Rome, 2010

UNFAO Fisheries Report No. 772, *Report of the Expert Consultation on Fishing Vessels Operating Under Open Registries and Their Impact on Illegal, Unreported and Unregulated Fishing,* UNFAO, Rome, 2004

UNFAO, *CITES Issues With Respect to International Fish Trade and the CITES/FAO MOU,* Tenth Session of the UNFAO Committee on Fisheries Sub-Committee on Fish Trade, Santiago de Compostela, May-June 2006

UNFAO, *Guidelines to Reduce Sea Turtle Mortality in Fishing Operations,* FAO Committee of Fisheries, Twenty-sixth Session, March 2005

UNFAO, *Historical Trends of Tuna Catches in the World,* Fisheries Technical Paper 467, UNFAO, Rome, 2004

UNFAO, *Implementation of the International Plan of Action to Prevent, Deter and Eliminate Illegal, Unreported and Unregulated Fishing*, FAO Technical Guidelines for Responsible Fisheries. No. 9. Rome, FAO. 2002

UNFAO, *Report of the Exert Consultation on Implementation Issues Associated With Listing Commercially Exploited Aquatic Species on CITES Appendices*, UNFAO Fisheries Report No. 741, Rome, 2004

UNFAO, *Report of the Expert Consultation on Fishing Vessels Operating Under Open Registries and Their Impact on Illegal, Unreported and Unregulated Fishing*, UNFAO Fisheries Report No. 722, Rome, 2004

UNFAO, *Report of the Expert Consultation on Legal Issues Related to CITES Commercially Exploited Aquatic Species*, UNFAO Fisheries Report No. 746, Rome, 2004

UNFAO, *Report of the Technical Consultation on the Measurement of Fishing Capacity*, UNFAO Fisheries Report No. 615, Rome, 2000

UNFAO, *Report of the Technical Consultation on the Suitability of the CITES Criteria for Listing Commercially-Exploited Aquatic Species*, UNFAO Fisheries Report No. 629, Rome, June 2000

United Nations Environmental Programme, *Environment and Trade: A Handbook*, 2nd Edition, UNEP/IISD, Winnipeg, 2005

United Nations General Assembly Report, *Sustainable Fisheries*, A/60/189, 2nd August 2005

Vasquez, Juan Carlos, *Compliance and Enforcement Mechanisms of CITES*, in Sara Oldfield (ed), *The Trade in Wildlife: Regulation for Conservation*, Earthscan Publications, London, 2003

Vukas, Budislav and Vidas, Davor, *Flags of Convenience and High Seas Fishing* in *Governing Highs Fisheries: The Interplay of Global and Regional Regimes*, Olav Scram Stokke (ed.), Oxford University Press, Oxford, 2001

Wells, Jane Marc, *Vessel Registration in Selected Open Registries*, 6 Mar. Law 221

World Trade Organisation, *Report by the Chairman of the Trade Negotiations Committee*, Committee on Trade and Environment, April 2011, Doc 11–2083

Willock, Anna and M. Lack, *Follow the Leader: Learning From Experience and Best Practice in Regional Fisheries Management Organisations*, WWF International and TRAFFIC

Willock, Anna, *Uncharted Waters: Implementation Issues and Potential Benefits of Listing Toothfish in Appendix II of CITES*, TRAFFIC International, Cambridge, 2002

Willock, Anna, *Using Trade and Market Information to Assess IUU Fishing Activities*, in *Fish Piracy: Combating Illegal, Unreported and Unregulated Fishing*, OECD, Paris, 2004

Winchester, Nik, *How the Squeeze on Standards Enables Small Flags to Flourish*, "The Sea", Issue 151, May/June 2001, Seafarers International Research Centre

WTO Information and Media Relations Division, *Understanding the WTO*, Geneva, 2005

Electronic Resources

(Unless otherwise stated all URLs remain intact as of May 2011)

The Advantages of the Panamanian Registry
http://www.embassy-avenue.jp/panama/adva.htm (site defunct)

American Bird Conservancy, *Sudden Death on the High Seas – Longline Fishing: A Global Catastrophe for Seabirds*
http://www.abcbirds.org/newsandreports/special_reports/seabird_report.PDF

Anderson, Sarah and Cavanagh, John, *Top 200. The Rise of Corporate Global Power*, December 2000
http://www.corpwatch.org/article.php?id=377

Bray, Kevin, *A Global Review of Illegal, Unreported and Unregulated Fishing*
http://www.fao.org/docrep/005/Y3274E/y3274e08.htm
CCAMLR IUU Vessel List
http://www.ccamlr.org/pu/e/sc/fish-monit/iuu-list-09.pdf
CCAMLR Member Contacts
http://www.ccamlr.org/pu/E/ms/contacts.htm
CCAMLR website
http://www.ccamlr.org/pu/e/gen-intro.htm
CCAMLR, *Incidental Mortality of Seabirds in Fisheries*
http://www.ccamlr.org/Pu/e/sc/imaf/ie-intro.htm
CCAMLR, *CCAMLR's Management of the Antarctic*
http://www.ccamlr.org/pu/e/e_pubs/am/man-ant/toc.htm
CIA World Factbook
https://www.cia.gov/library/publications/the-world-factbook/
CITES website
http://www.cites.org
Coalition of Legitimate Toothfish Operators
http://www.colto.org/index.htm
Crocodilian Biology Database
http://www.flmnh.ufl.edu/cnhc/cbd.html
Deep Sea Conservation Coalition, *Why the World Needs A Time-Out On High Seas Bottom Trawling*, DSCC. June 2005
http://www.savethehighseas.org/publicdocs/TimeOut_english.pdf
Department of the Environment, Food and Rural Affairs/Marine Fisheries Agency news release, *UK Beam Trawler Fined for Fishing in Closed Area*, 27th June 2006
http://www.defra.gov.uk/news/2006/060627e.htm (site defunct)
The Ecologist Online
http://www.theecologist.org
Environmental Justice Foundation, *ICCAT's Fight Against the Tuna Pirates*
http://www.ejfoundation.org/page268.html
EU Fisheries Commissioner Franz Fischler, *Illegal Fishing – A Threat to Our Common Heritage*
http://europa.eu.int/comm/archives/commission_1999_2004/fischler/illfish_en.htm (site defunct)
Fabra, Adriana, Gascón, Virginia and Werner, Rodolfo, *The Use of Port State Measures to Improve Fisheries Compliance*, National Environment Trust Paper, November 2006
http://www.illegal-fishing.info/item_single.php?item=document&item_id=154&approach_id=13
Findlay, Ken, *Historic Whaling in the Southern Hemisphere*, Indo-South Atlantic Consortium on Humpback Whales
http://www.ISACH.org/ (site defunct)
Franckx, Eric, *Applications of the Term "Introduction from the Sea"*
www.cites.org/eng/news/meetings/ifs-05/term_IFS.pdf
Franckx, Eric, *Legal and Institutional Implications of Listing Commercially-Exploited Aquatic Species*
www.cites.org/eng/news/meetings/ifs-05/IFS-05-implications.pdf
Gessar Fishery Company Ltd
http://www.gessar.ru/about/eindex.htm
Greenpeace IUU List
http://www.greenpeace.org/international/en/campaigns/oceans/pirate-fishing/Blacklist1/
IATTC IUU Vessel List
http://www.iattc.org/VesselRegister/IUU.aspx?Lang=en

ICCAT IUU Vessel List
http://www.iccat.es/en/IUU.asp
ICES, *Seamounts – Hotspots of Marine Life*
http://www.ices.dk/marineworld/seamounts.asp
Inter American Tropical Tuna Commission/Agreement on the International Dolphin Conservation Programme
http://www.iattc.org/DolphinSafeENG.htm
International Merchant Marine Registry of Belize
http://www.immarbe.com/fishing-regulations.html
International Shipping Directory
http://www.flagsofconvenience.com/page.php?pID=51
International Transport Workers' Federation, *FOC Countries*
http://www.itfglobal.org/flags-convenience/flags-convenien-183.cfm
International Transport Workers' Federation, *What do FOCs Mean to Seafarers?*
http://www.itfglobal.org/flags-convenience/flags-convenien-184.cfm
Joint Nature Conservation Committee, *Seabird Bycatch*
http://www.jncc.gov.uk/page-1565
Kim Rivera, *Incidental Catch of Seabirds in Longline Fisheries,* US National Marine Fisheries Service, Alaska, April 2002
http://www.waterbirdconservation.org/plan/rpt-NPOA.pdf
Lane, Calvin, *The African Squadron: The US Navy and the Slave Trade 1820–1862*
http://amistad.mysticseaport.org/discovery/themes/lane.navy.html (site defunct)
Lane, Tony, *Flags of Convenience: Is it Time to Redress the Balance?* Seafarer's International Research Centre, Cardiff University
www.sirc.cf.ac.uk/pdf/Flagcon.pdf
Le Gallic, Bertrand, *Using Trade Measures in the Fight Against IUU Fishing,* Paper Presented to International Institute of Fisheries Economics and Trade Conference, Japan, 2004
http://www.oecd.org/dataoecd/31/44/34227035.pdf
Lobach, Terje, *Port State Measures to Combat IUU Fishing: The FAO Model Scheme on Port State Measures,* Paper prepared for FOA/FFA Regional Workshop
ftp://ftp.fao.org/FI/DOCUMENT/tc-psm/Reg_Workshop_2006/Default.htm
Merchant Shipping Directorate, Malta Maritime Authority
http://www.dca.gov.mt/Page.aspx?pageid=470&lid=1
Mitchell, Daniel J., *The Threat to Global Shipping From Unions and High Tax Politicians: Restrictions on Open Registries Would Increase Consumer Prices and Boost the Cost of Government,* Prosperitas, The Centre for Freedom and Prosperity, August 2004, Vol. 9, Issue
http://www.freedomandprosperity.org/Papers/shipping/shipping.shtml (site defunct)
Mussa, Michael, Factors *Driving Global Economic Integration,* Presentation Paper for Symposium, *Global Economic Integration: Opportunities and Challenges,* August 2000
http://www.kc.frb.org/Publicat/sympos/2000/S00muss.pdf
NAFO IUU Vessel List
http://www.nafo.int/fisheries/frames/fishery-iuu.html
Nandan, Satya N., speech to the International Seabed Authority's Conference on the Governance of High Seas Fisheries and the United Nations Fish Agreement, Newfoundland and Labrador, May 2005, transcript available at
http://www.dfo-mpo.gc.ca/fgc-cgp/documents/presentations/nandan_e.pdf
NEAFC IUU 'A' Vessel List
http://www.neafc.org/measures/iuu-a-list.htm
NEAFC IUU 'B' Vessel List
http://www.neafc.org/measures/iuu-b.htm

Norwegian Fishing Directorate, IUU List
http://www.fiskeridir.no/english/fisheries/norwegian-black-list
Oceana, *Deep Sea Corals; Out of Sight, But No Longer Out of Mind*
http://www.oceana.org/north-america/publications/reports/deep-sea-corals-out-of-sight-but-no-longer-out-of-mind/
Oceana, *What Threat Does Trawling Pose?*
http://www.savecorals.com/trawling.html
Pautzke, Clarence G., *Russian Far East Fisheries Management,* Report to Congress of the North Pacific Fisheries Management Council, September 30th 1997
www.fakr.noaa.gov/npfmc/summary_reports/rfe-all.htm
Republic of Mauritius' Ministry of Public Infrastructure, Land Transport & Shipping
http://www.gov.mu/portal/site/mpisite/menuitem.c665e7efbc57b2368b1dd210a0208a0c/
Royal Society for the Protection of Birds
http://www.rspb.org.uk/supporting/campaigns/albatross/solutions.asp
Seafarer's International Research Centre, Cardiff University
http://www.sirc.cf.ac.uk/fsa.htm
Shipping Industry Flag State Performance Table, Maritime International Secretariat Services Ltd (in conjunction with BIMCO, Intercargo, International Chamber of Shipping, International Shipping Federation, Intertanko), London, 2006
http://www.marisec.org/flag-performance/FlagStatePerformanceTable06.pdf (site defunct)
Swan, Judith, *Port State Control: International Developments,* Paper prepared for UNFAO/FFA Regional Workshop to Promote the Full and Effective Implementation of Port State Measures to Combat IUU Fishing, Fiji, August/September 2006 and Doulman, David J., *Role of the Port State in Combating IUU Fishing and Promoting Long-Term Sustainability in Fisheries,* also prepared for UNFAO/FFA Regional Workshop.
Both available at
ftp://ftp.fao.org/FI/DOCUMENT/tc-psm/Reg_Workshop_2006/Default.htm
TRAFFIC International, *TRAFFIC Lauds Detention of Suspected 'Pirate' Toothfish Fishing Vessel*
http://www.traffic.org/news/pirate_toothfish.html (site defunct)
UK Foreign and Commonwealth Office
www.fco.gov.uk
UN Conference on Trade and Development
http://r0.unctad.org/ttl/docs-legal/unc-ml/status/Registration%20of%20Ships%201986.pdf
UN Department of Economic and Social Affairs
http://www.un.org/esa/sustdev/sids/sidslist
UN Oceans and the Law of the Sea website
http://www.un.org/Depts/los/index.htm
UNFAO Fisheries and Aquaculture Department, Technology Factsheets: Fishing Gear types, Set gillnets
http://www.fao.org/fishery/geartype/219/en
UNFAO Fisheries and Aquaculture RFMO Factsheet
http://www.fao.org/fi/website/FISearch.do?dom=rfb#rfb_map
UNFAO Fisheries Global Information System
http://www.fao.org/figis/servlet/static?dom=area&xml=Area51.xml
UNFAO Treaty Database for a list of Contracting Parties to the Compliance Agreement
http://www.fao.org/legal/treaties/012s-e.htm
UNFAO, IPOA-Seabirds
ftp://ftp.fao.org/docrep/fao/006/x3170e/X3170E00.pdf
UNFOA Fisheries Department, Country Profiles
http://www.fao.org/fi/fcp/en/RUS/profile.htm

United Nations Environmental Program, *Cold Water Coral Reefs: Out of Sight, No Longer Out of Mind*
http://www.unep.org/cold_water_reefs/comparison.htm
United Nations Fish Stocks Agreement
http://www.fao.org/legal/treaties/012s-e.htm
United Nations Food and Agriculture Organisation, Country Profiles
http://www.fao.org/fi/fcp/en/GEO/profile.htm
United Nations, Oceans and Law of the Sea
http://www.un.org/Depts/los/reference_files/chronological_lists_of_ratifications.htm#The%20United%20Nations%20Convention%20on%20the%20Law%20of%20the%20Sea
The Whale and Dolphin Conservation Society, *An Introduction to the Tuna-Dolphin Issue*
http://www.wdcs.org/dan/publishing.nsf/allweb/ADED9F368A73DC3280256E1B003F367C (site defunct)
The Whale and Dolphin Conservation Society, *The La Jolla Agreement: International Steps to Control Dolphin Fishing*
http://www.wdcs.org/dan/publishing.nsf/allweb/2C5AE8A85CD67CE980256E1B003F367D (site defunct)
Winchester, Nik and Alderton, Tony, *Flag State Audit 2003*, Seafarers International Research Centre
http://www.sirc.cf.ac.uk/fsa.html (site defunct)

Index

www.ingramcontent.com/pod-product-compliance
Lightning Source LLC
LaVergne TN
LVHW081515300926
849161LV00006B/1180
* 9 7 8 9 0 0 4 2 0 2 7 8 8 *